CONSUMER RELATED MATHEMATICS

AS YOU EXAMINE THIS TEXT, PLEASE NOTICE THAT:

1. The course begins with a review of WHOLE NUMBERS and the second chapter pertains to DECIMALS.

2. Throughout the text, stress is placed on computation skills which high school students need in solving consumer and business problems in everyday life.

3. Each topic to be studied begins at the top of a lesson page.

4. The four sections of each "block of lessons" consists of:

    a. Topic of study section

        (1) a vocabulary list
        (2) a short, easy-to-read essay

    b. Developing Skills section

        (1) lesson objective stated
        (2) lots of worked-out examples
        (3) practice exercises

    c. Applying Skills section

        (1) word problems which apply the skills learned
        (2) two-column format for ease of reading

    d. Maintaining Skills section

        (1) reinforcement exercises
        (2) each is keyed to lesson page

5. PRACTICE EXERCISES are plentiful. (Total 3,486 problems)

6. Each chapter features SPECIAL MATERIALS such as

    a. activities--each outlines interesting projects.
    b. consumer tips--each outlines helpful hints for shopping.
    c. careers--each brings awareness about different jobs.
    d. self-tests/chapter tests--diagnostic and assessment material.
    e. special topics.

7. ANSWERS to (1) odd-numbered exercises, (2) self-tests, and (3) cumulative reviews are given in back of the text (see pp. 365-376).

8. Topics of study are meaningful to students. For example, see Chapter 11 (OWNING A CAR) and Chapter 12 (OWNING A HOME).

9. STORY PROBLEMS: For immediate reinforcement, a double column format is used so that each problem in the right-hand column is like the one in the left-hand column.

10. Chapter 3 pertains to the METRIC SYSTEM.

11. The GLOSSARY, pp. 339-354.

12. SUPPLEMENTARY MATERIALS:

    a. Teacher's Guide (booklet, 60 pages)
    b. Duplicating Masters (package of 40; forms, chapter tests, cumulative reviews and activity sheets)

CONSUMER RELATED MATHEMATICS

Wallace W. Kravitz

Vincent Brant

CONSUMER RELATED MATHEMATICS

Holt, Rinehart and Winston, Publishers
New York, Toronto, London, Sydney

About the Authors

Wallace W. Kravitz formerly, a Business Teacher, Syosset, New York. Presently, Chairman of the Business Education Department, Mineola Public Schools, Mineola, New York.

Vincent Brant formerly, Coordinator of the Office of Mathematics, Grades K-12, Board of Education of Baltimore County, Towson, Maryland. Presently, a Mathematics Consultant and a Member of the Maryland Ad Hoc Committee on Metrication.

Photo credits are on page viii.

Copyright © 1976, 1971 by Holt, Rinehart and Winston, Publishers
All rights reserved
Printed in the United States of America

ISBN: 0-03-089716-5

78901234   071   9876543

CONTENTS

Acknowledgments for Photographs

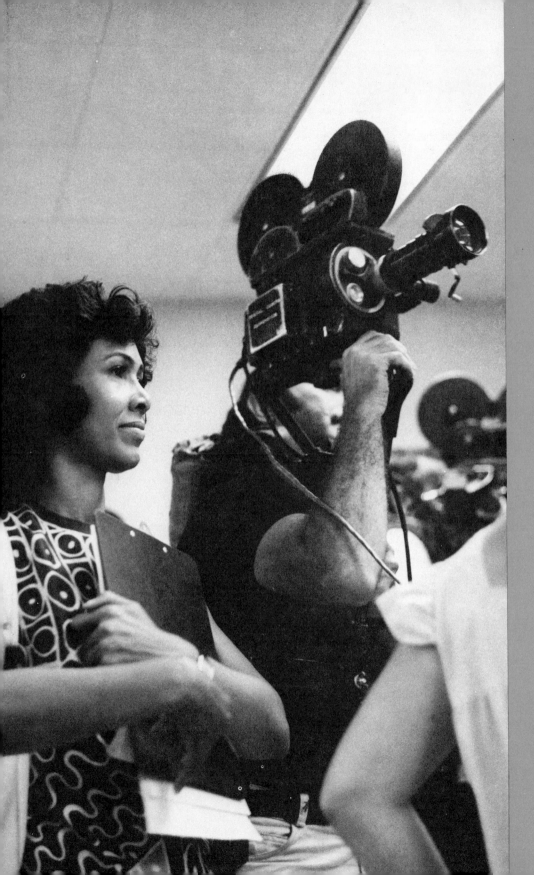

A TV commentator
and cameraman
covering a news event

Activities_____

Complete the square so that the sum in each column, row, and diagonal is 34. Use 4, 6, 7, 8, 10, 11, 12, 13, 14, and 15 once each.

16	2	9	
3			
5			
			1

Try making up several similar magic squares.

After school every day for a week, spend an hour at a busy street corner. Ask people who pass by what their favorite TV program is. Make a bar graph to show the results of your survey. Make a list of 5 questions that a friend can answer from your graph.

Plan a vacation trip of 1,000 to 2,000 miles by car. Record the name of the place at which you plan to spend each night; the distance you plan to drive that day; the cost of food and lodging for 2 people; and the costs of gas, oil, and car repairs. Find the average daily expense and the average speed at which you might have to travel.

Choose a job such as secretary, salesperson, bookkeeper, receptionist, or any other one which interests you. Find 5 different newspaper ads for that type of job. Clip the ads and paste them on a sheet of paper. Compare the salaries, fringe benefits, and expenses, such as travel and lunch. For which job would you apply? Why?

Skills in Addition

community college A community college is designed to serve a local area. It is usually a two-year college supported by local and state funds.

operate To operate means to use or run; for example, to operate an automobile.

frequency-of-repair Frequency-of-repair tells how often a machine has to be fixed.

estimate To estimate means to figure closely, but not exactly.

For Discussion

- In what year of high school is Ann Owens?

- What are her future plans?

- What is her problem?

- What is the first step in solving her problem?

"Dad, I'd like to buy a car in June," Ann Owens said one day in February.

"Well, Ann, do you really need a car?"

"Dad, I'm going to need a car for my job this summer, and to go to community college this fall."

"I guess you're right, Ann. What kind of car do you have in mind?"

"I like the new Spartan," Ann replied. "The consumer magazines, which rate cars in different ways, rated the Spartan as a Best-Buy in the small compact car field. They praised its low operating costs and low frequency-of-repair features."

"Ann, let's estimate the cost of a new Spartan by listing the equipment you want."

Basic car	$2,800
Automatic transmission	170
Power steering	90
White wall tires	40
Radio	60
Delivery charges	70
Total	$3,230

They sat back and looked at the total. What do you think their thoughts were?

DEVELOPING SKILLS

Commutative Property of Addition
Changing the order of the addends does not change the sum.

Replace *n* to make each sentence true. Do not add.

1. $19 + n = 6 + 19$ **2.** $49 + 12 = n + 49$ **3.** $n + 65 = 65 + 15$

Show that each sentence is true.

MODELS

$(5 + 9) + 6 = 5 + (9 + 6)$

$(5 + 9) + 6$	$5 + (9 + 6)$
$14 + 6$	$5 + 15$
20	20

$8 + (3 + 9) = (8 + 3) + 9$

$8 + (3 + 9)$	$(8 + 3) + 9$
$8 + 12$	$11 + 9$
20	20

4. $(4 + 7) + 9 = 4 + (7 + 9)$ **5.** $8 + (4 + 6) = (8 + 4) + 6$

Associative Property of Addition
Changing the grouping of the addends does not change the sum.

Group addends to make the additions easier.

6. $18 + 2 + 25$ **7.** $38 + 62 + 91$ **8.** $42 + 58 + 97$

Add.

9.	**10.**	**11.**	**12.**
98	847 mi	790 doz	$66,909
88	688 mi	925 doz	83,241
48	803 mi	114 doz	97,985
56	576 mi	783 doz	65,912
+ 76	15 mi	850 doz	1,308
	+ 1,149 mi	+ 52 doz	+ 276

Copy and complete. (Total sales = total cash sales + total charge sales.)

13.

SALES INVENTORY FOR MAY 12			
Department	Cash Sales	Charge Sales	Total Sales
Housewares	$350	$297	$ 647
Hardware	875	138	1,013
Drapery	286	67	353
Lamp	349	196	545
TOTALS			$2,558

14.

CAR OPERATING EXPENSES			
Month	Gas and Oil	Repairs	Total
September	$39	$12	
October	35	9	
November	43	14	
December	35	10	
TOTALS			$197

APPLYING SKILLS

1. Mr. Livero reported class enrollments of 31, 32, 29, 18, and 27. How many books should he order?

2. Ms. Michael's class enrollments were 36, 28, 24, 32, and 19. How many books should she order?

3. The number of students in the sophomore homerooms at Alpha High was:

43	44	27	38	37
36	23	31	27	26

How many seats are needed for the sophomore class assembly?

4. The number of students in the junior homerooms at Alpha High was:

32	46	27	29	41
45	23	38	37	36

How many seats are needed for the junior class assembly?

5. Students from 5 schools entered a state bowling tournament:

School	Entries
Packard Regional	134
Jackson Corners	298
Hampshire Heights	215
Mills Creek	178
Alpha Valley	137

Find the total number of entries.

6. Esther White Feather made the following deposits:

Date	Amount
September 2	$434
October 15	109
October 31	204
November 14	108
November 30	237

Find the total amount deposited.

7. Cash sales of the Imperial Clothiers for September 21 were:

Suits	$179	Topcoats	$406
Shoes	$219	Sportcoats	$387
Shirts	$ 79	Raincoats	$182

Find the total cash sales for that day.

8. The number of units of work Frank Boland completed last week was:

Monday	332	Thursday	319
Tuesday	371	Friday	371
Wednesday	407	Saturday	134

How many units did he produce last week?

Copy and complete. Check.

9.

LULA WASHINGTON'S BOUTIQUE			
Department	Cash Sales	Charge Sales	Total Sales
Coat	$5,377	$2,297	
Scarf	3,264	1,019	
Dress	2,989	6,290	
Sweater	3,798	4,650	
TOTALS			$29,684

10.

JACK LACY'S RETAIL STORE			
Department	Cash Sales	Charge Sales	Total Sales
Clothing	$2,400	$4,200	
Shoe	3,800	7,500	
Housewares	1,900	3,850	
Furniture	4,650	5,500	
TOTALS			$33,800

MAINTAINING SKILLS

Write word names. Use the place-value chart.

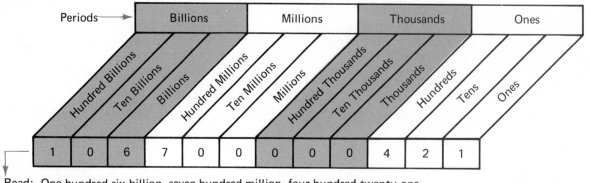

Periods →	Billions			Millions			Thousands			Ones		
	Hundred Billions	Ten Billions	Billions	Hundred Millions	Ten Millions	Millions	Hundred Thousands	Ten Thousands	Thousands	Hundreds	Tens	Ones
	1	0	6	7	0	0	0	0	0	4	2	1

Read: One hundred six billion, seven hundred million, four hundred twenty-one

1. 3,475   **2.** 63,009   **3.** 647,802,111   **4.** 215,703,006,000

Write numerals.

5. Sixty-five thousand, eight hundred seventy-five

6. Two hundred million, one thousand, two hundred

7. Twenty-four billion, twenty-four thousand, twenty-four

Copy and complete. [4]

8.

MIKE'S SALES RECORD			
Day	Cash	Charge	Total
Monday	$120	$110	
Tuesday	200	160	
Wednesday	160	140	
Thursday	320	290	
Friday	360	345	
Saturday	410	385	
TOTALS			$3,000

9.

JUDY'S SALES RECORD			
Day	Cash	Charge	Total
Monday	$22,380	$16,285	
Tuesday	17,190	19,514	
Wednesday	19,250	23,583	
Thursday	30,010	21,486	
Friday	17,620	19,715	
Saturday	32,710	42,417	
TOTALS			$282,160

Solve these problems. [4]

10. The enrollment at LaMesa High is 375 freshmen, 356 sophomores, 349 juniors, and 312 seniors. What is the total enrollment?

11. A carton with 4 packages was loaded on a pickup truck. Their weights were 270 lb, 298 lb, 316 lb, and 287 lb. What is the total weight?

Consumer Tips——

WHAT'S ON SALE WHEN

JANUARY
Cars • Beds • Tires • Furs • Fabrics •
Christmas Cards • Wrappings • TV's •
Furniture • Stationery • Linens •
Decorations • Notions • Lingerie •
Clothing and Accessories • Radios •
Decorating Accessories • Luggage •
Diamonds • Major Appliances •
Infant Needs • Floor Coverings

FEBRUARY
Decorating Accessories • Furniture •
Floor Coverings • Furs • Fabrics •
Major Appliances • Cars •
Men's Wear • Women's Stockings •
Women's Coats

MARCH
Housewares • China • Glassware

APRIL
Lingerie • Fabrics • Women's Coats •
Fashion Clearances • Diamonds •
Sleepwear • Children's Clothes

MAY
Decorating Accessories • Luggage •
Infant Needs • Clothing • Linens •
Housewares • Diamonds

JUNE
Summer Sportswear • Furniture •
Floor Coverings • Stockings • Beds •
Men's Clothing • Lingerie •
Sleepwear

JULY
Garden Equipment • Furniture • Beds •
Storm Windows • Garden Furniture •
Major Appliances • Jewelry • Tires •
Summer Fashions • Fabrics • Linens

AUGUST
Women's Accessories • Furniture •
Garden Equipment • Infant Needs •
Major Appliances • Beds • Linens •
Garden Furniture • Rugs • Furs • Cars

SEPTEMBER
Cars • Tires

OCTOBER
Women's Coats • Infant Needs •
Children's Clothes • Cars

NOVEMBER
Furs • Women's Coats

DECEMBER
Infant Needs • Decorations • Cards •
Women's Coats • Wrappings

Skills in Subtraction

itemize   To itemize means to list, in detail, each separate part or item.

accessories   Accessories are objects or devices which are not necessary but add to the beauty, comfort, or convenience of something else.

option   An option is a choice, something that can be chosen.

eliminate   To eliminate means to remove or discard.

For Discussion

- How did Scotty react to the car's cost?

- How can Scotty cut the car's costs?

- How was Ms. Walsh helpful to her son?

- What was Scotty hoping after they had reduced the costs?

Scotty Walsh and his mother looked at the price stickers on the windows of the new cars at the Garcia Motor Co. These stickers itemized the basic cost and the costs of accessories.

"Gosh, Mom," Scotty said sadly, "with these prices, I'll never get a new car."

Ms. Walsh, a very successful real estate executive, said, "Now don't get discouraged, Scotty. We can reduce the cost if we consider some options. Let's eliminate some accessories. You really don't need whitewall tires, power steering, and automatic transmission. Stick-shifting is very popular now. Look at these figures when we eliminate these accessories."

Cost of car on showroom floor	$3,500
Less whitewall tires	− 50
First option	$3,450
Less power steering	− 90
Second option	$3,360
Less automatic transmission	− 170
Third option	$3,190

Scotty said, "It still looks high. I hope I can afford the monthly payments."

DEVELOPING SKILLS

Subtract. Check.

MODELS

74	Check:	16		505	Check:	118
− 58		+ 58		− 387		+ 387
16		74		118		505

1. 42
− 27

2. 25
− 18

3. 83
− 65

4. 67
− 14

5. 354
− 125

6. 481
− 293

7. 152
− 38

8. 230
− 16

9. 5,091
− 1,728

10. 3,063
− 1,978

11. 1,449
− 349

12. 2,548
− 685

13. 7,572
− 608

14. 4,995
− 349

15. 6,003
− 4,879

16. 565 ft
− 497 ft

17. 1,297 mi
+ 145 mi

18. 1,283 in.
− 207 in.

19. 3,004 gal
− 897 gal

20. $358
− 185

21. $785
− 299

22. $3,609
− 3,355

23. $2,065
− 1,927

Copy and complete. Check. (Hint: total charges − total deductions = total net cost.)

24.

SIMSARIAN'S HARDWARE			
Item	Charges	Deductions	Net Cost
283	$246	$42	
487	387	62	
645	413	38	
TOTALS			$904

25.

FEORANZ'S FURNITURE			
Item	Charges	Deductions	Net Cost
563	$3,875	$987	
708	2,792	895	
810	1,056	290	
TOTALS			$5,551

26.

KOSEDNAR'S ELECTRIC			
Worker	Sales	Returns	Net Sales
Mr. Chu	$2,575	$198	
Ms. Day	2,483	207	
Mrs. Faye	2,550	386	
TOTALS			$6,817

27.

MALONE'S TIRES			
Worker	Sales	Returns	Net Sales
Mr. Robb	$1,805	$100	
Ms. Diaz	2,798	289	
Mrs. Gold	1,900	900	
TOTALS			$5,214

APPLYING SKILLS

1. Alice went shopping with $20 in her purse. She spent $11 for a scarf and a shirt. How much did she have left?

2. José went shopping with $19 in his wallet. He spent $12 for a scarf and a shirt. How much did he have left?

3. A truck weighs 5,175 pounds. When loaded, it weighs 12,180 pounds. What is the weight of the load?

4. A truck weighs 2,085 kilograms. When loaded, it weighs 5,290 kilograms. What is the weight of the load?

5. Abe reported sales of $252. Sheila reported sales of $404. Find the difference between their sales.

6. Willie Harris earned $531. Jack O'Dea earned $422. Find the difference between their earnings.

7. In a recent election, 14,321 votes were cast for the mayor. Two years before, 16,010 votes were cast for him. Did he gain or lose votes? How many?

8. In a recent election, 18,020 votes were cast for the mayor. Two years before, 15,983 votes were cast for her. Did she gain or lose votes? How many?

9. Carol bought a carload of radios for $3,763. She sold them for $4,250. The expenses in selling the radios amounted to $500. Find the amount of the loss.

10. Harry bought a truckload of rugs for $5,998. He sold them for $6,798. The expenses in selling the rugs amounted to $1,000. Find the amount of the loss.

Copy and complete. Check.

11.

JAY'S BOUTIQUE			
Item	Charges	Deductions	Net Cost
72	$174	$18	
68	134	11	
47	288	38	
TOTALS			$529

12.

ANGIE'S BOUTIQUE			
Item	Sales	Returns	Net Sales
384	$165	$19	
786	107	28	
485	39	15	
TOTALS			$249

13.

WEEKLY PAYROLL APRIL 3–7			
Worker	Gross Earnings	Total Deductions	Net Pay
Sharon	$185	$37	
Hal	170	34	
Ruby	210	42	
TOTALS			$452

14.

DAILY PRODUCTION RECORD			
Worker	Units Completed	Units Rejected	Units Accepted
Eiko	142	12	
Tony	136	14	
Mark	109	17	
TOTALS			344

MAINTAINING SKILLS

Copy and complete. Check. [4]

1.

CORA JOHNSON'S AUDIOVUE			
Department	Cash Sales	Charge Sales	Total Sales
Stereo	$15,898	$10,478	
Radio	625	595	
TV	22,000	4,000	
Record	300	100	
Cassette	850	410	
TOTALS			$55,256

2.

BRUNO HALL'S SHIPPING			
Order	Cost of Goods	Freight Charge	Total Cost
197	$1,250	$35	
158	750	18	
143	2,550	62	
519	880	19	
600	25,000	70	
TOTALS			$30,634

3.

SPENCER'S SUPPLY COMPANY			
Week	Cash Sales	Charge Sales	Total Sales
1st	$647	$1,500	
2nd	1,013	695	
3rd	2,985	800	
4th	900	250	
TOTALS			$8,790

4.

CHANG'S DEPARTMENT STORE			
Department	Cash Sales	Charge Sales	Total Sales
Notions	$500	$150	
Dress	3,587	2,750	
Suit	3,587	2,750	
Coat	4,035	8,000	
TOTALS			$25,359

Solve these problems. [9]

5. One week, a department store delivery truck used 82 gallons of gasoline. The next week, it used 109 gallons. How many more gallons of gasoline were used the second week?

6. A storage tank at the Ajax Service Center contains 2,260 liters of gasoline. When filled, the tank contains 10,260 liters. How many liters of gasoline are still needed to fill the tank?

7. Edna's Supermarket set a $3,500 weekly sales goal for the produce department. The sales were $3,478 for the 1st week, $3,836 for the 2nd week, and $3,486 for the 3rd week. By how much did the 1st week's sales fall short of the goal? By how much did the 2nd week's sales go over the goal?

8. Bart's Bindery set a weekly production goal of 29,000 completed units. The productions were 31,257 units for the 1st week, 24,021 units the 2nd week, and 24,035 units the 3rd week. By how much did the 1st week's production go over the goal? By how much did the 2nd week's production fall short of the goal?

Career/DATA PROCESSING

Computer technology has countless opportunities for data processing specialists. New uses and techniques are still being found for computers. This rela-
tively new area is important in the business world and in science and industry
as well.

Job Descriptions

- Machine operator—translates written programs and data into machine-
  readable codes; performs machine operations to yield the output.
- Tape librarian—maintains a current library of programs stored on mag-
  netic tape, punched cards, paper tape, or other machine-readable
  documents.
- Programmer—writes new programs and modifies existing programs in
  languages suited to the problems and the specific computer involved, for
  example, COBOL and FORTRAN.
- Systems analyst—oversees the operation of a complete program with full
  responsibility for a project.

Training

Many Data Processing Technicians receive training in high school programs.
Two-year programs are offered by most community colleges. Check the reli-
ability of private schools advertising such programs. While many jobs in this
area are routine, others require advanced training in computer technology.

Further Investigation

Arrange an interview with a data processing specialist. Ask about job qualifications, working conditions, possibilities for advancement, entry-level jobs.

Consult your guidance department about vocational training or post-high-
school technical courses in this area.

Skills in Multiplication

technician   A technician is a person who has skill and knowledge in an art or science.

budget   A budget is a plan for spending and saving a part of one's income.

personal expenses   Personal expenses refers to the paying out of money for one's own needs, such as clothes, cosmetics, and hobbies.

allowance   An allowance is an amount of money given each week or month by many parents to a young member of their family to use for certain needs.

For Discussion

- What is Rose's purpose in planning a budget?

- What sources of money does Rose plan to use to pay her expenses?

- What is the total income Rose estimated?

Rose Jackson showed her guidance counselor, Mr. Harris, a letter from the Howell School for X-Ray Technicians offering her a scholarship.

"Rose, I'm delighted," said Mr. Harris, "you earned it through your good work here at Douglas High School. Have you thought about your finances and budget?"

"Yes, Mr. Harris, I discussed this with my parents. I will need extra money for my school expenses, personal expenses, and car expenses. But I want to pay my own way as much as possible."

Mr. Harris looked at her with respect.

Rose continued, "You see, I have a part-time job now, and have been offered a full-time summer job. My parents will increase my allowance. Look at this estimate of my yearly income on this sheet."

Part-time	(21 weeks) 21 × $54 =	$1,134
Summer job	(10 weeks) 10 × $95 =	950
Allowance	(52 weeks) 52 × $10 =	+ 520
	Total yearly income	$2,604

Do you think that Rose will have enough income to do all that she plans?

DEVELOPING SKILLS

OBJECTIVE   **To multiply whole numbers**

Commutative Property of Multiplication
Changing the order of the factors does not change the product.

Replace n to make each sentence true. Do not multiply.

1. $12 \times n = 7 \times 12$

2. $36 \times 15 = n \times 36$

3. $n \times 43 = 43 \times 17$

Associative Property of Multiplication
Changing the grouping of the factors does not change the product.

Show that each sentence is true.

4. $(3 \times 5) \times 4 = 3 \times (5 \times 4)$

5. $8 \times (4 \times 6) = (8 \times 4) \times 6$

Show that each sentence is true.

MODELS

$5 \times (6 + 2)$	$(5 \times 6) + (5 \times 2)$
5×8	$30 + 10$
40	40

$5 \times (6 + 2) = (5 \times 6) + (5 \times 2)$

$7 \times (8 - 3)$	$(7 \times 8) - (7 \times 3)$
7×5	$56 - 21$
35	35

$7 \times (8 - 3) = (7 \times 8) - (7 \times 3)$

Distributive Property
Multiplication is distributive over addition and subtraction.

6. $9 \times (8 + 4) = (9 \times 8) + (9 \times 4)$

7. $8 \times (10 - 6) = (8 \times 10) - (8 \times 6)$

Multiply.

MODELS

$$\begin{array}{r} 3{,}951 \\ \times 62 \\ \hline 7\ 902 \\ 237\ 060 \\ \hline 244{,}962 \end{array}$$

$7\ 902 \longleftarrow (2 \times 3{,}951)$
$237\ 060 \longleftarrow (60 \times 3{,}951)$

$$\begin{array}{r} 2{,}505 \\ \times 37 \\ \hline 17\ 535 \\ 75\ 150 \\ \hline 92{,}685 \end{array}$$

$17\ 535 \longleftarrow (7 \times 2{,}505)$
$75\ 150 \longleftarrow (30 \times 2{,}505)$

8. $\begin{array}{r} 7{,}817 \\ \times 32 \\ \hline \end{array}$

9. $\begin{array}{r} 6{,}328 \\ \times 57 \\ \hline \end{array}$

10. $\begin{array}{r} 3{,}090 \\ \times 78 \\ \hline \end{array}$

11. $\begin{array}{r} 7{,}600 \\ \times 59 \\ \hline \end{array}$

12. $\begin{array}{r} 8{,}495 \\ \times 60 \\ \hline \end{array}$

Find the perimeter (distance around) each equilateral polygon.
(Hint: P = number of sides × length of 1 side.)

13. 3 sides each 380 centimeters long

14. 4 sides each 19 feet long

15. 5 sides each 17 centimeters long

16. 6 sides each 20 meters long

APPLYING SKILLS

Find the perimeter of each rectangle. Use $P = 2(\ell + w)$.

MODELS

Length: 28″
Width: 17″
$$P = 2(\ell + w)$$
$$= 2(28 + 17)$$
$$= 2 \times 28 + 2 \times 17$$
$$= 56 + 34, \text{ or } 90$$
So, the perimeter is 90 inches.

Length: 27 meters
Width: 16 meters
$$P = 2(\ell + w)$$
$$= 2(27 + 16)$$
$$= 2 \times 27 + 2 \times 16$$
$$= 54 + 32, \text{ or } 86$$
So, the perimeter is 86 meters.

1. Length: 13 in.
 Width: 7 in.

2. Length: 10 mi
 Width: 8 mi

3. Length: 37 meters
 Width: 15 meters

Find the area of each rectangle. Use $A = \ell \times w$.

MODELS

Length: 28′
Width: 12′
$$A = \ell \times w$$
$$= 28 \times 12$$
$$= 336$$
So, the area is 336 square feet.

$$\begin{array}{r} 28 \\ \times 12 \\ \hline 56 \\ 28 \\ \hline 336 \end{array}$$

Length: 23 centimeters
Width: 23 centimeters
$$A = \ell \times w$$
$$= 23 \times 23$$
$$= 529$$
So, the area is 529 square centimeters.

4. Length: 19 ft
 Width: 38 ft

5. Length: 28 yd
 Width: 17 yd

6. Length: 35 meters
 Width: 35 meters

Solve these problems.

7. Irving types addresses on envelopes at the rate of 85 per hour. How many can he address in 19 hours?

8. Betty places stamps on envelopes at the rate of 13 per minute. How many can she stamp in 38 minutes?

9. Margaret Ann Brant can sort 45 tickets in 1 minute. How many tickets can she sort in 3 hours?

10. Frank Black Hawk can seal 27 envelopes in 1 minute. How many can he seal in 2 hours?

11. The Pearl Harris Office Equipment Company needs 123 cars for its salespeople. Each car costs $3,175. What is the total cost?

12. The Joe Gomez Watch Company can make a wrist watch for $43. What is the total cost of 13,785 of these watches?

13. Dave wants to buy wall-to-wall carpeting for his 12′ × 15′ living room and 12′ × 12′ dining room. How much carpeting will he need?

14. Debbie wants to buy wall-to-wall carpeting for for her 15′ × 21′ living room and 15′ × 15′ bedroom. How much carpeting will she need?

MAINTAINING SKILLS

Copy and complete. Check. [9]

1.

PAYROLL FOR TOWN DECORATORS			
Worker	Gross Earnings	Total Deductions	Net Pay
D. Cross	$325	$65	
M. Gold	200	40	
H. Hunt	215	43	
K. Sato	300	60	
A. Tate	250	50	
TOTALS			$1,032

2.

PRODUCTION RECORD			
Worker	Units Completed	Units Spoiled	Units Accepted
Ms. Diaz	176	10	
Mr. Jones	175	9	
Mrs. Polk	158	10	
Mrs. Ring	162	12	
Mr. Sands	160	12	
TOTALS			778

3.

WEEKLY PAYROLL			
Worker	Gross Earnings	Total Deductions	Net Pay
A. Jackson	$275	$55	
B. Longo	210	42	
T. Rivera	275	55	
R. Stein	215	43	
TOTALS			$780

4.

WEEKLY PRODUCTION RECORD			
Worker	Units Completed	Units Rejected	Units Accepted
M. Bock	158	17	
P. Calise	162	19	
A. Ribik	203	26	
K. Tuite	149	10	
TOTALS			600

Solve these problems.

5. The gross income of Lucy Breen's Bake Shop
[9] was $1,759. Expenses amounted to $866. What was her net income?

6. The gross income of Ray Mason's Dress Shop
[9] was $1,507. Expenses amounted to $798. What was his net income?

7. What is the value of 37 bonds worth $75 each?
[15]

8. What is the value of 1,250 shares of stock worth
[15] $135 each?

9. Harry Rising Sun averages 18 miles to a gallon
[15] of gasoline. He used 396 gallons of gas on a vacation trip. How far did he travel?

10. Rose Ann Yates averages 11 kilometers to a liter
[15] of gasoline. She used 1,529 liters of gas on a vacation trip. How far did she travel?

Skills in Division

discount   A discount is a deduction from the original price of an article.

installment plan   An installment plan is a business arrangement to purchase goods by making regular payments over a period of time until the full amount is paid.

financing   Financing is a way that a buyer obtains money to purchase goods.

monthly payments   Monthly payments are the amounts paid until the installment debt has been paid.

average   The average of two or more numbers is obtained by finding the sum of the numbers and then dividing the sum by the number of addends.

For Discussion

- How does Fran expect to pay for the new equipment?
- How did Mr. Solomon calculate the monthly payments?

"Mr. Solomon, we've started a rock band at school and call ourselves *The Rolling Bones*," explained Fran Wang to the owner of the music store. "All of us need new and more powerful instruments and equipment."

"What kind of outfit are you looking for, Fran?" asked Mr. Solomon.

"I'd like to get a guitar, case, and an amplifier," Fran answered.

Mr. Solomon replied, "I can give you a good discount on those items. The guitar and case discounts for $512 and the amplifier discounts for $736, making a total of $1,248. Your installment plan over two years can be financed as follows."

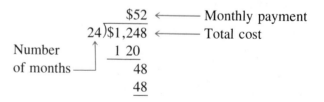

Fran said, "I can easily make 24 payments of $52 per month using the money I'll earn on the jobs we have already booked."

Would you advise her differently?

DEVELOPING SKILLS

OBJECTIVES   To divide whole numbers
To find the average of two or more numbers

Divide and check.

MODEL

$$36\overline{)15,948}$$

$$
\begin{array}{r}
443 \quad\longleftarrow \text{ Quotient} \\
36\overline{)15,948} \quad\longleftarrow \\
14\ 4 \qquad\qquad \longleftarrow \text{Dividend}\\
1\ 54 \\
1\ 44 \\
\hline
108 \\
108 \\
\hline
\end{array}
$$

Divisor

Check

$$
\begin{array}{r}
443 \\
\times\ 36 \\
\hline
2\ 658 \\
13\ 29 \\
\hline
15,948
\end{array}
$$

1. $9\overline{)3,843}$ **2.** $8\overline{)5,912}$ **3.** $50\overline{)49,350}$ **4.** $80\overline{)316,000}$

5. $36\overline{)35,100}$ **6.** $68\overline{)66,504}$ **7.** $181\overline{)15,385}$ **8.** $386\overline{)187,982}$

Find the quotient. Check.

MODEL $28,349 \div 45$

$$
\begin{array}{r}
629 \\
45\overline{)28,349} \\
27\ 0 \\
\hline
1\ 34 \\
90 \\
\hline
449 \\
405 \\
\hline
44
\end{array}
$$

Remainder (r) $\longrightarrow$ 44

Check

$$
\begin{array}{r}
629 \\
\times\ 45 \\
\hline
3\ 145 \\
25\ 16 \\
\hline
28,305 \\
+\quad 44 \\
\hline
28,349
\end{array}
$$

So, $28,349 \div 45 = 629$ r 44

9. $36,497 \div 57$ **10.** $65,720 \div 98$ **11.** $85,005 \div 193$

Find the average of these bowling scores.

MODEL   125, 135, 150, 165, 140

$$
\begin{array}{r}
125 \\
135 \\
150 \\
165 \\
140 \\
\hline
715
\end{array}
$$

$$
\begin{array}{r}
143 \quad\longleftarrow \text{ Average} \\
5\overline{)715} \\
\end{array}
$$

Number of games $\longrightarrow$ $\uparrow$ $\longleftarrow$ Sum of scores

12. 117, 143, 120, 110, 125   **13.** 185, 190, 175, 165, 170, 213

APPLYING SKILLS

1. In preparing for a party, Carl found that 18 pieces of candy would fit into a bag. How many bags can he fill with 252 pieces of candy?

2. Certain items are shipped in boxes of 36 items each. Joyce ordered 6,588 of these items. How many boxes will be shipped to her?

3. Linda averaged 42 miles an hour in driving from her home to Denver. The distance was 756 miles. How long did the trip take?

4. Cesar averaged 80 kilometers an hour in driving from his home to Reno. The distance was 1,200 kilometers. How long did the trip take?

5. Bill's car averages 21 miles to a gallon of gasoline. How much gas will he use in driving 1,575 miles?

6. Sheila's car averages 11 kilometers to a liter of gasoline. How much gas will she use in driving 2,224 kilometers?

7. Liz Olsen bought 14,850 feet of wire. She cut it into lengths of 165 feet each. How many pieces of wire did she get?

8. Kaoni Sato bought 12,240 meters of fabric. He cut it into lengths of 153 meters each. How many pieces of fabric did he get?

9. At Allen Tech, there are 6 junior homerooms with enrollments of 36, 32, 35, 33, 29, and 33. What is the average number of students in each homeroom?

10. On a vacation trip, the Harris family recorded daily mileages of 235, 255, 245, 270, 248, 250, 265, 270, 283, and 279. What was their average daily mileage?

11. An automobile agency sold 652 cars one year. The total sales were $1,787,784. What was the average price per car?

12. A real estate agency sold 125 houses one year. The total sales were $6,743,750. What was the average price per house?

Solve these problems.

MODEL   The Hall's food bills for 3 months were $200, $225, and $300. How much can they spend on food the next month in order to average $240 per month?

$240 ⟵——— Average per mo

×4 ⟵——— Number of mo

$960 ⟵——— Total for 4 mo

$200
225
300
Total for 3 mo ⟶ $725

$960
−725
$235 ⟶ Amount they can spend the next mo

13. Ruth Garcia's bowling scores for 5 games were 175, 160, 184, 167, and 165. What score does she need in the 6th game in order to average 170?

14. The number of units Bart Sands completed in 4 days was 252, 283, 267, and 305. How many does he need to complete the 5th day in order to average 262 units?

MAINTAINING SKILLS

Find the perimeter of each rectangle. Use $P = 2(\ell + w)$. [15]

1. Length: 4 meters
Width: 2 meters

2. Length: 5 meters
Width: 4 meters

3. Length: 34 meters
Width: 25 meters

4. Length: 62 meters
Width: 21 meters

Find the area of each rectangle. Use $A = \ell \times w$. [15]

5. Length: 8 meters
Width: 6 meters

6. Length: 9 meters
Width: 5 meters

7. Length: 88 meters
Width: 28 meters

8. Length: 36 meters
Width: 12 meters

Copy and complete. Check. [15]

9.

	PART-TIME PAYROLL		
Worker	Hourly Rate	Hours Worked	Gross Earnings
Arno, D.	$4	40	
Ford, F.	3	38	
Gray, G.	5	35	

10.

	PAYROLL		
Worker	Hourly Rate	Hours Worked	Gross Earnings
Sams, D.	$5	37	
Rays, F.	4	32	
Bott, G.	6	39	

Solve these problems.

11. Deborah wants to put a fence around her rectangular pool. The pool with its apron is 6 meters long and 4 meters wide. How much fencing does she need? [15]

12. Miguel wants to fence in his rectangular garden. His garden with a path around it is 4 meters long and 3 meters wide. How much fencing does he need? [15]

13. The Scudder Publishing Company plans to publish a 512-page textbook. There are 32 sections in the book. What is the average number of pages per section? [19]

14. Sheraton High School expects an enrollment of 1,400 students. There are 35 homerooms in the school. What is the average enrollment per homeroom? [19]

15. Larry Townsend's earnings for the first 3 weeks were $175, $150, and $200. How much must he earn the next week in order to average $167 per week? [19]

16. Sally reported weekly commissions of $125, $135, and $145. How much commission must she earn the next week in order to average $135 per week? [19]

17. Lumber cut into 5-foot lengths is on sale. How many lengths are needed to make a total of 105 feet? [19]

18. Roofing shingles are sold in bundles of 100 square feet. How many bundles are needed to cover a 2,800 square-foot roof? [19]

Self-Test: Chapter 1

Add. [4]

1.	$3,210
	1,568
	726
	4,009
	+ 985

2.	3,985
	1,568
	2,009
	4,210
	+8,726

Subtract. Check. [9]

3. $5,502
$-1,819$

4. 8,403
$- 729$

Multiply. [15]

5. 7,118
$\times 53$

6. 8,056
$\times 36$

Divide. Check. [19]

7. $72\overline{)70,200}$

8. $156\overline{)8,940}$

Find the average. [19]

9. 85, 90, 80, 65, 75

10. $175, $225, $270, $300, $215, $195

Copy and complete. Check.

11.
[4]

Worker	Cash Sales	Charge Sales	Total Sales
A. Baker	$1,978	$1,978	
L. Lopez	3,050	2,025	
K. Tate	879	423	
TOTALS			$10,333

12.
[9]

Item	Total Sales	Returns	Net Sales
327	$175	$59	
747	297	36	
402	400	85	
TOTALS			$692

Solve these problems.

13. Pat bought a carload of books for $3,856. He
[9] sold the books for $4,392. His expenses in selling the books amounted to $712. How much did he lose?

14. Sylvia reported weekly commissions of $82,
[19] $78, $96, and $85. How much commission must she earn the next week in order to average $91 per week?

Test: Chapter 1

Add.

1. $9,004
      2,310
        672
      8,615
        589

2. 3,007
      9,835
      1,568
      2,410
      7,862

Subtract. Check.

3. $7,803
      − 4,928

4. 6,504
       − 957

Multiply.

5. 8,276
      × 39

6. 9,807
      × 54

Divide. Check.

7. 36)12,600

8. 153)7,950

Find the average.

9. 65, 95, 85, 75, 85

10. $185, $235, $280, $320, $215, $265

Copy and complete. Check.

11.

Worker	Cash Sales	Charge Sales	Total Sales
M. Harris	$1,058	$1,058	
T. Finn	459	837	
P. Sudo	1,040	1,025	
TOTALS			$5,477

12.

Worker	Units Completed	Units Rejected	Units Accepted
L. Wang	857	29	
R. Rand	798	57	
G. Stein	600	43	
TOTALS			2,126

Solve these problems.

13. Jane bought a truckload of bricks for $2,856. She sold the bricks for $3,529. Her expenses in selling the bricks amounted to $713. How much did she lose?

14. Bill reported weekly commissions of $87, $93, $79, and $83. How much commission must he earn the next week in order to average $85 per week?

Rounding and Estimating

Round to the nearest 10.

MODELS

$$24$$
$$24 \atop \uparrow$$
Less than 5
So, $24 \doteq 20$
└── Read: is about

$$65$$
$$65 \atop \uparrow$$
5
So, $65 \doteq 70$

$$96$$
$$96 \atop \uparrow$$
More than 5
So, $96 \doteq 100$

1. 43 **2.** 102 **3.** 45 **4.** 555 **5.** 87 **6.** 299

Round to the nearest 100.

MODELS

$$646$$
$$646 \atop \uparrow$$
Less than 5
So, $646 \doteq 600$

$$853$$
$$853 \atop \uparrow$$
5
So, $853 \doteq 900$

$$1,572$$
$$1,572 \atop \uparrow$$
More than 5
So, $1,572 \doteq 1,600$

7. 136 **8.** 343 **9.** 754 **10.** 1,458 **11.** 999 **12.** 3,680

Estimate the sum to the nearest 10.

MODEL $99 + 128 + 103 + 117 + 58$

$99 \longrightarrow 100$
$128 \longrightarrow 130$
$103 \longrightarrow 100$
$117 \longrightarrow 120$
$\underline{58 \longrightarrow 60}$
$510 \longleftarrow$ Sum to the nearest 10

13. $175 + 230 + 186 + 79 + 325$ **14.** $109 + 211 + 999 + 36 + 902$

Estimate the sum to the nearest 100.

MODEL $2,550 + 3,842 + 410 + 73 + 4,378$

$2,550 \longrightarrow 2,600$
$3,842 \longrightarrow 3,800$
$410 \longrightarrow 400$
$73 \longrightarrow 100$
$\underline{46 \longrightarrow 0}$ (Hint: 4 is in the tens place.)
$6,900 \longleftarrow$ Sum to the nearest 100

15. $486 + 840 + 113 + 306 + 27$ **16.** $999 + 2,115 + 340 + 538 + 75$

DECIMALS

A scientist-aquanaut
gaining first hand
knowledge of ocean life

Activities

Copy the figure. Place each of the numerals 1, 2, 3, 4, 5, 6, 7 in a square so that the sum of the numbers in a straight line is 12.

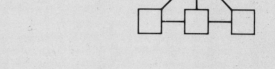

Form a committee to make a display on various careers. Ask your guidance counselor and librarian to help you locate materials for this activity.

Form a committee to make a bulletin-board display entitled "Decimals in Everyday Use." Bring newspapers, bulletins, and other publications showing the use of decimals in supermarkets, cars, sports (percentages), industry, banks, government, financial sections, advertisements, taxes, real estate, etc.

Make a broken line graph showing the position of your favorite record in the TOP FORTY ratings for a month or two. You may compare the rating of two or more records on the same graph by using different colors to represent the various records. Display your graphs on the bulletin board.

Begin a "Consumer Resource Corner" by obtaining various consumer reference pamphlets. A catalog listing many of these references may be obtained from the U.S. Post Office or by writing to Consumer Information, Public Documents Distribution Center, Pueblo, Colorado 81009.

The Meaning of Decimals

decimal   Decimal means "based on ten" or "base ten."

place value   A place-value chart for the decimal system shows the location of the place values.

PLACE-VALUE CHART				
Tens	Units	Tenths	Hundredths	Thousandths
10	1	.1	.01	.001

decimal point   A decimal point is a dot symbol placed immediately after the units place to show that place values to its right are less than 1. Place values to its left are equal to or greater than 1.

congruent   Congruent figures are figures which have the same size and the same shape.

For Discussion

- What does "decimal" mean?

- Where are decimals used?

- How would you describe .003?

"Can you give me some examples where decimals are used?" Harry asked his brother Bob.

Bob wrote a list and showed it to Harry.

Our sales tax is $.04 for each $1 spent.
I bought 16.3 gallons of gas for our car.
Some machine products are made so that they are accurate to .001 of an inch.
The metric system uses the decimal system.

Bob asked, "What does *decimal* mean?"

"*Decimal* means *based on 10* or *base 10*," replied Harry. "We use a place-value chart to help us name decimals. But I still can't imagine what .1 means."

Bob explained, "Imagine a strip of paper like this as being 1. Next, imagine the same strip divided into ten congruent parts. .1 means one small part, .2 means two small parts, and so on. Of course, 1 means 10 small parts. For .01, imagine the strip divided into 100 congruent parts." (See top of page.)

Do you think Bob's explanation is good?

DEVELOPING SKILLS

PLACE VALUE CHART

Whole numbers — Decimals

Hundred Thousands	Ten Thousands	Thousands	Hundreds	Tens	Ones	Tenths	Hundreths	Thousandths	Ten Thousandths	Hundred Thousandths
			5	7	3 •	1	0	9	2	

Read: Five hundred seventy-three   and   one thousand ninety-two ten thousandths

Write word names.

MODELS

.40 → Forty hundredths

25.045 → Twenty-five *and* forty-five thousandths

1. .8   **2.** .008   **3.** 71.6   **4.** 85.45   **5.** 8.376

Write decimals.

6. Four tenths   **7.** Four hundredths

8. One hundred five thousandths   **9.** Three and two hundred seven ten thousandths

Compare. Use =, >, or <.

MODELS

.3 and .30
Rename .3 as .30
.30 = .30
So, .3 = .30

.2 and .001
Rename .2 as .200
.200 > .001
So, .2 > .001
↑ greater than

5.2 and 5.23
Rename 5.2 as 5.20
5.20 < 5.23
So, 5.2 < 5.23
↑ less than

10. .1 and .15   **11.** .35 and .350   **12.** 7.3 and 7.23   **13.** .308 and .380

14. 8.0 and 7.5   **15.** .06 and .60   **16.** .3 and .045   **17.** .8 and .80

APPLYING SKILLS

Write word names.

1. 10.05 **2.** 7.048 **3.** 5.555 **4.** 55.55 **5.** 555.5

Write decimals.

6. Four and forty-one hundredths

7. Five thousandths

8. Sixty-five ten thousandths

9. One hundred six thousandths

10. Nine hundred seventy-eight and sixty-three thousandths

11. Forty-nine and one hundred forty-nine thousandths

12. Ten dollars and fifty-six cents

13. One hundred seven dollars and three cents

14. Eighteen and four tenths centimeters

15. Twenty-seven and five tenths inches

Compare. Which measure is larger?

16. 1.7 lb grapes; 1.2 lb apples

17. 4.6-lb turkey; 4.5-lb hen

18. 24.5-in. stick; 24.8-in. belt

19. 8.2-in. scissors; 8.9-in. nail file

20. 15.35 kilometers; 15.4 kilometers

21. 4.5 miles; 4.25 miles

Compare. Use =, >, or <.

22. .09 and .009 **23.** 13.05 and 13.50 **24.** 23.57 and 23.570 **25.** 25.1 and 2.51

List the decimals from largest to smallest.

26. .056, .15, .005

27. .095, .001, .015

28. .009, .909, .2

29. .151, .49, .08

30. .386, .683, .3864

31. 15.5, 15.05, 15.425

MAINTAINING SKILLS

Copy and complete Mr. Ho's sales record. Use the table to answer
exercises 1–4.   [19]

WEEKLY SALES RECORD FOR OCTOBER					
Day	First Week	Second Week	Third Week	Fourth Week	Total
Monday	$100	$125	$140	$110	
Tuesday	150	160	175	190	
Wednesday	180	170	300	50	
Thursday	170	175	125	200	
Friday	130	160	240	180	
TOTALS					$3,230

1. Find Mr. Ho's first week's average daily sales.

2. Find Mr. Ho's second week's average daily sales.

3. Find Mr. Ho's average Friday sales for the month of October.

4. Find Mr. Ho's average Monday sales for the month of October.

Compare. Write =, >, or <.   [28]

5. 1.573 and 15.73

6. $73.03 and $73.30

7. .003 and .03

8. 25.0405 and 26.04

9. 2.006 and 4.016

10. 60.89 and 70

11. .3456 and 1.003

12. 17.8 and 17.80

13. .46 and .046

14. 45.67 and 45.76

15. 82.97 and 82.79

16. .0004 and .00004

Solve these problems.

17. A traffic officer issued 525 tickets in 15 days.
[19] What was the average number of tickets issued per day?

18. A sales representative sold 960 toasters in 20
[19] days. What was the average number of toasters sold per day?

19. Coodus County reported the following number
[19] of seniors in each of its 6 senior high schools.

217; 103; 185; 201; 167; 129

Find the average number per school.

20. Whitney Shoe Co. has the following number
[19] of employees in each of its 5 factories.

452; 634; 598; 525; 490

Find the average number per factory.

21. Rachel and Bob own a bookstore. They sold
[4] 485 books in July, 500 books in August, and 976 books in September. How many books were sold in all three months?

22. The biology classes needed three buses to get
[4] to the zoo. The first bus held 49 students, the second 27, and the third 38. How many students went to the zoo?

Consumer Tips___

HOW TO BE A WISE SHOPPER

Consumer Information Act   Fair Credit Reporting Act

Federal Trade Commission

Consumer Credit Protection Act   TRUTH–IN–LENDING LAW

- Write for the federal publication index, *Consumer Information*, which lists many free and inexpensive publications of consumer interest.

  Address: Consumer Information
  Public Documents Distribution Center
  Pueblo, Colorado 81009

- Deal with stores, contractors, and services with good reputations.
- Study newspaper advertisements and consumer magazines.
- Use comparison shopping to get the best buy.
- Use unit pricing along with other standards of quality, size, and brand.
- Make a shopping list before shopping. Follow it closely.
- Check the labels of products before buying.
- Walk away from high pressure salespeople.
- Protect your credit rating by buying only those things you can afford.
- Study the features of the Truth-in-Lending law (Consumer Credit Protection Act). This states that the lender of credit must give:

    the finance charge
    the rate charged as the "annual percentage rate" or the
    "annual finance charge per $100 of unpaid balance."

- Learn your rights under the 1971 Fair Credit Reporting Act. Consult the Federal Trade Commission. If you are wrongfully denied credit, insurance, or employment, report it.
- Study carefully any contract before signing.
- Study carefully the warranties and guarantees before buying.
- Obtain a written estimate *before* repairs or improvements are made.
- Insist upon a written receipt upon payment in cash.

Adding & Subtracting Decimals

appliance An appliance is a device or machine, especially for household use.

interior decorator An interior decorator is a person who decorates and furnishes the inside of a room, apartment, house, etc.

list price The list price is the manufacturer's catalog price, usually the amount recommended to be charged consumers of those goods.

For Discussion

- What is Miguel's occupation?

- What is Maria's occupation?

- How did Miguel and Maria get information on prices of appliances?

- What was the saving on each of the appliances?

- Why did Miguel and Maria need the appliances?

Miguel Diaz and Maria Lopez were shopping for appliances at a nearby discount house. They planned to be married in 3 months. Miguel is a computer operator and Maria is an interior decorator.

Miguel and Maria had a pretty good idea of the list prices and the discount prices. They had studied the latest guides on discount buying in the local library.

They finally selected the appliances. Maria itemized the prices from the stickers.

Appliance	List Price	Discount Price
Refrigerator	$ 319.95	$ 290.95
Washer	249.95	206.80
Dryer	194.95	155.65
Dishwasher	249.00	204.75
TOTAL	$1,013.85	$ 858.15

Total of list prices	$1,013.85
Total of discount prices	− 858.15
Total savings	$155.70

Does it pay to be a good shopper?

DEVELOPING SKILLS

OBJECTIVE   To add and subtract decimals

Add. (Place the decimal point in the answer.)

MODELS $13.4 + 28.3$ $1.34 + 2.83$ $3 + 45.2 + 2.34 + .035$

Use vertical columns for "ragged" decimals.

```
    13.4              1.34          3    ────────→     3.000
  +28.3             +2.83          45.2  ────────→    45.200
   41.7              4.17          2.34  ────────→     2.340
                                 + .035  ────────→   + .035
    ↑                 ↑           50.575              50.575
 Line up the decimal points.
                                    ↑                   ↑
                                  Line up the decimal points.
```

1.   8.345
    + 5.142

2.   .3815
    + .1083

3.   1.314
      2.805
      7.891
   + 3.123

4. $121.17
     350.29
     115.63
  + 108.12

5. $44 + 13.2 + 32.47$ **6.** $11.7 + 25.34 + 22.0045$ **7.** $456.87 + 2.3 + 127$

Subtract. (Place the decimal point in the answer.)

MODELS $34.8 - 15.25$ $15 - 3.78$

```
    34.8            34.80          15   ────────→     15.00
  - 15.25         - 15.25        - 3.78             - 3.78
   19.55           19.55          11.22              11.22
     ↑               ↑              ↑                  ↑
 Line up the decimal points.     Line up the decimal points.
```

8.   9.88
   − 2.59

9.   57.9
   − 3.45

10.   4
    − 2.578

11.   328.427
    − 121.155

12. $5.91 - 3.78$ **13.** $49.7 - 24.08$ **14.** $129.8 - 7.455$ **15.** $9.537 - 4.8$

APPLYING SKILLS

Find the total cost of each auto.

1.	
4-door Economy Model	$2,646.00
Automatic transmission	177.40
Interior trim special	53.50
Padded dash and visor	31.80
Transportation charges	67.00
TOTAL	

2.	
Super 2-door Sedan	$3,546.00
Radio	67.00
Whitewall tires	39.90
Wheel covers	26.00
Padded dash and visor	31.30
TOTAL	

Find the balance after each deposit and withdrawal.

3.

Date	Deposit	With-drawal	Balance
Sept. 30			$250.00
Oct. 3	$476.83		
Oct. 10	58.47		
Oct. 17		236.98	
Oct. 24	300.04		

4.

Date	Deposit	With-drawal	Balance
June 1	$500.79		
Aug. 5	150.35		
Sept. 1		100.50	
Oct. 1	200.50		
Dec. 5	75.00		

Solve these problems.

5. Mr. Jacobs made the following purchases.

Suede coat	$160.00	Wallet	$14.98
Umbrella	$12.89	Shoes	$34.00
Leather bag	$46.99	Belt	$10.50

Find the total amount of his purchases.

6. Tamu purchased the following items.

Stamps	$ 5.00	Stationery	$3.95
Fabric	$27.52	Patterns	$3.75
Notions	$6.67	Labels	$4.00

Find the total amount of her purchases.

7. Before polishing, a steel plate was 2.342″ thick. After polishing, the steel plate was 2.087 inches. What amount of thickness was removed in the polishing?

8. Thomas Cohen bought 4.75 yards of material for a pair of pants. The pattern that Thomas bought calls for 3.125 yards. How much material will be left?

9. Rosalyn Baker started a trip with 18.5 liters of gasoline in her tank. She used 17.75 liters and then added 15 liters to the tank. How many liters does she have in the tank?

10. Rodriquez gave a store clerk a $50 bill for a $12.78 item. He then purchased another item that cost $8.15. How much is his change?

MAINTAINING SKILLS

Copy and complete each expense account.   [33]

Hint: Cash advance is money paid by company.

    Hotel + transportation + food + other expenses = total expenses.

    Cash advances − total expenses = balance due.

| | | | | | | | Total | Balance Due | |
	Worker	Cash Advances	Hotel Room	Trans-portation	Food	Other Expenses	Expenses	Company	Worker
1.	Pindle	$150.00	$18.96	$45.00	$23.00	$17.80	104.76	45.24	——
2.	Curran	200.00	$41.06	$87.90	$16.00	$ 9.00			
3.	Stanley	100.00	——	$18.00	$ 9.00	$38.00			
4.	Williams	300.00	$38.72	$157.00	$31.80	$55.00			
5.	Jones	250.00	$60.30	$189.00	$34.00	——			
6.	Hopkins	180.00	——	$14.00	$ 3.88	$73.50			
7.	Daniels	275.00	——	——	——	$189.00			
8.	George	100.00	——	$7.00	$12.00	$80.00			
	TOTALS	$1,555.00					$1,268.92		$33.30

EXPENSE ACCOUNTS—HALEY COMPANY
MONTH OF MAY 1974

Check totals using one of the following:

    Cash advances + bal. due worker − bal. due comp. = total expenses.

    Cash advances + bal. due worker − total expenses = bal. due comp.

    Cash advances − bal. due comp. + bal. due worker = total expenses.

Solve these problems.   [9]

9. Stan bought a truckload of dresses for $3,575. He sold the dresses for $4,298. His expenses amounted to $750. How much did he lose?

10. Pam bought a truckload of suits for $4,525. She sold the suits for $6,893. Her expenses amounted to $1,625. How much did she gain?

11. Alex Munoz's present salary is $9,000 a year. Last year his salary was $8,300. Find his increase in earnings.

12. A sculptor sold her first work for $2,300. Her next piece was sold for $1,700. Find the decrease in price.

13. A bookstore showed total sales for two months: $12,687 in May and $15,020 in June. What was the increase in sales for June?

14. A parking lot showed a profit of $1,426 in July and $1,962 in August. What was the increase in sales for August?

Career/ACCOUNTING

Accounting specialists are involved in the mainstream of all business and economic life. Our nation's economy has created an increasing demand for expert accounting controls. Many businesses require the services of a trained accountant to oversee their operations.

Job Descriptions

- Bookkeeper—keeps the records of a business; prepares payrolls; records information relating to the purchase and sale of merchandise; prepares customers' statements of account.

- Accountant—supervises the bookkeeper; advises management about procedures in operating its business.

- Auditor—verifies accounting records to determine legally acceptable procedures.

- Income tax accountant—prepares federal, state, and local tax returns for individuals and businesses.

- Certified public accountant—examines accounting records; advises management.

Training

Entry-level jobs may be prepared for in high school. Most two- and four-year colleges have business programs with an accounting major. A certified public accountant passes a comprehensive state examination in accounting theory, practice, and law.

Further Investigation

Arrange an interview with an accountant. Ask about job qualifications, working conditions, possibilities for advancement, entry-level jobs.

Consult your guidance department about business programs in your high school, and the post-high-school courses in this area.

Multiplying Decimals

finance contract   A finance contract is a legal form completed when a buyer arranges to repay a loan over a period of time.

factors   Factors are the numbers being multiplied. For example, in the statement, $2 \times 3 = 6$, both 2 and 3 are factors.

product   The product is the result obtained when numbers are multiplied. For example, in the statement, $5 \times 3 = 15$, the product is 15.

interest   Interest is the amount charged for a loan or the cost of borrowing money.

For Discussion

- What information did Mrs. Neumann want?

- Why is the true cost of an article higher than the cash price when buying on time?

- How did Tommy find the amount of interest being charged?

Carol Neumann, a mail carrier, asked the boat dealer, "What would be the finance contract for $2,520 for 24 months?"

The dealer made some calculations and said, "You would have to pay $130.20 per month for 24 months."

That night Carol told her twins, Tommy and Tess, about the boat dealer's offer.

Tommy asked, "How much interest are you being charged?"

"Well, Tommy, suppose you multiply $130.20 by 24," his mother suggested.

$$
\begin{array}{rl}
\$130.20 & \longleftarrow \text{ Monthly payment} \\
\times\,24 & \longleftarrow \text{ Number of months} \\
\hline
520\ 80 & \\
2\ 604\ 0 & \\
\hline
\$3,124.80 & \longleftarrow \text{ Cost and interest}
\end{array}
$$

"Next, subtract $2,520 from $3,124.80."

$$
\begin{array}{rl}
\$3,124.80 & \longleftarrow \text{ Cost and interest} \\
-\,2,520.00 & \longleftarrow \text{ Cost} \\
\hline
\$\ \ \ 604.80 & \longleftarrow \text{ Interest}
\end{array}
$$

"It costs money to borrow money," said Tommy. Are there advantages to paying cash?

DEVELOPING SKILLS

OBJECTIVE   To multiply decimals

Multiply.

MODEL   25.623 × 4.5

$$
\begin{array}{r}
25.623 \longleftarrow \text{3 decimal places plus} \\
\times\,4.5 \longleftarrow \text{1 decimal place} \\
\hline
12\,8115 \\
102\,492 \\
\hline
115.3035
\end{array}
$$

Place the decimal point here, 4 decimal places.

1.   640.7
       × 5.39

2. 3,449.62
       × .055

3.   3.127
       × 653.8

4. 9.0057
       × 32.48

5. $84.70
       × 36

6. $1,115.63
       × 100

7. $2,790.70
       × 7

8. 1,578
       × $.48

9. 32.9 × 1,000

10. .9568 × .46

11. 3.505 × 17

Find the area of each rectangle. Use $A = \ell \times w$.

MODELS   Length: 3.5 yd
              Width: 1.2 yd

$$
\begin{array}{r}
3.5 \\
\times\,1.2 \\
\hline
7\,0 \\
3\,5 \\
\hline
4.2\,0
\end{array}
$$

$A = \ell \times w$
$= 3.5 \times 1.2 \longleftarrow$
$= 4.20$

Length: 3.8 in.
Width: 2.5 in.

$$
\begin{array}{r}
3.8 \\
\times\,2.5 \\
\hline
1\,9\,0 \\
7\,6 \\
\hline
9.5\,0
\end{array}
$$

$A = \ell \times w$
$= 3.8 \times 2.5 \longleftarrow$
$= 9.50$

So, the area is 4.20, or 4.2 sq yd.

So, the area is 9.50, or 9.5 sq in.

12. Length: 26.8 in.
        Width: 9.5 in.

13. Length: 3.5 ft
        Width: 2.75 ft

14. Length: 9.2 yd
        Width: 6.3 yd

15. Length: 4.75 mi
        Width: 2.05 mi

APPLYING SKILLS

Copy and complete.

1.

PARAMOUNT HARDWARE			
Name	Hours Worked	Hourly Rate	Total Wages
C. Dara	38.5	$2.75	
J. Cole	40	3.50	
R. Rule	37.5	3.10	
B. Gong	40.5	2.99	
		TOTAL	

2.

PARAMOUNT HARDWARE			
Customer	Number of Items	Cost Per Item	Total Cost
J. B. Comp	72	$7.50	
Harvey's	36	3.73	
Lu's Wares	125	1.07	
T. Crant's	84	.96	
		TOTAL	

Solve these problems.

3. Mary Jackson can complete 3.5 units in 1 hour. How many units can she complete in 7.5 hours?

4. Larry Daniels walked for 2.5 hours at an average speed of 3.8 miles per hour. How far did Larry walk?

5. A woman earns $3.75 an hour. How much would she earn in a 7-hour day?

6. A man is paid $3.25 per hour. How much would he earn in a 40-hour week?

7. Joe is paid $1.50 for each delivery he makes. These are his deliveries for one week: 15 on Monday, 13 on Tuesday, 17 on Wednesday, 16 on Thursday and 18 on Friday. What were his total earnings for that week?

8. Valerie is paid $2.95 per hour. Last week, she worked 8 hours on Monday, 6.5 hours Tuesday, 7.25 hours on Wednesday, 4 hours on Thursday, and 6.75 hours on Friday. What were her total earnings for that week?

9. What is the total amount earned by a clerk who receives $2.80 per hour for a 37-hour week?

10. What is the total price of 7,540 toys sold by a wholesale dealer for $1.35 each?

Find the areas. $(A = \ell \times w)$

11.

Object	Length	Width	Area
Pool	27 ft	24.125 ft	
Handkerchief	8.5 in.	10 in.	
Sheet	4.3 yds	6.25 yd	
Desk top	3 ft	2.25 ft	

12.

Object	Length	Width	Area
Rug	12.25 ft	18 ft	
Table top	36 in.	38.2 in.	
Garden	10.75 ft	8.2 ft	
Bulletin board	1.2 yd	.5 yd	

MAINTAINING SKILLS

Write decimals. [28]

1. thirteen and twenty-six hundredths

2. nineteen and forty-two hundredths

3. four thousandths

4. three hundredths

5. three hundred six and one hundred ninety-two thousandths

6. nine hundred four and five hundred twelve thousandths

Which is larger? [28]

7. 3 lb chocolate or 2.9 lb chocolate

8. 4.8 kilograms or 5 kilograms

9. 3.782 kilometers or 36.2 kilometers

10. 16.7 miles or 1.678 miles

11. .046 centimeters or .06 centimeters

12. .007 grams or .0026 grams

Divide. [19]

13. $42\overline{)9,702}$

14. $35\overline{)9,380}$

15. $365\overline{)459,170}$

16. $234\overline{)249,912}$

Add. [33]

17.
```
  300
  31.80
   .57
+  1.568
```

18.
```
    .042
   1.83
 389.
+ 31.22
```

19.
```
 $500.87
  103.58
   97.70
+    .98
```

20.
```
 $ .1573
   .8119
  1.0001
+ 2.7390
```

Subtract. [33]

21.
```
 $4,495.27
 - 1,928.46
```

22.
```
 $5,468.35
 - 1,819.90
```

23.
```
  1.07559
 - .93838
```

24.
```
  87.3409
 - 9.9011
```

Solve these problems. [39]

25. Find the number of square feet in a room which measures 12.5 feet long by 10 feet wide.

26. A home movie screen measures 22.5" × 18." How many square inches does this screen contain?

27. What is the total cost of 1,500 items at $3.54 each?

28. What is the total cost of 550 books at $4.14 each?

29. What is the total cost of 60 dozen items if each item sells for 3.75 cents?

30. What is the total cost of 12 dozen items if each item sells for 5.4 cents?

Dividing Decimals

odometer   An odometer is an instrument which measures the distance traveled by a vehicle.

dividend, divisor, quotient, remainder   In the division process, the terms dividend, divisor, quotient, and remainder are used to describe the parts with which we are working.

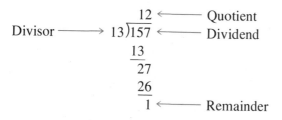

$$\text{Divisor} \longrightarrow 13\overline{)157} \longleftarrow \text{Dividend}$$

Quotient ⟵ 12

$$\begin{array}{r} \underline{13} \\ 27 \\ \underline{26} \\ 1 \longleftarrow \text{Remainder} \end{array}$$

checking division   Checking a division problem is based on this rule:

(divisor × quotient) + remainder = dividend

For Discussion

- What did Ms. Goodman explain to Jane?

- What types of driving were involved?

- Were the decimal points in Jane's divisions placed properly?

Ms. Goodman was explaining to her daughter, Jane, the way to check her gasoline mileage. She continued, "Since you are doing only city driving this week, keep a record of your mileage on the odometer. Also, fill your tank at the beginning and end of the week. Next divide the number of miles by the number of gallons. This is the gasoline mileage."

"That's easy," said Jane, "Since I am going to New York this weekend, I'll do the same to check my mileage on highway driving."

The following week Jane showed her mother her calculations.

City Driving

$$\begin{array}{r} 1\,4.5 \text{ mi/gal} \\ 18.6\overline{)269.7\,0} \text{ mi} \\ \underline{186} \\ 83\,7 \\ \underline{74\,4} \\ 9\,3\,0 \\ \underline{9\,3\,0} \end{array}$$

gal

Highway Driving

$$\begin{array}{r} 2\,1.8 \text{ mi/gal} \\ 11.5\overline{)250.7\,0} \text{ mi} \\ \underline{230} \\ 20\,7 \\ \underline{11\,5} \\ 9\,2\,0 \\ \underline{9\,2\,0} \end{array}$$

gal

"Jane, can you explain the difference?" What was Jane's answer?

DEVELOPING SKILLS

Divide.

MODELS

$$8\overline{)6.4} \qquad\qquad 8\overline{).64}$$

Line up the decimal points.

Whole
number
divisor $\longrightarrow$

$$\overset{.8}{8\overline{)6.4}} \leftarrow \text{Quotient}$$
$$\leftarrow \text{Dividend}$$

$$\overset{.08}{8\overline{).64}}$$

1. $5\overline{)37.860}$ **2.** $33\overline{).6270}$ **3.** $11\overline{)3.30}$ **4.** $121\overline{)72.600}$

5. $21\overline{)7.14}$ **6.** $42\overline{).966}$ **7.** $15\overline{)2.250}$ **8.** $459\overline{)1.377}$

Locate the decimal point in the quotient, then divide.

MODEL $3.14\overline{)77.558}$ $3.14\overline{)77.55\,8}$

$$
\begin{array}{r}
24.7 \\
314\overline{)7755.8} \\
628 \\
\hline
1475 \\
1256 \\
\hline
219\,8 \\
219\,8 \\
\hline
\end{array}
$$

9. $.62\overline{)39.4568}$ **10.** $1.7\overline{)268.09}$ **11.** $3.29\overline{).56917}$ **12.** $.0081\overline{)69.41943}$

13. $43\overline{)2.967}$ **14.** $.65\overline{)1781.65}$ **15.** $3.005\overline{)43.873}$ **16.** $71.25\overline{)527.25}$

Divide. Carry out to 3 decimal places. Round to nearest hundredth.

MODEL $.54\overline{)32.695}$

$$
\begin{array}{r}
60.546 \leftarrow \text{Quotient} \\
.54\overline{)32.69\,500} \leftarrow \text{Dividend} \\
32\,4 \\
\hline
29\,5 \\
27\,0 \\
\hline
2\,50 \\
2\,16 \\
\hline
340 \\
324 \\
\hline
16 \leftarrow \text{Remainder}
\end{array}
$$

Divisor

Add zeroes
to carry to
3 decimal
places.

So, $60.546 = 60.55$ to the nearest hundredth.

17. $.75\overline{).025}$ **18.** $.567\overline{)6.84}$ **19.** $23.3\overline{)125.6125}$ **20.** $.0347\overline{)7.8}$

APPLYING SKILLS

Divide.

1. $2.6\overline{)189.8}$ 2. $.14\overline{).938}$ 3. $.13\overline{)3563.3}$ 4. $43\overline{)2.967}$

5. $60.1\overline{)87.746}$ 6. $.082\overline{).0007872}$ 7. $1.425\overline{)1054.5}$ 8. $.009\overline{).23787}$

9. $35\overline{)\$187.60}$ 10. $9\overline{)\$29,510.19}$ 11. $7\overline{)\$3.43}$ 12. $12\overline{)\$178.32}$

13. $1,250 \div 10$ 14. $12.50 \div 10$ 15. $.015 \div 100$ 16. $98.7 \div 10$

Place the decimal point in the correct place in the quotient.

MODEL

$$51.03 \div 1.458 = 35.00$$

Dividend ÷ Divisor = Quotient

Check:

$$1.458 \times 35 = 51.03$$

Divisor × Quotient = Dividend

17. $16.159 \div 24.86 = 6500$

18. $36.9264 \div 75.36 = 4900$

19. $6103.9 \div 984.5 = 6200$

20. $7869.66 \div 84.62 = 9300$

21. $266,112 \div 985.6 = 2700$

22. $462.4 \div 6800 = 06800$

Solve these problems.

23. On a speed run of 1,120 miles, Ralph Forn's driving time was 13.25 hours. Find his average speed in miles per hour.

24. On a speed run of 1,120 miles, Sarah Well's driving time was 12.5 hours. Find her average speed in miles per hour.

25. Celeste sold 240 items for $500. What was the average price per item correct to the nearest whole cent?

26. A high school DECA club sold 125 tickets for $312.50. What was the average cost per ticket?

27. A strip of metal 135.44 inches long was cut into 32 equal parts. In the cutting process .56 in. was lost. How long was each part?

28. Material 160.38 yards long is cut into 25 equal pieces for clearance. In the cutting process .63 yd is lost. How long is each piece of material?

29. Suki sold a case of 24 cans of peanuts for $17.50. How much did each can cost, to the nearest cent?

30. A subscription costs $8.85 for 52 weeks. What is the single cost, to the nearest cent?

MAINTAINING SKILLS

Multiply. [39]

1. .320 × 100

2. .045 × 1,000

3. 4.595 × 25

4. 9.878 × 32

5. 36.4 × 82.9

6. 3.92 × 8.36

7. .308 × .421

8. .411 × .421

Divide. [43]

9. 8,562.84 ÷ 9.98

10. 5,416.32 ÷ 8.32

11. 4,367.52 ÷ 3.24

12. 5,940.9 ÷ 6.15

13. 10.187 ÷ 3.34

14. 10.807 ÷ 5.05

Solve these problems.

15. Find the total cost of 50 feet of shelving at $22
[39] a foot, 10 sheets of plaster board at $3.22 a
sheet, and 2 gallons of paint at $8.87 a gallon.

16. Find the total cost of purchasing 3 chairs at
[39] $17.50 a chair, 2 chests of drawers at $39.50
each, and a twin-size mattress for $57.50.

17. Ms. Jackson selected carpeting that cost $12
[39] per square meter for her office. How much
will it cost her to have wall-to-wall carpet if
her office is 4.3 meters x 3.9 meters?

18. Mr. Field wants to install wall-to-wall carpet-
[39] ing in his living room. The carpeting he selected
cost $10.50 per square meter. What will it cost
for the 5.6 meters by 4.1 meters room?

19. A super train travels 2,500 miles in 12.5 hours.
[43] How many miles does it travel in 1 hour? At that
rate, how many miles does it travel in 3 hours?

20. A plane travels 1,092 miles in 2.5 hours. How
[43] many miles does it travel in 1 hour? At that
rate, how many miles does it travel in 2 hours?

21. The Right Good Co. sold $4,038,697.50 worth
[43] of calculators last year. The cost of one calculator is $88.50. How many calculators were
sold?

22. The Time Sound Radio Co. sold $3,618,724.80
[43] worth of radios last year. The cost of one radio
is $45.60. How many radios were sold?

Copy and complete. [39]

23.

Name	Hourly Rate	Hours Worked	Gross Wages
J. Smith	$4.25	38.5	
H. Black	4.50	40.0	
P. White	6.70	39.5	

24.

Name	Hourly Rate	Hours Worked	Gross Wages
R. Wong	$6.35	37.5	
B. Wright	5.95	40.0	
C. Charles	6.50	35.0	

Self-Test: Chapter 2

Write word names. [28]

1. .0105

2. 1.46

Write decimals. [28]

3. Two and five hundredths

4. Four hundred seven thousandths

Compare. Use =, >, or <. [28]

5. 4.64 and 4.604

6. .0132 and .132

Add. [33]

7.   1.36
    + .061

8.   18.467
    +29.489

Subtract. [33]

9.   4.072
    − .961

10.   25
    − 1.32

Multiply. [39]

11. 4.23
    ×1.2

12. 6.431
    ×.014

Divide. [43]

13. .42)‾3864

14. 3.5)‾64.4

Find the area. $(A = l \times w)$ [39]

15.

Object	Length	Width	Area
Window	10 ft	4.5 ft	
Desk top	1.3 yd	.8 yd	
Rug	12.5 yd	10.2 yd	

Find the balance after each deposit. [33]

16.

Date	Deposit	Withdrawal	Balance
Dec 3			$482.36
Dec 18	$38.27		
Jan 2	81.36		

Solve these problems.

17. Bart bought $13.95 worth of merchandise. How
[33] much change did he receive from a $20 bill?

18. Sarah bought a record for $4.52. How much
[33] change did she receive from a $10 bill?

19. A subscription to a weekly magazine cost $5.98
[44] for 26 weeks. How much does it cost per week?

20. A street vendor sold 1,152 hot dogs last week.
[44] He worked 6 days. What was the average number sold per day?

Test: Chapter 2

Write word names.

1. 4.02

2. .1468

Write decimals.

3. Fourteen hundredths

4. Five and twenty-five thousandths

Compare. Use =, >, or <.

5. 4.681 and 4.68

6. .014 and .0041

Add.

7.
$$\begin{array}{r} 1.461 \\ +.032 \\ \hline \end{array}$$

8.
$$\begin{array}{r} .461 \\ +.992 \\ \hline \end{array}$$

Subtract.

9.
$$\begin{array}{r} 12 \\ -3.62 \\ \hline \end{array}$$

10.
$$\begin{array}{r} 8.46 \\ -.97 \\ \hline \end{array}$$

Multiply.

11.
$$\begin{array}{r} 4.38 \\ \times 1.22 \\ \hline \end{array}$$

12.
$$\begin{array}{r} .461 \\ \times .013 \\ \hline \end{array}$$

Divide.

13. $.37\overline{)32{,}227}$

14. $1.2\overline{)4.608}$

Find the area. $(A = l \times w)$

15.

Room	Length	Width	Area
Hall	24.6 ft	3.5 ft	
Den	14.4 ft	10.1 ft	
Kitchen	10.1 ft	9 ft	

Find the balance after each deposit.

16.

Date	Deposit	Withdrawal	Balance
Mar 4			$461.87
Mar 19	$461.91		
Apr 6	32.87		

Solve these problems.

17. Judy bought a dog for $75.42. She gave the clerk $80. How much change did she receive?

18. Hank bought a coat for $65.64. He gave the clerk $70. How much change did he receive?

19. Eugene White bought 22 display cases for his store. The cost was $9,355.50. What did one case cost?

20. Gloria Harris sold 516 charity sweepstakes tickets for $129. How much did one ticket cost?

Mental Multiplication

Multiply mentally.

MODELS

36×10	36×100	$36 \times 1,000$	$36 \times 10,000$
36	36	36	36
$\times 10$	$\times 100$	$\times 1,000$	$\times 10,000$
360	3,600	36,000	360,000
1 zero	2 zeros	3 zeros	4 zeros

1. 345×10 **2.** 190×10 **3.** 316×10 **4.** $1,440 \times 10$

5. 72×100 **6.** 106×100 **7.** 149×100 **8.** $1,500 \times 100$

9. $87 \times 1,000$ **10.** $217 \times 1,000$ **11.** $100 \times 1,000$ **12.** $506 \times 1,000$

13. $47 \times 10,000$ **14.** $111 \times 10,000$ **15.** $302 \times 10,000$ **16.** $93 \times 10,000$

Multiply mentally.

MODELS

2.6×10	2.6×100	$2.6 \times 1,000$
26.0, or 26	260.0, or 260	2,600.0, or 2,600
Moved 1 place to the right	Moved 2 places to the right	Moved 3 places to the right

17. 1.5×10 **18.** $.94 \times 10$ **19.** 23.4×10 **20.** $.003 \times 10$

21. 42.6×100 **22.** 2.35×100 **23.** 8.673×100 **24.** $.006 \times 100$

25. $.628 \times 1,000$ **26.** $86.26 \times 1,000$ **27.** $.0679 \times 1,000$ **28.** $.0038 \times 1,000$

Multiply mentally.

MODELS

$\$.53 \times 10$	$\$.53 \times 100$	$\$5.34 \times 10$
$\$5.30$	$\$53.00$, or $\$53$	$\$53.40$

29. $\$.39 \times 10$ **30.** $\$4.80 \times 10$ **31.** $\$2.25 \times 10$ **32.** $\$5.06 \times 10$

33. $\$.65 \times 100$ **34.** $\$7.23 \times 100$ **35.** $\$6.03 \times 100$ **36.** $\$.26 \times 1,000$

Multiply each number by 10, 100, and 1,000.

37. 576   **38.** 19.5   **39.** .006   **40.** $\$.36$ **41.** $\$9.36$

3

MEASUREMENT

Scientist taking a leaf
cutting for laboratory
examination

Activities

Place each of the numerals 1, 2, 3, 4, 5, 6, 7, 8, 9, 10, 11 in a square so that the sum of the numbers in one straight line totals 18.

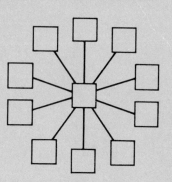

Make bulletin-board displays on the following:
1) Various sports and Olympic games which use metric measurement.
2) Industries and companies which are converting to the metric system, and some of their products which use metric measures.

Visit your local supermarket and make a list of the canned goods, packages, and medical products which indicate the quantity, size, or dosage in metric units.

Make a metric resource center in your library or another appropriate place. Collect the latest articles, books, magazines, and pamphlets dealing with the metric system. Also include some measuring devices as meter sticks, metric cups, metric scales, etc.

Make a survey of students and parents to find out what they know about the metric system and attitudes toward conversion to the metric system. Present your results to your class.

Conduct a debate on "The Metric System vs. The English System—Which Is Better?" Be sure that each side is aware of the advantages and disadvantages of both sides of the question.

Metric Units of Length

metric system   The metric system is a system of measurement based on the decimal system.

meter   The meter (m), sometimes spelled *metre,* is a unit of length in the metric system.

METRIC UNITS OF LENGTH			
1 kilometer	(km)	=	1,000 meters (m)
1 hectometer	(hm)	=	100 meters
1 dekameter	(dam)	=	10 meters
1 decimeter	(dm)	=	.1 meter
1 centimeter	(cm)	=	.01 meter
1 millimeter	(mm)	=	.001 meter

place-value chart   This place-value chart is helpful in renaming metric units of length.

km	hm	dam	m	dm	cm	mm

Each unit is 10 times the unit immediately to its right. Each unit is .1 of the unit immediately to its left.

For Discussion

- What course did Larry have to take?
- Why is the metric system simple?
- What U.S. companies and industries are changing over to the metric system?

Carl Schmidt, the service manager, said to Larry Bartolo, "I'm glad that you are going to work for us. Since you are a mechanic for foreign cars, your main concern with the metric system is to understand and use millimeters. Since you don't know the metric system, I want you to take a self-study course, *Metrics for Mechanics,* published by our company. If you have any trouble, come to me for help."

"I didn't realize that the metric system was so important," Larry commented.

"Well, Larry, the metric system is a very simple system," said Mr. Schmidt. "It is based on the decimal system, and it is used more than you think. For example, in Olympic events, on patterns for clothes, on labels of canned goods, and vitamin dosage we use metric measures. Many large U.S. companies and industries such as the copper, steel, and foreign cars are already changing over to the metric system. It is expected that the metric system will soon be the official measurement system in the U.S."

"You have really convinced me," said Larry.

DEVELOPING SKILLS

Measure each to the nearest centimeter and to the nearest millimeter.

1. _____   2. _____

3. _____   4. _____

Rename the metric measurements.

MODEL   975.6 mm = ___?___ m

Start with the decimal point immediately to the right of the given unit.   9   7   5   .6

km	hm	dam	m	dm	cm	mm

Then move the decimal point immediately to the right of the desired unit.   9   7   5   6

So, 975.6 mm = .9756 m

5. 5.6 m = ___?___ mm   **6.** 3,860 m = ___?___ km   **7.** 3 km = ___?___ m

8. 658 mm = ___?___ dm   **9.** 15.2 dam = ___?___ mm   **10.** 26.8 cm = ___?___ hm

11. 35,000 mm = ___?___ dm   **12.** 1.5 cm = ___?___ mm   **13.** 260 m = ___?___ km

Estimate the number of centimeters.

MODEL   An inch is a little more than 2.5 centimeters. About how
many cm are there in 5 in.? in 5 ft? [≐ means about]
$2.5 \times 5 = 12.5$ $2.5 \times 60 = 150.0$
So, 5 in. ≐ 12.5 cm   So, 5 ft ≐ 150 cm

14. 3 in.   **15.** 10 in.   **16.** 15 in.   **17.** 2 ft   **18.** 10 ft   **19.** 25 ft

Estimate the number of inches.

MODEL   A centimeter is a little less than .4 inch. About how many
in. are there in 12 cm? in 2 m?
$12 \times .4 = 4.8$ 2 m = 200 cm $200 \times .4 = 80.0$
So, 12 cm ≐ 4.8 in.   So, 2 m ≐ 80 in.

20. 10 cm   **21.** 15 cm   **22.** 25 cm   **23.** 1 m   **24.** 5 m   **25.** 10 m

APPLYING SKILLS

Measure to the nearest centimeter.

1. The length of your desk

2. The width of your desk

Measure to the nearest millimeter.

3. The length of your hand

4. The diameter of a quarter

Solve these problems.

5. Mr. and Mrs. Yoshida toured cities in the U.S. They followed this route:

San Francisco to Atlanta	3,442.4 km
Atlanta to Philadelphia	1,071.8 km
Philadelphia to Denver	2,541.2 km
Denver to San Francisco	1,527.3 km

How many kilometers did they travel? How many meters?

6. Mr. and Mrs. Mann toured the world. They followed this route:

New York to London	5,582.8 km
London to Cairo	3,516.4 km
Cairo to Hong Kong	8,153.0 km
Hong Kong to New York	12,971.4 km

How many kilometers did they travel? How many meters?

7. Mr. Frazer wants to put a wire fence around his evergreen seedling bed. The perimeter of the bed is 7.2 meters. Wire fencing costs $2.05 a m. How much will the fence cost?

8. Ms. Gimbel wants to put a plastic border around her triangular rock garden. The perimeter of the garden is 10.8 meters. Plastic border costs $1.95 a m. How much will the border cost?

9. A meter is a little more than a yard. About how many meters are there in 10 yards?

10. A meter is a little more than a yard. About how many meters are there in 24 yards?

11. A kilometer is a little more than .6 mile. About how many miles are there in 20 kilometers?

12. A kilometer is a little more than .6 mile. About how many miles are there in 60 kilometers?

13. Jack walked 3 miles. Dot walked 3 kilometers. Who walked farther? About how much farther?

14. Abni traveled 160 miles. Bart traveled 160 kilometers. Who traveled farther? About how much farther?

15. A mile is about 1.6 kilometers. About how many kilometers are there in 15 miles?

16. A mile is about 1.6 kilometers. About how many kilometers are there in 25 miles?

17. Ms. Blue Spruce drove at a speed of 50 mph. About how many km per hr did she drive?

18. Mr. Hernandes drove at a speed of 45 mph. About how many km per hr did he drive?

MAINTAINING SKILLS

Add using vertical columns.
Be sure to align the decimal points properly. [33]

1. 38.24; 560.31; 3.842; 56

2. 8.305; 2.61; 30.04; 2.1

3. 4.7; 9.6; .463; 1.24; 81.411

4. 3.8; 5.6; .26; 36.1; 89.094

5. 3,610.09; 92.382; 42,000.036; 4

6. 36.843; .086; 93,443.42; 10

Multiply. [15]

7. 463
× 42

8. 378
× 38

9. 746
× 82

10. 968
× 22

Solve these problems.

11. Morris spent the following amounts while on a [33] 3-day tour.

$7.97, $14.89, $.87, $5.00,
$10.10, $.98, and $.55

How much did he spend?

12. Last month Wilma spent the following amounts [33] on office supplies.

$.46, $1.29, $.38, $4.55,
$2.89, $.85, and $11.49

How much did she spend?

13. Last month Sara made deposits of $103.40, [33] $150.00, $45.63, $11.95, and $19.45. What was the total amount she deposited?

14. Ron's bill contained charges of $13.64, $52.98, [33] $77.80, $42.63, and $19.36. Find the total amount of his bill.

15. A factory sold 10,524 machines in one year at [15] $105 each. Find the total amount of sales.

16. A manufacturing company sold 12,836 fans in [15] one year at $78 each. Find the total amount of sales.

Copy and complete. [15]

17.

SUPPLY COMPANY			
Item Number	Number of Items	Cost Per Item	Total
A4367	146	$22	
A6434	55	14	
B7831	104	8	
D4002	25	54	

18.

HANDY HARDWARE			
Item Number	Number of Items	Cost Per Item	Total
436A	11	$19	
783H	47	47	
891E	194	7	
471E	117	11	

Consumer Tips———

ORGANIZATIONS THAT CAN HELP

2/4/74

To: Office of Consumer Affairs,
About 3 months ago, I ordered a radio
through the mail and I have never received it. One...

Do you need information? Or have a complaint? Or wish to report some deceptive or illegal selling practices? Start with your own local and state officials and agencies. You will find these listed in your telephone directory.

Still have a problem? Here are some national agencies to turn to:

Problems: All types of consumer problems.
Agency: Office of Consumer Affairs, Dept. of Health, Education, and Welfare, 330 Independence Avenue S.W., Washington, D.C. 20201

Problems: Complaints about obscene postal materials.
Use of mails to defraud.
Agency: Consumer Advocate, U.S. Postal Service, Room 5920, L'Enfant Plaza S.W., Washington, D.C. 20260.

Problems: Unsafe and dangerous tools, appliances, housewares, toys.
Agency: Consumer Product Safety Commission, Washington, D.C. 20207

Problems: Labeling and care of fabrics; fraudulent business methods.
Deceptive ads by companies in interstate business.
Agency: Federal Trade Commission, 6th and Pennsylvania Aves., Washington, D.C. 20580. (Local FTC in telephone directory.)

Problems: How to contact and obtain information about federal agencies.
Agency: Federal Information Center (see telephone directory)

Problems: Complaints about major appliances.
Failure to receive satisfaction from dealers and manufacturers.
Agency: Major Appliance Consumer Action Panel, 20 North Wacker Drive, Chicago, Illinois 60606.

Metric Units of Capacity

capacity   Capacity is the amount of liquid a container will hold.

volume   Volume is the amount of space inside an object.

liter   The liter (ℓ), sometimes spelled *litre,* is the basic unit of capacity in the metric system.

METRIC UNITS OF CAPACITY	
1 kiloliter (kl) =	1,000 liters
1 hectoliter (hl) =	100 liters
1 dekaliter (dal)=	10 liters
1 deciliter (dl) =	.1 liter
1 centiliter (cl) =	.01 liter
1 milliliter (ml) =	.001 liter

place-value chart   This place-value chart is helpful in renaming metric units of capacity.

kl	hl	dal	ℓ	dl	cl	ml

For Discussion

- What are the three most important metric units of capacity?

- What kind of geometric figure did Ms. Myers use to describe a liter?

"Before long, the capacity of measuring devices such as the cup and the teaspoon will be given in metric units," said Ms. Myers in her Foods II class. "Do you remember what capacity is, Tommy?" she asked her top student.

"Capacity tells how much liquid a container will hold," he answered.

She continued, "The most commonly used metric units are the liter, the milliliter, and the kiloliter. The other units are not used so often, but they are useful in the place-value chart we use to rename measurements."

She then asked Tommy to pour water from a liter container into a plastic cube-shaped container with length, width, and height each 10 centimeters.

Tommy said, "This cube has a volume of 1,000 cubic centimeters (cc) and holds 1 liter of water."

Ms. Myers wrote their findings on the chalkboard.

$$1 \ \ell = 1{,}000 \text{ cc} \qquad 1 \text{ ml} = 1 \text{ cc}$$

She continued, "For our work it is important to know that 1 cup has a capacity of 250 milliliters and 1 teaspoon has a capacity of 5 milliliters."

DEVELOPING SKILLS

Make true sentences.

MODELS

45 kl = ____?____ ℓ

kl	hl	dal	ℓ	dl	cl	ml

4 5 . 0 0 0

So, 45 kl = 4500 ℓ.

56 ml = ____?____ ℓ

kl	hl	dal	ℓ	dl	cl	ml

. 0 5 6 .

So, 56 ml = .056 ℓ.

1. 1 kl = ____?____ ℓ

2. 1 ℓ = ____?____ ml

3. 1 ℓ = ____?____ kl

4. 1 ml = ____?____ ℓ

5. 1 ml = ____?____ cl

6. 15 kl = ____?____ ℓ

7. 3.6 kl = ____?____ ℓ

8. 465 ml = ____?____ ℓ

9. 8,956 ℓ = ____?____ kl

10. 1,320 ml = ____?____ ℓ

11. 3.85 ℓ = ____?____ ml

12. 111,500 ℓ = ____?____ kl

Make true sentences. (Hint: 1 ℓ = 1,000 cc.)

13. 3 ℓ = _____ cc

14. 1 ml = _____ cc

15. 2,000 ml = _____ cc

Find the capacity in liters and in milliliters.

MODELS

21,450 cc
1 ℓ = 1,000 cc
21,450 ÷ 1,000 = 21.450
So, 21,450 cc = 21.45 ℓ,
or 21,450 ml.

30 cc
1 ℓ = 1,000 cc
30 ÷ 1,000 = .030
So, 30 cc = .03 ℓ, or
30 ml.

16. 37,000 cc

17. 42,800 cc

18. 50 cc

19. 75 cc

Estimate the number of liters.

MODEL   A liter is a little more than a quart. About how many liters are
there in 1 gallon?

Think: 1 gal = 4 qt and 1 ℓ ≐ 1 qt so, 1 gal ≐ 4 ℓ [≐ means is approximately equal to.]

20. 16 qt

21. 30 qt

22. 10 gal

23. 50 gal

24. 100 gal

Estimate the number of quarts and the number of gallons.

25. 4 ℓ

26. 12 ℓ

27. 20 ℓ

28. 30 ℓ

29. 50 ℓ

APPLYING SKILLS

Find the volume. (Use $V = \ell \times w \times h$.) Then find the capacity in liters and in milliliters.

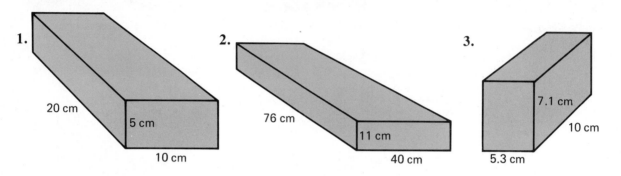

1. 20 cm, 5 cm, 10 cm

2. 76 cm, 11 cm, 40 cm

3. 7.1 cm, 10 cm, 5.3 cm

Solve these problems.

4. A can of juice holds 177 ml of juice. How many ℓ of juice does it hold?

5. A carton of milk holds 946 ml of milk. How many ℓ of milk does it hold?

6. A bottle has a capacity of .281 ℓ. What is its capacity in ml?

7. A mixing bowl has a capacity of .215 ℓ. What is its capacity in ml?

8. A gasoline tank truck has a volume of 31,037,000 cc. What is its capacity in ℓ? in kl?

9. A tanker has a volume of 21,960,000 cc. What is its capacity in ℓ? in kl?

10. A storage tank for acetic acid measures 400 cm by 300 cm by 200 cm. What is its capacity in ℓ? in kl?

11. Molasses was stored in a tank measuring 400 cm by 500 cm by 300 cm. What is its capacity in ℓ? in kl?

12. Milk sells for $1.40 a gal. About how much would 1 ℓ cost?

13. Liquid soap sells for $3.20 a gal. About how much would 1 ℓ cost?

14. Mary bought 4 gal of gas for $2.40. John bought 4 ℓ of gas for $.60. Who made the better buy?

15. Jake bought 5 qt of oil for $4.95. Lula bought 5 ℓ of oil for $4.95. Who made the better buy?

16. A bottle has a capacity of 20 ℓ. About what is its capacity in qt?

17. A bowl has a capacity of 60 ℓ. About what is its capacity in qt?

18. Miss Rose Chang bought 20 ℓ of gas. About how many gal of gas did she buy?

19. Mr. Bruce Kent bought 28 ℓ of gas. About how many gal of gas did he buy?

MAINTAINING SKILLS

Find the balance after each deposit or withdrawal. [33]

1.

Date	Deposit	Withdrawal	Balance
10/13			$432.86
10/14		$260.46	
10/16	$36.87		
10/20	306.42		
10/21		467.36	

2.

Date	Deposit	Withdrawal	Balance
2/23			$42.34
3/1	$242.00		
3/6		$106.42	
3/7	10.50		
3/11		96.43	

Copy and complete. Check. [33]

3.

WEEK ENDING MAY 10			
Employee	Gross Earnings	Total Deductions	Net Pay
Butter, A.	$155.42	$29.63	
Chu, W.	168.93	31.41	
Cohen, D.	104.96	10.85	
Outler, M.	203.91	42.81	
Ruth, J.	128.42	15.65	
TOTALS			$631.29

4.

WEEK ENDING MAY 31			
Employee	Gross Earnings	Total Deductions	Net Pay
Bear, G.	$242.97	$56.03	
Eagles, C.	196.81	36.42	
Fisher, N.	209.33	39.56	
Lyons, E.	214.64	41.83	
Robins, H.	186.23	29.81	
TOTALS			$846.33

Solve these problems.

5. Meg and Rose were cutting boards for book-
[33] shelves. Meg's board was 4.56 meters long.
Rose's board was 3.67 meters long. How much
longer was Meg's board?

6. Paul has a piece of wood 12.67 meters long. He
[33] needs a board 8.71 meters long. How much had
to be cut off to make the board the right length?

7. Sam needed 190 greeting cards. How many
[19] boxes of 24 cards each did he need to buy?

8. The Youth Club needs 175 name tags. How
[19] many packages of 16 name tags each will they
need to buy?

9. A truckload of 30 hogs weighed 7,020 pounds.
[19] Find the average weight of each hog.

10. A truckload of 48 bags of sand weighed 1,680
[19] pounds. Find the average weight of each bag.

11. How many bags of 24 apples each can be made
[19] from a truckload of 1,440 apples?

12. How many cartons of 16 reams each can be
[19] made from 800 reams of paper?

Career/GRAPHIC ARTS

Communications specialists work on radio, television, movies, and newspapers. Printing is one of the oldest forms of communication. It is rated the seventh largest industry in the United States. Graphic arts also involves illustrating, engraving, and packaging.

Job Descriptions

- Printing technician—assists in the actual production or manufacture of the printed product; operates and services printing machinery; understands how electronic computers aid in production.

- Production specialist—coordinates the procurement and delivery of all materials and equipment needed to manufacture the printed product; schedules the various operational steps in the manufacturing process; analyzes production problems and recommends solutions.

- Technical services specialist—tests materials used in manufacturing printed products; determines quality standards to meet each job; keeps up-to-date on new techniques and materials, keeps accurate records to develop higher quality products.

Training

Training may be available to high school graduates. Most career openings, however, are open to those who have completed at least a community or junior college program.

Further Investigation

Arrange an interview with a communications specialist. Ask about job qualifications, working conditions, possibilities for advancement, entry-level jobs.

Consult your guidance department about your high school programs suitable for training skills in this area. Ask about post-high-school programs in communications specialties.

Metric Units of Weight

tutor   A tutor is a person who teaches on an individual basis in special subjects.

relationship   A relationship is a connection or link between things.

gram   The gram (g) is a unit of mass. On earth we commonly use this unit for weight.

METRIC UNITS OF WEIGHT	
1 kilogram (kg) =	1,000 grams (g)
1 hectogram (hg) =	100 grams
1 dekagram (dag) =	10 grams
1 decigram (dg) =	.1 gram
1 centigram (cg) =	.01 gram
1 milligram (mg) =	.001 gram

place-value chart   This place-value chart is helpful in renaming metric units of weight.

kg	hg	dag	g	dg	cg	mg

For Discussion

- What are the 3 most important metric units of weight?
- What relationship involves metric length, capacity, and weight?

Charles Harris was explaining metric weight to George Cobb, who had been absent. As a member of the Dunbar High School Tutors' Club, Charles had helped many Dunbar students.

"George, the most important units are kilogram, gram, and milligram," Charles said. "There is an important relationship involving length, capacity, and weight. Our present system does not have this. Look here!"

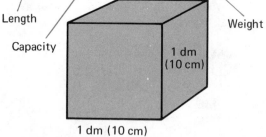

1 cu dm holds 1 ℓ of water which weighs 1 kg

Length

Capacity

Weight

1 dm (10 cm)

1 dm (10 cm)

"Now look at it this way, George, 1 cc holds 1 ml of water which weighs 1 g."

George said, "That's clear. It all fits."

DEVELOPING SKILLS

OBJECTIVES   To rename metric units of weight and use the relationship among volume, capacity, and weight
To change units of weight from English to metric and metric to English

Make true sentences.

MODELS

68.5 kg _____?_____ g

kg	hg	dag	g	dg	cg	mg

6 8 . 5   0   0

So, 68.5 kg = 68,500 g.

123 mg = _____?_____ g

kg	hg	dag	g	dg	cg	mg

1   2   3 .

So, 123 mg = .123 g.

1. 1 kg = _____?_____ g

2. 1 g = _____?_____ mg

3. 1 g = _____?_____ kg

4. 21.9 kg = _____?_____ g

5. 326 mg = _____?_____ g

6. 2,165 g = _____?_____ kg

7. 4,265 mg = _____?_____ g

8. 3.72 kg = _____?_____ mg

9. 90,000 mg = _____?_____ kg

Find the weight. Use these relationships.

1 cu dm holds 1 ℓ of water which weighs 1 kg
1 cc holds 1 ml of water which weighs 1 g

10. 1,052 ml of milk

11. 50 ℓ of water

12. 20 cc of juice

13. 15 cu dm of soup

Make true sentences. Use these relationships.

1 oz = 30 g   **1 lb = .5 kg**   **1 kg = 2 lb**

MODELS

25 oz $\doteq$ _____?_____ g
25 × 30 = 750
So, 25 oz $\doteq$ 750 g

140 lb $\doteq$ _____?_____ kg
140 × .5 = 70.0
So, 140 lb $\doteq$ 70 kg

18 kg $\doteq$ _____?_____ lb
18 × 2 = 36
So, 18 kg $\doteq$ 36 lb

14. 16 oz $\doteq$ _____?_____ g

15. 36 oz $\doteq$ _____?_____ g

16. 100 oz $\doteq$ _____?_____ g

17. 5 lb $\doteq$ _____?_____ kg

18. 175 lb $\doteq$ _____?_____ kg

19. 220 lb $\doteq$ _____?_____ kg

20. 65 kg $\doteq$ _____?_____ lb

21. 200 kg $\doteq$ _____?_____ lb

22. 1,300 kg $\doteq$ _____?_____ lb

APPLYING SKILLS

1. An object is placed on a pan of a balance. The object is balanced when weights of 500 g, 200 g, 100 g, and 50 g are placed on the other pan. What is the weight of the object in g? in kg?

2. An object is placed on a pan of a balance. The object is balanced when weights of 1,000 g, 500 g, 200 g, and 20 g are placed on the other pan. What is the weight of the object in g? in kg?

3. In a science lab identical cups are placed on the pans of a balance. An object is placed in one cup and balanced with water poured into the other. The cup contains 1,763 ml of water. What is the weight of the object in g? in kg?

4. In a science lab identical cups are placed on the pans of a balance. An object is placed in one cup and balanced with water poured into the other. The cup contains 2,050 ml of water. What is the weight of the object in g? in kg?

5. An object in a container is placed on a pan of a balance. An identical container on the other pan is filled with 8.6 ℓ of water. What is the weight of the object in kg? in mg?

6. An object in a container is placed on a pan of a balance. An identical container on the other pan is filled with 9.3 ℓ of water. What is the weight of the object in kg? in mg?

7. Don bought some hamburger which weighed 28 ounces. About how many grams did it weigh? About how many kilograms?

8. Lena bought some grapes which weighed 34 ounces. About how many grams did they weigh? About how many kilograms?

9. A foreign car weighs 1,800 kilograms. About how many pounds does the car weigh?

10. A football guard weighs 125 kilograms. About how many pounds does the guard weigh?

11. Jerry Goldberg wanted to buy 4 pounds of Swiss cheese. The cheese was selling for $4.50 per kilogram. About how much would he have to pay?

12. Ms. Agnes Blue Spruce wanted to buy 10 pounds of sugar. The sugar was selling for $1.05 per kilogram. About how much would she have to pay?

13. Mr. Bates bought 6 kilograms of beef for $22.68. About how much per pound did the beef cost?

14. Mrs. Romero bought 8 kilograms of coffee for $15.20. About how much per pound did the coffee cost?

15. Which would you rather have: a kilogram of gold, or a pound of gold?

16. Which would you rather have: a gram of gold, or an ounce of gold?

MAINTAINING SKILLS

Divide. [43]

1. 97.98 ÷ 46

2. 16.95 ÷ 15

3. 7,636 ÷ .08

4. 1,046 ÷ .04

5. 1.885 ÷ .13

6. 32.13 ÷ .42

Multiply. [39]

7. 11,842
× .06

8. 4,873
× .08

9. 735.15
× .11

10. 468.93
× .21

11. 3,416
× .025

12. 2,457
× .015

13. 3.52
× .21

14. 5.41
× .13

15. 480
× .9

16. 914
× .4

Find the total cost. [39]

17. 72 toys at 12.5 cents per toy

18. 98 bolts at 8.7 cents per bolt

19. 2.5 tons at $38 per ton

20. 4.7 kilograms at $12 per kilogram

21. 50 gallons at 67.8 cents per gallon

22. 75 liters at 90.5 cents per liter

23. 55 meters at 44 cents per meter

24. 90 feet at 20 cents per foot

Solve these problems.

25. George spent $159.50 on movie tickets. One
[43] ticket cost $2.75. How many tickets did he
buy?

26. Mary spent $39.15 on a surprise party. She
[43] spent $1.45 per guest. How many guests were
at her party?

27. Ben sold a case of 24 bottles of liquid cleaner
[43] for $23.04. How much did each bottle cost?

28. A subscription to a weekly magazine cost
[43] $14.56 for 52 weeks. What is the cost per
week?

29. A sales representative drove 412.6 miles on
[43] 18 gallons of gasoline. How many miles per
gallon (to the nearest tenth) was this?

30. Marita drove 362.8 miles on 14 gallons of gaso-
[43] line. How many miles per gallon (to the nearest
tenth) was this?

31. A strip of metal 1,616.44 centimeters long is
[43] cut into 44 equal parts. During the cutting
process, .76 centimeters is lost. How long is
each piece of metal?

32. A piece of copper wire 3,186.8 centimeters
[43] long is cut into 52 equal parts. During the cutting process, .24 centimeters is lost. How long
is each piece of wire?

Temperature

degree Celsius   Degree Celsius is the unit used in the metric system to measure temperature.

aptitude   Aptitude is a natural ability or talent.

calibrate   To calibrate is to place or adjust guide marks on dials or instruments to indicate degrees or quantity.

mechanical   Mechanical means having to do with machinery or tools.

For Discussion

- Why is it important for Mr. DuBois' students to learn about the Celsius thermometer?

- What are two key points on the Celsius thermometer?

"The change to the metric system is close at hand. It is very important that you become familiar with the Celsius thermometer." Mr. DuBois was talking to his Heating and Refrigeration class at Harden Technical Junior College. "In the metric system temperature is measured in degrees Celsius (°C). Zero degrees (0°C) is the point at which water freezes. One hundred degrees (100°C) is the point at which water boils. Can anyone suggest why the Celsius thermometer used to be called the Centigrade thermometer?"

Jane Curry, who has an excellent mechanical aptitude, answered, "There is a difference of 100 degrees between the freezing and boiling points of water, and *Centigrade* means *divided into hundreds*."

"Very good, Jane," remarked Mr. DuBois. "You will be seeing the dials for ovens calibrated with metric scales. The same thing is true for wall thermostats for heating and cooling. You will soon become used to the new units. It will seem strange at first to think of a temperature of 40°C as hot weather. However, we will get a lot of practice reading Celsius thermometers."

DEVELOPING SKILLS

OBJECTIVE   To read, interpret, and use Celsius temperatures

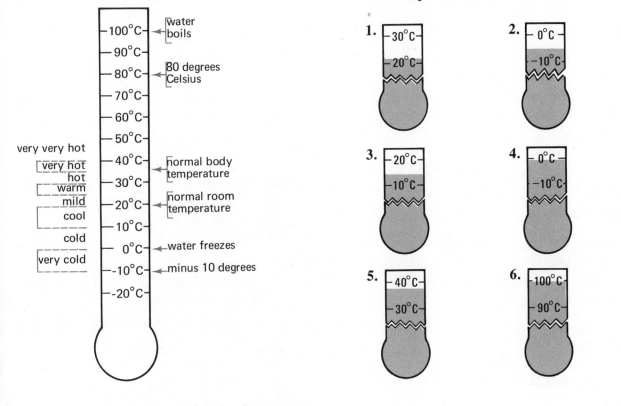

What temperature is shown?

Interpret the temperature. Use the thermometer.

MODELS   28° C   34° C   − 12° C
                28° C: warm   34° C: hot   − 12° C: very cold

7. 25° C   **8.** − 5° C   **9.** 15° C   **10.** 0° C   **11.** 38° C   **12.** 100° C

What is the change in temperature?

MODELS   From 20° C to − 5° C   From − 10° C to 5° C
                From 20° C to 0° C is a drop of 20°.   From − 10° C to 0° C is a rise of 10°.
                From 0° C to − 5° C is a drop of 5°.   From 0° C to 5° C is a rise of 5°.
                So, the temperature dropped 25°.   So, the temperature rose 15°.

13. From 25° C to 10° C   **14.** From 10° C to − 10° C   **15.** From − 5° C to − 15° C

APPLYING SKILLS

1. At dawn the temperature was 2° C. At 1 p.m. the temperature was 19° C. How many degrees did the temperature rise?

2. At noon the temperature was 17° C. At midnight the temperature was 2° C. How many degrees did the temperature drop?

3. At 1 p.m. the temperature was 6° C. By 9 p.m. it was −22° C. How many degrees did the temperature fall?

4. At 6 a.m. the temperature was −4° C. By noon it was 22° C. How many degrees did the temperature rise?

5. The lowest temperature recorded in Hawaii was −8° C on February 20, 1962. The highest recorded temperature was 38° C on April 27, 1931. What is the difference between these temperatures?

6. The lowest temperature recorded in Florida was −19° C on February 13, 1899. The highest recorded temperature was 43° C on June 29, 1931. Find the difference between these temperatures.

7. The lowest temperature recorded in Texas was −31° C on February 8, 1933. The highest recorded temperature was 49° C on August 12, 1936. Find the difference between these temperatures.

8. The lowest temperature recorded in California was −43° C on January 20, 1937. The highest recorded temperature was 57° C on July 10, 1913. Find the difference between these temperatures.

9. On November 8, 1974, the high temperature at Buffalo was 7° C. The high temperature at New Orleans was 19° C. Find the difference between these temperatures.

10. On November 8, 1974, the high temperature recorded at Anchorage was −3° C. The high temperature at Boston was 8° C. Find the difference between these temperatures.

11. At 1 p.m. the temperature was 8° C. At 9 p.m. the temperature had dropped 18°. What was the temperature at 9 p.m.?

12. At noon the temperature was −2° C. By midnight the temperature had dropped 17°. What was the temperature then?

13. At 6 p.m. the temperature was 6° C. By noon the temperature had risen 19°. What was the temperature at noon?

14. At 5 a.m. the temperature was −8° C. By noon the temperature had risen 29°. What was the temperature at noon?

Draw a bar graph.

15. Monthly Temperatures in Houston

Jan.	12° C	July	28° C
Feb.	13° C	Aug.	28° C
Mar.	16° C	Sept.	26° C
Apr.	21° C	Oct.	22° C
May	24° C	Nov.	16° C
June	28° C	Dec.	13° C

16. Monthly Temperatures in San Diego

Jan.	13° C	July	21° C
Feb.	13° C	Aug.	22° C
Mar.	15° C	Sept.	21° C
Apr.	17° C	Oct.	19° C
May	18° C	Nov.	17° C
June	19° C	Dec.	14° C

MAINTAINING SKILLS

1. Find the average of these test scores.

[19]
92	84	77	74
86	89	90	82
90	83	78	80

2. Find the average of these bowling scores.

[19]
172	181	164	189
204	175	182	164
190	174	169	175

3. Jane's scores on 6 tests were 85, 91, 76, 87,
[19] 85, and 80. Find her average test score.

4. Ben's scores on 4 tests were 76, 89, 92, and
[19] 95. Find his average test score.

Write decimals. [28]

5. Forty-six hundredths

6. Twelve hundredths

7. Six and fourteen thousandths

8. Four and twenty-five thousandths

9. One hundred three and eight tenths

10. Four hundred nine and three tenths

Compare. Use < and >. [28]

11. .81 and .18

12. 3.42 and 3.24

13. .042 and .24

14. .081 and .18

15. 4.046 and 5.01

16. 12.943 and 21.349

Copy and complete. Check. (See page 35.) [33]

		JUNE EXPENSE REPORT						Balance Due	
	Worker	Cash Advance	Hotel Room	Trans-portation	Food	Other Expenses	Total Expenses	Company	Worker
17.	Adam, H.	$200.00	$ 76.40	$ 26.00	$45.00	$ 56.00	$203.40	——	$3.40
18.	Brooks, S.	400.00	36.25	156.45	37.00	98.50			
19.	Collins, J.	40.00	——	10.42	15.50	10.90			
20.	Finch, L.	150.00	65.00	52.80	33.80	20.00			
21.	Goode, A.	350.00	120.00	80.25	75.00	41.50			
22.	Ito, K.	100.00	36.00	23.40	37.80	15.60			
23.	Lane, A.	50.00	25.50	——	11.80	36.40			
24.	Rath, E.	200.00	78.50	112.65	55.80	28.90			
25.	Stein, D.	160.00	54.60	97.75	40.30	6.30			
26.	Thomas, E.	250.00	97.82	74.80	87.60	112.45			
27.	Usler, H.	150.00	45.25	37.80	42.00	3.60			
28.	Wick, G.	75.00	19.00	48.72	23.50	10.00			
	TOTALS						2,320.61		

Self-Test: Chapter 3

Measure to the nearest centimeter. [52]

1. _____

Measure to the nearest millimeter. [52]

2. _____

Make true sentences. [52, 57, 63]

3. 42 m = _____ km

4. .4 cm = _____ mm

5. 3.62 m = _____ cm

6. 42 ml = _____ ℓ

7. 60 ℓ = _____ kl

8. 22 ℓ = _____ ml

9. 143 g = _____ kg

10. 1.4 kg = _____ g

11. 43 mg = _____ g

Estimate to make true sentences. [52, 57, 63]

12. 4 in. $\doteq$ _____ cm

13. 72 cm $\doteq$ _____ in.

14. 14 qt $\doteq$ _____ ℓ

15. 40 ℓ $\doteq$ _____ gal

16. 4 kg $\doteq$ _____ lb

17. 30 oz $\doteq$ _____ g

Interpret each temperature. [67]

18. $-10°$ C

19. 35° C

What is the change in temperature? [67]

20. From 10° C to $-5°$ C

Solve these problems.

21. A kilometer is a little more than .6 mile. About [52] how many miles are there in 50 kilometers?

22. Anna traveled 310 miles. Doug traveled 310 [52] kilometers. Who traveled farther? About how much farther?

23. Ms. Tanaka wants to put a wire fence around [52] her seedling bed. The perimeter of the bed is 10.2 meters. Wire fencing costs $2.15 a meter. How much will the fence cost?

24. An object in a container is placed on a pan of a [63] balance. An identical container on the other pan is filled with 1,462 ml of water. What is the weight of the object in kg?

25. Mr. Harris bought 3 kilograms of steak for $15. [63] About how much per pound did it cost?

26. Mary bought 4 gal of gas for $2.12. John bought [57] 4 ℓ of gas for $.55. What was the difference in price?

27. A mixing bowl has the capacity of 2.46 ℓ. What [57] is its capacity in ml?

28. The temperature went from $-4°$ C to 5° C. How [67] many degrees did the temperature rise?

Test: Chapter 3

Measure to the nearest centimeter.

1. _____

Measure to the nearest millimeter.

2. _____

Make true sentences.

3. 36 m = _____ km

4. .61 cm = _____ mm

5. 32.4 m = _____ cm

6. 48 ml = _____ ℓ

7. 90 ℓ = _____ kl

8. 36 ℓ = _____ ml

9. 419 g = _____ kg

10. 3.8 kg = _____ g

11. 96 mg = _____ g

Estimate to make true sentences.

12. 6 in. ≐ _____ cm

13. 56 cm ≐ _____ in.

14. 26 qt ≐ _____ ℓ

15. 96 ℓ ≐ _____ gal

16. 11 kg ≐ _____ lb

17. 61 oz ≐ _____ g

Interpret each temperature.

18. −1° C

19. 99° C

What is the change in temperature?

20. From 4° C to 16° C

Solve these problems.

21. A kilometer is a little more than .6 mile. About how many miles are there in 60 kilometers?

22. Kokayi traveled 27 miles. Hasanati traveled 27 kilometers. Who traveled farther? About how much farther?

23. Mr. Saito wants to put a wire fence around his garden. The perimeter of the garden is 15.9 meters. Wire fencing costs $2.10 a meter. How much will the fence cost?

24. An object in a container is placed on a pan of a balance. An identical container on the other pan is filled with 962 ml of water. What is the weight of the object in kg?

25. Mrs. Jones bought a 4-kilogram beef roast for $16.80. About how much per pound did it cost?

26. Sam bought 6 gal of gas for $3.30. Jane bought 6 ℓ of gas for $.84. What was the difference in price?

27. A pickle jar has the capacity of 1.62 ℓ. What is its capacity in ml?

28. The temperature went from 17° C to −1° C. How many degrees did the temperature fall?

Mental Division

Divide by 10.

MODELS

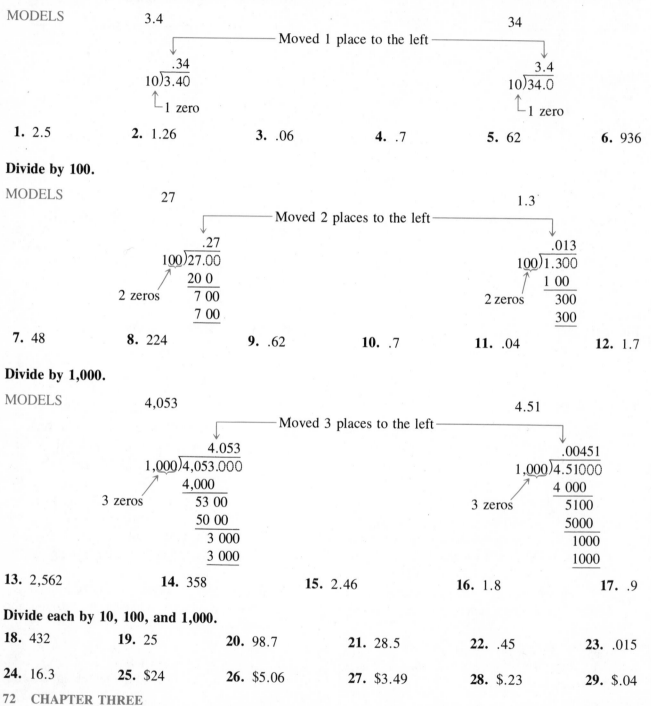

3.4

── Moved 1 place to the left ──

34

```
    .34
10)3.40
    └ 1 zero
```

```
    3.4
10)34.0
    └ 1 zero
```

1. 2.5   **2.** 1.26   **3.** .06   **4.** .7   **5.** 62   **6.** 936

Divide by 100.

MODELS

27

── Moved 2 places to the left ──

1.3

```
      .27
100)27.00
      20 0
2 zeros  7 00
      7 00
```

```
      .013
100)1.300
      1 00
2 zeros  300
      300
```

7. 48   **8.** 224   **9.** .62   **10.** .7   **11.** .04   **12.** 1.7

Divide by 1,000.

MODELS

4,053

── Moved 3 places to the left ──

4.51

```
        4.053
1,000)4,053.000
        4,000
3 zeros  53 00
        50 00
        3 000
        3 000
```

```
         .00451
1,000)4.51000
        4 000
3 zeros  5100
        5000
        1000
        1000
```

13. 2,562   **14.** 358   **15.** 2.46   **16.** 1.8   **17.** .9

Divide each by 10, 100, and 1,000.

18. 432   **19.** 25   **20.** 98.7   **21.** 28.5   **22.** .45   **23.** .015

24. 16.3   **25.** $24   **26.** $5.06   **27.** $3.49   **28.** $.23   **29.** $.04

Cumulative Review

Add.

1. 3,643
[4] 2,040
+ 3,652

2. 14.83
[33] 62.46
+ 11.41

Subtract.

3. 6,432
[9] − 2,821

4. 3.438
[33] − 1.309

Multiply.

5. 436
[15] × 12

6. 4.036
[39] × .02

Divide.

7. 42)‾546‾
[19]

8. 3.1)‾6.944‾
[43]

Make true sentences.

9. 50 m = _____ km
[52]

10. 1.8 cm = _____ mm
[52]

11. .36 ℓ = _____ ml
[57]

12. 45 ℓ = _____ cc
[52]

13. 45 mg = _____ g
[63]

14. 4.83 kg = _____ g
[63]

Estimate to make true sentences.

15. 8 in. ≐ _____ cm
[52]

16. 2 gal ≐ _____ ℓ
[57]

17. 8 lb ≐ _____ kg
[63]

Solve these problems.

18. The temperature went from − 10° C to 20° C.
[67] How many degrees did the temperature rise?

19. Marita traveled 346 miles. Omai traveled 346
[52] kilometers. Who traveled farther?

20. Maxina bought a baseball for $2.15. How much
[33] change did she receive from a $10.00 bill?

21. On a trip, Jim recorded daily mileages of 146,
[19] 205, 179, 186, and 194. What was his average
daily mileage?

Copy and complete.

22.
[39]

SMITH'S BOUTIQUE			
Name	Hours Worked	Hourly Rate	Total Pay
Abe, T.	38.5	$4.10	
Clark, K.	40	$3.30	
Dawn, S.	37.5	$2.56	
		TOTAL	

23.
[4]

HARRIS SPORTS SHOP			
Dept.	Cash Sales	Charge Sales	Total Sales
113	$1,468	$846	
205	$ 367	$251	
319	$ 962	$463	
TOTALS			$4,357

Reading Bar Graphs

Answer the questions about this vertical bar graph.

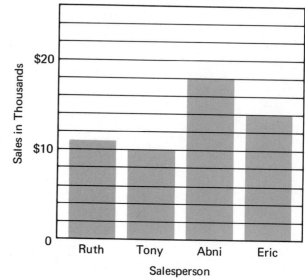

1. What is the title of the graph?

2. What is shown on the horizontal scale?

3. What is shown on the vertical scale?

4. What does 1 unit on the vertical scale mean?

5. Who sold the most? the least?

6. What is the difference in their sales?

7. What were the total sales that week?

8. What were the average sales that week?

Answer the questions about this horizontal bar graph.

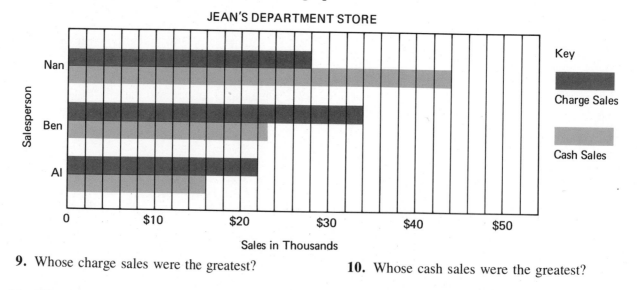

9. Whose charge sales were the greatest?

10. Whose cash sales were the greatest?

11. What were the total sales that week?

12. What were the average total sales that week?

13. What were the average charge sales?

14. What were the average cash sales?

4

FRACTIONS

A food inspector
checking the sugar
content in orange juice

Activities

Copy the puzzle at the right. Unscramble each word, one letter to each box. Then unscramble the circled letters to form a word to fill the boxes below.

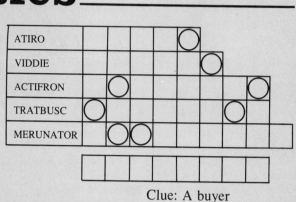

ATIRO					◯		
VIDDIE						◯	
ACTIFRON		◯					◯
TRATBUSC	◯						◯
MERUNATOR		◯	◯				

Clue: A buyer

Conduct a survey at your school to find out what part of the student body have part-time jobs. Your survey could sample the following:

1) What is your classification?

Sophomore _____
Junior _____
Senior _____

2) Do you have a part-time job?

Yes _____
No _____

3) If you work, do you have an early dismissal, or do you start work after school?

Early _____
After _____

4) What is your job? _____
   (What do you do?)

Keep a record of the answers. Report your findings for questions 1 and 2 in the form of a graph.

Make a report on agencies (i.e., Office of Consumer Affairs, Consumer Product Safety Commission, Major Appliance Consumer Action Panel, etc.) which can assist you or your parents in solving consumer problems and in registering complaints. Write for information and include your findings in the "Consumer Resource Corner" activity suggested on page 26.

Equivalent Fractions

fraction   A fraction is a way of expressing a value. It is made up of three parts: a horizontal bar, a whole number written above the bar, and a whole number greater than zero written below the bar; for example, $\frac{2}{3}$, $\frac{4}{5}$, $\frac{7}{8}$.

numerator   The numerator is the number written above the bar in a fraction. In the fraction $\frac{2}{3}$, the numerator is 2.

denominator   The denominator is the number written below the bar in a fraction. In the fraction $\frac{2}{3}$, the denominator is 3.

simplify a fraction   To simplify a fraction is to rename the fraction so that the only common factor of its numerator and denominator is 1.

equivalent fraction   An equivalent fraction is one which has been renamed by multiplying both numerator and denominator by the same non-zero number.

For Discussion

- How can you identify the numerator and denominator of a fraction?
- What procedure does Beth use to find equivalent fractions?

Karen Smith was working on her assignment. "We've been studying fractions," she told her sister, Beth. She showed her:

$$\frac{1}{4} \xleftarrow{\text{numerator}} \xrightarrow{} \frac{3}{8}$$
$$\xleftarrow{\text{denominator}} \xrightarrow{}$$

"We use diagrams to practice simplifying fractions," she explained.

"I had trouble in finding equivalent fractions when I had to rename in higher terms," she continued.

Beth asked, "Do you recall what happens to a number when you multiply it by 1?"

Karen replied, "The answer is the same as the original number." She wrote: $8 \times 1 = 8$, $750 \times 1 = 750$.

"Remember," Beth said, "There are many ways of writing the number 1 as a fraction." She wrote: $1 = \frac{2}{2}$, $1 = \frac{4}{4}$, $1 = \frac{5}{5}$, $1 = \frac{9}{9}$.

"Change the number 1 to a fraction in which both numerator and denominator are the same. Then multiply the fraction by this identity number. The result is a fraction in higher terms with the same value as the original fraction." She demonstrated: $\frac{2}{3} \times \frac{2}{2} = \frac{4}{6}$, "so $\frac{2}{3}$ and $\frac{4}{6}$ are equivalent."

DEVELOPING SKILLS

OBJECTIVE   To simplify fractions and to find equivalent fractions

Name each point using sixteenths, eighths, fourths, and/or halves.

MODELS   Point A represents $\frac{8}{16}$, $\frac{4}{8}$, $\frac{2}{4}$, and $\frac{1}{2}$.   Point E represents $\frac{28}{16}$, $\frac{14}{8}$, and $\frac{7}{4}$.

1.

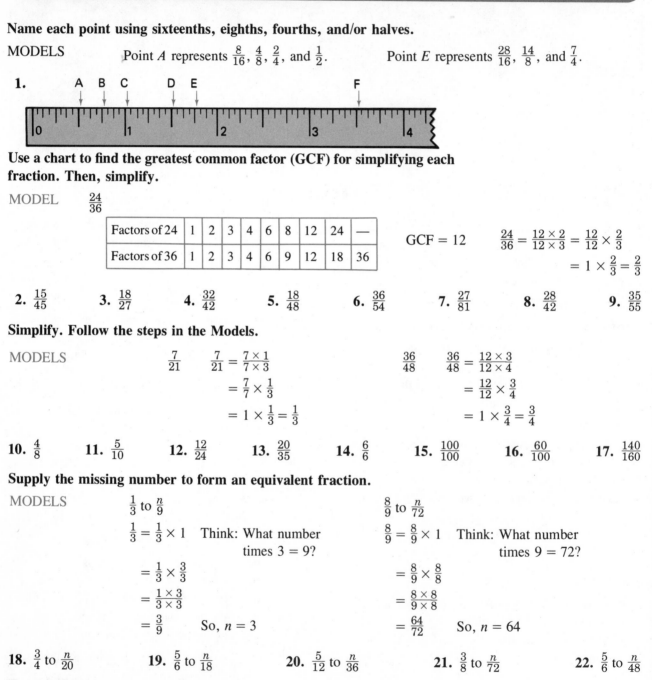

Use a chart to find the greatest common factor (GCF) for simplifying each fraction. Then, simplify.

MODEL $\frac{24}{36}$

Factors of 24	1	2	3	4	6	8	12	24	—
Factors of 36	1	2	3	4	6	9	12	18	36

GCF = 12 $\frac{24}{36} = \frac{12 \times 2}{12 \times 3} = \frac{12}{12} \times \frac{2}{3}$

$= 1 \times \frac{2}{3} = \frac{2}{3}$

2. $\frac{15}{45}$ **3.** $\frac{18}{27}$ **4.** $\frac{32}{42}$ **5.** $\frac{18}{48}$ **6.** $\frac{36}{54}$ **7.** $\frac{27}{81}$ **8.** $\frac{28}{42}$ **9.** $\frac{35}{55}$

Simplify. Follow the steps in the Models.

MODELS $\frac{7}{21}$ $\frac{7}{21} = \frac{7 \times 1}{7 \times 3}$ $\frac{36}{48}$ $\frac{36}{48} = \frac{12 \times 3}{12 \times 4}$

$= \frac{7}{7} \times \frac{1}{3}$ $= \frac{12}{12} \times \frac{3}{4}$

$= 1 \times \frac{1}{3} = \frac{1}{3}$ $= 1 \times \frac{3}{4} = \frac{3}{4}$

10. $\frac{4}{8}$ **11.** $\frac{5}{10}$ **12.** $\frac{12}{24}$ **13.** $\frac{20}{35}$ **14.** $\frac{6}{6}$ **15.** $\frac{100}{100}$ **16.** $\frac{60}{100}$ **17.** $\frac{140}{160}$

Supply the missing number to form an equivalent fraction.

MODELS $\frac{1}{3}$ to $\frac{n}{9}$ $\frac{8}{9}$ to $\frac{n}{72}$

$\frac{1}{3} = \frac{1}{3} \times 1$ Think: What number $\frac{8}{9} = \frac{8}{9} \times 1$ Think: What number
                              times 3 = 9?   times 9 = 72?

$= \frac{1}{3} \times \frac{3}{3}$ $= \frac{8}{9} \times \frac{8}{8}$

$= \frac{1 \times 3}{3 \times 3}$ $= \frac{8 \times 8}{9 \times 8}$

$= \frac{3}{9}$ So, $n = 3$ $= \frac{64}{72}$ So, $n = 64$

18. $\frac{3}{4}$ to $\frac{n}{20}$ **19.** $\frac{5}{6}$ to $\frac{n}{18}$ **20.** $\frac{5}{12}$ to $\frac{n}{36}$ **21.** $\frac{3}{8}$ to $\frac{n}{72}$ **22.** $\frac{5}{6}$ to $\frac{n}{48}$

APPLYING SKILLS

1. John Pirone and his 2 friends bought a pizza which they divided equally. How much did each boy receive?

2. Sue Hoffman and her 4 friends bought 2 pizzas which they divided equally. How much did each one receive?

3. Name each point using eighths.

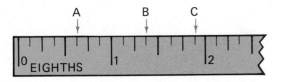

4. Name each point using fifths.

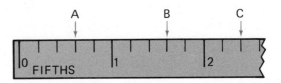

5. Name each point using sixteenths.

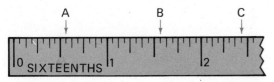

6. Name each point using tenths.

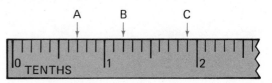

Simplify each answer.

7. Frank Hernandes has agreed to repay a loan in 8 months. This is equal to what part of a year?

8. It takes Gloria Green 18 minutes to walk to her job. What fractional part of an hour is 18 minutes?

9. Lisa spent 65 cents for a school notebook. What fractional part of a dollar did she spend?

10. Phil spent 80 cents for a ballpoint pen. What fractional part of a dollar did he spend?

11. On a 450-mile trip to Baltimore, Al had to stop for gas after driving 250 miles. What fractional part of the trip was completed?

12. On a 640-mile trip to Chicago, Beth stopped for lunch after driving 120 miles. What fractional part of the trip was completed?

Write 3 fractions equivalent to each.

MODEL

$\frac{1}{4}$

$\frac{1}{4} \times 1 = \frac{1}{4} \times \frac{2}{2}$

$\qquad = \frac{2}{8}$

$\frac{1}{4} \times 1 = \frac{1}{4} \times \frac{3}{3}$

$\qquad = \frac{3}{12}$

$\frac{1}{4} \times 1 = \frac{1}{4} \times \frac{4}{4}$

$\qquad = \frac{4}{16}$

13. $\frac{1}{2}$ **14.** $\frac{1}{5}$ **15.** $\frac{3}{4}$ **16.** $\frac{7}{8}$

MAINTAINING SKILLS

Find the area of each rectangle. [39]

1. Length: 2.3 m
Width: 1.2 m

2. Length: 14.5 cm
Width: 6.3 cm

3. Length: 12.6 m
Width: 9.4 m

4. Length: 1.06 m
Width: .92 m

Copy and complete. [39]

5.

Name	Hourly Rate	Hours Worked	Total Wages
J. Smith	$4.25	38.5	
H. Black	$4.50	40.0	
P. White	$6.70	39.5	
A. Ford	$5.15	37.0	

6.

Name	Hourly Rate	Hours Worked	Total Wages
R. Wong	$6.35	37.5	
B. Wright	$5.95	40.0	
C. Charles	$6.50	35.0	
H. Mott	$4.80	32.75	

Make true sentences. [52]

7. 4 km = _____ m

8. 8 km = _____ m

9. 423 m = _____ km

10. 1,978 m = _____ km

11. 136 mm = _____ cm

12. 42 mm = _____ cm

13. 43 cm = _____ m

14. 347 cm = _____ m

15. 8.7 m = _____ cm

Solve these problems.

16. Martha can complete 12.6 units in 1 hour. She
[39] is paid $.25 per unit. How much does she earn in 1 hour?

17. Bill can complete 9.2 units in 1 hour. He is
[39] paid $.30 per unit. How much does he earn in 1 hour?

18. Sam can complete 16.5 units in 1 hour. He is
[39] paid $.20 per unit. How much does he earn in an 8-hour day?

19. Jendayi can complete 15.4 units in 1 hour. She
[39] is paid $.22 per unit. How much does she earn in an 8-hour day?

20. Mrs. Harris plans to make a picture frame. The
[52] frame molding she selected cost $6.27 a meter. How much will the molding cost?

21. Mr. Cohen plans to put a short wire fence
[52] around his flower garden. The wire fencing cost $1.05 a meter. How much will the fence cost?

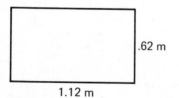

.62 m

1.12 m

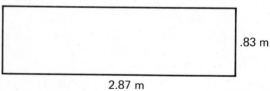

.83 m

2.87 m

Consumer Tips———

HOW TO CONSERVE ENERGY

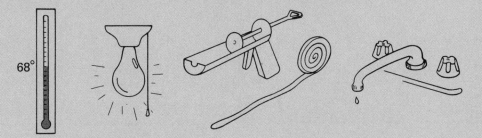

- Keep the thermostat at 68° during the day, 65° during the night.
- Change the filters in your heating and cooling system(s).
- Close the damper in your fireplace when not in use.
- Install storm doors and windows.
- Keep your storm doors and windows closed in winter, and when cooling during the summer.
- Close off unheated attics. If necessary, use caulking to seal.
- Close window drapes and shades at night during the winter and when cooling in the summer.
- Seal cracks and openings outside and inside your home. Apply caulking compound outside around doors and windows. Apply caulking rope inside around air conditioners and appliances.
- Turn off lights in rooms not being used.
- Use fluorescent lighting in bathrooms, laundries, kitchens, and garages. Fluorescent light uses only about one-fourth the electricity used by incandescent light.
- Use cold water in the washing machine. Hot water heaters are costly.
- Repair leaky faucets. A dripping hot water faucet will cause the water heater to operate more often, and use more fuel. Whether hot or cold, a dripping water faucet wastes hundreds of gallons of water a year.

Ratio and Proportion

credit union A credit union is a savings and loan organization formed by the employees of a company to serve its own members.

rate A rate is a relative amount, usually expressed as a ratio or a percent.

ratio A ratio is a comparison of numbers which shows the relationship of one to the other, usually stated as a fraction.

proportion A proportion is a statement of equality between 2 ratios.

For Discussion

- When a ratio is written as a fraction, which number is used as the numerator?

- Which number is used as the denominator?

- What is needed to set up a proportion?

Ben Carr wanted to borrow enough money to buy a camera. Sam, his older brother, belongs to a credit union.

Sam said, "The rate of interest on a loan from my credit union is $9 on every $100 borrowed. This means that the ratio of the interest to the amount of the loan is 9 to 100." He wrote:

$$\frac{9}{100} \quad \longleftarrow \text{Compared number} \longrightarrow 9{:}100$$
$$\qquad \longleftarrow \text{Compared-to number} \longrightarrow$$

"Each of these," he continued, "is read as 9 to 100."

"I see," said Ben, "since a ratio is a fraction, I can use the idea of equivalent fractions to find the interest on a loan of $125." He wrote:

$$\frac{9}{100} = \frac{n}{125}$$

Sam said, "You wrote a proportion which is read 9 is to 100 as n is to 125."

Ben figured the credit union charged $11.25 on a loan of $125. Was he right?

Sam said, "You can use a proportion to compare two fractions as well as to solve problems dealing with rates."

DEVELOPING SKILLS

Write a fraction for each ratio. Simplify when possible.

1. 3 to 12   **2.** 5 to 25   **3.** 3 to 6   **4.** 24 to 48   **5.** 54 to 90   **6.** 14 to 24

In every true proportion the product of the extremes equals the product of the means.

Extreme $\longrightarrow$ $\dfrac{7}{8} = \dfrac{21}{24}$ $\longleftarrow$ Mean $7 \times 24 = 8 \times 21$

Mean $\longrightarrow$ $\phantom{\dfrac{7}{8}}$ $\longleftarrow$ Extreme $168 = 168$

Copy and complete.

	Proportion	Extremes	Means	Product of Extremes	Product of Means	True Proportion
	$\frac{1}{2} = \frac{3}{6}$	1,6	2,3	6	6	Yes
7.	$\frac{3}{8} = \frac{5}{12}$					
8.	$\frac{4}{5} = \frac{12}{15}$					

Solve these proportions. Check.

MODEL $\dfrac{3}{4} = \dfrac{24}{n}$ $3 \times n = 4 \times 24$ Check: $\dfrac{3}{4} = \dfrac{24}{32}$

$3n = 96$ $3 \times 32 = 4 \times 24$

$3n \div 3 = 96 \div 3$ $96 = 96$

$n = 32$

9. $\frac{5}{7} = \frac{n}{63}$ **10.** $\frac{13}{21} = \frac{91}{n}$ **11.** $\frac{8}{15} = \frac{n}{105}$ **12.** $\frac{17}{n} = \frac{68}{100}$ **13.** $\frac{16}{25} = \frac{64}{n}$

Compare. Use <, =, or >.

MODELS $\frac{3}{5}$ and $\frac{3}{4}$ $\frac{5}{8}$ and $\frac{7}{16}$ $\frac{5}{6}$ and $\frac{7}{8}$

$3 \times 4 \, ? \, 5 \times 3$ $\frac{5}{8} = \frac{5}{8} \times 1 = \frac{5}{8} \times \frac{2}{2} = \frac{5 \times 2}{8 \times 2} = \frac{10}{16}$ $\frac{5}{6} = \frac{20}{24}$ and $\frac{7}{8} = \frac{21}{24}$

$12 \neq 15$ $\frac{10}{16} > \frac{7}{16}$ $\frac{20}{24} < \frac{21}{24}$

$12 < 15$ So, $\frac{5}{8} > \frac{7}{16}$ So, $\frac{5}{6} < \frac{7}{8}$

So, $\frac{3}{5} < \frac{3}{4}$

14. $\frac{9}{10}$ and $\frac{18}{20}$ **15.** $\frac{3}{5}$ and $\frac{3}{15}$ **16.** $\frac{5}{20}$ and $\frac{5}{200}$ **17.** $\frac{3}{8}$ and $\frac{7}{16}$ **18.** $\frac{7}{8}$ and $\frac{3}{4}$

APPLYING SKILLS

Solve. Use proportions.

MODEL   The tax rate is $45.22 per $1,000 of property value. Find the
taxes on a $14,000 home.

$$\text{compared number} \longrightarrow \frac{45.22}{1,000} = \frac{n}{14,000} \longleftarrow \text{compared-to number}$$

$$45.22 \times 14,000 = 1,000n$$
$$633,080 = 1,000n$$
$$633,080 \div 1,000 = 1,000n \div 1,000$$
$$633.08 = n$$

The taxes on a $14,000 home would be $633.08.

1. Casualty insurance rate of Company X is $.27 per $100. Find the insurance rate for a $17,000 property.

2. Casualty insurance rate of Company A is $.32 per $100. Find the insurance rate for a $26,500 property.

3. Six bags of cement will yield 32 cubic feet of concrete. How many cubic feet will 27 bags of cement yield?

4. A mixture of concrete calls for 180 kg of gravel for 7 bags of cement. How much gravel is needed for a 56-bag project?

5. Makay's hamburger stand estimates that 380 hamburgers are sold every 90 minutes. At that rate, how many hamburgers are sold in a regular 12-hour day?

6. Brown's taco stand estimates that 200 tacos are sold every 30 minutes. At that rate, how many tacos are sold in a regular 10-hour day?

7. A city of 22,000 grew to 26,000 in the last 5 years. At that rate, what will the population be 8 years from now?

8. A town of 6,500 grew to 7,200 in the last 2 years. At that rate, what will the population be 5 years from now?

9. A 252-meter coil of electrical cable weighs 96 kilograms. What length coil of the same cable will weigh 48 kilograms?

10. Seventy-five pounds of sliced turkey can serve approximately 330 people. How many people will 5 pounds of turkey serve?

11. Joan completed 1,800 units in an 8-hour workday. At that rate, find her weekly output for a 40-hour week.

12. Jake can assemble 25 boxes in 4 hours. At that rate, how many boxes can he assemble in a 40-hour work week?

13. Omari missed 2 out of 25 questions on a history test. On the next test he missed 3 out of 30 questions. Which result was better? (Hint: Which ratio is smaller?)

14. Kim scored 42 correct answers out of 50 on a math test. On another test she scored 63 out of 75 correct. Which score was better? (Hint: Which ratio is larger?)

MAINTAINING SKILLS

Supply the missing number to form an equivalent fraction. [78]

1. $\frac{1}{6} = \frac{n}{30}$

2. $\frac{2}{3} = \frac{n}{15}$

3. $\frac{3}{4} = \frac{n}{16}$

4. $\frac{2}{5} = \frac{n}{20}$

Simplify. [78]

5. $\frac{5}{10}$

6. $\frac{8}{16}$

7. $\frac{20}{25}$

8. $\frac{4}{12}$

9. $\frac{12}{36}$

10. $\frac{16}{48}$

Divide. [43]

11. $9.437\overline{)94.37}$

12. $.478\overline{)4.78}$

13. $.843\overline{)84.3}$

14. $62.31\overline{)623.1}$

Make true sentences. [57]

15. $.4\ \ell =$ _____ ml

16. $.250\ \ell =$ _____ ml

17. 1.3 kl = _____ ℓ

18. 4.1 kl = _____ ℓ

19. $1{,}463$ ml = _____ ℓ

20. $6{,}483$ ml = _____ ℓ

Solve these problems.

21. Emma drove 559.6 miles on her vacation. She
[43] used 32 gallons of gasoline. Find the mileage per gallon to the nearest tenth.

22. Uvaldo drove 561.7 km on his vacation. He
[43] used 96 liters of gasoline. How many kilometers did he drive on 1 liter of gasoline (to the nearest tenth)?

23. Beth earns $97.50 a week. She works 37.5
[43] hours. How much does she earn per hour?

24. Ron works 38.25 hours each week. He earns
[43] $91.80. How much does he earn per hour?

25. The high school Drama Club needs $210 to
[43] cover the expenses of their fall production. They also need to earn $150 for their scholarship fund. Tickets cost $1.25 each. How many tickets must they sell?

26. The Science Club is selling book covers. They
[43] earn 19 cents for each cover they sell. They must earn $20 to cover their operating expenses. In addition they need $75 for their project fund. How many covers must they sell?

27. The volume of a gasoline tank in a car is 81,450
[57] cc. What is its capacity in ℓ? in kl?

28. The volume of a large coffee maker is 12,225
[57] cc. What is the capacity in ℓ? in kl?

29. Ralph bought 6 gallons of gas for $3.23. Joan
[57] bought 6 liters of gas for $.73. What was the difference in price?

30. Taeko bought a gallon of milk for $1.79. Jack
[57] bought a liter of milk for $.47. What was the difference in price?

Addition

multiple A multiple of a given number is the product of that number and a whole number. A multiple of 3 is 6; a multiple of 4 is 12.

least common multiple The least common multiple (LCM) of two or more numbers is the smallest number that is a multiple of each given number.

number in mixed form A number in mixed form is a whole number and a fraction.

For Discussion

- How do you add fractions with unlike denominators?
- How do you add numbers in mixed form?
- How do you rename a fraction in which the numerator is larger than the denominator?

Reading

Pete told his mother that Cathy had helped him to understand fractions. He said to his sister, "To add fractions with the same denominator is no problem. I add the numerators and put the result over the denominator. But, I still have a problem when the fractions have different denominators."

Cathy replied, "The key is to rename the fractions so that the denominators are the same. For example, to add $\frac{1}{2}$ and $\frac{1}{3}$, find the least common multiple (LCM) of the denominators. I find making a chart helps." She wrote:

Multiples of 2	2	4	6	8	10	12	14	16	18	. . .
Multiples of 3	3	6	9	12	15	18	21	24	27	. . .

Common multiples of 2 and 3: 6, 12, 18, . . . The LCM of 2 and 3 is 6.

Pete said, "$\frac{1}{2}$ plus $\frac{1}{3}$ means $\frac{3}{6} + \frac{2}{6}$, or $\frac{5}{6}$. Please check to see if I have added these numbers in mixed form correctly."

$$\begin{array}{r} 1\frac{1}{2} \\ + 2\frac{2}{3} \\ \hline \end{array} = \begin{array}{r} 1 + \frac{1}{2} \\ 2 + \frac{2}{3} \\ \hline \end{array} = \begin{array}{r} 1 + \frac{3}{6} \\ 2 + \frac{4}{6} \\ \hline 3 + \frac{7}{6} \end{array}$$

Cathy pointed out that the fraction could be renamed. She explained, "$\frac{7}{6} = \frac{6}{6} + \frac{1}{6}$. Rename $\frac{6}{6}$ as 1 and add 1 to 3. So, the answer could be simplified to $4\frac{1}{6}$."

DEVELOPING SKILLS

Find the least common multiple (LCM). Make a chart to help you.

MODELS   3 and 4

Multiples of 3	3	6	9	12	15	. . .
Multiples of 4	4	8	12	16	20	. . .

LCM of 3 and 4 is 12.

12, 6, and 8

Multiples of 12	12	24	36	48	. . .
Multiples of 6	6	12	18	24	. . .
Multiples of 8	8	16	24	32	. . .

LCM of 12, 6, and 8 is 24.

1. 5 and 2   **2.** 6 and 4   **3.** 12 and 18   **4.** 6 and 8   **5.** 2, 8, and 10   **6.** 3, 5, and 6

Add.

MODELS

$$\frac{1}{5}$$
$$+\frac{2}{5}$$
$$\overline{\frac{3}{5}}$$

$$\frac{1}{2}=\frac{5}{10}$$
$$+\frac{1}{5}=\frac{2}{10}$$
$$\overline{\frac{7}{10}}$$

$$\frac{5}{8}=\frac{15}{24}$$
$$+\frac{1}{3}=\frac{8}{24}$$
$$\overline{\frac{23}{24}}$$

7. $\frac{5}{8}+\frac{2}{8}$ **8.** $\frac{1}{3}+\frac{1}{3}$ **9.** $\frac{2}{5}+\frac{1}{2}$ **10.** $\frac{1}{4}+\frac{1}{3}+\frac{1}{8}$

Rename in mixed form. Simplify.

MODELS $\frac{3}{2}=\frac{2}{2}+\frac{1}{2}=1+\frac{1}{2}=1\frac{1}{2}$ $\frac{52}{16}=\frac{48}{16}+\frac{4}{16}=3+\frac{1}{4}=3\frac{1}{4}$

11. $\frac{5}{4}$ **12.** $\frac{7}{6}$ **13.** $\frac{11}{3}$ **14.** $\frac{12}{5}$ **15.** $\frac{14}{4}$ **16.** $\frac{22}{8}$ **17.** $\frac{102}{48}$

Add. Simplify.

MODELS

$$\frac{3}{4}=\frac{3}{4}$$
$$+\frac{1}{2}=\frac{2}{4}$$
$$\overline{\frac{5}{4}=1\frac{1}{4}}$$

$$1\frac{1}{4}=1+\frac{3}{12}$$
$$+3\frac{1}{3}=3+\frac{4}{12}$$
$$\overline{4+\frac{7}{12}=4\frac{7}{12}}$$

$$1\frac{2}{3}=1+\frac{10}{15}$$
$$+8\frac{3}{5}=8+\frac{9}{15}$$
$$\overline{9+\frac{19}{15}=9+1+\frac{4}{15}=10\frac{4}{15}}$$

18. $\frac{2}{3}$
$+\frac{3}{4}$

19. $\frac{3}{5}$
$+\frac{5}{6}$

20. $4\frac{1}{2}$
$+8\frac{2}{3}$

21. $16\frac{2}{3}$
$+9\frac{3}{4}$

22. $\frac{2}{3}$
$\frac{1}{2}$
$+\frac{5}{6}$

23. $3\frac{1}{8}$
$2\frac{1}{2}$
$+8\frac{3}{5}$

APPLYING SKILLS

1. Chipo used $8\frac{1}{4}$ gallons of gas on a trip to Greenfield. She used only $7\frac{1}{2}$ gallons for her return trip. How much gas did she use in all?

2. Cesar runs $2\frac{1}{2}$ miles each morning before getting ready for school. After school he runs $5\frac{3}{8}$ miles before dinner. How many miles does he run each day?

3. One winter Princeton had $3\frac{1}{2}$ inches of snow in Dec., $4\frac{1}{2}$ inches in Jan., and $1\frac{1}{3}$ inches in Feb. How much snow did Princeton have in all?

4. Sac City had a storm that lasted 3 days. $3\frac{1}{2}$ inches of rain fell the first day, $1\frac{1}{8}$ inches the second, and $1\frac{11}{16}$ the third. How much rain fell in all?

5. The manager of Lacy's Men's Shop had $12\frac{1}{2}$ dozen shirts on hand. He ordered $16\frac{1}{2}$ dozen more, but only $14\frac{3}{4}$ dozen were delivered to him. How many dozen shirts did he have available to sell? How many dozen shirts did he originally plan to have on hand?

6. Rosemary's Fish Shop had $2\frac{1}{2}$ dozen goldfish on hand. She ordered $18\frac{1}{4}$ dozen more, but only $12\frac{1}{3}$ dozen were shipped to her. How many dozen goldfish did she have available to sell? How many dozen did she originally plan to have on hand?

7. Mr. Taylor bought a $3\frac{1}{2}$-lb box of chocolate and a $1\frac{1}{4}$-lb box of mints. How many pounds of candy did he buy in all?

8. Ms. Harris sold $3\frac{1}{2}$-lb copper kettle and a $4\frac{3}{4}$-lb copper pan to an antique dealer. How many pounds of copper did she sell?

Copy and complete. Check.

9.

WORK SCHEDULE				
Day	Sue	Joe	Jan	Total
Mon	$4\frac{1}{2}$ hr	$3\frac{3}{4}$ hr	$3\frac{1}{2}$ hr	
Tue	$5\frac{1}{3}$ hr	$4\frac{1}{6}$ hr	$5\frac{1}{2}$ hr	
Wed	$3\frac{5}{6}$ hr	$4\frac{1}{2}$ hr	$3\frac{1}{3}$ hr	
Thu	$4\frac{1}{4}$ hr	$5\frac{1}{3}$ hr	$4\frac{1}{6}$ hr	
Fri	$3\frac{1}{2}$ hr	$4\frac{5}{6}$ hr	$4\frac{3}{4}$ hr	
TOTALS				$64\frac{1}{4}$ hr

10.

SUMMER RAINFALL				
City	June	July	Aug	Total
Chicago	$3\frac{1}{2}$ in.	$3\frac{1}{4}$ in.	$2\frac{1}{2}$ in.	
Duluth	$3\frac{1}{8}$ in.	$3\frac{1}{2}$ in.	$2\frac{7}{8}$ in.	
Seattle	$\frac{3}{4}$ in.	$\frac{1}{2}$ in.	$\frac{7}{8}$ in.	
Miami	$5\frac{1}{2}$ in.	$6\frac{3}{4}$ in.	$7\frac{1}{8}$ in.	
Phoenix	$\frac{3}{8}$ in.	$\frac{3}{4}$ in.	$\frac{1}{2}$ in.	
TOTALS				$41\frac{7}{8}$ in.

MAINTAINING SKILLS

Solve these proportions. Check. [83]

1. $\frac{4}{5} = \frac{n}{25}$

2. $\frac{3}{4} = \frac{n}{24}$

3. $\frac{8}{6} = \frac{168}{n}$

4. $\frac{7}{4} = \frac{175}{n}$

5. $\frac{4}{25} = \frac{n}{1,000}$

Compare. Use <, =, or >. [83]

6. $\frac{6}{10}$ and $\frac{10}{20}$

7. $\frac{4}{5}$ and $\frac{9}{10}$

8. $\frac{1}{4}$ and $\frac{1}{3}$

9. $\frac{1}{5}$ and $\frac{3}{10}$

10. $\frac{7}{12}$ and $\frac{9}{16}$

Make true sentences. [63]

11. 2.73 kg = _____ g

12. 14.46 kg = _____ g

13. 346.7 g = _____ kg

14. 1,468.7 g = _____ kg

15. 1,248 mg = _____ g

16. 468 mg = _____ g

Copy and complete. Check. [4]

17.

SHARP DEPT. STORE				
Day	Coats	Suits	Jackets	Total
Mon	$1,426	$3,837	$2,100	
Tue	1,023	2,694	1,994	
Wed	2,041	4,012	2,546	
Thu	2,879	4,568	2,746	
Fri	4,878	8,036	4,464	
Sat	6,878	10,973	6,464	
TOTALS				$73,559

18.

SPORTS SHOP				
Day	Shoes	Equipment	Uniforms	Total
Mon	$146	$846	$178	
Tue	152	721	222	
Wed	148	967	467	
Thu	206	1,834	1,896	
Fri	315	2,012	456	
Sat	425	2,568	2,873	
TOTALS				$16,432

Solve these problems.

19. A city of 436,000 grew to 586,000 in the last 6
[83] years. At that rate, what will the population be
10 years from now?

20. A city of 278,000 grew to 312,000 in the last 4
[83] years. At that rate, what will the population be
6 years from now?

21. A cat weighs 11 pounds. About how many kilo-
[63] grams does it weigh?

22. A dog weighs 56 pounds. About how many
[63] kilograms does it weigh?

23. An object is placed on a pan of a balance. The
[63] object is balanced when weights of 500 g, 250
g, and 5 g are placed on the other pan. What is
the weight of the object in grams?

24. An object is placed on a pan of a balance. The
[63] object is balanced when weights of 1 kg, 500 g,
40 g, and 5 g are placed on the other pan. What
is the weight of the object in kilograms?

Subtraction

vocational program   A vocational program is a series of courses which a student takes to prepare for a skilled job. These courses prepare students to be electricians, carpenters, beauticians, secretaries, and so forth.

partnership   A partnership is a business owned by two or more people who share the responsibilities of operating the business and thus share the profits or losses which result.

addition   Addition may be described as:
$$\text{addend} + \text{addend} = \text{sum}$$

subtraction   Subtraction may be described as:
$$\text{sum} - \text{addend} = \text{missing addend, or difference}$$

For Discussion

- What vocational programs are available in your school?

- How did Molly explain subtracting numbers in mixed form?

- What relationship did Sheila use to check her subtraction?

"Dad," said Molly, "my guidance counselor tells me that the community college is offering several vocational programs. As you know, I'm interested in carpentry. My friend, Cleon Williams and I have been talking about forming a partnership in making cabinets someday."

"Why don't you sign up for one of the programs?" asked Mr. Malone.

At this point Sheila interrupted to bring up a question of her own. "Can you explain how to subtract and check this problem with numbers in mixed form?" She wrote:

$$8\tfrac{1}{2} - 4\tfrac{1}{3}$$

Molly reminded her that the first step was to find the least common multiple (LCM) of the denominators. She wrote:

$$8\tfrac{1}{2} - 4\tfrac{1}{3} = 8\tfrac{3}{6} - 4\tfrac{2}{6} = 4\tfrac{1}{6}$$

Sum   Addend   The difference

Sheila said, "I get it. Since addend plus addend equals sum, I can check like this."

Missing addend or difference $4\tfrac{1}{6} + 4\tfrac{1}{3} = 8\tfrac{3}{6}$, or $8\tfrac{1}{2}$

Addend   Sum

DEVELOPING SKILLS

OBJECTIVE   To subtract fractions and numbers in mixed form

Subtract. Simplify when possible.

MODELS

$\frac{5}{6} - \frac{1}{6}$

$\begin{array}{r} \frac{5}{6} \\ -\frac{1}{6} \\ \hline \frac{4}{6} = \frac{2}{3} \end{array}$

$\frac{1}{2} - \frac{1}{4}$

$\begin{array}{r} \frac{1}{2} = \frac{2}{4} \\ -\frac{1}{4} = \frac{1}{4} \\ \hline \frac{1}{4} \end{array}$

$\frac{5}{8} - \frac{1}{3}$

$\begin{array}{r} \frac{5}{8} = \frac{15}{24} \\ -\frac{1}{3} = \frac{8}{24} \\ \hline \frac{7}{24} \end{array}$

1. $\begin{array}{r} \frac{3}{5} \\ -\frac{1}{5} \\ \hline \end{array}$

2. $\begin{array}{r} \frac{7}{8} \\ -\frac{5}{8} \\ \hline \end{array}$

3. $\begin{array}{r} \frac{3}{4} \\ -\frac{3}{8} \\ \hline \end{array}$

4. $\begin{array}{r} \frac{7}{10} \\ -\frac{1}{5} \\ \hline \end{array}$

5. $\begin{array}{r} \frac{2}{3} \\ -\frac{1}{2} \\ \hline \end{array}$

6. $\begin{array}{r} \frac{3}{5} \\ -\frac{1}{2} \\ \hline \end{array}$

7. $\begin{array}{r} \frac{3}{5} \\ -\frac{1}{4} \\ \hline \end{array}$

8. $\begin{array}{r} \frac{6}{7} \\ -\frac{1}{6} \\ \hline \end{array}$

9. $\begin{array}{r} \frac{15}{16} \\ -\frac{3}{4} \\ \hline \end{array}$

10. $\begin{array}{r} \frac{5}{6} \\ -\frac{5}{12} \\ \hline \end{array}$

11. $\begin{array}{r} \frac{11}{12} \\ -\frac{2}{3} \\ \hline \end{array}$

12. $\begin{array}{r} \frac{9}{18} \\ -\frac{1}{6} \\ \hline \end{array}$

Rename in mixed form whose fractional part is greater than 1.

MODEL $3\frac{3}{4}$ $3\frac{3}{4} = \underline{2 + 1} + \frac{3}{4} = 2 + \frac{4}{4} + \frac{3}{4} = 2 + \frac{7}{4}$ or $2\frac{7}{4}$

13. $3\frac{2}{3}$ **14.** $5\frac{3}{8}$ **15.** $6\frac{1}{5}$ **16.** $7\frac{1}{6}$ **17.** $4\frac{2}{9}$ **18.** $9\frac{1}{4}$ **19.** $12\frac{4}{7}$ **20.** $15\frac{7}{16}$

Subtract. Simplify when possible. Check.

MODELS $4\frac{3}{4} - 2\frac{1}{2}$ Check:

$\begin{array}{r} 4\frac{3}{4} = 4 + \frac{3}{4} \\ -2\frac{1}{2} = 2 + \frac{2}{4} \\ \hline 2 + \frac{1}{4} = 2\frac{1}{4} \end{array}$

$\begin{array}{r} 2\frac{1}{4} = 2 + \frac{1}{4} \\ +2\frac{1}{2} = 2 + \frac{2}{4} \\ \hline 4 + \frac{3}{4} = 4\frac{3}{4} \end{array}$

$5\frac{1}{3} - 2\frac{1}{2}$ Check:

$\begin{array}{r} 5\frac{1}{3} = 5 + \frac{2}{6} = 4 + \frac{8}{6} \\ -2\frac{1}{2} = 2 + \frac{3}{6} = 2 + \frac{3}{6} \\ \hline 2 + \frac{5}{6} = 2\frac{5}{6} \end{array}$

$\begin{array}{r} 2\frac{5}{6} = 2 + \frac{5}{6} \\ +2\frac{1}{2} = 2 + \frac{3}{6} \\ \hline 4 + \frac{8}{6} = 5\frac{1}{3} \end{array}$

21. $\begin{array}{r} 4\frac{2}{3} \\ -2\frac{1}{3} \\ \hline \end{array}$

22. $\begin{array}{r} 8\frac{3}{4} \\ -2\frac{1}{4} \\ \hline \end{array}$

23. $\begin{array}{r} 9\frac{1}{8} \\ -5\frac{3}{4} \\ \hline \end{array}$

24. $\begin{array}{r} 10\frac{1}{6} \\ -5\frac{2}{3} \\ \hline \end{array}$

25. $\begin{array}{r} 7\frac{1}{3} \\ -2\frac{3}{4} \\ \hline \end{array}$

26. $\begin{array}{r} 16\frac{1}{6} \\ -4\frac{7}{8} \\ \hline \end{array}$

27. $\begin{array}{r} 5 \\ -1\frac{3}{4} \\ \hline \end{array}$

28. $\begin{array}{r} 6 \\ -4\frac{1}{3} \\ \hline \end{array}$

29. $\begin{array}{r} 8 \\ -\frac{5}{8} \\ \hline \end{array}$

30. $\begin{array}{r} 7 \\ -\frac{2}{5} \\ \hline \end{array}$

31. $\begin{array}{r} 4\frac{7}{8} \\ -2 \\ \hline \end{array}$

32. $\begin{array}{r} 7\frac{9}{10} \\ -5 \\ \hline \end{array}$

APPLYING SKILLS

1. Before it was washed, a piece of cloth measured $24\frac{1}{2}$ meters long. The cloth measured $23\frac{4}{5}$ meters after washing. How much did it shrink?

2. Joe had $14\frac{5}{16}$ gallons of milk in a milk can. He tipped it over and all but $2\frac{3}{4}$ gallons spilled out. How much milk did he spill?

3. How much longer is a board 10 meters long than a board $6\frac{47}{100}$ meters long?

4. How much greater is a distance of 54 miles than a distance of $38\frac{3}{4}$ miles?

5. A metal rod is $12\frac{3}{4}$ feet long. How much must be cut off to leave a rod $11\frac{1}{3}$ feet long?

6. A wire is $13\frac{1}{2}$ cm long. How much must be cut off to leave a wire $12\frac{3}{4}$ cm long?

7. Find the difference between a $\frac{3}{10}$ interest in a business and a $\frac{1}{3}$ interest in the same business.

8. Find the difference between a $\frac{4}{15}$ interest in a business and a $\frac{1}{3}$ interest in the same business.

9. One recipe for cake calls for $3\frac{1}{2}$ cups of flour. Another recipe calls for only $2\frac{1}{4}$ cups of flour. How much more flour is needed for the first cake?

10. Hamadi's recipe for caramel calls for $\frac{1}{3}$ cup of butter. Abni's recipe calls for $\frac{1}{2}$ cup of butter. How much more butter does Abni need?

11. The Junior Class is building a float. They need $32\frac{1}{3}$ yards of yellow crepe paper and 40 yards of red crepe paper. How many more yards of red paper than yellow do they need?

12. The dance committee has $27\frac{2}{5}$ meters of ribbon. They will need 45 meters of ribbon to make the decorations. How many more meters of ribbon do they need to buy?

13. From a filled 15-liter gasoline tank, $5\frac{3}{10}$ liters were used. How many liters were left?

14. From a filled 45-liter gasoline tank, $26\frac{7}{10}$ liters were used. How many liters were left?

15. Jack started a trip with $18\frac{1}{2}$ gallons of gasoline in his tank. He used $17\frac{3}{4}$ gallons and then added 15 gallons to the tank. How many gallons does he have in the tank?

16. Ruth had $18\frac{3}{4}$ gallons of paint. She used $14\frac{1}{4}$ gallons to paint a house. She then bought 20 gallons to replenish her supply. How many gallons does she now have on hand?

MAINTAINING SKILLS

Add. Simplify. [87]

1. $\frac{3}{4} + \frac{2}{3}$

2. $\frac{7}{8} + \frac{1}{3}$

3. $\frac{3}{10} + \frac{3}{4}$

4. $\frac{1}{2} + \frac{5}{8}$

Copy and complete. Check.

5.
[9]

WALTER'S MARKET			
	Sales	Returns	Net Sales
1st week	$14,467	$468	
2nd week	14,678	542	
3rd week	18,412	874	
4th week	16,487	648	
TOTALS			$61,512

6.
[9]

DOROTHY'S MARKET			
Employee	Sales	Returns	Net Sales
M. Caine	$1,678	$ 52	
J. Harris	1,367	142	
A. Malone	1,879	81	
C. Short	1,442	112	
TOTALS			$5,979

7.
[87]

PART-TIME WORK SCHEDULE				
Day	Joe	Ellen	Roy	Total
Mon	6 hr	$5\frac{1}{2}$ hr	$4\frac{1}{2}$ hr	
Tue	$2\frac{3}{4}$ hr	8 hr	$5\frac{1}{4}$ hr	
Wed	8 hr	—	$8\frac{1}{4}$ hr	
Thu	$3\frac{1}{4}$ hr	$6\frac{1}{2}$ hr	$6\frac{1}{4}$ hr	
Fri	$5\frac{1}{2}$ hr	5 hr	$5\frac{1}{4}$ hr	
Sat	$6\frac{1}{2}$ hr	7 hr	$2\frac{1}{2}$ hr	
TOTALS				96

8.
[87]

WORK SCHEDULE				
Day	Jose	Jane	Jill	Totals
Mon	8 hr	$7\frac{1}{4}$ hr	$7\frac{1}{2}$ hr	
Tue	—	8 hr	$8\frac{1}{2}$ hr	
Wed	$6\frac{3}{4}$ hr	—	$7\frac{1}{2}$ hr	
Thu	$9\frac{1}{4}$ hr	$7\frac{1}{2}$ hr	—	
Fri	$8\frac{1}{2}$ hr	$8\frac{1}{2}$ hr	8 hr	
Sat	10 hr	$9\frac{1}{2}$ hr	$8\frac{3}{4}$ hr	
TOTALS				$123\frac{1}{2}$

Solve these problems. [9]

9. In 1960 Homestead, Florida had a population of 9,152. In 1970 the population was 13,674. What was the population increase in that time?

10. Memorial Stadium in Maryland seats 52,137 people. The Astrodome in Texas seats 44,500 people. How many more people does Memorial Stadium hold?

Interpret each temperature. [67]

11. 0° C

12. −18° C

13. 30° C

14. 100° C

15. 200° C

16. 40° C

Career/REAL ESTATE

Real estate specialists transact business involving land development, homes, apartments, and commercial and industrial buildings. They bring together a seller and a buyer to arrange for purchasing, leasing, and financing. With our increasing population and limited land areas, a need for highly skilled people exists in this field.

Job Descriptions

- Real estate agent—computes the asking price for property based on size, appearance, age, and location.

- Salesperson and broker—obtains listings of property available for rental, lease, or sale.

- Appraiser—inspects property to determine the property's current market value.

- Mortgage and loan officer—prepares mortgages, makes title searches for the purchase of property.

Training

A real estate specialist has the ability to handle negotiations between buyer and seller. Licenses, required in some states, are usually obtained through written examinations. Many banks will train capable employees who have the ability to communicate in both written and oral form. Two- and four-year programs are available on the college level.

Further Investigation

Arrange an interview with a real estate specialist or banker who deals with mortgages. Ask about job qualifications, working conditions, possibilities for advancement, entry-level jobs.

Consult your guidance department about post-high-school programs of study in this area.

Multiplication

comparison shopping   Comparison shopping refers to checking and comparing the prices on similar merchandise.

product   The product of two or more numbers is found by multiplying the numbers.

For Discussion

- What two things did Karen and Kikuo have to know in order to buy enough material for the class?

- What steps did Karen take to find the product of a whole number and a number in mixed form?

- How did Kikuo know he needed nine 3-yard lengths?

- What costs did they compare in order to decide which was the better buy?

Karen and Kikuo, students in Mr. Garcia's play production class, were out comparison shopping for costume material. They checked prices at each of the two stores in their town. At one store the price of the material was $2.50 per yard. At the other store similar material was on sale for $4.75 for a 3-yard length.

Karen said, "There are 18 students in our class and I need a yard and a half of material for each costume. I need to find the product." She wrote:

$$18 \times 1\tfrac{1}{2} = \tfrac{18}{1} \times \tfrac{3}{2} = \tfrac{54}{2}, \text{ or 27 yd}$$

$$\text{and } \$2.50 \times 27 = \$67.50$$

She continued, "It will cost $67.50 at the first store."

Kikuo said, "If we buy the material at the other store, we need to buy nine of the 3-yard lengths." He wrote:

$$\$4.75 \times 9 = \$42.75$$

He continued, "This is definitely the better of the two prices."

DEVELOPING SKILLS

Find each product. Simplify.

MODELS $\frac{5}{8} \times \frac{3}{4} = \frac{5 \times 3}{8 \times 4} = \frac{15}{32}$ $\frac{5}{6} \times 7 = \frac{5}{6} \times \frac{7}{1} = \frac{5 \times 7}{6 \times 1} = \frac{35}{6}$, or $5\frac{5}{6}$

1. $\frac{2}{3} \times 2$ **2.** $3 \times \frac{5}{8}$ **3.** $\frac{3}{5} \times \frac{7}{8}$ **4.** $\frac{3}{4} \times \frac{1}{2}$ **5.** $\frac{5}{6} \times \frac{4}{5}$ **6.** $\frac{2}{3} \times \frac{3}{4}$

Rename as fractions.

MODELS $4\frac{1}{3} = 4 + \frac{1}{3} = \frac{12}{3} + \frac{1}{3} = \frac{13}{3}$ $3\frac{5}{8} = 3 + \frac{5}{8} = \frac{24}{8} + \frac{5}{8} = \frac{29}{8}$

7. $1\frac{5}{12}$ **8.** $1\frac{3}{5}$ **9.** $2\frac{3}{8}$ **10.** $3\frac{2}{3}$ **11.** $16\frac{1}{4}$ **12.** $19\frac{1}{5}$

Multiply. Simplify.

MODEL $2\frac{1}{2} \times 3\frac{1}{3} = \underbrace{\frac{5}{2} \times \frac{9}{3}}_{} = \frac{5 \times 9}{2 \times 2} = \frac{45}{4}$, or $11\frac{1}{4}$

⌐—Rename each factor as a fraction.

13. $3\frac{1}{2} \times 5\frac{1}{2}$ **14.** $2\frac{1}{2} \times 1\frac{1}{6}$ **15.** $5\frac{1}{4} \times 2\frac{1}{2}$ **16.** $6\frac{1}{2} \times 2\frac{1}{5}$

Multiply. Use the methods shown in the Models.

MODELS $\frac{3}{4} \times \frac{8}{9} = \frac{3 \times 8}{4 \times 9}$ Short Form $3\frac{1}{2} \times 5\frac{3}{5} = \frac{7}{2} \times \frac{28}{5}$ Short Form

$= \frac{3 \times 2 \times 4}{4 \times 3 \times 3}$ $\frac{\cancel{3}^{1}}{\cancel{4}_{1}} \times \frac{\cancel{8}^{2}}{\cancel{9}_{3}} = \frac{1 \times 2}{1 \times 3}$ $= \frac{7 \times 28}{2 \times 5}$ $3\frac{1}{2} \times 5\frac{3}{5} = \frac{7}{\cancel{2}_{1}} \times \frac{\cancel{28}^{14}}{5}$

$= \frac{4}{4} \times \frac{3}{3} \times \frac{2}{3}$ $= \frac{2}{3}$ $= \frac{7 \times 7 \times 2 \times 2}{2 \times 5}$ $= \frac{7 \times 14}{5}$

$= 1 \times 1 \times \frac{2}{3}$ $= \frac{2}{2} \times \frac{7 \times 7 \times 2}{5}$ $= \frac{98}{5}$

$= \frac{2}{3}$ $= 1 \times \frac{98}{5}$ $= 19\frac{3}{5}$

$= 19\frac{3}{5}$

17. $\frac{3}{8} \times \frac{2}{3}$ **18.** $\frac{5}{6} \times \frac{9}{10}$ **19.** $\frac{2}{3} \times \frac{5}{12}$ **20.** $\frac{7}{10} \times \frac{5}{8}$ **21.** $3\frac{1}{2} \times 4\frac{3}{4}$

22. $2\frac{1}{2} \times 12\frac{2}{3}$ **23.** $\frac{3}{4} \times 2\frac{1}{3}$ **24.** $8\frac{1}{2} \times \frac{4}{5}$ **25.** $\frac{3}{5} \times \frac{5}{8} \times 3\frac{1}{2}$ **26.** $\frac{3}{4} \times 2\frac{2}{3} \times \frac{4}{5}$

APPLYING SKILLS

1. The part-time cashier at the Old Time Diner worked $8\frac{1}{4}$ hours in one week. She is paid $2.50 an hour. What did she earn?

2. A part-time file clerk worked $17\frac{1}{2}$ hours last week. He earns $2.75 an hour. How much was he paid?

3. Mildred Kenny works $6\frac{3}{4}$ hours, six days a week. How many hours does she work?

4. Earl Jones works $9\frac{1}{3}$ hours, five days a week. How many hours does he work?

5. Jack decided to charge $1.20 an hour for baby-sitting. What should he receive for sitting 3 hours and 20 minutes?

6. Barbara charges $2.50 an hour for washing windows. How much should she receive for working 5 hours and 30 minutes?

7. One acre produced 36 bushels of wheat. How many bushels of wheat can be harvested from $12\frac{3}{4}$ acres?

8. There are $10\frac{1}{4}$ meters of material in a pair of curtains. How many meters of material are needed for 72 pairs?

Copy and complete.

9.

SIMPLEX MANUFACTURING COMPANY			
Employee	Hours Worked	Hourly Rate	Total Earnings
C. Abel	$32\frac{1}{2}$	$3	
R. Baker	$24\frac{1}{4}$	4	
B. Early	$34\frac{3}{4}$	5	
A. Jones	$28\frac{1}{4}$	6	
D. Metz	$38\frac{1}{4}$	4	
J. Thomas	$27\frac{3}{4}$	5	
S. Ward	$25\frac{1}{2}$	5	
J. Young	40	4	
TOTALS		—	

10.

JONES HARDWARE STORE			
Employee	Hours Worked	Hourly Rate	Total Earnings
J. Ball	$15\frac{1}{2}$	$2	
C. Diaz	$25\frac{1}{4}$	3	
E. Foote	$39\frac{1}{2}$	4	
A. Jones	$38\frac{1}{4}$	4	
E. O'Dea	$37\frac{1}{2}$	3.30	
G. Reid	$37\frac{1}{2}$	3.50	
M. Sands	$35\frac{3}{4}$	4	
T. Webb	35	5	
TOTALS		—	

Find the area of each rectangle.

11. Length: $6\frac{1}{3}$ ft
    Width: $2\frac{1}{2}$ ft

12. Length: $3\frac{1}{4}$ m
    Width: $1\frac{1}{2}$ m

13. Length: $8\frac{1}{3}$ yd.
    Width: $5\frac{5}{8}$ yd.

MAINTAINING SKILLS

Make true sentences. [52]

1. 4,678 m = _____ km

2. 17,248 m = _____ km

3. 36.42 km = _____ m

4. 4.873 km = _____ m

5. .087 m = _____ cm

6. 1.482 m = _____ cm

Multiply. [15]

7. 8,312
   $\times$ 128

8. 8,124
   $\times$ 361

9. 6,654
   $\times$ 314

10. 2,249
    $\times$ 543

Subtract. Simplify. [91]

11. $\frac{9}{10} - \frac{3}{10}$

12. $\frac{5}{11} - \frac{2}{11}$

13. $\frac{7}{8} - \frac{1}{4}$

14. $\frac{5}{6} - \frac{1}{3}$

Copy and complete. [15]

15.

WRIGHT'S DEPT. STORE			
Order Number	Number of Items	Cost Per Item	Total Cost
467J	42	$14	
678B	146	18	
478H	378	4	

16.

SONGLAND MUSIC STORE			
Order Number	Number of Items	Cost Per Item	Total Cost
H43	26	$421	
J47	14	583	
H37	4	1,467	

Solve these problems.

17. [91] How much greater is a distance of $13\frac{1}{8}$ miles than a distance of $6\frac{2}{3}$ miles?

18. [91] How much greater is a distance of $137\frac{47}{100}$ miles than a distance of $57\frac{81}{100}$ miles?

19. [91] A roll of carpeting contains $20\frac{1}{2}$ yards. Mrs. Walker cuts $6\frac{1}{3}$ yards from the roll. How much carpeting is left on the roll?

20. [91] A bolt of canvas contains $36\frac{1}{4}$ yards. Ms. Jackson cuts $12\frac{1}{2}$ yards from the bolt. How much canvas is left on the bolt?

21. [15] The Hudson Equipment Co. sold 463 typewriters. They made $22 profit on each. How much profit did they make on the sale?

22. [15] New Town Shoe Co. sold 15,869 pairs of shoes last month. Each pair sold for $17. What was the total amount of the sale?

23. [52] Ruth Williams drove 67 kilometers. About how many miles was this?

24. [52] Paul Smith hiked 25 kilometers. About how many miles was this?

Division

reciprocal   The product of a number and its reciprocal is 1. Since $\frac{2}{3} \times \frac{3}{2} = 1$, we can say $\frac{2}{3}$ is the reciprocal of $\frac{3}{2}$ and $\frac{3}{2}$ is the reciprocal of $\frac{2}{3}$.

complex   A complex fraction is a fraction in which the numerator, or the denominator, or both are fractions.

quotient   In the division process, the quotient is the result obtained.

multiplication   Multiplication may be described as factor × factor = product.

division   Division may be described as product ÷ factor = missing factor, or quotient.

For Discussion

- Why is multiplying a number by $\frac{1}{2}$ the same as dividing that number by 2?

- What is a rule for dividing fractions?

"Pete, I'm still confused when it comes to dividing fractions. Can you explain how to do this problem?" Margaret asked.

Pete answered, "Recall that the bar separating the numerator and the denominator of a fraction is a way of saying divided by. You can write a complex fraction for a division problem." He wrote:

$$\frac{2}{3} \div \frac{5}{8} = \frac{\frac{2}{3}}{\frac{5}{8}} \quad \longleftarrow \text{ Numerator}$$
$$\longleftarrow \text{ Denominator}$$

"Now," he continued, "if I multiply this complex fraction by 1, I'll get the same complex fraction." He asked Margaret to notice how to write the 1.

$$\frac{\frac{2}{3}}{\frac{5}{8}} \times \frac{\frac{8}{5}}{\frac{8}{5}} = \frac{\frac{2}{3} \times \frac{8}{5}}{1} = \frac{16}{15}, \text{ or } 1\frac{1}{15}$$

Shortcut: $\frac{2}{3} \div \frac{5}{8} = \frac{2}{3} \times \frac{8}{5} = \frac{16}{15}$, or $1\frac{1}{15}$

Margaret said, "Thanks, Pete, I understand now. I prefer using the shortcut."

DEVELOPING SKILLS

OBJECTIVES   To divide fractions
              To divide numbers in mixed form

Write the reciprocal of each fraction.

(Hint: The reciprocal of $\frac{1}{4}$ is $\frac{4}{1}$.)

1. $\frac{1}{2}$ **2.** $\frac{6}{7}$ **3.** $\frac{3}{4}$ **4.** $\frac{7}{8}$ **5.** $\frac{50}{72}$ **6.** $\frac{81}{92}$ **7.** $\frac{18}{6}$ **8.** $\frac{12}{3}$

Divide. Simplify.

MODELS

$$\frac{1}{2} \div \frac{3}{4}$$

$$\frac{1}{2} \div \frac{3}{4} = \frac{1}{2} \times \frac{4}{3}$$
$$= \frac{1 \times 4}{2 \times 3}$$
$$= \frac{1 \times 2 \times 2}{2 \times 3}$$
$$= \frac{2}{2} \times \frac{1 \times 2}{3}$$
$$= 1 \times \frac{2}{3}$$
$$= \frac{2}{3}$$

Short Form:

$$\frac{1}{2} \div \frac{3}{4} = \frac{1}{\cancel{2}} \times \frac{\cancel{4}}{3}$$
$$= \frac{1 \times 2}{1 \times 3}$$
$$= \frac{2}{3}$$

$$35 \div \frac{5}{8}$$

$$35 \div \frac{5}{8} = \frac{35}{1} \times \frac{8}{5}$$
$$= \frac{35 \times 8}{1 \times 5}$$
$$= \frac{5 \times 7 \times 8}{5 \times 1}$$
$$= \frac{5}{5} \times \frac{7 \times 8}{1}$$
$$= 1 \times 56$$
$$= 56$$

Short Form:

$$35 \div \frac{5}{8} = \frac{\cancel{35}^{7}}{1} \times \frac{8}{\cancel{5}_{1}}$$
$$= \frac{7 \times 8}{1 \times 1}$$
$$= \frac{56}{1}$$
$$= 56$$

9. $64 \div \frac{2}{3}$ **10.** $15 \div \frac{3}{4}$ **11.** $\frac{2}{3} \div 12$ **12.** $\frac{4}{5} \div 20$ **13.** $\frac{1}{4} \div \frac{3}{8}$

14. $\frac{3}{5} \div \frac{7}{10}$ **15.** $\frac{5}{8} \div \frac{3}{4}$ **16.** $\frac{3}{10} \div \frac{2}{5}$ **17.** $\frac{1}{4} \div \frac{1}{8}$ **18.** $\frac{1}{3} \div \frac{1}{6}$

Divide. Simplify.

MODEL

$$3\frac{5}{12} \div 1\frac{1}{4} = \frac{41}{12} \div \frac{5}{4} = \frac{41}{\cancel{12}_{3}} \times \frac{\cancel{4}^{1}}{5} = \frac{41 \times 1}{3 \times 5} = \frac{41}{15} \text{ or } 2\frac{11}{15}$$

19. $5\frac{1}{2} \div 3\frac{2}{3}$ **20.** $1\frac{1}{2} \div 2\frac{2}{5}$ **21.** $4\frac{1}{5} \div 4\frac{2}{3}$ **22.** $3\frac{1}{5} \div 1\frac{1}{3}$

APPLYING SKILLS

1. A scout leader bought a coil of rope 18 yards long. How many 27-inch sections can be cut from the rope?

2. A bin of soap powder contains 2,130 kg of soap. How many boxes, each weighing 120 g, can be filled from this bin?

3. How many 12-oz glasses can be filled from a 12-quart container of lemonade?

4. How many 6-ounce packs of bologna can be made from a 12-pound bologna roll?

5. A manufacturer uses $2\frac{3}{8}$ kg of copper to make a Model 37-2H motor. There is on hand a supply of 1,520 kg of copper. How many of these motors can be made with this supply?

6. Ms. Rossani owns 425 acres of land. She is going to divide this land into $2\frac{1}{2}$-acre plots for home development. How many plots does the land contain?

7. How many tiles each $\frac{3}{4}'$ long are needed for one row in a kitchen $15\frac{3}{4}'$ long?

8. How many chairs $\frac{3}{5}$ m wide are needed for one row in a theater $12\frac{3}{5}$ m wide?

9. Mr. Tracey drove 135 km in $2\frac{1}{4}$ hours. Find his average speed.

10. A plane traveled 4,280 km in $3\frac{1}{3}$ hours. Find its average speed.

11. Surveyors use a measure of length called a rod, which is equal to $16\frac{1}{2}$ ft. How many rods are there in a distance of 240 feet?

12. An airplane flew 845 miles in 2 hours and 30 minutes. Find the average speed in miles per hour. (Hint: 2 hr 30 min = $2\frac{1}{2}$ hr.)

13. A $12\frac{1}{2}$-lb. turkey cost $6.25. Find the price of the turkey per pound.

14. A $2\frac{2}{5}$-kg beef roast cost $15. Find the price of the beef per kilogram.

15. A grocer bought $55\frac{1}{2}$ lb of bacon. He used all this to make $\frac{1}{2}$-lb packages. How many packages did he make from his original purchase?

16. A butcher sells hamburger patties in $\frac{1}{4}$-lb packages. How many hamburger patties can she make from $42\frac{1}{2}$ pounds of hamburger?

17. During a period of $2\frac{1}{4}$ hours, the temperature dropped 13 degrees. How many degrees did the temperature drop each hour, on an average?

18. During a $4\frac{1}{2}$-hour period, $1\frac{1}{2}$ inches of rain fell. How many inches of rain fell each hour, on an average?

MAINTAINING SKILLS

Make true sentences. [57]

1. 36 ml = _____ ℓ

2. 149 ml = _____ ℓ

3. 42 ℓ = _____ ml

4. 142 ℓ = _____ ml

5. .78 kl = _____ ℓ

6. 1.782 kl = _____ ℓ

Divide. [19]

7. $48\overline{)9,648}$

8. $68\overline{)75,888}$

9. $82\overline{)304,056}$

10. $92\overline{)524,584}$

Multiply. Simplify. [97]

11. $\frac{1}{4} \times \frac{2}{3}$

12. $\frac{3}{4} \times \frac{2}{5}$

13. $\frac{48}{100} \times \frac{5}{12}$

14. $\frac{5}{16} \times \frac{24}{100}$

Solve these problems.

15. A TV network surveyed 1,632 people about
[19] program likes and dislikes. The office staff can process 34 completed forms each day. How long will it take to process the forms?

16. Workers at the Seacrest Berry Farm picked 672
[19] boxes of raspberries. They packed the berries in crates of 24 boxes each. How many crates of raspberries were picked?

17. Ida packs oranges, 8 to a box, from a crate of
[19] oranges which weighs 56 lb. There is an average of 4 oranges per pound. How many boxes can she pack from this crate?

18. Kaoni packs lemons, 12 to a box, from a crate
[19] of lemons which weighs 48 lb. There is an average of 6 lemons per pound. How many boxes can he pack from the crate?

19. Robert Harris bought 20 gallons of gas. About
[57] how many liters was this?

20. Amy Gray Eagle bought 3 gallons of paint.
[57] About how many liters was this?

21. **Complete this payroll form.** [97]

| | Hours Worked | | | | | | | | |
| UNEEDA WATCH COMPANY | | | | | | | | | |
Employee	Mon.	Tue.	Wed.	Thu.	Fri.	Sat.	Total Hours	Hourly Rate	Total Wages
L. Smith	$2\frac{1}{2}$	3	$4\frac{1}{4}$	$3\frac{1}{4}$	2	$5\frac{1}{4}$		$4	
R. Green	3	$3\frac{3}{4}$	$3\frac{3}{4}$	$1\frac{1}{2}$	$3\frac{1}{2}$	$4\frac{1}{2}$		3	
T. Jones	$4\frac{1}{4}$	3	$2\frac{1}{2}$	$4\frac{1}{2}$	$2\frac{3}{4}$	$3\frac{3}{4}$		4	
TOTALS							61		224

Scale Drawings

template A template is a pattern or mold used as a guide in a design.

scale drawing A scale drawing of an object is a drawing whose shape is similar to the object.

scale A scale refers to the ratio used to make a scale drawing of an object. A scale may be expressed in terms such as 1 in. = 10 ft, 1 cm = 10 m, 2 cm = 100 km, and so on.

representative ratio The representative ratio is the simplified ratio of the scale. If the scale is 1 cm = 2 m, the representative ratio is $\frac{1}{100 \times 2}$, or $\frac{1}{200}$.

For Discussion

- Why are scale drawings used by designers?
- How does a designer choose a scale?
- How can templates save time in arranging furniture?
- What scale lengths will Melba use in her drawing?

Mr. Williams asked Melba and Kent to help him rearrange the living-room furniture.

Melba asked, "Kent, will you make templates for the furniture while I make a scale drawing of the room? I'll indicate the doors, windows, heating vents, and electrical outlets on the drawing."

Kent asked, "What scale will you use? How long will you draw the segments representing the length and width of the room?"

"The room is 540 cm long and 380 cm wide. I'm using a representative ratio of 1 to 100. Now, to find the scale lengths in my drawing, I'll set up proportions. Remember, I'm using centimeters, so the real lengths must be in centimeters." She wrote:

Length: $\frac{n}{540} = \frac{1}{100}$ Width: $\frac{n}{380} = \frac{1}{100}$

$100n = 540 \times 1$ $\qquad 100n = 380 \times 1$

$n = \frac{540}{100}$ $\qquad\qquad n = \frac{380}{100}$

$n = 5.4$ $\qquad\qquad\quad n = 3.8$

"In the scale drawing the length will be 5.4 cm and the width will be 3.8 cm," Melba said.

DEVELOPING SKILLS

Find the representative ratio.

MODEL   Scale: $\frac{1}{2}$ in. = 10 ft   Scale length (in.) $\longrightarrow$
Real length (in.) $\longrightarrow$ $\dfrac{\frac{1}{2}}{10 \times 12} = \frac{1}{2} \div 120 = \frac{1}{2} \times \frac{1}{120} = \frac{1}{240}$

Representative ratio $= \frac{1}{240}$

1. $\frac{1}{4}$ in. = 1 ft   **2.** $\frac{1}{2}'' = 1''$ **3.** 1 cm = 100 m   **4.** 1 cm = 5 km

The scale for a scale drawing is $\frac{1}{2}$ in. = 10 ft. Find the scale lengths for these real lengths.

MODEL   30 ft   Find the representative ratio. (See Model above.)

Let n = scale length. $\dfrac{n}{30 \times 12} = \dfrac{1}{240}$

Set up a proportion and solve. $240n = 360 \times 1$

$n = \dfrac{360}{240}$

$n = 1\frac{1}{2}$ The scale length is $1\frac{1}{2}$ in.

5. 20 ft   **6.** 32 ft   **7.** 48 ft   **8.** 87 ft   **9.** 50 ft   **10.** 90 ft

Find the real lengths for these scale lengths. Scale: 1 cm = 6 m

MODEL   18 cm $\dfrac{18}{n} = \underbrace{\dfrac{1}{6 \times 100}}$ $\longleftarrow$ $\boxed{\dfrac{\text{cm}}{\text{m} \times 100} = \dfrac{\text{cm}}{\text{cm}}}$

$\rule{1cm}{0pt}$ Representative ratio.

$18 \times 600 = n \times 1$
$10,800 = n$ The real length is 10,800 cm, or 108 m.

11. 12 cm   **12.** 24 cm   **13.** 21 cm   **14.** 15 cm   **15.** 72 cm   **16.** 60 cm

Choose a scale for making a scale drawing of each of the following. Allow for a 1.5-cm margin.

MODEL   Building 105 m $\times$ 50 m   Paper 38 cm $\times$ 23 cm
Amount of usable paper: 35 cm $\times$ 20 (38 − 3 = 35; 23 − 3 = 20)

Possible scale for horizontal real lengths: $\dfrac{35}{105 \times 100} = \dfrac{35}{10,500} = \dfrac{1}{300}$

Possible scale for vertical real lengths: $\dfrac{20}{50 \times 100} = \dfrac{20}{5,000} = \dfrac{1}{250}$

Use the smaller ratio: $\frac{1}{300}$, or 1 cm = 3 m

17. Lot 125 m $\times$ 75 m   Paper 28 cm $\times$ 18 cm   **18.** Store 252 m $\times$ 175 m   Paper 39 cm $\times$ 28 cm

APPLYING SKILLS

1. A scale drawing is to be made of a room with dimensions $16' \times 12'$. The scale is $\frac{1}{8}'' = 1'$. Find the scale lengths of the dimensions. Construct a scale drawing using the given scale. Label all parts.

2. A blueprint is to be drawn for a rectangular building $174' \times 120'$. The scale is $\frac{1}{4}'' = 12'$. Find the scale lengths of the dimensions. Construct a scale drawing using the given scale. Label all parts.

Some dictionaries show pictures of animals and the corresponding representative ratios. Measure the longest dimension, then find the approximate real length.

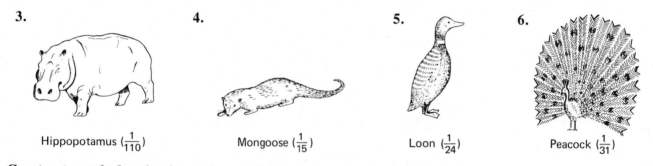

3. Hippopotamus $(\frac{1}{110})$

4. Mongoose $(\frac{1}{15})$

5. Loon $(\frac{1}{24})$

6. Peacock $(\frac{1}{31})$

Construct a scale drawing for each room listed. Choose a scale that allows for a 1″ margin on 11″ × 8″ paper.

7. Living room: $24' \times 18'$

8. Kitchen: $15' \times 12'$

9. Dining room: $18' \times 12'$

10. Bedroom: $12' \times 12'$

Find the real length for each dimension lettered _a_ through _f_.

Find the real length for each dimension lettered _a_, _b_, and _c_.

11. Scale: $\frac{1}{4}'' = 6'$

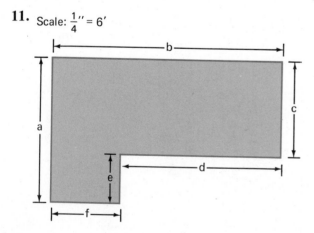

12. Scale: 1cm = 10 cm

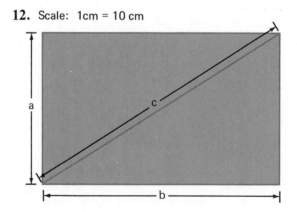

MAINTAINING SKILLS

Make true sentences. [63]

1. 42 kg = _____ g

2. 831 kg = _____ g

3. 1,467 g = _____ kg

4. 3,870 mg = _____ g

5. 33 mg = _____ g

6. 87 mg = _____ g

Divide. Simplify. [101]

7. $\frac{1}{2} \div \frac{3}{4}$

8. $\frac{5}{6} \div \frac{1}{4}$

9. $3\frac{1}{4} \div 1\frac{1}{3}$

10. $5\frac{1}{3} \div 1\frac{1}{2}$

Solve these problems.

11. Doug Marshall's typing speed-test records [19] showed:

24	32	35	34
25	30	34	36
30	28	29	35

Find his average typing speed (words per minute).

12. Jayne's bakery uses 100-pound sacks of flour. [19] The number of sacks used were:

Sunday, 20	Wednesday, 18
Monday, 19	Thursday, 20
Tuesday, 21	Friday, 22

Find the average number of sacks needed per day.

13. Sherry's ice cream parlor reported a week's [19] sales as follows:

Sunday	$437	Thursday	$340
Monday	$280	Friday	$373
Tuesday	$301	Saturday	$410
Wednesday	$197		

Find the average daily sales.

14. Ernesto's bakery reported a week's sales as [19] follows:

Sunday	$467	Thursday	$315
Monday	$281	Friday	$394
Tuesday	$301	Saturday	$451
Wednesday	$297		

Find the average daily sales.

15. A band marches about $1\frac{3}{4}$ miles in an hour dur- [101] ing a parade. How many hours would it take the band to parade 6 miles?

16. An insect walks about $7\frac{1}{2}$ meters in an hour. [101] How many hours would it take the insect to walk 42 meters?

17. A piece of wood measures 12 feet long. How [101] many $\frac{4}{5}$-foot long pieces can be cut from this wood?

18. A group hiked 8 miles. They rested every $2\frac{1}{2}$ [101] miles. How many times did they stop to rest?

19. Evian has 10,000 grams of grass seed. She [63] needs a total of 13 kilograms of seed for her front lawn. How many more grams of grass seed does she need?

20. Vicente is making fruit cocktails for his party. [63] He has 1.71 kg apples, 1.5 kg peaches, and 1.54 kg cherries. How many grams of fruit does he have in all?

Self-Test: Chapter 4

Simplify. [78]

1. $\frac{4}{6}$

2. $\frac{15}{20}$

Write 3 fractions equivalent to each. [78]

3. $\frac{1}{3}$

4. $\frac{2}{5}$

Solve these proportions. [83]

5. $\frac{7}{8} = \frac{21}{n}$

6. $\frac{2}{5} = \frac{n}{100}$

Compare. Use $<$, $=$, or $>$. [83]

7. $\frac{1}{2}$ and $\frac{2}{5}$

8. $\frac{1}{4}$ and $\frac{2}{8}$

Add. [87]

9. $\frac{1}{2} + \frac{1}{4}$

10. $2\frac{1}{2} + 1\frac{1}{5}$

Subtract. [91]

11. $\frac{5}{8} - \frac{1}{4}$

12. $2\frac{1}{2} - 1\frac{3}{4}$

Multiply. Simplify. [97]

13. $\frac{1}{2} \times \frac{3}{5}$

14. $1\frac{1}{4} \times 2\frac{1}{2}$

Divide. Simplify. [101]

15. $\frac{1}{4} \div \frac{1}{3}$

16. $2\frac{1}{2} \div \frac{3}{4}$

Find the scale lengths for these real lengths. Scale: 1 cm = 3 m. [105]

17. 36 m

18. 45 m

Find the real lengths for these scale lengths. Scale: 1 in. = 2 ft. [105]

19. 6 in.

20. 3.5 in.

Solve these problems.

21. Ruth Williams used $5\frac{1}{2}$ gallons of gas on a trip to
[87] Forest Park. She used only $4\frac{9}{10}$ gallons for her return trip. How much gas did she use in all?

22. George Jones had $16\frac{1}{2}$ gallons of gas in his car.
[91] He drove to Dallas and used $15\frac{3}{10}$ gallons. How much gas did he have left in his car?

23. Martha works $4\frac{1}{2}$ hours a day, 5 days a week.
[97] How many hours does she work in a week?

24. Rudy walked $4\frac{1}{2}$ miles in $3\frac{1}{4}$ hours. Find his
[101] average speed, in miles per hour.

25. Make a scale drawing of a bedroom. The length
[105] is 12 ft and the width is $10\frac{1}{2}$ ft. Use the scale $\frac{1}{2}$ in. = 1 ft.

26. A dictionary picture of a possum measures $1\frac{1}{4}$
[105] inches. The representative ratio is $\frac{1}{12}$. Find the approximate real length.

Test: Chapter 4

Simplify.

1. $\frac{6}{9}$

2. $\frac{10}{20}$

Write 3 fractions equivalent to each.

3. $\frac{4}{5}$

4. $\frac{1}{6}$

Solve these proportions.

5. $\frac{3}{9} = \frac{15}{n}$

6. $\frac{1}{20} = \frac{n}{100}$

Compare. Use <, =, or >.

7. $\frac{1}{3}$ and $\frac{4}{12}$

8. $\frac{4}{5}$ and $\frac{7}{8}$

Add.

9. $\frac{2}{3} + \frac{1}{4}$

10. $1\frac{5}{8} + 2\frac{1}{4}$

Subtract.

11. $\frac{9}{10} - \frac{1}{2}$

12. $2\frac{3}{4} - 1\frac{1}{3}$

Multiply. Simplify.

13. $\frac{2}{3} \times \frac{1}{5}$

14. $4\frac{1}{2} \times 1\frac{1}{3}$

Divide. Simplify.

15. $\frac{2}{3} \div 2$

16. $4\frac{1}{2} \div 1\frac{2}{3}$

Find the scale lengths for these real lengths. Scale: 1 in. = 2 ft.

17. 42 ft

18. 15 ft

Find the real lengths for these scale lengths. Scale: 1 cm = 3 m.

19. 26 cm

20. 14 cm

Solve these problems.

21. James Hargis used $7\frac{1}{2}$ gallons of gas on a trip to Center City. He used $6\frac{7}{10}$ gallons on the return trip. How much gas did he use in all?

22. Shirley Anderson had $17\frac{1}{2}$ gallons of gas in her car. She drove to work and used $1\frac{3}{10}$ gallons. How much gas did she have left in her car?

23. Joe works $6\frac{1}{2}$ hours a day, 5 days a week. How many hours does he work in a week?

24. Linda walked $3\frac{3}{4}$ miles in $2\frac{1}{2}$ hours. Find her average speed, in miles per hour.

25. Make a scale drawing of a bedroom. The length is 4 m and the width is $3\frac{1}{2}$ m. Use the scale 2 cm = 1 m.

26. A dictionary picture of a king penguin measures 3 cm. The representative ratio is $\frac{1}{30}$. Find the approximate real length.

Drawing Bar Graphs

Draw a bar graph.

MODEL

WEEKLY PAYROLL	
Name	Earnings
A. Adams	$125
C. Chen	150
S. Davis	125
L. Gomez	200
F. Sudo	150
R. Toth	175

Step 1 Draw a vertical line and mark the earnings along the line by 25's.

Step 2 Draw a horizontal line and mark the names.

Step 3 Draw bars of the correct height to represent the earnings. The bars should be the same width and should be equally spaced.

Step 4 Complete the rectangle. Give the graph a title and label the scales.

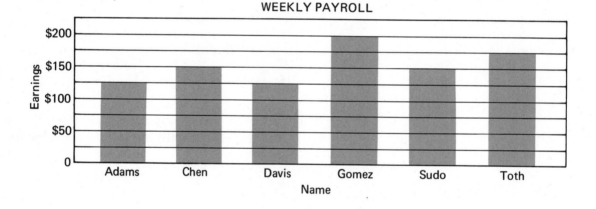

1.	JOE WASHINGTON'S SALES RECORD	
	Week	Sales
	1	$1,600
	2	$2,000
	3	$1,200
	4	$1,400
	5	$1,600
	6	$2,000
	7	$1,800
	8	$1,900
	9	$2,200
	10	$2,400

2.	EVA BLUE SPRUCE'S SALES RECORD	
	Week	Sales
	1	$2,000
	2	$1,500
	3	$1,700
	4	$1,700
	5	$2,000
	6	$2,300
	7	$2,500
	8	$2,400
	9	$2,800
	10	$3,000

5
PERCENT

An airline crewman
helping to direct the
pilot into the terminal

Activities

Copy the puzzle at the right. Unscramble each word, one letter to each box. Then unscramble the circled letters to form a word to fill the boxes below.

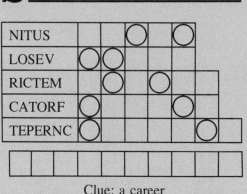

NITUS

LOSEV

RICTEM

CATORF

TEPERNC

Clue: a career

Set up two or three budgets based upon a $600 monthly income. Specify whether your budget is for one person or a family of two, three, etc. Let each budget try to meet different needs. For example:

    1) saving for a new car, clothing, and the like;

    2) large expenditures for food, rent, and so on;

    3) large amounts needed for meeting the expense of credit purchases and bank loans.

Conduct a survey among your friends, members of your family, and other people that you know well. See if you can find the reasons they do or do not have a budget. Share your findings with the class. As a result of your survey, what recommendations would you make to a person who is considering a budget?

Plan a one-week winter's vacation in a place of your choice. Set up two separate budgets for this vacation. Prepare a budget of expenses for an economy rate and a first-class rate. Example: take a bus, stay at a budget hotel; fly, stay at a medium priced hotel; or vice versa, etc.

Meaning of Percent

percent   Percent means hundredths. The symbol for percent is %.

interest   Interest is a charge made for a loan of money or goods of value.

For Discussion

- How does Abe change a percent to a decimal?

- What did Mr. Kartch ask?

- How did Abe answer Mr. Kartch's question?

- How did Marcia answer Mr. Kartch's question?

- When might Marcia's method be used?

"I arranged for a 9% loan at the bank," Ms. Kartch said.

"What does that mean?" asked Marcia.

Abe explained, "Percent means hundredths, so Mom will have to pay $9 interest for each $100 she borrows."

Marcia said, "I think I understand."

$9\% = 9$ hundredths $= 9 \times .01$, or $.09$

$150\% = 150$ hundredths $= 150 \times .01$, or 1.50

$8.6\% = 8.6$ hundredths $= 8.6 \times .01$, or $.086$

Abe said, "I use a shortcut to change a percent to a decimal. I drop the percent symbol and move the decimal point two places to the left."

Marcia said, "To change a decimal to a percent, I could move the decimal point two places to the right and write the percent symbol."

Mr. Kartch asked, "How would you change a fraction to a percent?"

Abe replied, "I'd set up a proportion to find an equivalent fraction with a denominator of 100. Then I'd change to percent."

Marcia said, "First, I'd divide to change the fraction to a decimal. Then, I'd change to percent."

DEVELOPING SKILLS

Change to percents.

MODELS

	.07	1.83	.086
	.07 = 7 × .01	1.83 = 183 × .01	.086 = 8.6 × .01
	= 7 hundredths	= 183 hundredths	= 8.6 hundredths
	= 7%	= 183%	= 8.6%

1. .25   **2.** .003   **3.** .63   **4.** 1.45   **5.** 3.00   **6.** .875

Change to percents.

MODEL

$$\frac{9}{25}$$

$$\frac{9}{25} = \frac{9}{25} \times \frac{4}{4}$$

$$= \frac{36}{100}, \text{ or } 36\%$$

$$\frac{9}{25} = \frac{n}{100}$$

$$25 \times n = 900$$

$$n = 36$$

$$\frac{36}{100} = 36\%$$

$$\frac{9}{25} = 9 \div 25$$

$$\begin{array}{r} .36 \\ 25\overline{)9.00} \\ 75 \\ \hline 150 \\ 150 \\ \hline \end{array} \longrightarrow 36\%$$

7. $\frac{1}{2}$ **8.** $\frac{3}{4}$ **9.** $\frac{1}{6}$ **10.** $\frac{1}{50}$ **11.** $\frac{3}{8}$ **12.** $\frac{3}{20}$

Change to decimals.

MODELS

	7%	183%	8.6%
	7% = 7 × .01	183% = 183 × .01	8.6% = 8.6 × .01
	= .07	= 1.83	= .086

13. 28%   **14.** 5%   **15.** .1%   **16.** 32.8%   **17.** 140%   **18.** 65%

Change to fractions. Simplify when possible.

MODELS

	7%	36%	$16\frac{1}{2}\%$
	7% = 7 × .01	36% = 36 × .01	$16\frac{1}{2}\% = 16.5\%$
	= 7 hundredths	= 36 hundredths	= 16.5 × .01
	$= \frac{7}{100}$	$= \frac{36}{100}, \text{ or } \frac{9}{25}$	= 165 thousandths
			$= \frac{165}{1,000}, \text{ or } \frac{33}{200}$

19. 5%   **20.** 68%   **21.** 1%   **22.** $4\frac{1}{2}\%$ **23.** 140%   **24.** 10%

APPLYING SKILLS

Copy and complete.

	Fraction	Decimal	Percent
	$\frac{4}{5}$	.80	80%
1.	$\frac{1}{4}$		
2.		.003	
3.		.75	
4.			60%
5.			12.3%
6.	$\frac{180}{720}$		
7.	$1\frac{45}{100}$		
8.		.066	

	Fraction	Decimal	Percent
	$\frac{2}{3}$	$.66\frac{2}{3}$	$66\frac{2}{3}\%$
9.	$\frac{1}{3}$		
10.		.1	
11.		.88	
12.			2%
13.			6.4%
14.	$\frac{80}{200}$		
15.	$\frac{72}{100}$		
16.		1.34	

Solve these problems.

17. Ms. Mason traveled 28% of a trip. Write the fraction for the part she traveled.

18. Mr. Hayes ate 60% of the cupcakes he baked. Write the fraction for the part he ate.

19. Mark used 50% of the supplies given him. Write a decimal for the amount he used.

20. Edna washed 40% of her new car. Write a decimal for the amount she washed.

21. Mr. Stein invited some people to a party. He expects at least $\frac{1}{2}$ of them to come. What percent does he expect to come?

22. On Monday $\frac{3}{4}$ of Mrs. Rosen's students attended geometry class. What percent attended class on Monday?

23. Tesse used .45 of the gasoline in her plane. What percent of gasoline did she use?

24. Roger built .65 of the fence around his house. What percent of the fence has he built?

25. Angelo played 85% of a basketball game before he was replaced by Jason. Write a fraction for the part of the game Jason played.

26. Marie planted 46% of her flower seeds before lunch. Write a fraction for the amount of seeds she must plant after lunch.

MAINTAINING SKILLS

The scale for a scale drawing is 1 cm = 5 m. Find the scale lengths for these real lengths. [105]

1. 14 m **2.** 18 m **3.** 100 m **4.** 50 m **5.** 84 m **6.** 78 m

The scale for a scale drawing is $\frac{1}{8}'' = 5'$. Find the real lengths for these scale lengths. [105]

7. $1\frac{1}{2}''$ **8.** $2\frac{3}{8}''$ **9.** $\frac{7}{8}''$ **10.** $\frac{3}{4}''$ **11.** $10''$ **12.** $15''$

Divide. Round each quotient to the nearest tenth. [43]

13. $.46\overline{)8.736}$ **14.** $.91\overline{)46.487}$ **15.** $4.6\overline{)4.874}$ **16.** $5.2\overline{)5.787}$

Simplify. [78]

17. $\frac{52}{100}$ **18.** $\frac{42}{100}$ **19.** $\frac{25}{100}$ **20.** $\frac{75}{100}$ **21.** $\frac{40}{100}$ **22.** $\frac{60}{100}$

Solve these problems. [43]

23. Pat bought 3.25 kg of meat for $7.93. How much did the meat cost per kilogram?

24. Randy bought 8.5 kg of wax for $11.22. How much did the wax cost per kilogram?

25. Susan drove 215.7 km on 19.7 liters of gasoline. How many kilometers per liter was this (to the nearest tenth)?

26. Frank drove 817.8 km on 72.8 liters of gasoline. How many kilometers per liter was this (to the nearest tenth)?

Make a scale drawing of each of the following. Use the scales given. [105]

27. Living room: 4.6 m × 3.1 m
Scale: 1 cm = .5 m

28. Garage: 19 ft × 17 ft
Scale: .5 in. = 1 ft

Find the approximate real lengths for each picture. Representative ratios are given. [105]

29.

Gorilla $(\frac{1}{40})$

30.

Fox $(\frac{1}{28})$

31.

Emu $(\frac{1}{60})$

Consumer Tips———

POSTAL SERVICES

There are four major classes of mail which you can use.

1ST CLASS:
Letters, typed or handwritten matter less than 70 lb, and less than 100 in. length and girth (distance around)

2ND CLASS:
Newspapers, periodicals

3RD CLASS: ("advertising mail")
Circulars, books, catalogs, merchandise, seeds, cuttings, bulbs, plants, less than 16 oz

4TH CLASS: ("Parcel Post")
Packages less than 40 lb and less than 84 in. (length and girth)

All rates are given in the pamphlet entitled, "Domestic Postage, Rates, Fees Information," which you may obtain at your local post office.

These are certain postal services which offer fast delivery:

Airmail; Priority Mail (Airmail between 9 oz and 70 lb)

Aerogramme — special overseas correspondence

Express Mail – overnight delivery in certain areas only

Special Delivery – immediate delivery from the destination post office

Mailgram – early delivery of telegrams the next business day

Special postal handling of valuables is available through Insured Mail, Registered Mail, C.O.D. Mail, Money Orders, and International Money Orders.

Proof of mailing and delivery is obtained by a Certificate of Mailing, Certified Mail, and a Return Receipt.

Percent Problems

compared number   The compared number is the numerator of the fraction equivalent to a given ratio.

compared-to number   The compared-to number is the denominator of the fraction equivalent to a given ratio.

related rate   The related rate is the percent equivalent to a given ratio.

financial aid   Financial aid refers to some type of loan or gift which may be available to qualified students.

For Discussion
- How does Doreen solve all percent problems?
- What general pattern can be used to solve all percent problems?
- How would you check to see if Doreen and Charles got the correct answers?

Reading
Doreen Gorski mentioned that 960 students at King Memorial High School were planning to continue their education after graduation.

"There are 1,600 students enrolled this year," said her brother Charles. "What percent does that represent?"

Doreen answered, "The related rate, or percent is a ratio, so I solve all percent problems by using a proportion. You can use this pattern." She wrote:

$$\frac{\text{Compared number}}{\text{Compared-to number}} = \text{Related rate (percent)}$$

$$\text{Proportion: } \frac{960}{1,600} = \frac{n}{100}$$

She continued, "n is 60, so 60% of the students plan to continue their education."

Charles said, "My guidance counselor said that 65% of the students enrolled at the local community college get some type of financial aid. The enrollment is 5,000."

"How many students are receiving aid?" asked Mrs. Gorski.

Charles wrote:

$$\begin{array}{l}\text{Compared number} \longrightarrow \\ \text{Compared-to number} \longrightarrow\end{array} \quad \frac{n}{5,000} = \frac{65}{100}$$

He answered, "3,250 students are receiving aid."

DEVELOPING SKILLS

Compute.

MODEL   25% of 48 is what number?

$$25\% = \frac{n}{48} \longleftarrow \text{Compared number}$$
$$\longleftarrow \text{Compared-to number}$$

$$\frac{25}{100} = \frac{n}{48}$$
$$25 \times 48 = 100n$$
$$1{,}200 = 100n$$
$$12 = n$$

$$\begin{array}{r} 48 \\ \times\ .25 \\ \hline 2\ 40 \\ 9\ 60 \\ \hline 12.00, \text{ or } 12 \end{array}$$ So, 25% of 48 is 12.

1. 40% of 75

2. 37.5% of 64

3. 50% of 38

4. 150% of 48

5. 13% of 65

6. 75% of 24

Compute.

MODEL   16 is what percent of 40?

$$n = \frac{16}{40} \longleftarrow \text{Compared number}$$
$$\longleftarrow \text{Compared-to number}$$

$$n = \frac{2}{5}$$
$$= 40\%$$

So, 16 is 40% of 40

$$\frac{16}{40} = \frac{n}{100}$$
$$1{,}600 = 40n$$
$$40 = n$$
$$\frac{16}{40} = \frac{40}{100}, \text{ or } 40\%$$

7. 24 is what percent of 30?

8. 36 is what percent of 90?

9. 30 is what percent of 15?

10. 60 is what percent of 160?

Compute.

MODEL   12 is 25% of what number?

$$25\% = \frac{12}{n} \longleftarrow \text{Compared number}$$
$$\longleftarrow \text{Compared-to number}$$

$$\frac{25}{100} = \frac{12}{n}$$
$$25n = 1{,}200$$
$$n = 48$$

$$.25 \times n = 12$$
$$n = \frac{12}{.25}$$
$$n = 48$$ So, 12 is 25% of 48.

11. 40 is 25% of what number?

12. 18 is 75% of what number?

13. 70 is 12.5% of what number?

14. 20 is 40% of what number?

APPLYING SKILLS

1. *Like* magazine will award a prize to all sales-people who increase their list of subscribers by at least 15%. Mike Felser has 400 subscribers. How many new subscribers will qualify him for an award?

2. An airline anticipates a 35% increase in passenger traffic because of new equipment. The present average passenger load is 48,000 a month. Find the expected passenger increase.

3. A suit is reduced to sell for $48. This price is 75% of the original price. Find the original price.

4. Ms. Yamamoto donated 10% of her net weekly earnings to charity. Her donation was $25. Find her net earnings.

5. Out of a total inventory of 3,000 books, a book store did not sell 900 books. What percent was not sold?

6. A lawnmower was originally listed at $60. The price was reduced by $12. What percent was it reduced?

7. A used car lot advertises 20% off the listed price of any car. What is the sale price of a car listed at $1,500?

8. A printing press produced 400 newspapers. 16% were unclear and had to be thrown away. How many were thrown away?

9. Margie made a down payment of $45 on a pair of skis marked $150. What percent of the selling price did she already pay?

10. James typed 600 envelopes. A total of 1,500 must be typed. What percent has James typed?

11. Earl Jackson receives 4% commission on all his sales. Last week his commission was $150. Find the amount of his sales.

12. This month Maria Lopez received a $1,240 commission. Her rate of commission is 8%. Find her sales for this month.

13. Bill receives 5.5% commission on all his sales. Last week, his sales were $1,766. Find his commission last week.

14. This month Ameid earned $2,468 for selling books. She receives 6% commission. What was her commission this month?

15. A radio tagged $70 was reduced by $14. By what percent was it reduced?

16. A coat tagged $120 was reduced by $30. By what percent was it reduced?

17. Omari paid $75 for security on an apartment. This was 30% of his monthly rent. What does he pay each month for rent?

18. Janet paid an installment fee of $45 for her carpet. This was 15% of the price of the carpet. Find the price of the carpet.

19. Bill White Feather's heating costs are down 15% since last month. Find this month's bill if last month's bill was $53.

20. MODERN'S runs a special sale reducing all goods by 25%. Find the sale price of a pair of curtains at $12.00 a pair.

MAINTAINING SKILLS

Change to percents. [114]

1. .26   **2.** .35   **3.** .3   **4.** 1.4   **5.** .008   **6.** .446

7. $\frac{4}{5}$ **8.** $\frac{3}{10}$ **9.** $\frac{3}{8}$ **10.** $\frac{7}{8}$ **11.** $\frac{1}{3}$ **12.** $\frac{5}{6}$

Change to fractions. Simplify. [114]

13. 10%   **14.** 40%   **15.** 12%   **16.** 32%   **17.** 150%   **18.** $37\frac{1}{2}$%

Change to decimals. [114]

19. 67%   **20.** 42%   **21.** 160%   **22.** 250%   **23.** .5%   **24.** .25%

Add. Simplify. [87]

25. $\frac{1}{4} + \frac{3}{5}$ **26.** $\frac{7}{8} + \frac{2}{3}$ **27.** $1\frac{1}{2} + 3\frac{3}{4}$ **28.** $7\frac{1}{4} + 6\frac{1}{3}$

Multiply. Simplify. [97]

29. $\frac{1}{2} \times \frac{3}{4}$ **30.** $\frac{1}{4} \times \frac{7}{10}$ **31.** $1\frac{1}{4} \times 3\frac{1}{5}$ **32.** $2\frac{1}{2} \times 3\frac{3}{10}$

Solve these problems.

33. Youngtown High School basketball team won
[114] the championship game. Seven-tenths of the student body went to the game. What percent went to the game?

34. Jackson High School presented an all-school
[114] musical. Three-fifths of the student body worked to make it a success. What percent was this?

35. A special election was held in Springfield.
[114] Forty-seven percent of the registered voters voted. Write a fraction for this amount.

36. A new editor was found for the high school
[114] paper. Sales went up forty percent. Write a fraction for the increase in sales.

37. Jake drove $3\frac{2}{5}$ miles to the store. From there he
[87] drove $8\frac{1}{10}$ miles to the park. He then drove $6\frac{1}{2}$ miles home. How far did he drive in all?

38. Helen walks $1\frac{3}{10}$ miles to work. At lunch time
[87] she walks $\frac{1}{2}$ mile. After work she takes another route home, walking $2\frac{1}{5}$ miles. How far does she walk each day?

Find the area. [97]

39. Length: $4\frac{1}{2}$ ft

    Width: $2\frac{1}{3}$ ft

40. Length: $10\frac{1}{4}$ in.

     Width: $6\frac{1}{2}$ in.

41. Length: $100\frac{1}{2}$ m

     Width: $46\frac{1}{4}$ m

Career/DISTRIBUTION

Distribution plays an ever increasing role in our nation's economy. Our country produces a major share of the world's goods. Firms involved in distribution are providing jobs for almost 60 percent of the labor force. Career opportunities for young people are now open to high school graduates in the areas of marketing.

Job Descriptions

- Stock clerk—sorts, stores, packages, and in general keeps track of merchandise as it is sent out or arrives.

- Sales personnel—sells merchandise by convincing customers that a product fills their needs.

- Buyer—selects the merchandise to be sold by the firm; visits the producer to examine goods; keeps record of goods on hand, and what is "open to buy."

- Promotion—prepares the advertising materials for either newspapers, magazines, radio, or television; arranges goods for sale to attract customers.

Training

Entry-level jobs in this field are often open to high school graduates. High school distributive education programs offer good preparation. Post-high-school programs are available in most junior and community colleges. Full four-year college programs are offered by many universities.

Further Investigation

Arrange an interview with a buyer or other expert in the area of distribution. Ask about job qualifications, working conditions, possibilities for advancement, entry-level jobs.

Consult your guidance department about vocational training (work–experience programs) or post-high-school courses in this area.

Percent Change

inventory   Inventory refers to a list of articles or merchandise on hand at any time.

accountant   An accountant is a professionally trained person who keeps, inspects, or adjusts business records. Accountants advise clients about the financial operations of their businesses.

overstocking   Overstocking of supplies means having a greater quantity of supplies on hand than needed at the time.

For Discussion

- Why was Ms. Blue Spruce's company concerned about inventory?

- How is inventory information used by the managers of a business?

- What affect would overstocking inventory have on a business?

- When would overstocking be an advantage?

As stockroom manager, Ms. Blue Spruce was asked to prepare a report dealing with inventory control. "Our accountants want a report in which last year's inventory is compared with this year's," she announced one evening at dinner. "I have to calculate the percent change for every inventory item."

"What will the accountants do with that information?" asked her son, Paul.

His mother explained, "We are overstocked. Too much money is tied up in unsold goods. Our accountants want to know which items have not moved. When they look at these figures, they will be able to tell us which items might cause future problems."

"Will inventory controls now increase chances of future profits?" asked Lucy.

"Sure thing," replied Ms. Blue Spruce. "I've got to find an easy way to calculate percent increase or percent decrease."

Paul answered, "Subtract one from the other to find what the change was. Then set up a proportion to find the percent. Use the change or difference as the compared number and last year's inventory as the compared-to number."

DEVELOPING SKILLS

OBJECTIVE To compute percent increase or decrease

Find the percent increase.

MODEL   This Year's Price: $2,500; Last Year's Price: $2,000

This year's price: $2,500

Last year's price: 2,000 ⟵——— Compared-to number

Difference: $ 500 ⟵——— Compared number

$$\% \text{ increase} = \frac{500}{2,000} \begin{array}{l} \longleftarrow \text{ Compared number} \\ \longleftarrow \text{ Compared-to number} \end{array}$$

$$= \frac{1}{4}, \text{ or } 25\%$$

This Year's Price	Last Year's Price		This Year's Price	Last Year's Price
1. $250	$200	**2.**	$240	$160
3. $1,500	$1,200	**4.**	$15,000	$9,000
5. $4,800	$3,200	**6.**	$23,520	$21,000
7. $480	$400	**8.**	$9,720	$9,000

Find the percent decrease.

MODEL   Last Year's Orders: 3,000; This Year's Orders: 2,500

Last year's Orders: 3,000 ⟵——— Compared number

This year's Orders: 2,500

Difference: 500 ⟵——— Compared-to number

$$\% \text{ decrease} = \frac{500}{3,000} \begin{array}{l} \longleftarrow \text{ Compared-to number} \\ \longleftarrow \text{ Compared number} \end{array}$$

$$= \frac{1}{6}, \text{ or } 16\frac{2}{3}\%$$

Last Year's Orders	This Year's Orders		Last Year's Orders	This Year's Orders
9. 75,000	50,000	**10.**	5,400	1,800
11. 320	160	**12.**	50,000	40,000
13. 2,400	1,800	**14.**	1,000	900
15. 48,000	40,000	**16.**	7,500	7,000

APPLYING SKILLS

1. The Boonsville Public Library circulation last month was 24,000 books. This month the circulation was 28,000 books. What is the compared number? What is the compared-to number? Find the percent increase.

2. Mary Jackson paid $26.00 for her electric bill last month. This month she paid $28.08 for her electric bill. What is the compared number? What is the compared-to number? Find the percent increase.

3. At the end of the summer, Ace Motors reduced the price of a Super 8 from $5,500 to $4,950. By what percent has the price been reduced?

4. Enrollment in one high school in Galveston decreased from 1,500 students to 1,200 students. Find the percent decrease in enrollment.

5. Last month Mary Pelligrino's salary was $90. This month it increased to $100.80. Find the percent increase.

6. The number of employees in a company increased from 100 to 130. Find the percent increase.

7. In May the monthly sales of used cars were 860,000. In June the monthly sales of used cars were 774,000. What was the percent change?

8. Last week most shirts at Miguel's boutique sold for $15.00. This week they are selling for $13.50. Find the percent change.

9. A shoe manufacturer produced 860,000 pairs of shoes last year and 774,000 pairs the year before. Find the percent change in production.

10. On her vacation this year, Judy Robinson drove 168 miles to a resort. Last year she drove 112 miles to a mountain lodge. Find the percent change.

11. The population of Locust Valley is 68,775. Five years ago the population was 65,500. Find the percent change in the 5-year period.

12. In one hour Martin typed 2 pages of his term paper. In the next hour he typed an additional 3 pages. Find the percent change.

Copy and complete.

13.

Last Year	This Year	Change (+ or −)	Percent
$400.	$500.		
1.00	.20		
2,400.	2,700.		
250.	125.		

14.

Last Year	This Year	Change (+ or −)	Percent
$20.	$8.		
40.	52.		
3,200.	800.		
55.	82.50		

MAINTAINING SKILLS

Compute. [119]

1. 50% of 300

2. 45% of 150

3. 37.3% of 4,763

4. 84.6% of 2,836

5. 84 is what percent of 200?

6. 42 is what percent of 84?

7. 40 is 10% of what number?

8. 25 is 20% of what number?

Subtract. Simplify. [91]

9. $\frac{1}{2} - \frac{1}{3}$

10. $\frac{3}{4} - \frac{2}{3}$

11. $3\frac{1}{3} - 1\frac{3}{4}$

12. $6\frac{1}{5} - 2\frac{1}{2}$

Divide. Simplify. [101]

13. $\frac{1}{2} \div \frac{1}{5}$

14. $\frac{3}{5} \div \frac{1}{3}$

15. $3\frac{1}{2} \div \frac{2}{3}$

16. $7\frac{1}{4} \div \frac{1}{2}$

Solve these problems.

17. Janice ran the 100 meter dash in $16\frac{3}{10}$ sec. Julie [91] ran it in $15\frac{7}{10}$ sec. How much less time did Julie take?

18. Phil broad-jumped $4\frac{7}{12}$ ft. Lon broad-jumped [91] $4\frac{13}{36}$ ft. How much shorter was Lon's broad jump?

19. Last year, Overton Motors gave an across-the-[119] board 7% increase in salary to each employee. The average salary was $8,760 the year before. Find the average salary after the increase.

20. Newton's General Steel Works experienced a [119] decrease in profits of 10% this year. The profits made the previous year were $20,180. What profit did the company make this year?

21. Miss Harris has $49.80 taken out of her pay [119] each month for savings. This is 6% of her monthly salary. How much does she earn?

22. The amount of taxes withheld from Joe's [119] paycheck each week is $35.20. This is 25% of his weekly salary. How much does he earn?

23. Elena's weekly salary is 15% more than Dave's. [119] Dave earns $230. How much does Elena earn?

24. New car prices will be increased by 5% next [119] month. A car now cost $3,510. How much will it cost next month?

25. Lou White Feather pays $1,800 a year for rent [119] on his apartment. He earns $9,000 a year. What percent of his yearly salary does he spend for rent?

26. Mason School invited 450 people to its annual [119] play. There were 306 people at the play. What percent of the people invited came to the play?

Budgeting

budget   A budget is a plan for spending one's income.

necessity   A necessity is an item without which one cannot get along.

fixed expenses   Fixed expenses are certain necessary living costs that occur regularly.

variable expenses   Variable expenses are those items which are likely to change from time to time.

For Discussion

- What solution did Mr. Williams suggest when his wife said they might not be able to pay all of their bills?

- Which items in a family budget are fixed?

- Which items are variable expenses?

Reading

Luann Williams had just returned from shopping at the supermarket. "If prices keep going up, we will barely have money enough to pay last month's bills," she told her husband.

"We had better start planning for the future now," he said. "Even though I expect a salary increase the first of the year, the cost of living trend is not very encouraging. We need to revise our family budget. If we set aside a definite amount regularly for necessities, we might find that we have more money to spend on items we plan to cut down on."

"Let's look at our fixed expenses, first, and include a definite amount for savings. Then we can plan some variable expenses, no matter how small they might be," said Luann.

Food	$75
Clothing	30
Housing	60
Household Expense	10
Insurance	15
Transportation	20
Savings	10
Recreation	10
Personal Allowance	15
Emergency Fund	5
Weekly net income	$250

"I wonder what percent of our weekly net income is spent on food?" sighed Joe, their son.

DEVELOPING SKILLS

OBJECTIVE **To prepare a budget**

Find the amount spent on each item.

MODEL   Yearly Net Income: $8,000

Item	Percent	Amount
Food	20%	$1,600
Clothing	15%	$1,200
Housing	25%	$2,000
Transportation	12%	$ 960
Insurance	10%	$ 800
Recreation	8%	$ 640
Savings	10%	$ 800
TOTALS	100%	$8,000

$\longrightarrow$ 20% of $8,000

$\begin{array}{r} \$8,000 \\ \times\ .20 \\ \hline \$1600.00 \end{array}$

So, 20% of $8,000 = $1,600 (amount spent on food)

1. Yearly Net Income: $6,750

Item	Percent
Food	30%
Clothing	30%
Housing	10%
Transportation	5%
Insurance	10%
Recreation	7%
Savings	8%

2. Yearly Net Income: $17,500

Item	Percent
Food	10%
Clothing	12%
Housing	20%
Transportation	10%
Insurance	15%
Recreation	10%
Savings	23%

Find the percent for each amount.

MODEL   Monthly Net Income: $420

Food	$126	30%
Housing	$105	25%
Clothing	$ 84	20%
Transportation	$ 42	10%
Recreation	$ 21	5%
Savings	$ 42	10%

$\longrightarrow \frac{126}{420} = \frac{n}{100}$

$420n = 12,600$

$n = 30$

$\frac{30}{100} = 30\%$ (percent spent on food)

3. Monthly Net Income: $600

Food	$150
Housing	$200
Clothing	$ 75
Transportation	$ 75
Recreation	$ 60
Savings	$40

4. Monthly Net Income: $840

Food	$210
Housing	$252
Clothing	$126
Transportation	$126
Recreation	$ 84
Savings	$42

APPLYING SKILLS

1. Ted has a new job which gives him a net monthly income of $360. Make up a budget using: food, 35%; housing, 25%; transportation, 10%; clothing, 15%; savings, 10%; recreation, 5%.

2. Fola has a business which gives her a net monthly income of $16,400. Make up a budget using: rent, 26%; operating expenses, 8%; salaries, 19%; advertising, 5%; stock, 32%; profit, 10%.

3. Alfonso received a $5,500 scholarship for his freshman year at college. Make up a budget using: tuition and books, 50%; room and board, 33%; clothing, 10%; transportation, 3%; recreation, 4%.

4. Francis has a yearly net income of $9,400. Make up a budget using: food, 30%; housing, 25%; clothing, 15%; transportation, 7%; recreation, 8%; insurance, 5%; savings, 10%.

5. Alan Schroeder's net income is $110 per week. Alan lives at home and has agreed to give his parents $33 per week for his room and board. Other items in his weekly budget are: clothing, $22; recreation, $11; lunches, $11; savings, $33. What percent is budgeted for each item?

6. Judy Stewart is a buyer for her uncle's bookstore. Judy's net take home pay amounts to $120 per week. She prepared a budget using: room and board, $40; clothing, $34; recreation, $20; savings, $14; lunches, $12. What percent is budgeted for each item?

7. Peggy has a yearly net income of $13,500. She planned a budget using: food, $3,375; clothing, $2,025; housing, $4,050; transportation, $1,350; insurance, $1,080; recreation, $945; savings, $675. What percent is budgeted for each item?

8. Peter's business has a monthly net income of $14,600. He has a budget using: rent, $3,650; operating expenses, $1,314; salaries, $2,920; advertising, $292; stock, $4,818; profit, $1,606. What percent is budgeted for each item?

9. Maxine has a yearly net income of $18,600. Complete her budget.

Item	Percent	Amount
Food	15%	
Clothing	10%	
Housing	20%	
Transportation	12%	
Insurance	15%	
Recreation	13%	
Savings	15%	
TOTALS		

10. Ron has a monthly net income of $1,200. Complete his budget.

Item	Percent	Amount
Food	20%	
Clothing	15%	
Housing	18%	
Transportation	5%	
Insurance	7%	
Recreation	10%	
Savings	25%	
TOTALS		

MAINTAINING SKILLS

Solve these proportions.   [83]

1. $\frac{5}{8} = \frac{75}{n}$

2. $\frac{4}{5} = \frac{96}{n}$

3. $\frac{1}{3} = \frac{n}{450}$

4. $\frac{1}{4} = \frac{n}{144}$

Compare. Use <, =, or >.   [83]

5. $\frac{1}{5}$ and $\frac{1}{10}$

6. $\frac{1}{4}$ and $\frac{1}{3}$

7. $\frac{3}{4}$ and $\frac{3}{5}$

8. $\frac{7}{8}$ and $\frac{7}{10}$

Find the percent increase.   [125]

	Last Year's Price	This Year's Price		Last Year's Orders	This Year's Orders
9.	$.45	$.60	10.	2,000	2,250
11.	$.96	$1.08	12.	4,500	4,950
13.	$.50	$.60	14.	4,600	5,106

Find the percent decrease.   [125]

	Last Year's Price	This Year's Price		Last Year's Orders	This Year's Orders
15.	$6.50	$5.85	16.	64,000	15,360
17.	$20.00	$19.00	18.	460	368
19.	$.40	$.38	20.	86,400	76,032

Solve these problems. Use proportions.   [83]

21. A bookstore sells 15 books every half hour. At this rate, how many books are sold in 8 hours?

22. A 40-acre field yields 500 bushels of wheat. At this rate, how many bushels would a 100-acre field yield?

23. A town grew from 6,225 to 7,500 in the last 3 years. At that rate, what will the population be 10 years from now?

24. A city grew from 846,000 to 848,600 in the last 4 years. At that rate what will the population be 5 years from now?

Solve these problems.   [125]

25. An automobile decreased in value from a $2,980 to $2,235. Find the percent decrease.

26. The price of 5 pounds of sugar increased from $1.80 to $1.98. Find the percent increase.

27. Holt High School had 680 students enrolled last year. This year it has 782 students. Find the percent increase in enrollment.

28. Last year the Wayne High School Band had 140 members. This year its membership dropped to 133. Find the percent decrease in membership.

Self-Test: Chapter 5

Change to percents. [114]

1. .07 **2.** .009 **3.** 4.00 **4.** $\frac{3}{4}$ **5.** $\frac{2}{3}$ **6.** $3\frac{1}{2}$

Change to decimals. [114]

7. 42.6% **8.** 5.7% **9.** .7%

Change to fractions. Simplify. [114]

10. 7% **11.** $14\frac{1}{2}$% **12.** 180%

Compute. [119]

13. 72% of 120

14. 115% of 400

15. 16 is what percent of 64

16. 100 is what percent of 1,600

17. 72 is 25% of what number

18. 24 is 37.5% of what number

Find the percent increase. [125]

19. Last year's income: $10,000 This year's income: $11,000

Find the percent decrease. [125]

20. Last year's price: $8.50 This year's price: $8.33

Copy and complete this budget. [129]

21.

YEARLY NET INCOME: $10,400		
Item	Percent	Amount
Food	28%	
Rent	24%	
Clothing	16%	
Transportation and recreation	15%	
Savings and insurance	17%	
TOTALS		

Solve these problems. [119]

22. Mr. Brooks receives a 4% commission on all sales. Last week his sales totaled $1,567. How much commission did he receive?

23. Miss Roberts earns $200 per week. After deductions her take home pay is $174. What percent of her earnings is her take home pay?

Test: Chapter 5

Change to percents.

1. .08　　　　**2.** .002　　　　**3.** 5.00　　　　**4.** $\frac{5}{8}$　　　**5.** $\frac{1}{3}$　　　**6.** $1\frac{3}{4}$

Change to decimals.　　　　　　　　　　　**Change to fractions. Simplify.**

7. 92.3%　　　**8.** 3.2%　　　**9.** .5%　　　**10.** 3%　　　**11.** $6\frac{1}{2}$%　　　**12.** 150%

Compute.

13. 54% of 80　　　　　　　　　　　　　**14.** 125% of 300

15. 32 is what percent of 80　　　　　　　**16.** 90 is what percent of 45

17. 14 is 50% of what number　　　　　　　**18.** 20 is 12.5% of what number

Find the percent increase.

19. Last year's salary: $5,000　　　　　This year's salary: $6,000

Find the percent decrease.

20. Last year's sales: $8,000　　　　　This year's sales: $7,200

Copy and complete this budget.

21.

YEARLY NET INCOME: $9,400		
Item	Percent	Amount
Food	30%	
Rent	25%	
Clothing	20%	
Transportation and recreation	15%	
Savings and insurance	10%	
TOTALS		

Solve these problems.

22. Ms. Nelson receives 3% commission on all sales. Last week her sales amounted to $4,872. How much commission did she receive?

23. Mr. Brill earns $180 per week. After deductions his take home pay is $162. What percent of his earnings is his take home pay?

Aliquot Parts

An aliquot part of a number is an exact divisor of the number. \$.25 is an
aliquot part of \$1.00 because \$1.00 ÷ \$.25 = 4.

Find what aliquot part of \$1 each is.

MODELS

20¢
Think \$1 = 100¢
$\frac{20}{100} = \frac{1}{5}$
So, 20¢ is \$$\frac{1}{5}$, or $\frac{1}{5}$ of a dollar.

$33\frac{1}{3}$¢
$\frac{33\frac{1}{3}}{100} = 33\frac{1}{3} \div 100$
$= \frac{100}{3} \times \frac{1}{100}$, or $\frac{1}{3}$

1. 10¢

2. 50¢

3. 75¢

4. $66\frac{2}{3}$¢

5. $16\frac{2}{3}$¢

6. $83\frac{1}{3}$¢

7. $12\frac{1}{2}$¢

8. $37\frac{1}{2}$¢

9. $62\frac{1}{2}$¢

10. $87\frac{1}{2}$¢

Find the cost. Use aliquot parts.

MODELS

56 @ $37\frac{1}{2}$¢
$37\frac{1}{2}$¢ = \$$\frac{3}{8}$
$\overset{7}{\cancel{56}} \times \$\frac{3}{8} = \$21$
$\underset{1}{}$

160 @ \$$1.87\frac{1}{2}$
\$$1.87\frac{1}{2}$ = \$1 + \$.$87\frac{1}{2}$, or \$1 + \$$\frac{7}{8}$
$\overset{20}{\cancel{160}} \times \$\frac{15}{8} = \$300$
$\underset{1}{}$

11. 28 @ 25¢

12. 48 @ 25¢

13. 56 @ 75¢

14. 24 @ $12\frac{1}{2}$¢

15. 96 @ $12\frac{1}{2}$¢

16. 36 @ $16\frac{2}{3}$¢

17. 54 @ $16\frac{2}{3}$¢

18. 27 @ $33\frac{1}{3}$¢

19. 144 @ $33\frac{1}{3}$¢

20. 64 @ \$.$62\frac{1}{2}$

21. 252 @ \$.$83\frac{1}{3}$

22. 144 @ \$.$83\frac{1}{3}$

23. 160 @ \$.$87\frac{1}{2}$

24. 720 @ \$.$66\frac{2}{3}$

25. 360 @ \$.$66\frac{2}{3}$

26. 480 @ \$1.25

27. 4,000 @ \$1.$62\frac{1}{2}$

28. 2,400 @ \$2.$87\frac{1}{2}$

6

BANKING
SERVICES

A Bureau of Indian
Affairs agent relating
job information

Activities

Ask each student in your class for his or her weight. Use the table for arranging the numbers. Use a tally mark to show each person's weight. Find the approximate, mean, median, and mode of the weights.

Weight in pounds	Number of students
Under 100 lb	
101–110	
111–120	
121–130	
131–140	
141–150	
151–160	
Over 160 lb	

Investigate different interest rates. Form a committee to visit several banks, credit unions, and savings and loan associations to obtain information and brochures regarding the special features of their savings plans. Be sure to obtain materials (such as pamphlets, deposit slips and withdrawal slips) from many banks and not from just one bank because of the variety of plans offered and the different interest rates.

Arrange a bulletin-board display in your classroom showing the information you have collected from the banks, etc., above. You may also want to include a display on "Reconciling a Bank Statement."

Interest on Loans

lending agency A lending agency is an organization that is in business to loan money.

interest Interest is the cost of borrowing money. This formula may be used to compute interest.

$$I \quad = \quad p \quad \times \quad r \quad \times \quad t$$

Amount of interest — Amount borrowed — Rate of interest — Length of time to repay loan

principal The principal of a loan is the original amount borrowed, or the unpaid balance still owed.

amount due The amount due is the sum of the principal and interest. It may refer to the monthly payment or the total payment due on the loan.

For Discussion

- How did Mavis Spradley offer to help her brother?

- How are interest rates usually stated?

- What will be the amount due on Jimell's loan?

"Jimell," said Marvis Spradley, "if you really want to buy a new electric typewriter and don't have the money, I can lend you some. My savings account isn't very large, but there's enough to help you."

"Thanks, Mavis, I don't think I'll need it."

"Where will you get the money?" she asked. "Is Mother going to lend it to you?"

"No," he answered. "I'm 18 years old now and have a steady job. I checked with the local bank. They are willing to let me borrow $300. I must repay it with interest in eight months. Their interest charge on a small loan is 9%."

To find the amount of interest due, Jimell wrote:

$$I = p \times r \times t$$

$$I = \frac{\overset{3}{\cancel{300}}}{1} \times \frac{\overset{3}{\cancel{9}}}{\underset{1}{\cancel{100}}} \times \frac{\overset{2}{\cancel{8}}}{\underset{\underset{1}{\cancel{4}}}{\cancel{12}}}$$

$$= \frac{3 \times 3 \times 2}{1 \times 1 \times 1} = 18$$

He continued, "The interest charge is $18."

"What will be the total amount due the bank eight months from now?" asked Mavis.

DEVELOPING SKILLS

Find the interest and the amount due on each loan.

MODEL $1,800 @ 8% for 9 months

Using Fractions

$1,800 @ 8% for 9 months

Interest = principal × rate × time

$$I = 1,800 \times 8\% \times \frac{3}{4} \leftarrow \left(\frac{9}{12} = \frac{3}{4}\right)$$

$$I = 1,\overset{18}{800} \times \frac{\overset{2}{8}}{\underset{1}{100}} \times \frac{3}{\underset{1}{4}}$$

$$= \$108$$

Using Decimals

$1,800 @ 8% for 9 months

Interest = principal × rate × time

$$I = 1,800 \times .08 \times .75 \leftarrow \left(\frac{9}{12} = \frac{3}{4} = .75\right)$$

$$\begin{array}{r} \$1,800 \\ \times\ .08 \\ \hline 144.00 \\ \times\ .75 \\ \hline 7\ 20\ 00 \\ 100\ 80\ 0 \\ \hline 108.00\ 00, \text{ or } \$108 \end{array}$$

Amount due = principal + interest

A = $1,800 + $108

= $1,908

Amount due = principal + interest

A = $1,800 + $108

= $1,908

1. $1,500 @ 7% for 3 yr
4. $350 @ 8% for 6 mo
7. $470 @ $7\frac{1}{2}$% for 2 yr

2. $200 @ 6% for 2 yr
5. $225 @ 7% for 4 yr
8. $900 @ $8\frac{1}{2}$% for 3 yr

3. $2,000 @ 8% for 9 mo
6. $800 @ 9% for 18 mo
9. $670 @ 8% for $2\frac{1}{2}$ yr

Find the interest and the total amount due. Use banker's interest.

MODEL $1,400 at 9% for 60 days

$$I = p \times r \times t$$

$$= 1,\overset{14}{400} \times \frac{\overset{3}{9}}{\underset{1}{100}} \times \frac{\overset{1}{60}}{\underset{\underset{1}{2}}{360}}$$

$$= \$21$$

$$A = p + I$$
$$= \$1,400 + \$21$$
$$= \$1,421$$

10. $920 @ 4% for 90 days
13. $624 @ 8% for 120 days
16. $1,260 @ 8% for 240 days

11. $4,250 @ 5% for 180 days
14. $600 @ 5% for 36 days
17. $900 @ 9% for 120 days

12. $500 @ 6% for 60 days
15. $150 @ 6% for 30 days
18. $810 @ 9% for 60 days

APPLYING SKILLS

1. Ms. Jackson borrowed $1,500 at 6% for 1 yr. How much interest must be paid?

2. Jeff Kowalski borrowed $750 at 7% for 2 years. How much interest must be paid?

3. Mr. Sullivan borrowed $500 from his savings bank. The loan was paid 18 months later with 7% interest. How much interest was paid?

4. Emily Brown borrowed $2,400 from her credit union. The loan was repaid 27 months later with 5% interest. How much interest was paid?

5. James Chan borrowed $4,600 from a bank to start a business of his own. The loan is due in 2 years, with 6% interest. How much will be due at the time of payment?

6. Ms. Kent borrowed $800 from a loan association to finance her vacation. The loan is due in 2 years with 9% interest. How much will be due at the time of payment?

7. Donna Alverone borrowed $3,000 at $4\frac{1}{2}$% interest to cover graduate school expenses. The loan must be paid in 4 years. Find the amount due.

8. Mr. Clark borrowed $5,000 at $7\frac{1}{4}$% interest to pay for home improvements. The loan must be paid in 6 years. Find the amount due.

9. Mr. Waller borrowed $440 for 2 years at $6\frac{1}{2}$%. Find the interest charge on this loan. Find the total amount due.

10. Anna Davis borrowed $300 for $1\frac{1}{2}$ years at 9%. Find the interest charge on this loan. Find the total amount due.

11. Marge Glass borrowed $1,500 from a finance company at $1\frac{1}{2}$% interest per month. She was able to repay the loan in 30 days. What amount was due?

12. Joe Malone borrowed $130 from his employer at 1% interest per month. In the meantime, he received his income tax refund check and was able to repay the loan in 60 days. What amount was due?

13. Mr. Jameson borrowed $600 from his bank. He signed a note promising to repay it with 9% interest in 90 days. Find the amount due.

14. Ms. Klein borrowed $1,800 from her bank. She signed a note promising to repay it with 8% interest in 120 days. Find the amount due.

15. Mrs. Esposito borrowed $300 for a freezer. The rate of interest was 10% and she repaid the loan in 60 days. What amount was due?

16. Mr. Matthews borrowed $780 for a stereo. The rate of interest was $9\frac{1}{2}$% and he repaid the loan in 180 days. What amount was due?

MAINTAINING SKILLS

Change to percents. [114]

1. $\frac{1}{4}$ 2. $\frac{1}{5}$ 3. $\frac{3}{5}$ 4. $\frac{3}{4}$ 5. $\frac{35}{60}$ 6. $\frac{12}{25}$

7. .43 8. .52 9. 1.4 10. 1 11. .485 12. .003

Change to fractions. [114]

13. 14% 14. 54% 15. 10% 16. 30% 17. .5% 18. 1.06%

Change to decimals. [114]

19. 87% 20. 63% 21. .03% 22. .5% 23. 200% 24. 150%

Make true sentences. [52]

25. .46 mm = _____ cm

26. 1.56 m = _____ cm

27. 164 cm = _____ m

28. 10 cm = _____ m

29. 42 mm = _____ cm

30. 87 mm = _____ cm

Estimate the number of meters, centimeters, or kilometers. [52]

31. 14 yd $\doteq$ _____ m

32. 42 in. $\doteq$ _____ cm

33. 4 mi $\doteq$ _____ km

Copy and complete. Check. [129]

34.

MONTHLY NET INCOME: $1,200		
Budget Item	Amount	Percent of Salary
Mortgage payment	$240	
Food	216	
Clothing	96	
Insurance	72	
Medical	48	
Household Operating	156	
Automobile	120	
Contributions	36	
Recreation	60	
Savings	108	
Gifts	48	
TOTALS		100%

35.

YEARLY NET INCOME: $8,000		
Budget Item	Amount	Percent of Salary
Mortgage Payment	$2,000	
Food	1,920	
Clothing	720	
Insurance	400	
Medical	480	
Household Operating	720	
Automobile	960	
Contributions	80	
Recreation	240	
Savings	160	
Gifts	320	
TOTALS		100%

Consumer Tips___

FABRICS AND THEIR CARE

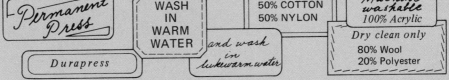

A law enforced by the Federal Trade Commission (FTC) requires that labels be attached to fabric products. These specify the fibers used and care needed. The manufacturer's name or FTC code number should be on or near the label.

- Fiber labels on furs should give:
  - the correct English name of the animal
  - the animal's native country, if imported fur
  - whether the fur is natural, bleached, or dyed
  - from what part of the animal the fur was taken

- Fiber labels on natural fibers must tell:
  - whether the fabric is cotton, wool, linen, or silk
- Often there will be descriptions such as re-used wool, cashmere, vicuna.

- Fiber labels on man-made fibers must designate:
  - acetate, acrylic, anidex, azlon, glass, metal, modacrylic, nylon, nytril, olefin, polyester, rayon, rubber, saran, spandex, vinal, vinyon

The FTC created these 17 names to show chemical composition and other features such as cleanability, durability, fade-resistence, and durable press. FTC ruled that these names be on labels of fabrics with 5% or more of these fibers. "Other Fibers" is used for fabrics with less than 5%.

- Care labels must give:
  - the method for cleaning the product safely
- Directions apply only for regular care, not for spot removal.

The FTC rule does not apply to headwear, handwear, footwear, disposable items, fur, leather, items needing no maintenance, and mill ends.

Promissory Notes

promissory note   A promissory note is a written agreement to repay a loan at the end of a definite time period.

maker   The maker of a promissory note is usually the borrower who, by signing the note, promises to repay the amount due.

payee   The payee of a note is usually the lender to whom the amount due is to be repaid. This may be a person, a bank, a credit union, and so on.

date of maturity   The date of maturity is the date on which payment is due.

banker's interest   Banker's interest is calculated on the basis of a 360-day year, assuming 30 days per month.

For Discussion

- Why does the borrower sign a promissory note?
- Why is a promissory note usually referred to as a "2-party" instrument?
- By what method did Bill compute the interest?

Agnes and Bill were talking about borrowing money.

"When I arrange for my loan, the lender will probably require that I sign a promissory note," Agnes said.

"What is that?" asked Bill.

"Just what the name says it is," she replied. "It is a written promise to repay the amount due after a certain period of time. Let me find you an illustration."

She found one in her math textbook.

Agnes continued, "The lender, or payee, is the Fifth National Bank. The borrower, or maker, is Willard B. Forest."

Bill said, "The amount borrowed is $1,500 and the interest rate is 8%."

Agnes said, "The time of the note is 90 days and the date of maturity is February 1, 1976. Can you compute the interest?"

Bill wrote:

$$I = \frac{\overset{15}{\cancel{1,500}}}{1} \times \frac{\overset{2}{\cancel{8}}}{\underset{1}{\cancel{100}}} \times \frac{\overset{1}{\cancel{90}}}{\underset{1}{\cancel{360}}}$$

"The interest is $30," he said.

DEVELOPING SKILLS

Answer the questions about this promissory note.

$ 500	Rockford, New Jersey	April 3 19 75
	30 days after date ____ I promise to pay	

to the order of _____ General Trust of New Jersey _____

_____ Five hundred _____ Dollars

Payable at _____ General Trust of New Jersey _____

Value received at 7% interest

No. 4231 Due May 3, 1975   Evelyn Roldema

1. Who is the maker of this note?

2. Who is the payee?

3. What is the rate of interest?

4. What is the principal?

5. What is the time of the loan?

6. What is the date of maturity of the note?

Find the time of the note.

MODEL Date of note, July 3;
maturity date, September 1

July,   31 days
        − 3 days (beginning date of note)
        —————
        28

Aug. + 31 days
        —————
        59

Sept. + 1 day (due date)
        —————
        60 days

7. Date of note: Aug. 8
   Maturity date: Nov. 2
8. Date of note: Sept. 3
   Maturity date: Oct. 31

Find the date of maturity for each note.

MODELS A. Date of note, Mar. 30; Time, 50 days
        March,   31 days
                − 30 (date of note)
                —————
                1
        April, + 30
                —————
                31

        50 (time of note)
      − 31 (days left in March and April)
        —————
        19 (days in May)
Maturity date: May 19

        B. Date of note, Oct. 31; Time, 4 mo
        Maturity date: February 28

9. Date of note, May 18, Time 30 days
10. Date of note, Dec. 1, Time 40 days
11. Date of note, Jan. 30, Time, 1 mo
12. Date of note, Dec. 31, Time 4 mo

APPLYING SKILLS

1. On April 1, George Thomas signed a $600 promissory note due in 30 days with 8% interest. On what day will the note become due? What amount will be due?

2. On Sept. 8, Alice Saunders signed a $500 promissory note due in 45 days with 6% interest. On what day will the note become due? What amount will be due?

3. Ms. Zorel borrowed $1,000 from a savings bank on Sept. 22. She repaid the loan on Nov. 1 with 5% interest. How much did she pay?

4. Mr. Kilpatrick borrowed $900 from his credit union on May 24. On Aug. 22, he repaid the loan with 4% interest. How much did he pay?

5. In order to pay some emergency bills, Don Vecchio borrowed $900 on March 8. He repaid the loan on June 6 with 5% interest. How much did he pay?

6. In order to pay her tuition, Susan Robinson borrowed $500 on Sept. 9. She repaid the loan on Nov. 8 with 12% interest. How much did she pay?

7. Janet Delgato signed a promissory note on Jan. 3 for $360, payable in 60 days. The interest rate was 7%. On what day was the note due? What amount did she pay?

8. James Brown Eagle signed a promissory note on July 19 for $300, payable in 180 days. The interest rate was 6%. On what day was the note due? What amount did he pay?

9. Dr. Jones borrowed $1,800 for new office furnishings on Nov. 7. She was to repay the loan in 6 months with 6% interest. What is the date of maturity of the loan? How much is due?

10. Mr. Svenson borrowed $900 for a new motorcycle on March 31. He was to repay the loan in 3 months with 6% interest. What is the date of maturity of the loan? How much is due?

Find the amount due on the date of maturity.

11.

$ _375_	_Twin Forks, Colorado_ _January 27_ 19 _75_

60 days _____ after date ___✓ promise to pay

to the order of _Central Bank of Twin Forks_

Three hundred seventy five _____ Dollars

Payable at _Central Bank of Twin Forks_

Value received at _8% interest_

No. _15642_ Due _March 28, 1975_ _Howard Adams_

MAINTAINING SKILLS

Make true sentences.   [57]

1. 14 kl = _____ ℓ

2. 2 kl = _____ ℓ

3. 36 ℓ = _____ ml

4. 42 ℓ = _____ ml

5. 36 ml = _____ ℓ

6. 178 ml = _____ ℓ

Compute.   [119]

7. 16% of 18

8. 24% of 92

9. 8 is what percent of 40?

10. 9 is what percent of 900?

11. 8 is 2% of what number?

12. 24 is 6% of what number?

Find the interest and amount due.   [138]

13. $46,000 @ 9% for 2 yr

14. $51,000 @ 8% for 1.5 yr

15. $4,500 @ 15% for 6 mo

16. $6,480 @ 10% for 12 mo

17. $300 @ 12% for 3 mo

18. $800 @ 11% for 9 mo

Find the interest and amount due. Use banker's interest.   [133]

19. $600 @ 8% for 60 days

20. $3,200 @ 9% for 90 days

21. $1,500 @ 7.5% for 120 days

22. $440 @ 6.5% for 180 days

Solve these problems.

23. Sara Lewis borrowed $1,530 from a bank at 9%
[138] interest. The loan was repaid in 30 days. What
amount was paid?

24. Kikuo Ito borrowed $4,560 from a bank at 12%
[138] interest. The loan was repaid in 120 days. What
amount was paid?

25. Mrs. Cano borrowed $13,000 to start a new
[138] business. She paid the loan in 4 years plus interest at 12%. How much interest did she pay?

26. Mr. Stuart borrowed $10,000 to expand his
[138] business. He paid the loan in 5 years plus interest at 10%. How much interest did he pay?

27. A sofa was reduced to $350. This was 80% of
[119] the original price. What was the original price?

28. A bike is on sale for $92.50. This is 75% of the
[119] original price. What is the original price?

29. There are 320 students in the Junior Class at
[119] City High. Forty-eight are members of the
drama club. What percent is this?

30. Mrs. Arnold has a 450-acre farm. She has a 90-
[119] acre pasture. What percent of the farm is pasture?

Career/TRANSPORTATION

Traffic and transportation specialists work for efficient movement of freight and people. All sorts of goods, from vegetables to machinery, move by rail, truck, water, or air. The transportation specialist makes possible the physical distribution system which helps us to achieve the highest standard of living in the world.

Job Description

- Rate clerk—prepares rate statements; quotes rates and charges; audits freight bills.

- Traffic representative—contacts business firms to sell freight business; quotes rates; settles complaints.

- Traffic manager—manages all activities concerning the shipment of goods; has thorough knowledge of state and federal laws and regulations.

- Terminal manager—supervises all workers in loading, unloading, storing, and crating of goods.

Training

Entry-level jobs are available to capable high school graduates. Sometimes licenses or certificates are required. Those with career goals should pursue a one- or two-year college program in transportation.

Further Investigation

Arrange an interview with a traffic or transportation specialist. Ask about job qualifications, working conditions, possibilities for advancement, entry-level jobs.

Consult your guidance department about any special requirements by your state or by federal bodies (i.e., Federal Aviation Administration). Also ask about post-high-school courses in this area.

Checking Accounts

checking account   A checking account is an arrangement made between a depositor and a bank whereby payment orders will be made to third parties by the bank from the depositor's account balance.

commercial bank   A commercial bank is a bank that specializes in handling funds for its depositors, including making payments for them by cashing checks, which are payment orders.

overdrawn   A checking account is overdrawn if the depositor writes checks for more money than there is in the account.

For Discussion

- In working with a checkbook, what items are to be added to the checkbook balance?

- In working with a checkbook, what items are to be subtracted from the checkbook balance?

- Why is a check called a "3-party" instrument?

- What advantages does making payments by check have compared to making payments by cash?

Darrin and Charlene Marks had just opened a joint checking account at their local commercial bank.

Charlene said, "Paying by check is certainly more convenient than paying cash."

"I'll feel a lot safer carrying a checkbook, rather than a wallet full of cash," Darrin said. "But let's be sure we keep the check stub accurately. Remember, every time we draw a check, we have to subtract its amount from our checkbook balance."

"If we get careless with the check stub record, we might discover our account is overdrawn," Charlene said. "If that happens, the bank will probably refuse to cash our check. If it happens too often, the bank might ask us to close our account."

Darrin and Charlene examined a sample check and stub. "Let's assume we have a balance of $375 in our account," Darrin said. "If we draw a check for $35 to pay the gas and electric bill, we'll have $340 left for the next check."

DEVELOPING SKILLS

OBJECTIVE   To fill out deposit slips and check stubs

Total these deposits.

1.

	DOLLARS	CENTS
BILLS	224	00
COIN	7	62
CHECKS	375	89
"	423	53
"	89	57
TOTAL		

2.

	DOLLARS	CENTS
BILLS	347	00
COIN	11	24
CHECKS	575	23
"	328	72
"	79	78
TOTAL		

3.

	DOLLARS	CENTS
BILLS	151	00
COIN	3	26
CHECKS	10	75
"	8	21
"	13	54
TOTAL		

Find the missing entries and balances on these check stubs.

MODEL

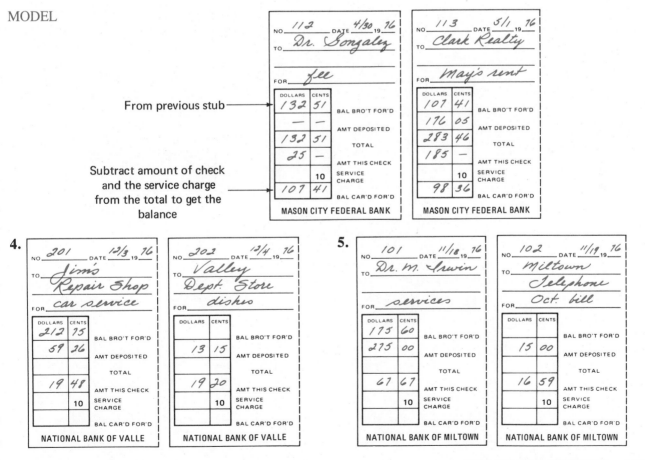

From previous stub →

Subtract amount of check and the service charge from the total to get the balance →

MODEL stubs:

NO. 112   DATE 4/30 19 76
TO Dr. Gonzalez
FOR fee

DOLLARS	CENTS	
132	51	BAL BRO'T FOR'D
—	—	AMT DEPOSITED
132	51	TOTAL
25	—	AMT THIS CHECK
	10	SERVICE CHARGE
107	41	BAL CAR'D FOR'D

MASON CITY FEDERAL BANK

NO. 113   DATE 5/1 19 76
TO Clark Realty
FOR May's rent

DOLLARS	CENTS	
107	41	BAL BRO'T FOR'D
176	05	AMT DEPOSITED
283	46	TOTAL
185	—	AMT THIS CHECK
	10	SERVICE CHARGE
98	36	BAL CAR'D FOR'D

MASON CITY FEDERAL BANK

4.

NO. 201   DATE 12/3 19 76
TO Jim's Repair Shop
FOR car service

DOLLARS	CENTS	
212	15	BAL BRO'T FOR'D
59	26	AMT DEPOSITED
		TOTAL
19	48	AMT THIS CHECK
	10	SERVICE CHARGE
		BAL CAR'D FOR'D

NATIONAL BANK OF VALLE

NO. 202   DATE 12/4 19 76
TO Valley Dept. Store
FOR dishes

DOLLARS	CENTS	
		BAL BRO'T FOR'D
13	15	AMT DEPOSITED
		TOTAL
19	20	AMT THIS CHECK
	10	SERVICE CHARGE
		BAL CAR'D FOR'D

NATIONAL BANK OF VALLE

5.

NO. 101   DATE 11/18 19 76
TO Dr. M. Irwin
FOR services

DOLLARS	CENTS	
175	60	BAL BRO'T FOR'D
275	00	AMT DEPOSITED
		TOTAL
67	67	AMT THIS CHECK
	10	SERVICE CHARGE
		BAL CAR'D FOR'D

NATIONAL BANK OF MILTOWN

NO. 102   DATE 11/19 19 76
TO Miltown Telephone
FOR Oct. bill

DOLLARS	CENTS	
		BAL BRO'T FOR'D
15	00	AMT DEPOSITED
		TOTAL
16	59	AMT THIS CHECK
	10	SERVICE CHARGE
		BAL CAR'D FOR'D

NATIONAL BANK OF MILTOWN

APPLYING SKILLS

Find the total amount of the deposit.

1. Straub's Music Center sent the following bills, coins, and checks to the bank to be deposited:

3 twenty-dollar bills	17 quarters
27 ten-dollar bills	13 dimes
15 five-dollar bills	7 nickels
42 one-dollar bills	19 pennies
Checks: $24.47	$49.95
31.37	76.80
8.19	47.89

2. Vartin's Hardware Store sent the following bills, coins, and checks to the bank to be deposited:

1 fifty-dollar bill	24 quarters
4 twenty-dollar bills	26 dimes
15 ten-dollar bills	15 nickels
19 five-dollar bills	31 pennies
36 one-dollar bills	
Checks: $13.47	$23.98
16.91	56.02

Find the missing entries.

3.

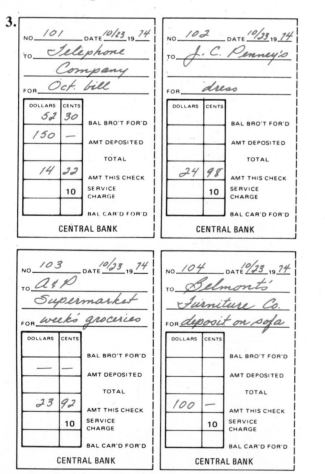

4.

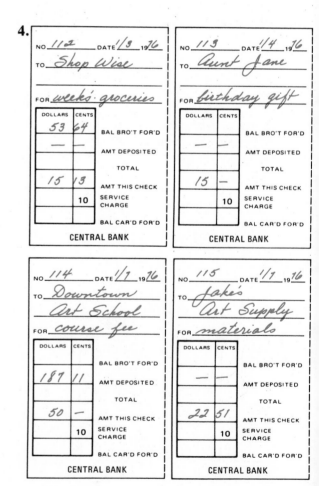

MAINTAINING SKILLS

Make true sentences. [63]

1. .46 g = _____ mg

2. 1.86 g = _____ mg

3. 48 g = _____ kg

4. 53 g = _____ kg

5. 1.36 kg = _____ g

6. 46.4 kg = _____ g

Solve these problems.

7. Mr. Fallon earned $7,890 in 1972. In 1973 he [125] earned $6,469.80. What was the percent increase in his earnings?

8. Mrs. Jane White Feather earned $8,400 last [125] year. The year before she earned $8,000. What was the percent increase in her earnings?

9. Sara Williams sells for the Greenwood Book [125] Company. She increased her commission from $7,200 last year to $8,400 this year. What was the percent increase?

10. The population of Nassau County, New York [125] in 1960 was 1,575,000. By 1970, the population was 1,811,250. What percent increase did this represent?

11. In a science lab identical cups are placed on the [63] pans of a balance. An object is placed in one cup and balanced with water poured into the other. The cup contains 4.6 ℓ of water. What is the weight of the object in kg?

12. An object in a container is placed on a pan of a [63] balance. An identical container on the other pan is filled with 3.8 ℓ of water. What is the weight of the object in kg?

13. Fumiko bought 17 ounces of chocolate. About [63] how many grams did it weigh?

14. Ralph bought 24 ounces of fish. About how [63] many grams did it weigh?

15. Emma Jackson borrowed $500 from a savings [143] bank on June 8. The note was due in 60 days. Find the date of maturity for this loan.

16. Walt Harris borrowed $650 from a loan company [143] on March 3. The note was due in 90 days. Find the date of maturity for the loan.

17. Ron Clear Water borrowed $1,800 to add a new [143] room to his home. The note was dated December 4 and was due in 5 months. The interest rate was 8%. Find the date of maturity of the loan. How much was due?

18. Barb White borrowed $2,500 to add a garage to [143] her home. The note was dated August 5 and was due in 6 months. The interest rate was 9%. Find the date of maturity of the loan. How much was due?

Reconciling a Bank Statement

reconciliation statement A reconciliation statement is a form prepared to find the amount of money available in a checking account. This amount should agree with the checkbook balance as shown on the last check stub used.

canceled checks Canceled checks are checks that have been paid by the bank and returned to the depositor.

numerically Numerically refers to the arrangement of items by their numbers.

outstanding checks Outstanding checks are checks that have been drawn but not yet cashed at the bank where the account is kept.

service charge A service charge is a deduction from the checking account balance made by the bank for handling the account.

For Discussion

- Why did Ms. Sterling want to make a reconciliation statement?
- What adjustments may have to be made to the bank statement to find the correct balance?
- What adjustments may have to be made to the checkbook record to find the correct balance?

"Al," Ms. Sterling said to her son, "Did you learn to prepare a bank reconciliation statement as part of your school work?"

He answered, "Yes, I did in several of my business education classes."

"Our checkbook balance does not agree with the bank statement which arrived in the mail today," she told him. "I don't want to overdraw our account, so I'd appreciate your help in finding the correct available balance."

Al's first step was to arrange the canceled checks numerically. These were returned with the bank statement. He compared each canceled check with its matching check stub to make certain that the amount written on the check agreed with the amount written on the matching stub. In this way, he located the stubs for which no canceled checks had been returned. He listed the outstanding checks, totaled them and deducted this total from the bank statement balance.

Next, he subtracted the amount of the bank service charge from the last check-stub balance. With these two adjustments, Al found that the checkbook balance and the bank balance agreed.

DEVELOPING SKILLS

OBJECTIVE   To reconcile bank statements with checkbook balances

Prepare a reconciliation statement.

MODEL

    Present checkbook balance: $259.75
    Bank statement balance: 121.31
    Service charge: .96
    Outstanding checks: #162, $4.50 #187, $16.25
                         #185, $9.95 #188, $3.82
    Deposits not shown on statement: $150, $12

RECONCILIATION STATEMENT
August 10th 19 _75_

A. Outstanding Checks

No./Date	Amount				
1. *162*	4	50	**B.** Closing balance shown on this statement	121	31
2. *185*	9	95	**C.** PLUS deposits made after last entry on this statement	150 / 12	
3. *187*	16	25	**D.** Total (B & C)	283	31
4. *188*	3	82	**E.** MINUS total of outstanding checks (A)	34	52
5.			**F.** Your bank balance (D minus F)	248	79
6.			**G.** Checkbook balance	249	75
Total (A)	$ 34	52	**H.** Service charge		96
			I. Correct checkbook balance (G minus H)	248	79

1. Bank statement balance $211.24
   Present checkbook balance   172.00
   Service charge   1.38
   Outstanding   #15, $37.95 #22, $6.90
   checks: #19, $8.27 #23, $37.50
   Deposits not shown on statement $50.00

2. Bank statement balance $349.90
   Present checkbook balance   401.92
   Service charge   1.39
   Outstanding   #57, $21.32 #63, $8.85
   checks: #62, $2.28 #64, $16.92
   Deposits not shown on statement $100.00

3. Present checkbook balance $125.68
   Bank statement balance   109.57
   Deposits not shown on statement   80.00
   Outstanding   #312, $13.60 #317, $17.75
   checks: #313, $4.89, #318, $30.00
   Service charge   2.35

4. Present checkbook balance $348.65
   Outstanding   #180, $35.84 #190, $17.88
   checks: #188, $3.00 #194, $20.75
   Bank statement balance $234.47
   Deposits not shown on statement $190.00
   Service charge $1.65

APPLYING SKILLS

1. Linda Chin's checkbook balance was $1,650.50. Her bank statement showed a balance of $1,661.75 with a service charge of $1.25. There were two outstanding checks, #44 for $3.50 and #46 for $9.00. Prepare a reconciliation statement.

2. Roy Carter's checkbook balance was $400.20. His bank statement showed a balance of $411.35 with a service charge of $.85. There were two outstanding checks, #105 for $3.10 and #111 for $8.90. Prepare a reconciliation statement.

3. On June 1, Marilyn Walsh received her bank statement which indicated a balance of $365, with a service charge of $1.10. Her checkbook record indicated a balance of $439.80. After matching canceled checks with check stubs, she found these checks outstanding: #211 for $7.00, #213 for $7.30, #217 for $6.80, #218 for $5.20. Also, a deposit of $100 was not shown on the bank statement. Prepare a reconciliation statement.

4. Kelly Motors received its bank statement which indicated a balance of $9,266.45 with a service charge of $4.45. The checkbook balance was $8,922.86. The outstanding checks were #132, $84, #134 for $93.27, #135 for $86.50, #137 for $119.27 and #138 for $165. Also, a deposit of $200.00 was not shown on the bank statement. Prepare a reconciliation statement.

5. Howard Simon found that his bank balance on November 30 was $340. His checkbook balance on that date was $263. He found the following checks had not been cashed and returned by the bank: #167, $14, #170, $18, and #171, $46. The bank deducted $1 for a service charge. Find the correct available checkbook and bank balance.

6. Greenpoint Stationers found that its bank balance on May 31 was $1,987. The last check stub showed a balance of $1,536. The following checks had not been cashed and returned by the bank: #408, $128, #511, $136 and #514, $192. The bank deducted $5 for a service charge. Find the correct available checkbook and bank balance.

7. Ed Harris' present checkbook balance is $1,041.02. His bank indicates a balance of $1,605.92, with a service charge of $2.10. His outstanding checks were: #93, $115.50, #95, $116.50, #97, $135.00, #98, $272.80, #99, $27.20. He noted that his last deposit of $100 was not shown on his bank statement. Prepare a reconciliation, and indicate the correct, available checkbook and bank balance.

8. Suzannah Stern's present checkbook balance is $1,116.98. Her bank indicates a balance of $2,013.57, with a service charge of $2.75. Her outstanding checks were #204, $230.10, #207, $208.04, #208, $40.00, #210, $451.20, #212, $20.00. A deposit she had made of $50 was not shown on the bank statement. Prepare a reconciliation, and indicate the correct, available checkbook and bank balance.

MAINTAINING SKILLS

Interpret each temperature.   [67]

1. 14° C

2. −5° C

3. 35° C

4. 90° C

Find the amount spent on each.   [129]

5. Yearly Net Income: $8,500

Food	25%
Housing	30%
Clothing	20%
Transportation	12%
Insurance	8%
Recreation	4%
Savings	1%

6. Yearly Net Income: $12,000

Food	20%
Housing	26%
Clothing	18%
Transportation	10%
Insurance	12%
Recreation	8%
Savings	6%

Find the missing entries and balances on these check stubs.   [149]

7.

8.

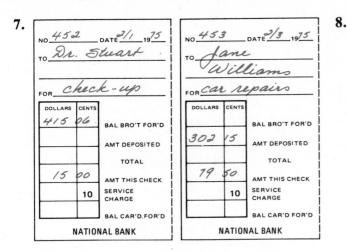

Find the total amount of the deposit.   [149]

9. Jones' Leather Goods Store sent the following bills, coins, and checks to the bank to be deposited:

4 twenty-dollar bills	54 quarters
28 ten-dollar bills	28 dimes
17 five-dollar bills	4 nickels
26 one-dollar bills	39 pennies

Checks: $24.32, $86.49, $37.83

10. Goldberg's Malt Shop sent the following bills, coins, and checks to the bank to be deposited:

11 twenty-dollar bills	10 quarters
21 ten-dollar bills	41 dimes
14 five-dollar bills	21 nickels
52 one-dollar bills	45 pennies

Checks: $41.42, $12.82, $39.56

Self-Test: Chapter 6

Find the interest and amount due. [138]

1. $1,560 at $8\frac{1}{2}\%$ for 5 yr

2. $280 at $7\frac{1}{2}\%$ for 60 da

Find the time of the note. [143]

3. Date of note: June 4
Maturity date: Aug. 3

Find the maturity date. [143]

4. Date of note: Nov. 8
Time: 90 days

Find the missing entries on these check stubs. [149]

5.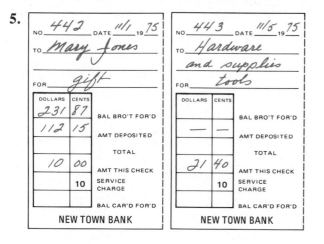

6.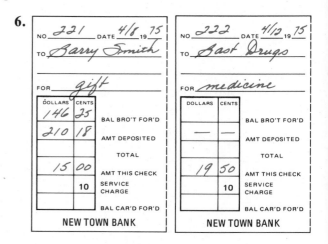

Find the amount of this deposit. [149]

7. 6 ten-dollar bills   20 dimes
12 five-dollar bills   36 nickles
36 one-dollar bills   82 pennies
Checks: $42.51, $18.26, $9.30, $146.82

Prepare a reconciliation statement. [153]

8. Bank statement balance, $437.18; checkbook balance, $252.52; outstanding checks, #872, $150.67; #874, $15.89; #875, $20.00; bank service charge, $1.90.

Solve these problems.

9. Cesar Gomez borrowed $750 from a savings
[143] bank on Oct. 5. He repaid the loan on Dec. 4 with 6% interest. How much did he repay?

10. Margarita Diaz borrowed $900 on May 8, pay-
[143] able in 90 days. The interest rate was 6.5%. On what day was the note due? What amount did she pay?

11. Mr. Barker borrowed $450 from a bank. He
[138] signed a note promising to repay it with 8% interest in 60 days. Find the amount due.

12. Mrs. Spencer borrowed $350 for a vacation.
[138] The rate of interest was 9.5%. She repaid the loan in 120 days. What amount was due?

Test: Chapter 6

Find the interest and the amount due.

1. $2,600 at 9% for 2 yr

2. $120 at 7% for 90 da

Find the time of the note.

3. Date of note: July 13
   Maturity date: Sept. 11

Find the maturity date.

4. Date of note: March 21
   Time: 50 days

Find the missing entries on these check stubs.

5.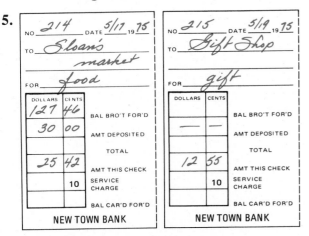

6.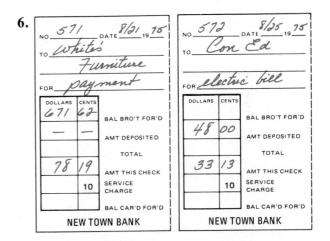

Find the total amount of this deposit.

7. 5 twenty-dollar bills   15 quarters
   23 ten-dollar bills   12 dimes
   15 five-dollar bills   23 pennies
   Checks: $21.32, $16.93, $8.85, $25.43

Prepare a reconciliation statement.

8. Bank statement balance, $328.85; checkbook balance, $317.59; outstanding checks: #73, $2.13; #75, $4.18; #80, $8.65; bank service charge, $3.70.

Solve these problems.

9. Barb Smith borrowed $800 from a savings bank on Sept. 2. She repaid the loan on Dec. 1 with 5% interest. How much did she repay?

10. John Van Patten borrowed $500 on March 24, payable in 60 days. The interest rate was 5.5%. On what day was the note due? What amount did he pay?

11. Mrs. Williams borrowed $600 from a bank. She signed a note promising to repay it with 9% interest in 90 days. Find the amount due.

12. Mr. Jones borrowed $250 for a vacation. The rate of interest was 9.5%. He repaid the loan in 180 days. What amount was due?

The 6%, 60-Day Method

To find banker's interest at 6% for 60 days, move the decimal point 2 places to the left in the principal.

MODELS

Interest on $1,000 @ 6% for 60 days ⟶ $10.00, or $10

Interest on $1,250 @ 6% for 60 days ⟶ $12.50

Notice that r is 6%, or $\frac{6}{100}$ and t is $\frac{60}{360}$, or $\frac{1}{6}$ so, $r \times t = \frac{6}{100} \times \frac{1}{6}$, or $\frac{1}{100}$. To divide by 100, move the decimal point 2 places to the left.

What is the interest @ 6% for 60 days? Use the shortcut.

1. $100

2. $6,000

3. $1,765

4. $3,584

5. $7,809

6. $955.50

7. $2,550.02

8. $7,809

Find the interest at 6%.

MODELS

$500 for 30 days

30 da $= \frac{30}{60}$, or $\frac{1}{2}$

$5.00 ⟵ I for 60 da

$\frac{1}{2}$ of $5.00 = $2.50 ⟵ I for 30 da

$1,000 for 36 days

36 da $= \frac{36}{60}$, or $\frac{3}{5}$

$10 ⟵ I for 60 da

$\frac{3}{5}$ of $10 = $6 ⟵ I for 36 da

9. $750 for 20 da

10. $2,800 for 15 da

11. $5,000 for 6 da

12. $640 for 45 da

Find the interest at 6%.

MODELS

$1,200 for 120 da

120 da $= (2 \times 60)$ da

$12 ⟵ I for 60 da

$2 \times $12 = $24 ⟵ I for 120 da

$8,500 for 90 da

90 da $= (60 + 30)$ da

$85.00 ⟵ I for 60 da

$+ 42.50$ ⟵ I for 30 da $\left(\frac{1}{2} \text{ of } \$85\right)$

$127.50 ⟵ I for 90 da

13. $1,640 for 120 da

14. $900 for 90 da

15. $450 for 120 da

16. $8,000 for 180 da

Cumulative Review

Add.

1. 134.24
[33]   34.89
  + 64.12

2. $2\frac{1}{2}$
[87] $+3\frac{3}{4}$

Subtract.

3. 3,648
[9] −   464

4. $4\frac{1}{8}$
[91] $-1\frac{3}{4}$

Multiply.

5. 304 × 28
[15]

6. $6\frac{1}{2} \times 4\frac{1}{3}$
[97]

Divide.

7. 36.48 ÷ 12
[43]

8. $8\frac{1}{2} \div 4\frac{1}{4}$
[101]

Compare. Use > or <.

9. .013 and .13
[28]

10. $\frac{5}{8}$ and $\frac{3}{4}$
[83]

Solve these proportions. [83]

11. $\frac{4}{15} = \frac{n}{60}$

12. $\frac{3}{25} = \frac{n}{100}$

Find the interest and amount due.

13. $1,500 @ 7.5% for 2 yr
[138]

Find the maturity date.

14. Date of note: Dec. 2 Time: 60 da
[143]

Compute. [119]

15. 85% of 1,300

16. 12 is 25% of what number

Find the percent increase.

17. Last year's price: $10
[125] This year's price: $12

Find the percent decrease.

18. Last year's income: $15,000
[125] This year's income: $13,500

Make true sentences.

19. .4 cm = _____ m
[52]

20. .36 kl = _____ ℓ
[57]

21. 118 g = _____ kg
[63]

Find the real lengths for these scale lengths. Scale: 1 cm = 2 m [105]

22. 4.5 cm

23. 7 cm

Find the percent for each amount.

24. Monthly net income: $700
[129]

Item	Amount
Food	$175
Housing	$210
Clothing	$105
Transportation	$140
Other	$70

Prepare a reconciliation statement.

25.
[153]

Bank statement balance	$368.32
Checkbook balance	$379.92
Service charge	$2.10
Outstanding checks #487	$18.50
#489	$25.60
#490	$96.40
Deposit not shown on statement	$150.00

Broken-Line Graphs

Answer these questions about the broken-line graph.

1. What is the title of the graph?

2. What is shown on the horizontal scale?

3. What is shown on the vertical scale?

4. What does 1 unit on the vertical scale represent?

5. Why is there a break on the vertical scale?

6. What was the highest price per share?

7. What was the lowest price per share?

8. When was the stock selling for $26\frac{3}{8}$ per share?

CLOSING PRICE PER SHARE OF BON STOCK

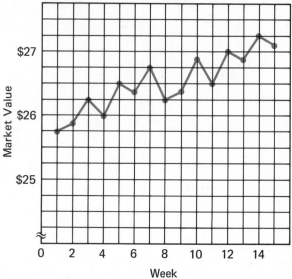

9. When was the stock selling for $26\frac{7}{8}$ per share?

10. What was the change in value between the 1st and 10th weeks?

11. What was the change in value between the 5th and 12th weeks?

12. Mack bought 15 shares of this stock the 5th week. How much did he pay?

13. Jane bought 10 shares of this stock the 4th week. How much did she pay?

14. Tamu Thomas bought 100 shares of this stock the 1st week. She sold the shares the 7th week. How much profit, not excluding the brokerage fee, did she make?

15. Paul Marks bought 100 shares of this stock the 4th week. He sold the shares the 8th week. How much profit, not excluding the brokerage fee, did he make?

Draw broken-line graphs.

16. MIDVILLE'S SCHOOL TAX

Year	Rate Per $1,000
1	$16.25
2	23.75
3	25.00
4	28.75
5	30.00

17. PRICE PER SHARE OF REX STOCK

Week	Market Value
1	$30.25
2	33.75
3	38.00
4	36.00
5	37.25

A musical instrument
technician assembling
an electric guitar

Activities_____

The figure on the right has 4 dots on each side.
Rearrange the dots to form a new figure with 5
dots on each side.

Form committees to visit insurance agencies to obtain information and pamphlets on the various types of life insurance and health insurance. Arrange, if possible, to have some insurance agent or agents visit your class and discuss the various types of insurance. You can also write the following agencies for information on insurance. Explain that your class is studying this topic.

Educational Division   Institute of Life Insurance
Insurance Information Institute   Educational Division
110 William Street   277 Park Avenue
New York, N. Y. 10038   New York, N. Y. 10017

Arange a bulletin-board display in the front lobby of your school or in your classroom, showing the information you have collected from the insurance companies. Be sure that the material is from many companies and not just one company, since there are many different plans for insurance.

Study the stock market pages in your newspaper and select a stock which you think is promising. Pretend that you have purchased 50 shares of that stock. At the end of each week for 3 months, calculate how much you have gained or lost. Make a line graph showing the performance of your stock. Compare your results with a classmate who selected a different stock. You may wish to invite a representative from a brokerage or investment company to discuss stocks and bonds with your class.

Savings Accounts

commercial bank   A commercial bank offers a variety of banking services, including checking accounts.

savings bank   A savings bank offers savings accounts, loans, and other banking services, but not checking accounts.

savings and loan associations   Savings and loan associations are similar to savings banks; however, they are organized differently and operate under different regulations.

compound interest   Compound interest is interest based on deposits plus previous interest payments which remained in the depositor's account.

For Discussion

- How did Betty caution Mary regarding the amount of money to be saved?
- What kind of savings institutions did Betty name?
- What were some of the differences among these institutions?

Mary Blue Spruce had just received her first pay envelope on her new job. Excitedly, she turned to the friendly supervisor of her department, Betty Krause.

"It feels so good to have earned this money," Mary said. "I want to save a part of it. Can you tell me the best way to save money and where I can invest it?"

Betty answered, "It's best to deposit money on a regular basis, but be sure that you leave yourself enough for living expenses. As to where to invest your money, you have several choices: commercial banks, savings banks, savings and loans associations, our own company credit union, and don't forget, United States Savings Bonds."

"Do these places differ?" asked Mary. "Or doesn't it make any difference where I invest?"

Betty answered, "They differ in the services they offer, in the rate of interest they offer, and in the method of compounding interest. Why don't you come to my house tonight? I'll show you a good consumer book which explains the advantages and disadvantages of these savings institutions."

DEVELOPING SKILLS

OBJECTIVE   To compute the amount on deposit in a compound interest account

Find the amount of interest earned at the end of 6 months. The rate is 5% compounded semiannually.

MODELS $345.62

$345 ← Compound interest is paid on whole dollars only. Do not round off. → $1,583

$$\frac{.05 \text{ (rate)}}{\$17.25}$$

$$\times .5 \ (\tfrac{1}{2} \text{ year})$$

$8.6250, or $8.63 ← Round interest to the nearest cent. → $39.5750, or $39.58

$1,583.20

$1,583

$$\frac{.05 \text{ (rate)}}{\$79.15}$$

$$\times .5 \ (\tfrac{1}{2} \text{ year})$$

1. $575.00   **2.** $820.00   **3.** $624.59   **4.** $1,380.15

Find the amount of interest earned at the end of 3 months. The rate is 5% compounded quarterly.

5. $4,500.00   **6.** $1,752.44   **7.** $867.94   **8.** $550.99

Find the amount of money on deposit in each of the following accounts. Use the compound interest table on page 329.

MODELS $500 for 5 yr @ 6% $500 for 5 yr @ 6% $500 for 5 yr @ 6%
                Compounded annually   Compounded semiannually   Compounded quarterly

Table entry   Table entry   Table entry
for 6% interest and   for $\frac{6\%}{2}$, or 3% and   for $\frac{6\%}{4}$, or $1\frac{1}{2}\%$ and
$n = 5$ is 1.3382 $n = 5 \times 2$, or 10 $n = 5 \times 4$, or 20

$$\frac{1.3382}{\underset{669.1000}{\times 500}}$$

$$\frac{1.3439}{\underset{671.9500}{\times 500}}$$

$$\frac{1.3469}{\underset{673.4500}{\times 500}}$$

On deposit: $669.10   On deposit: $671.95   On deposit: $673.45

9. $500 for 2 years @ 6% interest compounded semiannually

10. $600 for 18 months @ 5% interest compounded quarterly

11. $750 for 2 years @ 5% interest compounded quarterly

12. $800 for 3 years @ 6% interest compounded semiannually

13. $1,000 for 5 years @ 6% interest compounded semiannually

14. $935 for 6 years @ 5% interest compounded quarterly

APPLYING SKILLS

1. Carol Stillman received $100 on her birthday. She put the money in a savings bank which pays 5% interest compounded semiannually. She made no deposits and no withdrawals. Find the balance after 18 months.

2. John Gonzalez received a $321 refund on his taxes. He put the money in a savings bank which pays 6% interest compounded quarterly. He made no deposits or withdrawals. Find the balance after 6 months.

3. George Robertson's savings account earns 5% interest compounded quarterly. On January 2, he had a balance of $200. Find the account balance on January 2 of the following year.

4. Judy Rossiter's savings account earns 7% interest compounded semiannually. On July 1, she had a balance of $400. Find the account balance on July 1 of the following year.

5. Laura Gray Eagle has $450 in her savings account. The account pays 6% interest compounded annually. Find the account balance after 3 years.

6. Paul Goldberg has $230 in his savings account. The account pays 5% interest compounded annually. Find the account balance after 6 years.

7. Tom McCarthy put $500 in a special savings account. He may not make any withdrawals for 3 years. The account earns 8% interest, compounded quarterly. How much is the account worth after 3 years?

8. Joanna Martino put $1,000 in a special savings account. She may not make any withdrawals for 5 years. The account earns 7% interest, compounded semiannually. How much is the account worth after 5 years?

9. Miss Lynch has kept $1,200 in a savings account for 6 years. The account earns 7% interest compounded semiannually. How much is the account worth?

10. Mr. Jenkins has kept $900 in a savings account for 5 years. The account earns 6% interest compounded quarterly. How much is the account worth?

11. Steve Schroeder deposited $500 in one savings account which earns 6% compounded quarterly. He deposited $800 in another account which earns 7% compounded semiannually. Both amounts were then kept on deposit for 2 years. What is the total value of both accounts?

12. Amy La Due deposited $700 in one savings account which earns 5% compounded semiannually. She deposited $900 in another account which earns 6% compounded quarterly. Both amounts were then kept on deposit for 3 years. What is the total value of both accounts?

13. Which earns the higher interest after 1 year: $1,000 @ 6% compounded semiannually, or $1,000 @ 6% compounded quarterly?

14. Which earns the higher interest after 5 years: $500 @ 5% compounded semiannually, or $500 @ 5% compounded quarterly?

MAINTAINING SKILLS

Change to percents. [114]

1. $\frac{1}{2}$
2. $\frac{1}{4}$
3. $\frac{1}{3}$
4. $\frac{2}{3}$
5. $1\frac{1}{6}$
6. $2\frac{3}{8}$

7. .50
8. .46
9. 1.3
10. 4.8
11. .001
12. .0016

Add. [33]

13.
$$4678.42$$
$$+\ \ 361.87$$

14.
$$4811.31$$
$$+\ \ \ 26.02$$

15.
$$48.6872$$
$$+41.487$$

16.
$$643.8721$$
$$+\ \ 46.0143$$

Add. [87]

17.
$$\frac{1}{3}$$
$$\frac{1}{2}$$
$$+\frac{1}{4}$$

18.
$$\frac{1}{2}$$
$$\frac{1}{4}$$
$$+\frac{3}{8}$$

19.
$$4\frac{1}{2}$$
$$16\frac{3}{4}$$
$$+12\frac{1}{8}$$

20.
$$19\frac{3}{8}$$
$$10\frac{3}{4}$$
$$+\ 6\frac{1}{2}$$

21.
$$8\frac{1}{3}$$
$$6\frac{1}{4}$$
$$+12\frac{5}{8}$$

22.
$$14\frac{1}{5}$$
$$6\frac{1}{2}$$
$$+11\frac{3}{4}$$

Find the balance after each deposit. [33]

23.

Date	Deposit	Withdrawal	Balance
Sept. 4			$378.46
Sept. 11	$52.46		
Sept. 18	34.97		
Sept. 25	81.13		
Oct. 2	14.81		

24.

Date	Deposit	Withdrawal	Balance
Jan. 8			$41.86
Jan. 15	$42.97		
Jan. 22	146.91		
Jan. 29	52.61		
Feb. 5	71.82		

Prepare a reconciliation statement. [153]

25.
Present checkbook balance	$56.42
Bank statement balance	229.64
Service charge	2.85
Outstanding checks: #361	41.86
#364	38.75
#365	102.60
#366	12.86
Deposit not shown on statement	20.00

26.
Present checkbook balance	$83.72
Bank statement balance	266.79
Service charge	3.25
Outstanding checks: #578	48.36
#580	12.50
#581	110.46
#582	50.00
Deposit not shown on statement	35.00

Consumer Tips____

AIR CONDITIONING

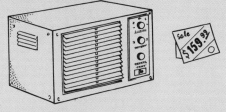

If you plan to buy an air conditioner, you should consider the amount of cooling needed, the purchase price, and the efficiency of the air conditioner.

The amount of cooling needed is expressed in BTU's (British Thermal Units). It depends upon: the amount of space to be cooled; the number of inside and outside walls; the number of windows; the type of roof or ceiling.

The efficiency of an air conditioner is measured by the energy efficiency ratio (EER). It is calculated by dividing the air conditioner's cooling capacity (measured in BTU's) by the wattage (number of watts).

Consult your local gas and electric company to determine the number of BTU's needed to cool the space.

Both the number of BTU's and the wattage may be found on the name plate of the air conditioner.

The resulting EER number tells the number of BTU's delivered for each watt of electricity. The more efficient it is, the higher the EER.

Consider the most efficient air conditioner to do the job. Do not buy an oversized air conditioner. It will run less frequently because it removes heat and humidity rapidly. But people in the room will be uncomfortable due to the noticeable changes in heat and humidity.

You can reduce operating costs further by:
- closing the window drapes and shades to keep the sun out
- using the exhaust fan in the kitchen and in the bathroom
- cleaning the air conditioner filter frequently
- setting the thermostat at 78°

Investing in Bonds

bond   A bond is evidence of a debt issued by a corporation or government that promises repayment at a definite time.

par value (face value)   Par value, or face value, is an amount printed, stamped, or written on the investment certificate.

return on an investment   The return on an investment is the amount earned on the investment.

securities   Bonds may be referred to as securities.

market price   Market price is the price at which a bond or stock is currently selling.

For Discussion

- What are some ways of investing money?
- Why is the purchaser of a bond considered as a lender of money?
- What is the advantage of buying bonds?

Mr. Johnson, a broker, was talking to the Morton family about investing in bonds.

"There are many ways of investing money," said Mr. Johnson. "Having a savings account is one way; buying bonds is another way."

"What is a bond?" Mr. Morton's son, Jerry asked.

"A bond is evidence of a debt," answered Mr. Johnson. "Buyers of bonds lend their money to the corporation, government, or agency that is selling the bonds. The par value of the bond is the amount that the bondholder will collect when the bond is due to be paid. The bondholder is paid interest in each interest period as long as he or she owns the bond."

"How does the interest on bonds compare with return on other investments?" asked Mr. Morton.

"Usually bonds yield more interest than savings accounts," replied Mr. Johnson. "However, savings accounts are a very safe investment. One advantage of bonds is that interest must be paid, even if the business has not earned a profit."

"That is a good feature," said Mr. Morton.

DEVELOPING SKILLS

OBJECTIVE   To determine the selling price and the annual interest on a bond

Find the market price or selling price of each of these $1,000 par value bonds.

MODEL   Con Edis @ $58\frac{1}{2}$ (Hint: $58\frac{1}{2}$ quote means $58\frac{1}{2}$% of the par value.)

$$\$1,000 \times .585 = \$585 \text{ market price}$$

1. Alcoa @ $72\frac{1}{2}$

2. AmT & T @ $94\frac{1}{4}$

3. GMot Acc @ $92\frac{1}{4}$

4. Norf & West @ $45\frac{1}{2}$

5. Nor Pac @ $32\frac{1}{4}$

6. Oak Elect @ $45\frac{1}{4}$

7. Otis E @ $74\frac{1}{2}$

8. PanAm A @ $67\frac{3}{8}$

9. Phil El @ $99\frac{1}{4}$

10. TWA @ 85

11. Allied Ch @ 78

12. East Air Lin @ 32

Find the annual interest on each of these $1,000 par value bonds.

MODEL   US Steel $4\frac{1}{2}$s (Hint: the rate of interest is given immediately after the name of the issue with the letter, s.)

$$\$1,000 \times .045 = \$45 \text{ interest}$$

13. Am Airlin 11s

14. G Mot Acc 5s

15. Ohio Edis 10s

16. Am M Fdy $4\frac{1}{4}$s

17. Nat Steel $8\frac{1}{4}$s

18. Pac G E $4\frac{3}{8}$s

19. Oneida $5\frac{1}{2}$s

20. U S Steel $4\frac{3}{4}$s

21. Am Cyan $7\frac{3}{8}$s

Find the selling price and the annual interest. Par value is $500.

22. Dayco Corp 6s, 51

23. Gen Elec 4s, 94

24. Exxon 7s, 80

25. Ampx Cp $5\frac{1}{2}$s, 34

26. Chrysl $8\frac{3}{4}$s, $98\frac{1}{2}$

27. N Dist $4\frac{1}{2}$s, $57\frac{3}{4}$

28. M G M 9s, $72\frac{1}{4}$

29. Fairch $4\frac{3}{8}$s, 37

30. Feddrs 5s, $29\frac{1}{2}$

APPLYING SKILLS

Find the costs and the annual interest earned for each investment. Par value is $1,000.

MODEL   7 Beth St $4\frac{3}{4}$s, $69\frac{1}{2}$ (Hint: Cost to buyer equals the selling price.)

$$\begin{aligned} \text{Cost} &= 7 \times (\$1,000 \times .695) \\ &= 7 \times \$695 \\ &= \$4,865 \end{aligned} \qquad \begin{aligned} \text{Interest} &= (7 \times \$1,000) \times .0475 \\ &= \$7,000 \times .0475 \\ &= \$332.50 \end{aligned}$$

1. 8 Pennzl $7\frac{1}{2}$s, 73

2. 2 Sear Roe $6\frac{3}{4}$s, 84

3. 5 Am Brands $9\frac{5}{8}$s, $105\frac{1}{2}$

4. 1 McCrory $7\frac{1}{2}$s, $27\frac{1}{4}$

5. 3 Texaco $7\frac{3}{4}$s, 91

6. 2 Food Fair 4s, $69\frac{1}{2}$

Solve these problems.

7. Mr. Sheridan wishes to purchase three $1,000 Oneida bonds. They are quoted at $52\frac{1}{2}$. Find the market price of these bonds.

8. Ms. Walker wishes to buy ten $500 General Motors bonds. They are quoted as $91\frac{1}{2}$. Find the market price of these bonds.

9. Beth has held five $1,000 Cons Mot 6s bonds for 3 years. How much interest have the bonds earned?

10. Harry has held four $500 Otis E 7s bonds for 5 years. How much interest have the bonds earned?

11. Mr. Santiago has three $1,000 So Blt bonds quoted at $84\frac{1}{2}$ and two $500 Good Yr bonds quoted at 92. He decides to sell all 5 bonds. What is the total market price?

12. Mrs. Yoshida has six $500 Uni Man bonds quoted at $87\frac{1}{4}$ and three $1,000 ATT bonds quoted at 76. She decides to sell all 9 bonds. What is the total market price?

13. Ellen Robinson bought seven $1,000 G & O 6s bonds at $86\frac{1}{2}$. She kept these bonds for 2 years and then sold them at $92\frac{1}{4}$. Find her total gain from owning these bonds.

14. Jerry Duncan bought eight $500 UnAirL 4s bonds at $57\frac{1}{2}$. He kept these bonds for 3 years and then sold them at 62. Find his total gain from owning these bonds.

MAINTAINING SKILLS

Change to fractions. [114]

1. 5% **2.** 8% **3.** 2.5% **4.** .5% **5.** $33\frac{1}{3}\%$ **6.** $66\frac{2}{3}\%$

Change to decimals. [114]

7. 4% **8.** 9% **9.** $5\frac{1}{4}\%$ **10.** $6\frac{4}{5}\%$ **11.** .3% **12.** $\frac{1}{2}\%$

Subtract. [33]

13. 481.42
  − 67.81

14. 381.46
  − 21.91

15. 32.8783
  − 1.6782

16. 47.3981
  − 12.0125

Subtract. [91]

17. $\frac{7}{8}$
$-\frac{1}{4}$

18. $\frac{3}{4}$
$-\frac{1}{12}$

19. $2\frac{1}{4}$
$-\frac{1}{3}$

20. $7\frac{7}{8}$
$-1\frac{3}{4}$

21. $27\frac{1}{2}$
$-1\frac{3}{4}$

22. $38\frac{3}{4}$
$-2\frac{1}{8}$

**Find the amount of money on deposit in each of the following accounts.
Use the table on page 329.** [164]

23. $800 for 2 years @ 5% interest compounded quarterly

24. $1,000 for 3 years @ 6% interest compounded quarterly

25. $950 for $2\frac{1}{2}$ years at 6% interest compounded semiannually

26. $750 for $1\frac{1}{2}$ years at 5% interest compounded semiannually

Solve these problems.

27. Miss Blake has kept $1,500 in a savings ac-
[164] count for 3 years. The account earns 6% interest compounded quarterly. How much is the account worth?

28. Mr. Williams has kept $500 in a savings ac-
[164] count for 10 years. The account earns 5% interest compounded semiannually. How much is the account worth?

29. Which earns the highest interest after 3 years:
[164] $1,000 @ 6% compounded semiannually or $1,000 @ 6% compounded quarterly?

30. Which earns the highest interest after 2 years:
[164] $1,500 at 5% compounded quarterly or $1,500 at 5% compounded annually?

31. Rodney bought a sweater for $15.49 and a pair
[33] of slacks for $16.50. He gave the cashier two $20 bills. How much change did he receive?

32. Thelma bought 2 chairs for $49.00 each and a
[33] lamp for $19.95. She gave the cashier six $20 bills. How much change did she receive?

Investing in Stocks

share of stock A share of stock represents part ownership in a corporation.

board of directors The Board of Directors of a corporation is a group elected by the stockholders to manage the business.

shareholder (stockholder) A shareholder, or stockholder, is a person who buys shares of stocks, thus becoming one of the owners of the corporation.

dividends Dividends are earnings, or profits, which the Board of Directors of a corporation may decide to pay to its stockholders.

brokerage fee A brokerage fee is the commission the broker receives for buying and selling stocks.

For Discussion

- Do stockholders have any responsibility in managing the business of the corporation?
- When are dividends paid to stockholders?
- What will Ruth's class study tomorrow?

As her project for consumer mathematics class, Ruth Dawkins was interviewing Miss Sarah Keys, vice-president of a well-known securities company.

"When you buy a share of common stock, you become a part owner of the company that is issuing the stock," said Miss Keys. "Then you may take part in electing the Board of Directors which manages the business. You have one vote for each share you own. The control of the business often rests with those having the most shares, or votes."

"That's fair," commented Ruth. "Persons investing the most money should have the most say."

"Exactly," continued Miss Keys. "You should also know that stockholders receive earnings, called *dividends,* if the Board of Directors feels that enough profits were made. Dividends are usually lower if the business needs money for operating costs or expansion."

"This is a big help, Miss Keys. I'll report this information to my class. Tomorrow, we are going to learn how to read and understand the stock exchange reports that appear on the financial pages of our newspapers."

DEVELOPING SKILLS

Answer the questions below on this stock listing.

| Year | | Stocks and Div in Dollars | Sales | | High | Low | Last | Net Chg |
High	Low		P/E	100's				
$25\frac{1}{2}$	$15\frac{1}{2}$	Indian Gas 2	6	3	16	16	16	. . .
$25\frac{7}{8}$	12	Indpl PL 1.82	8	57	$16\frac{1}{4}$	16	$16\frac{1}{4}$	. . .
28	10	Indl Nat 1.20	4	78	$10\frac{1}{4}$	10	$10\frac{1}{8}$	$+\frac{1}{8}$
$14\frac{3}{8}$	$4\frac{3}{8}$	Inexco Oil	7	50	$5\frac{3}{4}$	$5\frac{5}{8}$	$5\frac{5}{8}$	$-\frac{1}{4}$

| Year | | Stocks and Div in dollars | Sales | | High | Low | Last | Net Chg |
High	Low		P/E	100's				
$25\frac{1}{2}$	$15\frac{1}{2}$	Indian Gas 2	6	3	16	16	16	. . .

Quotes this year — Dividends pd in dollars — Price earnings ratio (%) — 300 shares sold — Today's quotes — Difference between yesterday's "Last" and today's

1. How much in dividends would you receive from 1 share of Indpl PL?

2. What was the highest quote this year for a share of Inexco Oil?

3. What is the price-earnings ratio for Indl Nat?

4. How many shares of Indpl PL were traded?

Find the cost including the brokerage fee. Use the last price from stock listing.

MODEL   30 shares of Indpl PL; brokerage fee, $14.15

$16.25 From listing
$\times 30$
$487.50
$+ \; 14.15$ Brokerage fee
$501.65 Cost

5. 25 shares of Indian Gas,
   Brokerage fee: $12.40

6. 100 shares of Inexco Oil,
   Brokerage fee: $17.65

Find the dividends earned on the following holdings. Use the stock listing above.

MODEL   200 shares of Indian Gas $200 \times \$2.00 = \$400$ Total dividends earned

7. 125 shares of Indl Nat

8. 50 shares of Indpl PL

APPLYING SKILLS

Answer the questions below on this stock listing.

| Year | | Stocks and Div. | | | | | | Net |
High	Low	in Dollars	P/E	100's	High	Low	Last	Chg
$13\frac{3}{8}$	$3\frac{1}{4}$	Am Motors	5	215	$3\frac{3}{8}$	$3\frac{1}{8}$	$3\frac{1}{2}$	$+\frac{1}{4}$
$38\frac{1}{4}$	$20\frac{3}{8}$	Cor GW 2.50	4	45	$27\frac{1}{2}$	$26\frac{1}{8}$	27	$+\frac{3}{4}$
179	$84\frac{1}{2}$	duPont 1.25	7	172	89	$87\frac{5}{8}$	$88\frac{1}{4}$	$+\frac{7}{8}$
20	$12\frac{1}{4}$	Firestone 1.60	5	159	$13\frac{5}{8}$	13	$13\frac{1}{4}$	$-\frac{1}{8}$
$28\frac{3}{4}$	$13\frac{1}{2}$	Gen Dynam 1	5	56	$17\frac{3}{4}$	$17\frac{3}{8}$	$17\frac{3}{8}$	$+\frac{1}{8}$
$9\frac{7}{8}$	$3\frac{5}{8}$	Magnvox 1.20	. . .	17	$4\frac{1}{2}$	$3\frac{3}{4}$	4	$-\frac{1}{4}$

1. Mrs. Dwight owns 300 shares of Magnvox. How much will she earn in dividends after 1 year?

2. Mr. Jordan owns 250 shares of Firestone. How much will he earn in dividends after 1 year?

3. What is the cost of 300 shares of Am Motors? Include a brokerage fee of $51.86.

4. What is the cost of 400 shares of Cor GW? Include a brokerage fee of $177.85.

Solve these problems.

5. Eve Johnson invested $2,250 in Eastman Kodak stock when the shares were listed at 75. How many shares does she own?

6. David Weiss invested $525 in American Zinc stock when the shares were listed at 21. How many shares does he own?

7. Mr. Sanchez invested $3,400 in Dan River stock when the shares were listed at 17. That year, the stocks earned dividends of $2 per share. How many shares does he own? How much did his investment yield?

8. Ms. Wilson invested $2,500 in Collins Radio stock when the shares were listed at 25. That year, the stocks earned dividends of $3 per share. How many shares does she own? How much did her investment yield?

9. Alice Klein purchased 100 shares of Westinghouse Electric stock at $67\frac{1}{4}$. The following year, she sold the stock at $72\frac{1}{2}$. She received dividends of 80 cents per share. What was her total gain?

10. George Ferguson purchased 80 shares of Gar Wood stock at $8\frac{3}{4}$. The following year, he sold the stock at $10\frac{1}{2}$. He received dividends of $1 per share. What was his total gain?

MAINTAINING SKILLS

Simplify. [78]

1. $\frac{45}{900}$

2. $\frac{30}{1,200}$

3. $\frac{12}{72}$

4. $\frac{300}{1,500}$

5. $\frac{65}{910}$

6. $\frac{50}{640}$

Solve these proportions. [83]

7. $\frac{70}{280} = \frac{n}{100}$

8. $\frac{48}{5,000} = \frac{n}{100}$

9. $\frac{32}{6,400} = \frac{n}{100}$

10. $\frac{480}{6,000} = \frac{n}{100}$

Find the annual interest on each of these $1,000 par value bonds. [169]

11. Am Mot 6s

12. S Pac $4\frac{1}{4}$s

13. Wyly $7\frac{1}{4}$s

14. SCM $5\frac{1}{2}$s

15. RdgB $6\frac{1}{2}$s

16. Ray $10\frac{7}{8}$s

Find the selling price and annual interest on these bonds. Par value is $500.
[169]

17. N Ind 10s, 99

18. TVA $9\frac{1}{4}$s, 95

19. Tapp $5\frac{1}{2}$s, 94

20. St. Oln 9.7s, 89

21. RapA $7\frac{1}{2}$s, 85

22. Seagr $7\frac{3}{4}$s, 96

Solve these problems.

23. Mr. Jackson wishes to purchase five $1,000
[169] PGE bonds. They are quoted at 78. Find the market price of these bonds.

24. Ms. Iverson wishes to buy ten $1,000 Tx Ind
[169] bonds. They are quoted at 92. Find the market price of these bonds.

25. Sue has held five $1,000 Unv O $6\frac{5}{8}$s bonds for
[169] 6 years. How much interest have the bonds earned?

26. John has held eight $1,000 PAA $4\frac{1}{2}$s bonds for
[169] 10 years. How much interest have the bonds earned?

27. The tax rate is $35.50 per $1,000 of property
[83] value. Find the taxes on a $15,000 home.

28. The tax rate is $54 per $1,000 of property value.
[83] Find the taxes on a $26,000 home.

29. The casualty insurance rate of Company B is
[83] $.42 per $100. Find the insurance rate for an $18,000 property.

30. The casualty insurance rate of Company C is
[83] $.32 per $100. Find the insurance rate for an $18,000 property.

Career/TEXTILES

Man-made fibers and combinations of synthetic and natural fibers have created limitless opportunities in the textile industry. Major work areas are (1) research and development, (2) quality control and production, and (3) customer service and sales. In these areas, the textile specialist uses a high degree of knowledge to create new markets.

Job Descriptions

- General laboratory technician—tests cloth samples to determine strengths and weaknesses; runs tests to determine characteristics of various fibers.

- Evenness tester technician—operates testing equipment; analyzes the results; uses sophisticated instruments to maintain quality control.

- Production control technician—gathers data and makes calculations to keep materials moving evenly through the production operations.

- Job study technician—makes time and motion studies; sets fair job loads; determines piece rates for different operations.

Training

Entry-level jobs may be available to high school graduates. Many two- and four-year colleges offer programs. High school graduates without advanced training will find it difficult to progress upward.

Further Investigation

Arrange an interview with a textile specialist. Ask about job qualifications, working conditions, possibilities for advancement, entry-level jobs.

Consult your guidance department about suitable programs in your high school. Also ask about post-high-school technical programs available in this career area.

Rate of Return

profitable investment   A profitable investment is an investment that pays a steady, or sizable, income.

rate of return   The rate of return is a way of describing how profitable an investment is in terms of a percent, rather than in dollars and cents.

$$\text{Rate of return} = \frac{\overset{\text{Compared number}}{\underset{\downarrow}{\text{return for 1 year}}}}{\underset{\underset{\uparrow}{\text{Compared-to number}}}{\text{cost of investment}}}$$

For Discussion

- What facts would an investor usually want to know before making an investment?

- How did Mr. Mikulski explain finding the rate of return on an investment?

- Is the most profitable investment the one which returns the largest dollar amount?

"Mr. Mikulski, how can I really tell which kind of investment is most profitable?" asked Harry Cervantes in his evening school class.

"As an investor, you should know something about the company, its history with respect to payments of dividends, its future prospects," replied Mr. Mikulski. "You should also know how to calculate the rate of return on your investment."

"How do you do that?" asked Harry.

"Very simply. Compare the dollar amount of the return to the amount invested and express the ratio as a percent. For example, a $50 dividend on a $1,000 investment is a 5% return. A $30 dividend on an investment of $300 is a 10% return. The most profitable investment has the highest percent of return."

Harry interrupted, "I see what you mean. The investment which returns the largest dollar amount is not always the most profitable investment. Looking at the 5% return and the 10% return, it is easy to see that the $300 investment is more profitable."

DEVELOPING SKILLS

Find the annual rate of return on each investment. Disregard brokerage fees. Round answers to the nearest .1%.

MODEL
A 5%, $1,000 bond purchased at 80
return = $1,000 × .05 = $50
cost = $1,000 × .80 = $800

By Formula
$$\text{rate} = \frac{\text{return}}{\text{cost}}$$
$$= \frac{50}{800}$$
$$= \frac{1}{16}$$
$$= .0625, \text{ or } 6.3\%$$

By Proportion
$$\frac{50}{800} = \frac{n}{100}$$
$$800n = 5,000$$
$$n = 6.25$$
$$\text{rate} = 6.3\%$$

1. A $4\frac{1}{2}$%, $1,000 bond @ 90

2. A $6\frac{1}{2}$%, $1,000 bond @ 91

3. A 6s, $1,000 bond @ 72

4. A 5s $1,000 bond @ 64

5. A 7s $500 bond @ $85\frac{1}{2}$

6. A 6s $500 bond @ $80\frac{3}{4}$

7. 10 shares of stock purchased at 75 per share, paying annual dividends of $6 per share

8. 20 shares of stock purchased at 105 per share, paying semiannual dividends of $3 per share

9. 30 shares of stock purchased at $48\frac{1}{2}$ per share, paying semiannual dividends of $2.50 per share

10. 40 shares of stock purchased at $20\frac{1}{2}$ per share, paying annual dividends of $8 per share

11. 100 shares of stock purchased at 75 per share, paying annual dividends at 5% of the par value of $100

12. 50 shares of stock purchased at 95 per share, paying annual dividends at 4% of the par value of $100

13. 200 shares of stock purchased at 80 per share, paying semiannual dividends at 6% of the par value of $100

14. 150 shares of stock purchased at 75, paying semiannual dividends at 5% of the par value of $100

APPLYING SKILLS

Solve these problems. Disregard brokerage fees. Round answers to the nearest .1%.

1. Anne Washington has a $4\frac{1}{2}\%$, $1,000 bond which she purchased at 80. What is the annual rate of return on her investment?

2. Bob Wilson has a $6\frac{1}{2}\%$, $500 bond which he purchased at 91. What is the annual rate of return on his investment?

3. Mrs. Goldman purchased a share of stock at 98. The stock pays a semiannual dividend of $4 per share. What is the annual rate of return on this stock?

4. Mr. Stanton purchased a share of stock at 86. The stock pays a semiannual dividend of $3 per share. What is the annual rate of return on this stock?

5. Mr. Forlini bought a $5\frac{1}{2}$s, $1,000 bond at 75. A year later, he sold it at 82. Find the total gain on his investment.

6. Ms. Whittier bought a $4\frac{3}{4}$s, $1,000 bond at 80. A year later, she sold it at 87. Find the total gain on her investment.

Which is the more profitable investment?

7. A 4%, $1,000 bond @ 110, or a 5%, $1,000 bond @ 160

8. A 6%, $500 bond @ 83, or a 7%, $500 bond @ 80

9. A share of stock listed at 37 and paying an annual dividend of $5, or a share of stock listed at 75 and paying a quarterly dividend of $2

10. A share of stock listed at 60 and paying an annual dividend of $4, or a share of stock listed at 32 and paying a semiannual dividend of $3

Solve these problems.

MODEL   A certain investment returns $30. This represents a 6% rate of return. Find the cost of the original investment.

Let n = cost of investment

$$.06 = \frac{30}{n}$$
$$.06n = 30$$
$$n = \frac{30}{.06}$$

or

$$\frac{6}{100} = \frac{30}{n}$$
$$6n = 3000$$
$$n = \frac{3000}{6}$$

So, the original investment cost $500.   = 500   ·   = 500

11. An office building owner made a net profit of $12,000 from rentals last year. The rate of return on his investment was 8%. Find the cost of this investment.

12. A stockholder made a net profit of $22,000 from her investments last year. The rate of return on her investments was 11%. Find the cost of these investments.

MAINTAINING SKILLS

Multiply. [39]

1. 48.67
   × 3.87

2. 93.90
   × 4.86

3. 4,678
   × .0125

4. 6,107
   × .0355

5. 1.4721
   × .02

6. 4.1287
   × .04

Multiply. Simplify. [97]

7. $\frac{1}{4} \times \frac{1}{5}$

8. $\frac{3}{4} \times \frac{2}{3}$

9. $1\frac{1}{4} \times 3\frac{1}{2}$

10. $6\frac{1}{3} \times 1\frac{1}{4}$

11. $\frac{1}{2} \times \frac{3}{4} \times \frac{1}{5}$

12. $\frac{1}{4} \times \frac{2}{3} \times \frac{2}{5}$

13. $1\frac{4}{5} \times 6\frac{1}{3} \times 1\frac{1}{2}$

14. $4\frac{1}{2} \times 3\frac{1}{4} \times 1\frac{2}{3}$

Find the cost of these stocks, excluding the brokerage fees. [173]

15. 30 shares of Upjohn @ $46\frac{1}{8}$

16. 50 shares of Trans @ $59\frac{1}{2}$

17. 136 shares of Tennc @ $87\frac{1}{4}$

18. 150 shares of StJoeM @ $37\frac{3}{4}$

Copy and complete. [39]

19.

	OUTLER ELECTRIC		
Name	Hours Worked	Hourly Rate	Gross Wages
Beth	36.5	$3.25	
Cora	40	2.75	
May	38.5	3.00	
Stan	37.75	2.95	
TOTAL	—	—	

20.

	CARBONE APPLIANCES		
Name	Hours Worked	Hourly Rate	Gross Wages
John	26.25	$2.75	
Julia	30.5	3.00	
Sally	40	2.50	
Steve	35.5	2.85	
TOTAL	—	—	

Solve these problems. Disregard brokerage fees. [173]

21. Martha Jackson invested $3,479 in Shell Oil stock. Shares were listed at 49. How many shares does she own?

22. George Wong invested $1,998 in Xerox Corp. stock. Shares were listed at 54. How many shares does he own?

23. Last year, Warnaco paid dividends at the rate of $.80 a share. Mr. Blackwell owns 200 shares. Find his annual dividends that year.

24. Last year, Stevens Company paid dividends at the rate of $1.20 per share. Mrs. Arnold owns 250 shares. Find her annual dividends that year.

Life Insurance

life insurance   Life insurance provides financial protection for the insured and for those who have a financial interest in the life of the insured party.

term insurance   Term insurance provides protection for a limited time and has no cash surrender value.

cash surrender value   The cash surrender value of a policy is an amount which can be collected by the insured if the policy is cashed in before the protection ends.

beneficiary   A beneficiary is a person to whom the proceeds of a policy will be paid.

premium   The premium of an insurance policy is its cost. It may be paid on a monthly, quarterly, semiannual, or annual basis.

For Discussion

- Compare the advantages and disadvantages of term insurance and straight-life insurance.
- Why do you think that term insurance is less expensive than straight-life?

Tommy and Louise Robinson, a recently married couple, were in the library. Tommy is a clothing designer and Louise is a computer systems analyst. They were looking for articles on life insurance so that they could determine which type of policy would be best for them.

"This magazine is great," whispered Louise. "It describes all types of insurance: term, straight-life, endowment, limited payment life, and other types. It seems that we should choose either term insurance or straight-life. Term insurance is low cost and usually renewable. Straight-life protects for life. Term insurance has no cash surrender value, but straight-life does. Also, at age 90 the proceeds of straight-life are paid to the insured."

"How do the costs compare?" asked Tommy.

"Term premiums are less expensive but increase each time the policy is renewed. Straight-life premiums stay the same," answered Louise.

"Louise, let's check these books out and take them home to study over the weekend."

DEVELOPING SKILLS

OBJECTIVE   To determine annual premiums and periodic premium payments on life insurance policies

Use the table to determine the annual premium for each policy.

Age At Issue	Term		Straight Life	Limited Payment		Endowment Policy	
	5-Year	10-Year		20-Year	30-Year	20-Year	30-Year
	ANNUAL PREMIUMS PER $1,000						
15	—	—	$15.75	$28.10	$22.10	$49.50	$31.90
20	$ 7.75	$ 8.10	17.60	30.60	24.00	49.80	32.40
25	8.50	9.10	20.00	33.30	26.25	50.30	33.20
30	9.70	10.60	22.80	36.50	28.90	51.10	34.40
35	11.50	12.80	26.40	40.15	32.15	52.30	36.20
40	14.30	16.30	31.00	44.50	36.25	54.15	39.00
45	18.50	21.50	36.80	49.70	41.60	57.05	43.20

MODEL   Straight-life policy for $5,000, issued at age 25

From the table ⟶ $20.00 (for $1,000)

$$\frac{\times 5}{\$100.00 \text{ (for } \$5,000)}$$

The annual premium is $100.

1. Five-year term policy for $2,000 issued at age 20

2. Twenty-year limited payment policy for $5,000 issued at age 35

3. Thirty-year endowment policy for $10,000 issued at age 25

4. Straight-life policy for $15,000 issued at age 45

Find the periodic premium payment. Use the schedule.

MODEL   Find the monthly premium on a $5,000, 10-year term policy purchased at age 30.

From table ⟶ $10.60 (for $1,000)

$$\frac{\times 5}{\$53.00} \text{ (Annual premium for } \$5,000)$$

From schedule ⟶ $\times .087$ (Rate for monthly payment)

37100

4 2400

$4.61100, or $4.61 per month

PERIODIC PAYMENT SCHEDULE	
Period	Multiply Annual Premium By
Monthly	.087
Quarterly	.26
Semiannually	.51

5. Find the quarterly premium on a $10,000 straight-life policy, issued at age 40.

6. Find the semiannual premium on a $5,000, 30-year limited policy, issued at age 30.

APPLYING SKILLS

Solve these problems.

MODEL   John Armstrong is 30 years old. He purchased a $5,000 straight-life insurance policy. What total amount of premiums will he have paid if he dies at age 60?

$22.80 Annual premium for $1,000

× 5

$114.00 Annual premium for $5,000

× 30 Years from purchase to death

$3,420.00 Total amount of premiums

1. Raul Nunez purchased a $10,000 20-year limited payment life insurance policy at the age of 30. He died at age 35. What total amount of premiums had he paid?

2. Nancy Richardson purchased a $20,000, 30-year endowment life insurance policy at the age of 25. She died at age 40. What total amount of premiums had she paid?

3. Mrs. Mueller took out a $15,000 straight-life insurance policy at the age of 40. She agreed to pay semiannual premiums. She died at age 50. How much had she paid in premiums?

4. Mr. Duffy took out a $10,000, 20-year endowment life insurance policy at the age of 35. He agreed to pay semiannual premiums. He died at age 52. How much had he paid in premiums?

5. James Osborne took out a $7,000, 5-year term life insurance policy at the age of 25. He agreed to pay quarterly premiums. What total amount of premiums had he paid at the end of 5 years?

6. Lucy Samson took out a $5,000, 10-year term life insurance policy at the age of 20. She agreed to pay quarterly premiums. What total amount of premiums had she paid at the end of 10 years?

7. Laura Chan, age 25, bought a $12,000 straight-life insurance policy and agreed to pay annual premiums. She died at age 68. How much more did her beneficiary collect, compared to the premiums she paid for the insurance?

8. Bill Oliveri, age 30, bought a $10,000 straight-life insurance policy and agreed to pay annual premiums. He died at age 56. How much more did his beneficiary collect, compared to the premiums he paid for the insurance?

9. Mr. Mahoney purchased a $15,000 straight-life insurance policy at the age of 30. He paid annual premiums. This policy contained a double indemnity clause which pays twice the face value in the event of accidental death. At the age of 44, Mr. Mahoney was killed in a traffic accident. How much more did his beneficiary collect, compared to the premiums he paid for this insurance?

10. Ms. Dorline purchased a $20,000 straight-life insurance policy at the age of 25. She paid annual premiums. This policy contained a double indemnity clause, which pays twice the face value in the event of accidental death. At the age of 52, Ms. Dorline was killed in a plane crash. How much more did her beneficiary collect, compared to the premiums she paid for this insurance?

MAINTAINING SKILLS

Divide. Simplify. [101]

1. $1 \div \frac{1}{3}$

2. $2 \div \frac{2}{3}$

3. $\frac{1}{2} \div \frac{1}{4}$

4. $\frac{1}{2} \div \frac{1}{8}$

5. $7\frac{1}{2} \div \frac{1}{2}$

6. $6\frac{1}{2} \div \frac{1}{4}$

7. $92\frac{1}{2} \div 1\frac{1}{8}$

8. $51\frac{1}{3} \div 1\frac{3}{4}$

Compute. [119]

9. 80% of 92

10. 45% of 75

11. 18 is what percent of 30?

12. 15 is what percent of 75?

13. 14 is 50% of what number?

14. 32 is 80% of what number?

Find the annual rate of return on each investment. Disregard brokerage fees. Round answers to the nearest .1%. [179]

15. a $3\frac{3}{4}$%, $1,000 bond @ 86

16. a $4\frac{1}{2}$%, $1,000 bond @ 88

17. a 5s, $500 bond @ 75

18. a 6s, $500 bond @ 92

19. a $6\frac{1}{2}$ s, $1,000 bond @ 72

20. a $7\frac{1}{4}$s, $500 bond @ 82

21. 30 shares of stock, purchased at 96 per share paying annual dividends of $8 per share

22. 25 shares of stock purchased at 46 per share, paying annual dividends of $4 per share

Solve these problems.

23. Barb made a down payment of $50 on a television set. The set cost $125. What percent of the selling price did she pay?
[119]

24. Andrew made a down payment of $25 on a chair. The chair cost $80. What percent of the selling price did he pay?
[119]

25. An apartment building owner made a net profit of $14,000 from rentals last year. The rate of return on her investment was 7%. Find the cost of the investment.
[179]

26. A stockholder made a net profit of $13,500 last year. The rate of return on her investment was 9%. Find the cost of this investment.
[179]

Health Insurance

health insurance Health insurance provides money to pay the medical expenses of hospitals and surgeons.

surgical Surgical refers to using instruments to treat disease or injury.

hospital and surgical insurance Hospital and surgical insurance offers different plans and coverages for in-hospital charges and certain surgical expenses.

major medical insurance Major medical insurance provides money to pay for very serious and long illnesses or accidents.

For Discussion

- Why does disability income insurance appear to be an important type of health insurance?

"Now that you're married, Neal, you should consider buying health insurance," said Mrs. Swenson to her son, a steelworker.

"What kinds are there, Mom?"

"One type covers hospital expenses and certain surgeons' expenses which are options," replied his mother. "Then you should consider major medical to take care of very expensive costs of serious and long-term illnesses or accidents. A third type is disability income insurance to take care of replacing pay lost due to an accident or illness."

"How does major medical insurance work, Mom?" asked Neal.

"In general, major medical takes over when your basic hospital and surgical insurance has been used up and it cannot pay for other expenses. You would pay the first $100, after which major medical would pay about 80% of your eligible expenses. You should join your steel company's group insurance plan because group plans are cheaper."

"That's a good idea, Mom."

DEVELOPING SKILLS

Make and complete a chart for each of the following hospital bills. Use Insurance Plan A,
stated at the right.(Note: Medical policies do not
cover television and telephone expenses.)

INSURANCE PLAN A		
Room Expenses	In-hospital Expenses	Surgical Plan
$40 per day for 60 days	Maximum of $500	Maximum of $200

MODEL   Hospital room and board – 20 days at $50 per day; medicine
and X-rays – $200; operating room – $75; anesthetics – $85;
surgeon's fee – $300

	Items	Cost	Company Pays	You Pay
Room	20 days @ $50	$1,000	$800	$200
In-hospital	Medicine, X-ray	$ 200		
	Operating room	75		
	Anesthetics	85		
	Total	$ 360	$360	$0
Surgical	Surgeon's fee	$ 300	$200	$100

Room: Company pays $40 per day.
$40 × 20 days = $800
In-hospital: Company pays $500 maximum.
$360
Surgical: Company pays $200 maximum.
$200

You pay costs over coverage.
$1,000 − $800 = $200
You pay costs over coverage.
$0
You pay costs over coverage.
$300 − $200 = $100

1. Hospital room and board–30 days at $45 per
day; operating room–$120; surgical supplies–
$125; blood–$75; medicine and X-rays–$170;
surgeon's fee–$250

2. Hospital room and board–15 days at $55 per
day; blood plasma–$75; anesthetics–$80;
medicine, X-rays–$180; operating room–$90;
ambulance–$20; surgeon's fee–$275

3. Hospital room and board–45 days at $40 per
day; blood–$80; operating room–$110; surgical supplies–$55; surgeon's fee–$200; television, telephone–$35

4. Hospital room and board–25 days at $60 per
day; blood–$100, operating room–$150; surgical supplies–$70; surgeon's fee–$300; television, telephone–$40

APPLYING SKILLS

1. Mr. Dean's hospital room and board bill is listed as 25 days at $65 per day. His medical insurance provides coverage for 60 days at $50 per day. How much does it cost the insurance company? Mr. Dean?

2. Ms. Kuhn's hospital room and board bill is listed as 45 days at $70 per day. Her medical insurance provides coverage for 90 days at $60 per day. How much did it cost the insurance company? Ms. Kuhn?

3. Alice Spear's in-hospital expenses were $70 for blood, $100 for the operating room, $20 for medicine and X-rays, $5 for phone calls and $15 television rental. Her medical insurance plan pays $600 maximum for in-hospital expenses. How much did the insurance company pay?

4. Harry Ames' in-hospital expenses were $75 for blood, $90 for the operating room, $40 for medicine and X-rays, $2 for phone calls and $25 television rental. His medical insurance plan pays $400 maximum for in-hospital expenses. How much did the insurance company pay?

5. Mr. Bono's hospital bill is $5,500. He has a major medical insurance policy. After he pays a deductible amount of $500, the insurance company pays 80% of the remaining balance up to $30,000 and Mr. Bono pays 20%. How much does the insurance company pay?

6. Ms. Carnes' hospital bill is $12,500. She has a major medical policy. After she pays a deductible amount of $500, the insurance company pays 80% of the remaining balance up to $50,000, and Ms. Carnes pays 20%. How much does the insurance company pay?

7. Miss Thomas' hospital bill is $8,500. She has a major medical insurance policy. After she pays a deductible amount of $500, the insurance company pays 80% of the remaining balance up to $50,000 and Miss Thomas pays 20%. How much does Miss Thomas pay?

8. Mr. Stanley's hospital bill is $10,500. He has a major medical insurance policy. After he pays a deductible amount of $500, the insurance company pays 80% of the remaining balance up to $75,000 and Mr. Stanley pays 20%. How much does Mr. Stanley pay?

9. Mr. Turner's hospital bill is $8,900. He has a major medical insurance policy. After he pays a deductible amount of $500, the insurance company pays 80% of the first $5,000 and Mr. Turner pays 20%; thereafter, the insurance company pays 100% of the remaining balance. How much did the insurance company pay? How much did Mr. Turner pay?

10. Mrs. Penn's hospital bill is $11,200. She has a major medical insurance policy. After she pays a deductible amount of $1,000, the insurance company pays 80% of the first $5,000, and Mrs. Penn pays 20%; thereafter, the insurance company pays 100% of the remaining balance. How much did the insurance company pay? How much did Mrs. Penn pay?

MAINTAINING SKILLS

Divide.   [43]

1. $12\overline{)4,275.6}$

2. $25\overline{)6,357.5}$

3. $2.3\overline{)839.5}$

4. $6.5\overline{)1,267.5}$

Find percent decrease.   [125]

	Last Year's Orders	This Year's Orders
5.	4,000	3,500
7.	2,000	1,800
9.	450	405
11.	9,500	8,075

Find percent increase.   [125]

	Last Year's Orders	This Year's Orders
6.	2,400	3,000
8.	4,500	4,725
10.	300	375
12.	19,000	23,370

Find the annual premium for each policy. Use the table on page 183.   [183]

13. Twenty-year limited payment policy for $6,000 issued at age 25

14. Ten-year term policy for $15,000 issued at age 40

15. Straight-life policy for $12,000 issued at age 35

16. Twenty-year endowment policy for $15,000 issued at age 45

Solve these problems.

17. The number of jobs at a company increased [125] from 150 to 165. Find the percent increase.

18. Monthly sales of used cars went from 16,000 [125] to 20,000 in Nov. Find the percent increase.

19. A boat manufacturer produced 75,000 boats [125] last year. This year it produced only 70,000 boats. Find the percent decrease.

20. Last year 240 students enrolled in business [125] education. This year only 210 students enrolled. Find the percent decrease.

21. Mr. Brown purchased a $15,000 straight-life [183] insurance policy at the age of 25. He paid annual premiums. The policy contained a double indemnity clause, paying twice the face value in the event of accidental death. At the age of 60, Mr. Brown was killed in a plane crash. How much more did his beneficiary collect, compared to the premiums paid for this insurance? (Use the table on page 183.)

22. Mrs. Wong purchased a $10,000 straight-life [183] insurance policy at the age of 30. She paid annual premiums. The policy contained a double indemnity clause, paying twice the face value in the event of accidental death. At age 55, Mrs. Wong was killed in a boating accident. How much more did her beneficiary collect, compared to the premiums paid for this insurance? (Use the table on page 183.)

Self-Test: Chapter 7

Find the amount of money on deposit in each of the following accounts. Use the compound interest table on page 329. [164]

1. $550 for 6 yr @ 6% compounded semiannually

2. $500 for 3 yr @ 5% compounded quarterly

Find the selling price and annual interest on these bonds. Par value is $1,000. [169]

3. ATT, $4\frac{3}{8}$s, 85

4. B & O $6\frac{1}{2}$s, 97

Find the cost of these stocks including the brokerage fees. [173]

5. 50 shares of RevcoDS @ 19
Brokerage fee: $26.55

6. 75 shares of Wach @ 30
Brokerage fee: $46.63

Copy and complete. [173]

	Number of Shares	Stocks and Dividends in Dollars	Total Dividends Earned
7.	300	Safewy 1.80	
8.	150	Wall Bus .55	

Solve these problems. Disregard brokerage fees. Round answers to the nearest .1%. [179]

9. Susan Blumberg has a 5%, $1,000 bond which she bought at 75. What is the annual rate of return?

10. David Johnson bought 10 shares of stock at 36. The stock pays a semiannual dividend of $1.50 per share. What is the annual rate of return?

Solve these problems.

11. Gerald Henry purchased a $15,000, 30-year
[183] limited payment life insurance policy at age 25. The annual premiums were $26.25 per $1,000. What was the annual premium of his policy?

12. Barb Swanson's hospital board and room bill is
[187] listed as 30 days at $65 per day. Her insurance provides coverage for 80 days at $60 per day. How much does Barb have to pay?

13. A 25-year-old woman purchased a $12,000
[183] straight-life insurance policy. The annual premium was $17.60 per $1,000. The rate for monthly payments was .087 of the annual premium. Find the amount of her monthly payments.

14. Bill Harris' in-hospital expenses were $125 for
[187] blood, $100 for the operating room, $52 for medicine and X-rays, and $20 for television rental. His medical insurance pays $400 maximum for in-hospital expenses. How much did the insurance company pay?

Test: Chapter 7

Find the amount of money on deposit in each of the following accounts. Use the compound interest table on page 329.

1. $1,400 for 3 yr @ 5% compounded semiannually

2. $700 for 5 yr @ 6% compounded quarterly

Find the selling price and annual interest on these bonds. Par value is $1,000.

3. AInvt $9\frac{1}{2}$s, 76

4. Case $5\frac{1}{2}$s, 90

Find the cost of these stocks including brokerage fees.

5. 100 shares of Stw @ 17
Brokerage fee: $40.51

6. 75 shares of WhelPit @ 42
Brokerage fee: $57.44

Copy and complete.

	Number of Shares	Stocks and Dividends in Dollars		Total Dividends Earned
7.	175	Raybest	1.50	
8.	250	SupmkG	.20	

Solve these problems. Disregard brokerage fees. Round answers to the nearest .1%.

9. Sara Williams has a 6%, $1,000 bond which she purchased at 90. What is the annual rate of return on her investment?

10. Bob White Feather purchased 15 shares of stock at 45. The stock pays annual dividends of $.60 per share. What is the annual rate of return?

Solve these problems.

11. Geraldine White purchased a $20,000, 20-year, endowment life insurance policy at age 30. The annual premiums were $51.10 per $1,000. What was the amount of her premium?

12. Jack Hilmer's hospital board and room bill is listed as 40 days at $75 per day. His insurance provides coverage for 90 days at $50 per day. How much did Jack have to pay?

13. A 45-year-old man purchased a $15,000, 10-year term life insurance policy. The annual premium was $21.50 per $1,000. The rate for semiannual payments was .51 of the annual premium. Find the amount of his semiannual payments.

14. Sharon Allen's in-hospital expenses were $150 for blood, $175 for the operating room, $45 for medicine and X-rays, and $15 for a telephone in her room. Her medical insurance pays $450 maximum for in-hospital expense. How much did the insurance company pay?

Circle Graphs

Answer the questions. Use the circle graph.

1. What is the Drew's net monthly income?

2. What percent is budgeted for clothing?

3. What is the measure of the central angle that represents clothing? (Hint: Use a protractor to measure.)

4. What percent is budgeted for food?

5. What is the measure of the central angle that represents food?

6. What percent is budgeted for rent?

7. What is the measure of the central angle that represents rent?

8. What percent is budgeted for each of the remaining items?

9. What is the measure of each of the remaining central angles?

10. What is the sum of the percents?

11. What percent does the circle represent?

12. What is the sum of the measures of the central angles?

13. How many degrees does the entire circle represent?

THE DREW'S MONTHLY BUDGET

Clothing $50

Operating Expenses $150

Recreation $60

Savings and Insurance $75

Rent $140

Food $125

Copy and complete. Then draw a circle graph.

14.

NET MONTHLY INCOME $720			
Item	Amount	Percent	Degrees in Central Angle on Graph
Food	$180	$\frac{180}{720} = \frac{1}{4} = 25\%$	25% of $360 = \frac{1}{4} \times 360 = 90$
Rent	216		
Clothing	144		
Recreation	72		
Savings	108		
TOTALS			

8
BUYING GOODS AND SERVICES

A microbiology lab technician detecting impurities in cosmetics

Activities

In the figure at the right there are 25 boxes containing numbers picked at random. Copy the figure. Connect any three boxes that touch each other horizontally, vertically, or diagonally and whose numbers add to 40.

30	9	17	31	16
3	6	21	23	3
19	11	3	14	7
20	25	28	17	9
16	4	18	9	30

Obtain a time table for a bus or train that services your area. Figure out whether it would be financially worthwhile to take a job in another town or city and commute daily if your pay is about $20 more per week working there, compared to working in your hometown area. Consider such questions as: How long does it take to make the trip one way? Is there a commuter's discount ticket available? etc.

Choose national brand items on sale at local supermarkets or grocery stores. List the names of at least 3 to 5 stores where these items can be purchased and the price at each store. Make a chart to present the results of your comparison shopping.

Begin a ''Consumer Aware: Sales and Bargains'' section for your classroom bulletin board by noting markdowns, money-savers, and rip-offs by local dealers. Prepare charts which will serve as a shoppers' guide for particular items (such as albums, tennis shoes, furniture, clothes, etc.). Select different types of shops—independent, department, discount, etc. Form committees to update this section each week or month with accurate or surveyed information on markdowns, money-savers, and rip-offs.

Pricing Goods

business administration   Business administration concerns the management and operations of a business. Some colleges offer programs in business administration.

net income   A business earns a net income or profit when its cost and expenses are less than its income from sales or services.

net income = selling price − cost − expenses

net loss   A business suffers a net loss when its cost and expenses are greater than its income.

markup   Markup is an amount added to the cost price of goods to set a selling price. This amount is also known as the margin or gross profit.

markdown   A markdown is the amount of reduction in selling price, usually because of a special sale.

For Discussion

- Why was Manuel interested in attending the community college in his area?
- How would the selling price of a new car be set?
- Why would an automobile dealer reduce the price of a new car?

Manuel and Carlos Gomez hoped one day to have a new-car dealership. Carlos was completing his studies in auto mechanics, and Manuel expected to attend the community college to study business administration.

Mr. Gomez said, ''I notice you have a college catalog. Have you looked over the course offerings to be sure that you can meet your career goals?''

Manual assured him that he had.

''This afternoon, we are going down to Montoya's showroom to look over the business,'' Carlos said.

''A dealership is a big business,'' their father said. ''I wonder how much profit is made on the sale of a new car?''

''I don't know,'' Carlos answered, ''but the markup must be large enough to cover all costs and expenses and still leave a profit.''

''By the way,'' Mrs. Gomez added, ''I understand the best time to buy a new car is at the end of the summer. Dealers want to make space for the new models coming out in the fall.''

''This means a markdown of the selling price to attract buyers,'' Manuel said.

DEVELOPING SKILLS

OBJECTIVE   To find selling price, gross profit, and net profit

Find the selling price.

Selling price = cost + markup

MODELS   Cost: $35.50   Markup: $22.95   Cost: $16   Margin: 25%
Selling price = cost + markup   25% of $16 = $4.00
= $35.50 + $22.95   Selling price = $16 + 4
= $58.45   = $20

1. Cost: $53.44   Markup: $20.55   **2.** Cost: $48.20   Margin: $14.79

3. Cost: $96   Margin: 50%   **4.** Cost: $72   Markup: 40%

Find the sale price. Use sale price = selling price − markdown.

5. Selling price: $100   Markdown: $24.50   **6.** Selling price: $299.99   Markdown: $55.99

7. Selling price: $250   Markdown: 20%   **8.** Selling price: $48   Markdown: 25%

Find the gross profit.

Gross profit = selling price − cost

9. Selling price: $32.50   **10.** Selling price: $12.75
Cost: $25.00   Cost: $7.60

Find the net profit.

Net profit = gross profit − expenses

MODELS   Selling price   Cost   Expenses   Selling Price   Cost   Expenses
$75 $50 $15 $25 $18   30% of cost
$75 $25 $25   30% of $18 = $5.40
− 50   − 15   − 18   Expenses—↑
$25 ← Gross profit $10 ← Net profit $ 7 ← Gross profit
$7 − $5.40 = $1.60←Net profit

	Selling Price	Cost	Expenses		Selling Price	Cost	Expenses
11.	$12,000	$8,000	$2,500	**12.**	$21,460	$15,200	$3,800
13.	$15.50	$10.50	30% of cost	**14.**	$11.88	$9.00	25% of cost

APPLYING SKILLS

Copy and complete.

	Selling Price	Cost	Gross Profit	Expenses	Net Profit
1.	$1.50	$.90		$.35	
2.	$7.50	5.25		1.75	
3.		3.00		1.50	$1.00
4.		6.85	$3.40		1.50
5.	15.00		10.00	7.50	

	Selling Price	Cost	Gross Profit	Expenses	Net Profit
6.	$6.50	$4.00		$1.50	
7.	9.75	7.25		1.95	
8.		2.50		1.00	$.50
9.		5.95	$2.00		1.00
10.	25.00		7.00	4.50	

Solve these problems.

11. A sweater that cost a retailer $14.50 has a 20% markup. What is the selling price?

12. A pair of shoes that cost $22 has a 25% markup. What is the selling price?

13. A suit that was selling for $56 was marked down 15%. What was the sale price?

14. A couch that was selling for $159.95 was marked down 20%. What was the sale price?

15. A bathing suit cost retailer Willie Johnson $10. He sold it for $16. His expenses were 40% of the cost. What was his gross profit? What was his net profit?

16. A watch cost jeweler Myra Carlsen $32. She sold it for $48. Her expenses were 30% of the cost. What was her gross profit? What was her net profit?

17. Ray Duncon sold $12,000 worth of merchandise. The total cost of this merchandise was $6,700. Operating expenses amounted to $3,400. What was his gross profit? What was his net profit?

18. Leslie Kerns sold $16,350 worth of merchandise. The total cost of this merchandise was $9,400. Operating expenses amounted to $5,500. What was her gross profit? What was her net profit?

19. Zelda sold a dress that cost her $16 for $24. Her expenses were 25% of the cost. What was the net profit on the sale?

20. Zane sold a shirt that cost him $9 for $15. His expenses were 50% of the cost. What was the net profit on the sale?

21. A lamp selling for $51 was marked down $33\frac{1}{3}\%$. The lamp cost the dealer $30. What was the gross profit?

22. A calculator selling for $75 was marked down $33\frac{1}{3}\%$. The calculator cost the dealer $40. What was the gross profit?

MAINTAINING SKILLS

Add. [4]

1.	**2.**	**3.**	**4.**	**5.**
361	487	308	491	381
487	891	192	613	216
+946	+978	+653	+184	+341

Make true sentences. [52]

6. 14 m = _____ cm

7. 8.2 km = _____ m

8. 46 mm = _____ cm

9. .82 mm = _____ cm

10. .46 km = _____ m

11. 8.23 m = _____ cm

12. 82 cm = _____ m

13. 14.6 cm = _____ m

14. 46 m = _____ mm

Solve these problems.

15. Mr. Sean's hospital room and board bill is listed
[187] as 20 days at $70 per day. His medical insurance provides coverage for 70 days at $60 per day. How much will it cost the insurance company? How much will it cost Mr. Sean?

16. Mrs. Hall's hospital room and board bill is listed
[187] at 50 days at $65 per day. Her medical insurance provides coverage for 55 days at $70 per day. How much will it cost the insurance company? How much will it cost Mrs. Hall?

17. Jean Thomas' in-hospital expenses were $90 for
[187] blood, $110 for the operating room, $40 for medicine, $2 for phone calls, and $20 for television rental. Her medical insurance plan pays $600 maximum for in-hospital expenses. How much did the insurance company pay?

18. Leroy William's in-hospital expenses were $80
[187] for blood, $125 for the operating room, $50 for medicine and X-rays, and $10 for a telephone in his room. His medical insurance plan pays $450 maximum for in-hospital expenses. How much did the insurance company pay?

19. John needs 382 centimeters of gold braid for a
[52] centennial costume. The braid sells for $2.42 a meter. What will the braid for John's costume cost?

20. Margaret needs 54 centimeters of wire to hang
[52] a picture. The wire sells for 52¢ a meter. How much will 54 centimeters of wire cost?

21. Mr. Estacio's daily coat sales were $464, $843,
[4] $964, $465, and $789. What were his total sales for the week?

22. June Harris' daily income was $48, $55, $47,
[4] $62, and $59. What was her total income for the week?

Consumer Tips‎___

BUYING APPLIANCES

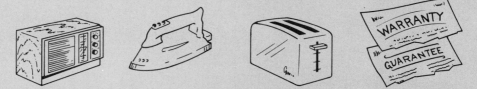

- Consult ratings from consumer and household magazines.
- Buy name brands. Parts are usually easier to get and may often be obtained locally for do-it-yourself repairs.
- Make sure that the appliance has a warranty or guarantee. Study it. Fill it in and return it soon after purchase.
- Check to see that the carton containing the appliance was unopened.
- Check the voltage required by the appliance. If wiring is necessary, contact a reliable electrical contractor.
- Insist that delivery, installation, and warranty be included in the total price.
- Be cautious about "wholesale prices" offered by a retail dealer.
- Comparison shop. Consider repair service as a part of "best buy."
- Read the instruction manual before operating the appliance.
- Ask for facts about the electrical power used by the appliance.

Below are some common appliances. The first number represents the average number of watts of power the appliance requires. The second is an estimate of the number of kilowatt hours of energy used in a year by a consumer.

Appliance	No. of Watts	No. of kwh	Appliance	No. of Watts	No. of kwh
Waterheater	2,475	4,519	Range/Oven	12,200	1,175
Refrig/freezer	326	1,137	TV (color)	200	440
Dishwasher	1,201	363	Iron (hand)	1,008	144
Coffeemaker	894	106	Washing Machine	512	103
Radio	71	86	Toaster	1,146	39

Comparison Shopping

comparison shopping Comparison shopping is a way of determining the best price for similar merchandise selling at several different stores.

competitive product A competitive product is one that is similar in quality and price to other similar items.

unit price Unit price refers to the price of an item in terms of a familiar unit. For example, the unit price of a 4-ounce can of fish selling for 53¢ may be stated as $2.12 per pound.

For Discussion

- What kind of job does Mrs. Kickingbird have?
- How would she comparison shop for the merchandise sold in her store?
- What methods did Carol suggest for comparing prices?

Reading

Ellen Kickingbird has a job as an assistant buyer for the Ortiz Clothing Store. One of the exciting parts of her job is to comparison shop at similar stores in the area.

"There are so many clothing stores in our town," she explained to her husband Chet. "Many of them carry the same type and quality of merchandise. As a result, we must be sure our prices are competitive. If our prices are higher, we'll lose customers. On the other hand, if our prices are too low, we may not have a net income large enough to stay in business."

"It sounds as if you have to find the right combination of quality, price, and service to your customers in order to keep them happy," Chet said.

Their son Frank overheard this conversation and said, "I had a similar problem this afternoon when I went shopping for jam. A 10-ounce jar was priced at 79 cents. Another brand was priced at 89 cents for 12 ounces. I was confused as to which was the better buy."

His sister Carol explained two ways to decide. One way involved comparing the unit prices of the two jars. The other involved writing a proportion to find how much 12 ounces of the first brand would cost.

DEVELOPING SKILLS

Find the unit price to the nearest tenth of a cent.

MODEL   45 g for $.59

Two Ways

$$\begin{array}{r} \$.0133 \\ 45\overline{)\$.5900} \\ \underline{45} \\ 140 \\ \underline{135} \\ 50 \end{array}$$

$$\frac{45}{.59} = \frac{1}{p}$$
$$45\,p = .59$$
$$p = .59 \div 45$$
$$p = .013$$

So, the unit price is about 1.3¢ per gram.

1. 65 g for $.75
2. 12 oz for $.89
3. 3 lb for $2.50
4. 2 kg for $1.75
5. 6.5 lb for $9
6. 8.4 kg for $6.80

Which is the better buy?

MODEL   A 15-oz jar for $1.39 or a 12-oz jar for $.89

Two Ways

Find the unit price of each.

$$\begin{array}{r} \$.0926 \\ 15\overline{)\$1.3900} \\ \underline{1\,35} \\ 40 \\ \underline{30} \\ 100 \end{array} \qquad \begin{array}{r} \$.0741 \\ 12\overline{)\$.8900} \\ \underline{84} \\ 50 \\ \underline{48} \\ 20 \end{array}$$

Find the cost of 12 oz of the 1st brand.

$$\frac{15}{1.39} = \frac{12}{n}$$
$$15\,n = 16.68$$
$$n = 1.112$$

7.4¢ per oz is less than 9.3¢ per oz.
So, the 12-oz jar for $.89 is the better buy.

12 oz of the 1st brand would cost $1.11.
So, the 12-oz jar for $.89 is the better buy.

7. Wafers: 45-g box for $.59
or 65-g box for $.75

8. Fish: 12-oz can for $.55
or 1-lb can for $.61

9. Juice: 6-oz can for $.45
or 10-oz can for $.65

10. Soap: 3 bars for $.89
or 4 bars for $1.15

Which is the best buy?

11. Coffee: .5-kg can for $.95
1-kg can for $1.87
1.5-kg can for $2.79

12. Cheese: 4-oz jar for $.59
8-oz jar for $.79
12-oz jar for $1.40

APPLYING SKILLS

Find the unit price to the nearest tenth of a cent.

1. 8 oz for $3.65

2. 9 oz for $4.29

3. 12 oz for $1.85

4. 15 oz for $2.25

5. 30 g for $12.59

6. 20 g for $16.79

7. 3.5 m for $3.50

8. 2.5 m for $4.65

9. 12.31 for $3.80

Solve these problems.

10. Sharon Callahan sells bananas at 3 pounds for 56 cents. What is the unit price?

11. Rod Galloway sells cherries at 2 pounds for 85 cents. What is the unit price?

12. Don Willoughby sells orange juice in a 6-ounce container for 45 cents. He sells a 10-ounce container for 65 cents. Which is the better buy?

13. Sheila Greenberg sells cream cheese in a 4-ounce package for 59 cents. She sells a 7-ounce package for 89 cents. Which is the better buy?

14. A 2.5-liter container of antifreeze coolant costs $7.44. A 3.5-liter container costs $8.75. Which is the better offer?

15. A 2.5-lb box of candy at Wong's Sweet Shop costs $4.75. A 3.5-lb box of candy costs $5.95. Which is the better offer?

16. Colonel Smithfield's fried chicken is priced at 21 pieces for $8.25. A bucket with 16 pieces sells for $6.85. Which is the better offer?

17. Colonel Blimp's fish and chips is priced at 3 pieces for $1.39. An order of 5 pieces is priced at $1.99. Which is the better offer?

18. A 6-pack of cola sells for $1.19. A comparable 8-pack sells for $1.45. Which is the better offer?

19. Tomato juice is priced at 3 cans for 89 cents. A comparable brand is priced at 4 cans for $1.19. Which is the better offer?

Which is the best offer?

20. 3 meters for $1.25
4 meters for $1.65
5 meters for $1.89

21. 3 ounces for 49¢
6 ounces for 99¢
10 ounces for $1.43

22. 1.5 liters for $3.50
1.8 liters for $4.35
2.2 liters for $5.40

23. 4.5 liters for $2.70
5.2 liters for $3.10
7.3 liters for $4.15

MAINTAINING SKILLS

Find the selling price. [196]

1. Cost: $23.50   Markup: 40%

2. Cost: $16.00   Markup: 45%

Find the gross profit. [196]

3. Selling price: $34   Cost: $24

4. Selling price: $47   Cost: $32

Find the net profit. [196]

	Selling price	Cost	Expenses		Selling price	Cost	Expenses
5.	$14.00	$10.00	30% of cost	**6.**	$22.00	$16.00	25% of cost

Subtract. [9]

7.   48,736
    − 1,483

8.   38,478
    − 3,421

9.   87,467
    − 1,682

10.   37,482
    − 13,874

Make true sentences. [57]

11. 42 ml = _____ ℓ

12. 14.5 ml = _____ ℓ

13. 36 ℓ = _____ kl

14. 1,472 ℓ = _____ kl

15. 48 ℓ = _____ ml

16. 9.6 ℓ = _____ ml

Solve these problems.

17. A sweater that costs $10.50 has a 40% markup. [196] What is the selling price?

18. A pair of skis that costs $30 has a 50% markup. [196] What is the selling price?

19. A bottle of cola holds 78 ml of cola. How many [57] liters of cola does it hold?

20. A cup holds .036 liter of liquid. How many [57] milliliters does it hold?

Copy and complete. Check. [9]

21.

CLOTHING MARKET			
Dept.	Sales	Returns	Net Sales
401	$4,467	$ 482	
403	6,473	1,021	
601	5,093	876	
TOTALS			$13,654

22.

FIVE AND DIME			
Dept.	Sales	Returns	Net Sales
972	$361	$25	
981	496	91	
940	124	13	
TOTALS			$852

Installment Purchases

installment purchase   An installment purchase is a way of buying. The purchaser makes a part payment each week or month until the total price has been paid.

carrying charge   A carrying charge is the additional charge on a long term loan or when buying on the installment plan.

down payment   A down payment is a certain amount that is usually paid at the time the goods or services are purchased on the installment plan.

minor   A minor is a person who has not reached the age of legal responsibility for making business agreements.

For Discussion

- How was Larry planning to get money to pay for his stereo system?
- Why would Mr. or Mrs. Weiser's signature be needed by Larry if he borrows money?

The Weiser brothers were working on a project at home. When Abe heard Larry say he wanted to buy a stereo system for his car, he said, "How do you think we'll be able to afford this?"

"I know," Larry answered. "Even though I have a full-time job lined up for this summer, that money will go for tuition and books. I'll need a loan to pay for the stereo."

"Have you discussed this with anyone yet?" Abe asked.

"Dad and I talked about borrowing from the savings and loan where he and mother have an account," Larry replied. "I'll use the borrowed money to pay the full cash price of the stereo. It means saving the carrying charge I'd have to pay if I buy on the installment plan."

"Remember, Larry, you're a minor. If you borrow money while you are a minor, you'll need an adult's signature," Abe said.

DEVELOPING SKILLS

OBJECTIVE   To determine installment, carrying charge, and total installment price in installment purchases

Find the amount of each installment payment.

MODELS   A used car
Cash price: $600   Down payment: $60
Carrying charge: $45   No. of payments: 10

Cash price	$600
Down payment	$-\ 60$
	$540
Carrying charge	$+\ 45$
Total amount due	$585

$$\text{Amount of payment} = \frac{\text{Total amount due}}{\text{No. of payments}}$$
$$= \frac{\$585}{10}$$
$$= \$58.50$$

So, each payment is $58.50.

A television set
Cash price: $400   Down payment: 15%
Carrying charge: $50   No. of payments: 10

$$15\% \text{ of } \$400 = \text{Down payment}$$
$$\$60 = \text{Down payment}$$

$400	Cash price
$-\ 60$	Down payment
$340	
$+\ 50$	Carrying charge
$390	Total amount due

$$\frac{\$390}{10} = \$39.00$$

So, each payment is $39.00.

1. A stove
Cash price: $375   Down payment: $40
Carrying charge: $25   No. of payments: 8

2. A sofa
Cash price: $300   Down payment: 10%
Carrying charge: $30   No. of payments: 15

Find the total installment price and the carrying charge.

MODEL   A set of luggage for $180 cash or $10.95 down and $12.50 a month for 14 mo

Monthly installment	$ 12.50
Number of payments	$\times 14$
Balance yet due	$175.00
Down payment	$+\ 10.95$
Total installment price	$185.95

Total installment price	$185.95
Cash price	$-\ 180.00$
Carrying charge	$\ \ 5.95$

So, the installment price is $185.95 and the carrying charge is $5.95.

3. A desk for $85.90 cash or $10.00 down and $10.00 a month for 8 mo

4. A radio for $95 cash or $11.00 down and $13.00 a month for 7 mo

5. A coat for $125.40 cash or $40.00 down and $9.00 a month for 11 mo

6. A chair for $150 cash or $35.00 down and $11.00 a month for 12 mo

APPLYING SKILLS

Copy and complete.

	Cash Price	Down Payment	Balance	Carrying Charge	Amt Yet To Pay	Number of Payments	Amt of Payment	Installment Price
1.	$ 229.50	$ 19.50		$ 25.00	$235.00	20		$ 254.50
2.	1,250.00	150.00		64.00		24		1,314.00
3.	750	10%		33.75		18		783.75
4.	675	67.50		20.25	627.75		31.39	
5.	1,350	150.00	1,200			24	52.50	
6.	1,500	10%				30	47.25	
7.	599.88	100.00		24.99		15		
8.	3,000	10%		162.00		36		

Find the total installment price and the amount of each payment.

9. A vacuum cleaner
Cash price: $75   Down payment: 15%
Carrying charge: 6% No. of payments: 12

10. Bedroom suite
Cash price: $456   Down payment: 15%
Carrying charge: 8% No. of payments: 12

11. A set of 15 reference books
Cash price: $10   Down payment: $16.50
per book
Carrying charge: $15 No. of payments: 25

12. A set of 6 gold chrome chairs
Cash price: $300   Down payment: $270
per chair
Carrying charge: $61.20 No. of payments: 30

Solve these problems.

13. Ms. Champ purchased a new carpet.
Terms: $320 cash or $48 down and $16.20 a month for 18 mo. What was the carrying charge?

14. Mr. Ash purchased a diamond ring.
Terms: $550 cash or $160 down and $18.50 a month for 24 mo. What was the carrying charge?

15. A diamond ring was priced at two jewelers.
1st offer: $245 cash or $45 down and 16 payments of $13.50 each.
2nd offer: $245 cash or $15 down and 52 payments of $5 each.
Which is the better installment offer? The cash price is how much less than the better offer?

16. A washer/dryer was priced at two stores.
1st offer: $500 cash or $70 down and 12 payments of $41.25 each.
2nd offer: $500 cash or $70 down and 20 payments of $25.50 each.
Which is the better installment offer? The cash price is how much less than the better offer?

MAINTAINING SKILLS

Multiply. [15]

1. 478
   $\times\,32$

2. 781
   $\times\,41$

3. 361
   $\times\,141$

4. 912
   $\times\,322$

Make true sentences. [63]

5. 46 kg = _____ g

6. 1.6 kg = _____ g

7. 87 g = _____ mg

8. 1.8 g = _____ mg

9. 4,467 g = _____ kg

10. 472 g = _____ kg

Find the unit price to the nearest tenth of a cent. [201]

11. 46 g for 65¢

12. 247 g for 89¢

13. 2 kg for $2.46

14. 4 kg for $1.46

Which is the best buy? [201]

15. Milk: quart for $.45
   half-gallon for $.79
   gallon for $1.69

16. Detergent: 12 oz for $.59
   32 oz for $1.29
   48 oz for $2.09

Solve these problems.

17. A 6-pack of cola sells for $1.08. A comparable
[201] 8-pack sells for $1.35. Which is the better offer?

18. Oranges are priced 3 for $.59 or a package of 10
[201] for $1.98. Which is the better offer?

19. An object in a container is placed on a pan of a
[63] balance. An identical container on the other pan
   is filled with 789 ml of water. What is the weight
   of the object in g?

20. An object in a container is placed on a pan of a
[63] balance. An identical container on the other pan
   is filled with 1,679 ml of water. What is the
   weight of the object in kg?

Find the areas. [15]

21. Length: 42 m
   Width: 37 m

22. Length: 81 cm
   Width: 64 cm

23. Length: 102 cm
   Width: 88 cm

24. Length: 130 mm
   Width: 90 mm

Career/HOME FURNISHINGS

Home furnishing specialists create certain effects through elements of design. These specialists are also called interior decorators and interior designers. As long as there is a desire to combine comfort and beauty, there will continue to be career opportunities in this field. Today interior designers work closely with architects in homes, businesses, and industry.

Job Descriptions

- Home planner—offers decorating services with retail purchases; visits homes to consult with clients.

- Consultant—provides customers in retail stores with advice on one phase of decorating: floor coverings, draperies and upholstery, furniture, or lighting fixtures.

- Display specialist—plans and develops promotion of merchandise for displays within a retail store.

- Buyer—specializes in a particular department of a retail store: draperies, housewares, linen, china, etc.; purchases all merchandise for the department; trains salespeople.

Training

Entry-level jobs are available to some high school graduates with a distributive education background. Many community and junior colleges offer programs. Four-year college programs in design are available.

Further Investigation

Arrange an interview with a home furnishings specialist. Ask about job qualifications, working conditions, possibilities for advancement, entry-level jobs.

Consult your guidance department about distributive education programs in your high school. Also ask for post-high-school courses in this area.

Sales Taxes

levy   To levy is to raise or collect money by government authority.

sales tax   A sales tax is a levy set by a local or state government on many goods and services. It is usually paid by the consumer of items.

excise tax   An excise tax is a levy set by a government on certain articles sold and produced within its own borders.

For Discussion

• Why are sales taxes levied in many states?

• If Charles waits until June to buy his friend a gift, why will it cost more?

• How did Charles find the amount of sales tax without doing any written calculations?

Charles Johnson read the headline in his local newspaper, "Governor Signs 2% Increase in State Sales Tax; New Levy to Take Effect June 1."

"I guess this means just about everything we buy, except food purchased in a grocery store, will become more expensive," he said to his father.

"You're right," Mr. Johnson replied. "If there is any major purchase to be made, we should consider it now, before the increase goes into effect."

"I guess I should buy Ella the graduation gift I want to give her," Charles said. "I've been saving all winter for it. She needs a watch, so I have decided to get her a self-winding, calendar watch. The price at O'Hara's Jewelry Store is $100, plus 5% sales tax, or a total of $105. If I wait until June, it will cost me a couple of dollars more."

"That's a pretty expensive graduation gift," Mr. Johnson said. "Does that mean that you and Ella are going steady, or that you are engaged?"

DEVELOPING SKILLS

Find the sales tax at 4% for each item.

MODEL   A pair of shoes @ $12.95
                        Two Ways

$12.95   1% tax = $.1295   (Decimal point is moved 2
$\times .04$ $\times 4$ places to the left.)
$.5180 = $.52   4% tax = $.5180 = $.52

1. A dress @ $26.00   **2.** A pen @ $.39   **3.** A book @ $7.25

4. A shirt @ $5.99   **5.** A tie @ $1.79   **6.** A wallet @ $6.50

Find the price including 6% excise tax.

MODEL   A used car @ $1,200
                $1,200 $1,200
                $\times .06$ $+\quad 72$
                $72.00 \longleftarrow$ Tax $1,272 \longleftarrow$ Price including tax

7. A brief case @ $15.95   **8.** A watch @ $58.49   **9.** A camera @ $39.90

10. A coat @ $62.50   **11.** A suit @ $90.00   **12.** A hairdryer @ $24.95

Find the price including 3% sales tax and 7% excise tax.

MODEL   A suit @ $172.49

                    1% of $172.49 = $1.7249

        $1.7249 $1.7249
          $\times 3$ $\times 7$
        5.1747 12.0743

                $172.49 \longleftarrow$ Original price
                    5.17 $\longleftarrow$ 3% sales tax
                  12.07 $\longleftarrow$ 7% excise tax
                $189.73 \longleftarrow$ Total price

13. A suitcase @ $24.75   **14.** A diamond ring @ $650   **15.** A record @ $3.99

APPLYING SKILLS

Complete the sales slips.

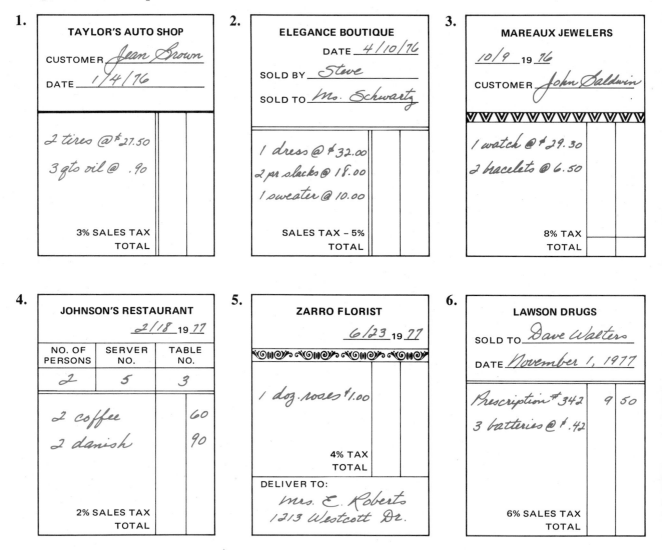

1.

TAYLOR'S AUTO SHOP

CUSTOMER *Jean Brown*

DATE *1/4/76*

2 tires @ $27.50
3 qts oil @ .90

3% SALES TAX
TOTAL

2.

ELEGANCE BOUTIQUE

DATE *4/10/76*

SOLD BY *Steve*

SOLD TO *Ms. Schwartz*

1 dress @ $32.00
2 pr slacks @ 18.00
1 sweater @ 10.00

SALES TAX – 5%
TOTAL

3.

MAREAUX JEWELERS

10/9 19 *76*

CUSTOMER *John Baldwin*

1 watch @ $29.30
2 bracelets @ 6.50

8% TAX
TOTAL

4.

JOHNSON'S RESTAURANT

2/18 19 *77*

NO. OF PERSONS	SERVER NO.	TABLE NO.
2	5	3

2 coffee 60
2 danish 90

2% SALES TAX
TOTAL

5.

ZARRO FLORIST

6/23 19 *77*

1 doz. roses $1.00

4% TAX
TOTAL

DELIVER TO:
Mrs. E. Roberts
1213 Westcott Dr.

6.

LAWSON DRUGS

SOLD TO *Dave Walters*

DATE *November 1, 1977*

Prescription #342   9 50
3 batteries @ $.42

6% SALES TAX
TOTAL

7. Mr. Allen's motel bill cost $16.00 plus 4% state sales tax. How much was he charged?

8. Ms. Bakker's new coat cost $112.00 plus 5% sales tax. How much was she charged?

9. The list price of Goodstore tires is $44.59 each at Sam's Auto Supplies. Sales tax in this area is 3%. How much would 4 tires cost?

10. The list price of Super socks is $1.49 a pair at Betty's Shop. Sales tax in this area is 8%. How much would 3 pairs cost?

MAINTAINING SKILLS

Divide. [19]

1. $48\overline{)18,576}$

2. $72\overline{)22,896}$

3. $41\overline{)17,015}$

4. $96\overline{)77,952}$

Find the interest and amount due on each loan. [138]

5. $1,000 @ 8% for 2 yr

6. $400 @ 7% for 6 mo

7. $1,300 @ $6\frac{1}{2}$% for 3 yr

8. $1,400 @ 8% for $2\frac{1}{2}$ yr

Find the interest and amount due. Use banker's interest. [138]

9. $400 @ 8% for 90 days

10. $1,500 @ 7% for 120 days

11. $500 @ $9\frac{1}{2}$% for 30 days

12. $900 @ $7\frac{1}{2}$% for 60 days

Copy and complete. [205]

	Cash Price	Down Payment	Balance	Carrying Charge	Amt Yet To Pay	No. of Payments	Amt of Payment	Installment Price
13.	$1,000	$100		$150		24		
14.	500	125		65		11		
15.	1,200	15%				18	$69.50	
16.	600	20%				12	47.50	

Solve these problems.

17. Mark Jackson borrowed $500 at 8% for 1 year.
[138] How much interest must be paid?

18. Sarah Black borrowed $700 at 7% for 2 years.
[138] How much interest must be paid?

19. Mr. Barker borrowed $540 from his bank. He
[138] signed a note promising to repay it with 8% interest in 60 days. Find the amount due.

20. Ms. Walker borrowed $1,000 from her bank.
[138] She signed a note promising to repay it with 9% interest in 240 days. Find the amount due.

21. Mrs. Diaz purchased a new desk. The terms
[205] were $250 cash or $35 down and $16.50 a month for 15 months. What was the carrying charge?

22. Mr. Suzuki purchased a new refrigerator. The
[205] terms were $650 cash or $100 down and $26.50 a month for 24 months. What was the carrying charge?

Charge Accounts

consumer   A consumer is the one who finally uses the services or goods produced.

retail   The retail price of goods is the amount paid by the consumer.

charge account   A consumer with a good credit rating may be allowed to open a charge account. A charge account permits a consumer to pay for purchases at a future date, but allows immediate possession and use of the goods.

credit card   A credit card is issued to qualified consumers of goods and services who sign for the purchase and agree to pay within a certain period of time.

For Discussion

- What are the advantages and disadvantages in using credit cards?
- Why would a retail store encourage consumer credit buying?
- How can a store protect itself in the event a customer does not pay what is owed within a reasonable period of time?

Celia and Tom Kelly were shopping at Stear's Department store. Celia said, "I need a new winter coat. They are on sale this week. This one looks very nice on me and is a good buy."

"I think so, too," Tom agreed. "But we must be careful right now. We have already charged several items here this month. The bill will be quite large. When we pay our other charge accounts at the end of this month, we might find ourselves short of funds."

"Wise consumers buy what they need at a price they can afford," Celia said. "I think if we limit our future purchases this month, we'll be able to manage within our budget."

The sales clerk asked Ms. Kelly for her credit card. After checking the account number against a list of charge accounts that had been discontinued, the clerk wrote up the sales slip. Ms. Kelly signed the form.

The clerk then wrapped the package and put a copy of the charge sales slip inside the package. Keeping these copies will help the Kellys to check the accuracy of their bill when it arrives later in the month.

DEVELOPING SKILLS

OBJECTIVE To find the balance due on a charge account statement, including interest charges on unpaid balances

Prepare a charge account statement and find the balance due. There is a $1\frac{1}{2}\%$ monthly interest charge on unpaid balances.

MODEL Account of John and Jane Carey: previous balance $75.98; payment, April 3, $25.00; purchases: April 10, blouses, $19.76; April 17, slacks, $17.95; April 24, shoes, $21.99

JOSEPHSON'S DEPARTMENT STORE					
ACCOUNT OF: JOHN AND JANE CAREY BILLING DATE: 5/1/76					
DATE	DESCRIPTION				AMOUNT
4 10	BLOUSES				19 76
4 17	SLACKS				17 95
4 20	PAYMENT				-25 00
4 24	SHOES				21 99

PREVIOUS BALANCE	PAYMENTS & CREDITS	BALANCE	FINANCE CHARGE	NEW PURCHASES	NEW BALANCE
75 98	25 00	50 98	76	59 70	111 44

PAYMENT MUST REACH US BY 5/25/76

$75.98	Previous balance
− 25.00	Payment
$50.98	Balance
.015	Finance charge rate
$ .76	Finance charge
$19.76	
17.95	
21.99	
$59.70	New purchases
50.98	Balance
.76	Finance charge
$111.44	New Balance

1. Account of Martin Jasper: no previous balance; purchases: April 12, jacket, $35; April 19, shoes, $15.95; April 21, wallet, $7.67

2. Account of Melissa Green: no previous balance; purchases: April 13, blouse, $8.99; April 20, hose, $1.19; April 22, perfume, $8.50

3. Account of Ms. F. Daley: previous balance, $45.79; payment, May 2, $30.00; purchases: May 5, dress, $25.25; May 5, evening gown, $49.12

4. Account of Mr. K. Tanaka: previous balance, $57.05; payment, June 4, $40; purchases: June 9, tennis racket, $18.50; June 9, racket cover, $2.50

5. Account of Jack Micheck: Previous balance, $14.60; payment June 3, $10; purchases: June 11, shirts, $17.99; June 12, slacks, $11.63; June 14, jacket, $44.15

6. Account of Sue Washington: Previous balance $35.32; payment, July 2, $25; purchases: July 3, bathing suit, $29.79; July 5, sunglasses, $6.50

APPLYING SKILLS

Solve these problems. There is a $1\frac{1}{2}\%$ monthly interest charge on unpaid balances.

1. Charles Gary's March balance was $63.74. On April 1, he made a payment of $50.00. During April, he charged these items:
   April 14, socks, $3.12
   April 16, handkerchiefs, $2.78
   April 23, wallet, $10.75
   Find his new balance.

2. Miriam Silver's March balance was $57.60. On April 3, she made a payment of $20.00. During April, she charged these items:
   April 11, handbag, $13.63
   April 20, skirts, $29.37
   April 20, dress, $41.99
   Find her new balance.

3. Gail Sanchez's April balance was $50.25. On May 5, she made a payment of $15.25. During May, she charged these items:
   May 2, shoes, $23.50
   May 9, dresses, $45.21
   On May 11, she returned one of the dresses for a credit of $26.14. Find her new balance.

4. Nick Cummings' April balance was $76.24. On May 6, he made a payment of $56.24. During May he charged these items:
   May 5, shoes, $25.13
   May 23, ties, $11.34
   On May 7, he returned the shoes for a credit of $25.13. Find his new balance.

5. Joe Lemmler's April balance was $25.13. On May 3, he made a payment of $25.13. During May, he charged these items:
   May 4, cologne, $6.78
   May 14, slacks, $25.10
   May 14, shirts, $15.12
   On May 20, he paid $30 on account. Find his new balance.

6. Eve Winn's April balance was $9.75. On May 2, she made a payment of $9.75. During May, she charged these items:
   May 8, hose, $4.19
   May 17, dresses, $35.26
   May 17, shoes, $17.98
   On May 19, she paid $20 on account. Find her new balance.

7. Susan Morton's May balance was $34.19. On June 2, she made a payment of $24.19. During June, she charged these items:
   June 1, skirt, $14.96
   June 1, blouse, $9.42
   June 9, bathing suit, $16.49
   On June 12, she returned the blouse for a credit of $9.42. Find her new balance.

8. Dave Kickingbird's May balance was $74.29. On June 3, he made a payment of $50.00. During June, he charged these items:
   June 3, shirt, $15.32
   June 14, jacket, $25.86
   June 14, boots, $18.13
   On June 15, he returned the jacket for a credit of $25.86. Find his new balance.

MAINTAINING SKILLS

Answer these questions about this promissory note. [143]

$ 2,250.00	Albany, New York May 6 1975

30 days _____ after date _I_ promise to pay

to the order of _Jean Rising Sun_

Two thousand two hundred fifty and 00/100 ———— Dollars

Payable at _Valley Trust Company_

Value received at _8% interest_

No. _538_ Due _June 5, 1975_   _John Sutterfield_

1. Who is the maker of this note?

2. Who is the payee?

3. What is the rate of interest?

4. What is the principal?

5. What is the time of the loan?

6. What is the date of maturity?

Find the time of each note. [143]

7. Date of note: May 1
   Maturity date: June 30

8. Date of note: Oct. 15
   Maturity date: Dec. 13

Find the date of maturity for each note. [143]

9. Date of note: June 5   Time: 45 da

10. Date of note: April 25   Time: 120 da

Solve these problems.

11. Mr. Marshall bought $42.00 worth of mer-
[211] chandise at a gift shop. He had to pay a 5% state sales tax. How much tax was due?

12. Miss Sanders bought a used car for $1,100. She
[211] had to pay a 7% excise tax on the purchase. How much tax did she pay?

13. Jack Harris bought a set of tires for $180. He
[211] had to pay a 4% excise tax and a 5% sales tax. What was the total cost of the tires?

14. Ruth Jackson bought a train ticket to Denver.
[211] The ticket cost $87 plus an 8% excise tax and a 4% sales tax. What was the total cost of the ticket?

15. Julie's test scores were 82, 88, 91, 79, and 85.
[19] What was her average score?

16. Kirk's test scores were 92, 88, 78, 83 and 84.
[19] What was his average score?

Self-Test: Chapter 8

Find the selling price. [196]

1. Cost: $2.50   Markup: $1.00

2. Cost: $36.00   Margin: 45%

Find the gross profit and the net profit. [196]

3. Selling price: $15,000   Cost: $11,000
Expenses: $2,400

4. Selling price: $4.98   Cost: $3.50
Expenses: 30% of cost.

Find the unit price to the nearest tenth of a cent. [201]

5. 10 oz for $.79

6. 480 g for $1.44

Find the amount of each payment. [205]

7. Freezer
Cash price: $395   Down payment: $50
Carrying charge: $70   No. of payments: 10

8. Bedroom furniture
Cash price: $695   Down payment: $90
Carrying charge: $121   No. of payments: 12

Find the total installment price and carrying charge. [205]

9. A trail bike for $350.00 cash or $70 down and
$30 for 11 months.

10. A sofa for $225 cash or $45 down and $14.00
for 15 months.

Find the sales tax at 4% for each item. [211]

11. A book @ $4.95

12. A belt @ $6.50

Find the price including a 5% sales tax. [211]

13. A car @ $2,500

14. A tennis racket @ $17.95

Solve these problems.

15. Salad oil is sold 10 oz for $.75, 24 oz for $1.25,
[201]   or 42 oz for $2.09. Which is the best buy?

16. Laundry detergent is sold 14 oz for $.54, 2 lb
[201]   10 oz for $1.19, or 5 lb for $2.45. Which is the
best buy?

17. Marie Morales' May charge account balance
[215]   was $85.23. On May 5, she paid $25 on her
account. On May 8, she charged a coat for
$69.50. There is a $1\frac{1}{2}\%$ interest charge on her
unpaid balance. Find her new balance.

18. Roger Finley's July charge account balance was
[215] $76.40. On July 5, he paid $20 on his account.
On July 10, he charged a suit for $90. There is
a $1\frac{1}{2}\%$ interest charge on his unpaid balance.
Find his new balance.

Test: Chapter 8

Find the selling price.

1. Cost: $5.00   Markup: $2.00

2. Cost: $24.00   Margin: 40%

Find the gross profit and the net profit.

3. Selling price: $14,000   Cost: $10,000
   Expenses: $3,000

4. Selling price: $8.98   Cost: $4.50
   Expenses: 20% of cost

Find the unit price to the nearest tenth of a cent.

5. 3 lb for $1.05

6. 845 g for $1.69

Find the amount of each payment.

7. Desk
   Cash price: $250   Down payment: $30
   Carrying charges: $14   No. of payments: 6

8. Television
   Cash price: $350   Down payment: $50
   Carrying Charges: $48   No. of payments: 12

Find the total installment price and carrying charge.

9. Carpeting for $420 or $80 down and $39 for 10 months.

10. Chairs for $250 or $40 down and $22 for 11 months.

Find the sales tax at 3% for each item.

11. Shoes @ $14.95

12. A sweater @ $12.98

Find the price including a 4% sales tax.

13. A lamp @ $24.50

14. A plant @ $2.50

Solve these problems.

15. Flour is sold in a 2 lb bag for $.45, 5 lb bag for $.75 or 10 lb bag for $1.53. Which is the best buy?

16. Cola is sold in 32 oz bottles for $.55, 48 oz bottles for $.72, and 69 oz bottles for $.99. Which is the best buy?

17. Mark Wagner's May charge account balance was $64.49. On May 10, he paid $15 on his account. On May 17, he charged a shirt for $12.42. There is a $1\frac{1}{2}\%$ interest charge on his unpaid balance. Find his new balance.

18. Rose Marcus' June charge account balance was $45.10. On June 5, she paid $10.00 on her account. On June 15, she charged a pair of slacks for $18.49. There is a $1\frac{1}{2}\%$ interest charge on her unpaid balance. Find the new balance.

Estimating Temperatures

Estimate the temperature in degrees Fahrenheit. Use the graph.

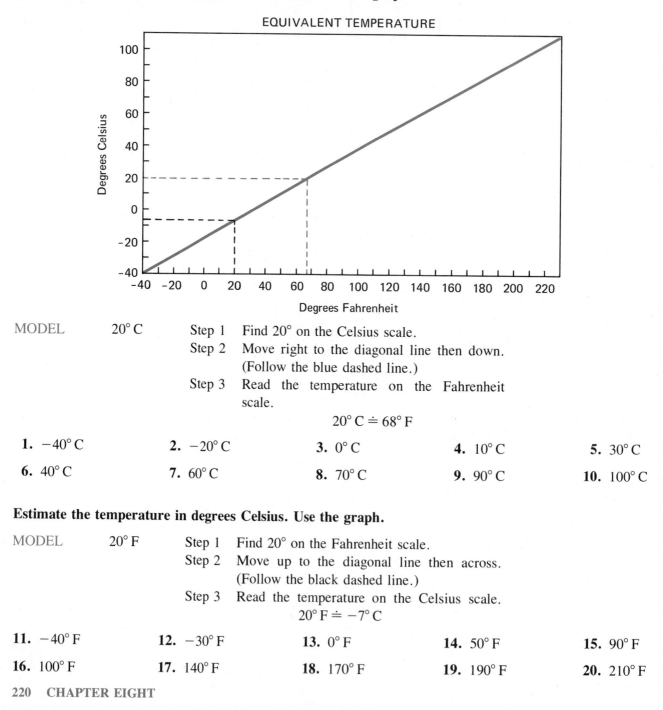

MODEL   20° C   Step 1   Find 20° on the Celsius scale.

                                 Step 2   Move right to the diagonal line then down. (Follow the blue dashed line.)

                                 Step 3   Read the temperature on the Fahrenheit scale.

$$20° \text{ C} \doteq 68° \text{ F}$$

1. $-40°$ C   **2.** $-20°$ C   **3.** 0° C   **4.** 10° C   **5.** 30° C

6. 40° C   **7.** 60° C   **8.** 70° C   **9.** 90° C   **10.** 100° C

Estimate the temperature in degrees Celsius. Use the graph.

MODEL   20° F   Step 1   Find 20° on the Fahrenheit scale.

                                 Step 2   Move up to the diagonal line then across. (Follow the black dashed line.)

                                 Step 3   Read the temperature on the Celsius scale.

$$20° \text{ F} \doteq -7° \text{ C}$$

11. $-40°$ F   **12.** $-30°$ F   **13.** 0° F   **14.** 50° F   **15.** 90° F

16. 100° F   **17.** 140° F   **18.** 170° F   **19.** 190° F   **20.** 210° F

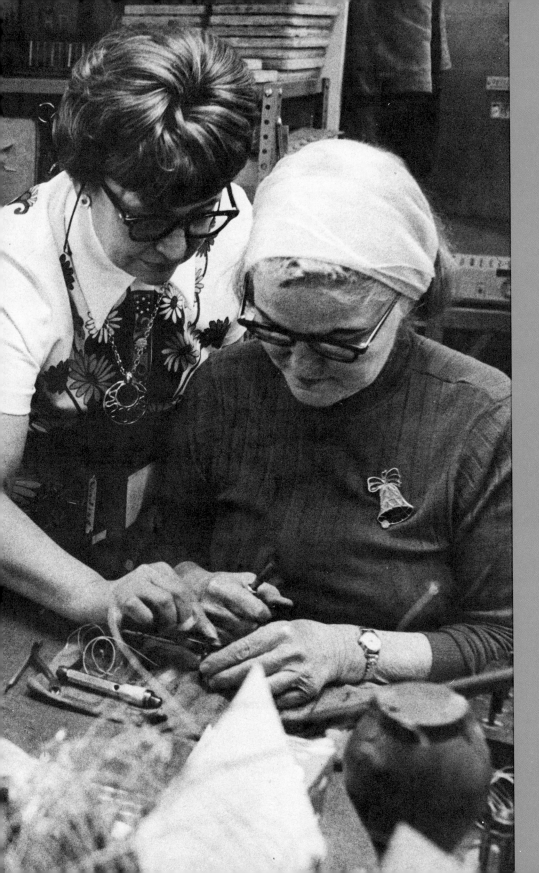

A technician overseeing
the adjustment of a
centrifugal blower

Activities

Copy the puzzle at the right. Unscramble each word, one letter to each box. Then un-scramble the circled letters to form a word to fill the boxes below.

HARGP			○		○
DORRE				○	
TACRH				○	
CERROD			○		

Clue: One who defrauds

Use the yellow pages of your local telephone directory to find the names and telephone numbers of 5 firms handling the following:

1) Blacktop for driveways   2) Home insulation
3) Cesspool or septic tank cleaners

Make a report or bulletin-board display (or both) using some of the references listed below. Many of these references are free. When ordering, be sure to specify the title and item number. Order from Consumer Information, Public Documents Distribution Center, Pueblo, Colorado 81009.

Title	Item Number	Price
Don't Be Gypped	063B	Free
Clothing Repairs	054B	60¢
Clothing and Fabric Care Labeling	053B	Free
Removing Stains from Fabrics	056B	40¢
Quackery	074B	Free
Truth in Lending	075B	Free
How to Conduct a Clean-up Campaign	079B	Free
New Look in Food Labels	086B	Free
Food and Your Money	228B	Free
Brand vs. Generic Drugs	139B	Free
Standards for Meat and Poultry Products	115B	Free

Investigate the terms: F.O.B. Shipping Point and F.O.B. Destination

Trade Discounts

list price   A manufacturer's catalog describes goods for sale and recommends a list price as the amount which the consumer should pay.

trade discount   A trade discount is a reduction in the list price of goods, usually given by the manufacturer to dealers selling the goods.

wholesaler   A wholesaler is a dealer who buys large quantities of goods from a manufacturer. The wholesaler may store the goods, repackage them, and sell them in smaller quantities to other dealers, or in some cases directly to the consumer.

retailer   A retailer is a merchant who buys small quantities of goods from a wholesaler, or possibly the manufacturer, for sale to the final consumer.

invoice   An invoice is a billing statement prepared by the seller of goods.

For Discussion

- Why does the manufacturer offer a wholesaler a trade discount?

- Why is a wholesaler called a *middleman*?

In a window of the Apex Rug and Carpet Company, Cora Wilcox had noticed a sign which read, "Quality Rugs at Discount Prices." She was interested in buying a rug for her children's bedroom, so she went in and was looking through the manufacturer's catalog.

"The rugs you are looking at" said the salesperson, "are selling at a $33\frac{1}{3}\%$ trade discount off the recommended list price."

The salesperson explained that Apex sold directly from its huge warehouse and therefore could save the consumer part of the middleman's markup. Since the retailer is by-passed, the retailer's share of the distribution costs could be saved.

The sale was closed when the salesperson showed Cora this invoice:

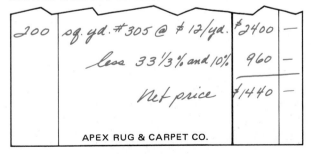

200	sq. yd. #305 @ $12/yd.	$2400	—
	less 33 1/3% and 10%	960	—
	Net price	$1440	—

APEX RUG & CARPET CO.

DEVELOPING SKILLS

Find the invoice price.

MODEL   List price: $360   Discount: $33\frac{1}{3}\%$

$$33\frac{1}{3}\% \text{ of } \$360 = \frac{1}{3} \times 360, \text{ or } 120$$

$$\$360 - \$120 = \$240 \longleftarrow \text{Invoice Price}$$

1. List price: $500
Discount: 40%

2. List price: $1,200
Discount: 30%

3. List price: $1,570
Discount: $33\frac{1}{3}\%$

Find the invoice price.

MODEL   List price: $300   Discounts: 25% and 20%

Step 1   25% of $300 = $75   Step 2   20% of $225 = $45

$300 ←——— List price $225 ←——— Price after 1st discount

− 75 ←——— 1st discount   − 45 ←——— 2nd discount

$225 ←——— Price after 1st discount $180 ←——— Invoice price

4. List price: $500
Discounts: 20% and 25%

5. List price: $1,200
Discounts: $33\frac{1}{3}\%$ and 10%

6. List price: $2,400
Discounts: 20%, 10%, and 5%

Find the single discount that is equivalent to the chain of trade discounts.

MODEL   25% and 20%

Method A   Step 1   Step 2   Step 3

100% ←⎰ List   20% of 75% = .2 × 75%, or 15%   100%

− 25% ⎱ Price   75%   − 60%

75%   −15% ⎰ Part of   40%

60% ←⎱ list price paid

Equivalent single discount ————————↑

Method B   25% + 20% = .25 + .2 = .45 ←——— Sum of discounts

25% × 20% = .25 × .2 = .05 ←——— Product of discounts

.45 − .05 = .40 = 40% ←——— Sum − product

Note: Method B works with 2 discounts only.

7. 20% and 10%   **8.** 25% and $33\frac{1}{3}\%$ **9.** $33\frac{1}{3}\%$ and 10%   **10.** 25%, 20%, and 5%

APPLYING SKILLS

1. The list price for a certain cologne is $1.95 per bottle. A druggist purchased 12 bottles of this cologne. The trade discount was $33\frac{1}{3}\%$. What was the invoice price?

2. The list price for a certain tire is $34.50 per tire. A gasoline station owner purchased 30 tires. The trade discount was $33\frac{1}{3}\%$. What was the invoice price?

3. A manufacturer offers a trade discount of 20% on desks listed at $239.80 each. Beth Schmidt, Inc., purchased 30 desks. What was the invoice price?

4. A wholesaler offers a trade discount of 25% on tables listed at $219.62 each. Rod Harris, Inc., purchased 10 tables. What was the invoice price?

5. Edith Blue Spruce's Sportswear receives a trade discount of 20% less 5% on all purchases. What single discount is equivalent to this chain of discounts?

6. John Carl Mack's Rainwear receives a trade discount of 45% less 10% on all purchases. What single discount is equivalent to this chain of discounts?

7. The W. Ho Company buys books at 20% less 10% less 5%. What single discount is equivalent to this chain of discounts?

8. The Bright Company buys candy at 40% less 30% less 2%. What single discount is equivalent to this chain of discounts?

9. Anita's Supermarket buys meats at 30% less 20%. Anita purchased $12,000 worth of meats. What was the total discount? What was the invoice price?

10. Pete's Sweet Shop buys candy at 40% less 10%. Pete purchased $14,000 worth of candy. What was the total discount? What was the invoice price?

11. Turk, Inc., buys pianos at $33\frac{1}{3}\%$ less 20%. Turk purchased $150,000 worth of pianos. What was the invoice price?

12. Rand, Inc., buys books at $12\frac{1}{2}\%$ less 10%. Rand purchased $240,000 worth of books. What was the invoice price?

13. A stationery company buys paper at 20% less 15% less 5%. What is the invoice price for $10,500 worth of paper?

14. A merchant buys dresses at 30% less 10% less 5%. What is the invoice price for $12,800 worth of dresses?

15. Everwhite toothpaste lists at $.57 per tube. A supermarket can buy the toothpaste at $33\frac{1}{3}\%$ less 15% whenever it buys 200 or more tubes. What is the invoice price for 350 tubes of this toothpaste?

16. Everbrite polish lists at $.69 per tube. A supermarket can buy the polish at 25% less $12\frac{1}{2}\%$ whenever it buys 144 or more tubes. What is the invoice price for 225 tubes of this polish?

MAINTAINING SKILLS

Solve these proportions. [83]

1. $\frac{n}{40} = \frac{1}{4}$

2. $\frac{n}{60} = \frac{3}{5}$

3. $\frac{4}{5} = \frac{60}{n}$

4. $\frac{6}{10} = \frac{36}{n}$

Solve these problems about charge accounts. There is a $1\frac{1}{2}\%$ monthly interest charge on unpaid balances. [215]

5. Mrs. Walker's April balance was $25.97. On May 2, she made a payment of $10.00. During May, she charged these items:
   May 8, blanket, $15.63
   May 17, glasses, $4.98
   May 19, coat, $89.42
   Find her new balance.

6. Mr. Samuels' July balance was $87.96. On August 4, he made a payment of $50.00. During August, he charged these items:
   August 10, slacks, $40.56
   August 19, shirts, $14.72
   August 19, jacket, $49.00
   Find his new balance.

Find the total amount of the deposit. [149]

7. Smith's Dress Shop sent the following bills, coins, and checks to the bank to be deposited:
   14 twenty-dollar bills   8 quarters
   15 ten-dollar bills   15 dimes
   20 five-dollar bills   36 nickels
   Checks: $36.48, $92.51, $32.87

8. Robinson's Shoe Store sent the following bills, coins, and checks to the bank to be deposited:
   11 twenty-dollar bills   12 quarters
   14 ten-dollar bills   36 dimes
   8 five-dollar bills   30 nickels
   Checks: $87.42, $61.92, $25.00

Find the missing entries. [149]

9.
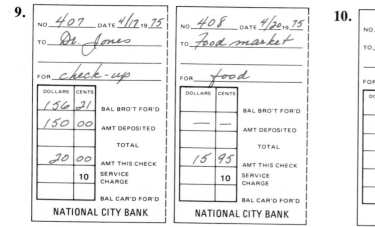

10.
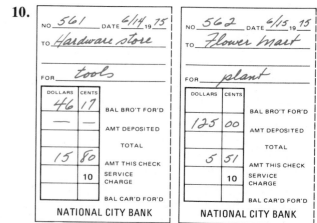

Consumer Tips___

TRAVEL

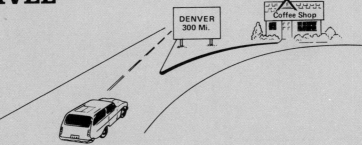

If you wish to plan a vacation trip:

- Use the free tour-planning services of major oil companies.

- Ask for maps showing the most direct route or a scenic route.

- Make hotel and motel reservations in advance. Several large hotel and motel corporations make reservations free of charge.

- Notify friendly neighbors and the police of your trip so that they may look out for your property.

- On the road, drive steadily at a moderate rate of speed.

- Do most of your driving in the early morning or afternoon hours.

- Use budget-motels which do not have special facilities. Their rates are 25% to 50% lower than regular motels.

- Visit historic sights, museums, and lesser known national parks nearby for short, inexpensive trips.

- Contact the chamber of commerce in the places you plan to travel.

- Obtain information about inexpensive motels, hotels, restaurants, and places to see. Get a chambers of commerce list from:
  Chamber of Commerce of the United States
  1615 H. Street, N.W.
  Washington, D.C. 20006.

If you select a travel agent, choose one in good standing with the American Society of Travel Agents.

The Cost of Goods Sold

inventory   An inventory is a listing of all goods on hand with their estimated or actual values.

cost of goods sold   The cost of goods sold is the estimated or actual cost value of merchandise which has been sold.

retail price   The retail price of merchandise is the actual price at which goods are sold to the consumer.

For Discussion

- What job did Theodore have to do after school?
- What information is needed to calculate the gross profit of a business?
- How do you find the cost of goods sold?

Reading

Theodore Baines said to his grandmother, "I'll be home later than usual this afternoon. I'm going to help take inventory at the school store."

"I've noticed signs in store windows advertising inventory sales," she said. "Does this have anything to do with what you'll be doing at school?"

Theodore explained that their store, like most stores, tries to keep the inventory low. Every month an overstocked item is marked down. "Since reducing a price will usually increase sales, the store's gross profit is actually increased," he said. "The purpose of taking an inventory is to find the cost of goods sold." He wrote:

$$\text{Cost of Goods Sold} = \frac{\text{Beginning}}{\text{Inventory}} + \text{Purchases} - \frac{\text{Ending}}{\text{Inventory}}$$

He continued, "Because we take inventory at the end of every year, we start the next year with that amount. We add to that our total purchases to find the value of the goods available for sale. We then deduct the new ending inventory to find the cost of goods sold." He wrote:

Starting inventory Jan. 1	$1,000
Total purchases for year	+ 2,500
Value of goods available for sale	3,500
Ending inventory Dec. 31	− 900
Cost of goods sold	$2,600

"We deduct this cost from the total retail sales to find the amount of gross profit," he said.

DEVELOPING SKILLS

Copy and complete the inventory charts.

MODEL

INVENTORY			
Quantity	Item	Unit Cost	Value
75	Helmets	$10.50	$ 787.50
2	Footballs #413	6.25	12.50
40	Shoulder pads	5.00	200.00
		TOTAL	$1,000.00

Value = Quantity × Unit Cost

1.

Quantity	Item	Unit Cost	Value
78	A Albums	$2.59	
141	B Albums	3.39	
187	C Albums	4.27	
		TOTAL	

2.

Quantity	Item	Unit Cost	Value
6	Record racks	$ 6.01	
5	Hi Fi units #08	50.07	
48	Record disks	.35	
		TOTAL	

Find the cost of goods sold.

MODEL   Starting inventory $1,000   Purchases $2,500   Final inventory $800

Cost of goods sold = starting inventory + purchases − final inventory

$$\begin{array}{r} \$1,000 \\ +\,2,500 \\ \hline 3,500 \\ -\ \ 800 \\ \hline \$2,700 \end{array}$$ ← Value of goods available for sale

← Cost of goods sold

3. Starting inventory: $7,000
Purchases: $12,000
Final inventory: $1,700

4. Starting inventory: $785
Purchases: $12,000
Final inventory: $3,000

5. Starting inventory: $1,300
Purchases: $28,800
Final inventory: $4,500

Find the gross profit.

MODEL   Total retail sales: $15,000   Cost of goods sold: $2,700

$15,000 − $2,700 = $12,300 Gross profit

6. Total retail sales: $38,000
Cost of goods sold: $17,000

7. Total retail sales: $3,000
Cost of goods sold: $1,289

8. Total retail sales: $103,000
Cost of goods sold: $68,000

APPLYING SKILLS

1. Deca Club members of Edison School sell school supplies. They began with $125 worth of supplies and purchased $150 more. At the end of the term, an inventory was taken. Complete the chart.

Item	Quantity	Unit Cost	Value
Pencils #2	54	$.05	
Ball Point Pens	12	.47	
Shorthand Pads	23	.39	
Book Covers	308	.10	
Protractors	14	.31	
Rulers	11	.26	
		TOTAL	

Find the cost of goods sold.
Retail sales amounted to $385.60. Find the gross profit.

2. A neighborhood grocer sells dairy products. The store began with $65 worth of products and purchased $95 more. At the end of the week, an inventory was taken. Complete the chart.

Item	Quantity	Unit Cost	Value
Skim Milk (qt)	11	$.28	
Homogenized Milk			
Quarts	18	.33	
Half Gallons	9	.53	
Buttermilk (qt)	5	.26	
Chocolate (qt)	4	.30	
		TOTAL	

Find the cost of goods sold.
Retail sales amounted to $235.70. Find the gross profit.

3. Lee's Mart wanted to determine how successfully it had been operating. This information was obtained: beginning inventory, $18,000; merchandise purchased, $50,000; final inventory, $15,000; retail sales to date, $75,000. Find the cost of goods sold. What was the gross profit?

4. Catherine Gales wanted to determine how successfully her firm had been operating. She obtained this information: final inventory, $65,114.50; merchandise purchased, $248,968.30; beginning inventory, $42,238.75; retail sales to date, $325,000. Find the cost of goods sold. What was the firm's gross profit?

5. Each item is what percent of the cost of goods sold? (The cost is the compared-to number.)

	Dollars	Percent
Sales	$20,000	$166\frac{2}{3}\%$
Cost of Goods Sold	$-12,000$	100%
Gross Profit	8,000	$66\frac{2}{3}\%$
Operating Expenses	$-6,000$	
Net Profit	$2,000	

6. Each item is what percent of the sales? (The sales is the compared-to number.)

	Dollars	Percent
Sales	$20,000	100%
Cost of Goods Sold	$-12,000$	
Gross Profit	8,000	
Operating Expenses	$-6,000$	
Net Profit	$2,000	

MAINTAINING SKILLS

Find the real lengths of *a*, *b*, and *c*. [105]

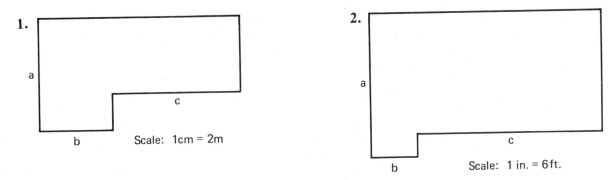

1.

a

c

b

Scale: 1cm = 2m

2.

a

b

c

Scale: 1 in. = 6 ft.

Find the scale lengths for these real lengths. Scale: $\frac{1}{2}$ in. = 6 in. [105]

3. 3 ft 9 in.

4. 4 ft 6 in.

5. 30 in.

Find the single discount that is equivalent to the chain of discounts. [224]

6. 40% and 10%

7. 35% and 20%

8. 25% and 15%

Solve these problems.

9. Hines Sportswear Co. receives a trade discount
[224] of 30% on all purchases. Six suits were purchased at $49.50 each. Find the invoice price.

10. Wong Office Supply Co. receives a trade dis-
[224] count of 35% on all purchases. Ten calculators
were purchased at $79 each. Find the invoice
price.

11. Mike Nichols found that his bank balance on
[153] November 18 was $125.14. His last check stub
showed a balance of $118.04. He found that
the following checks had not been cashed and
returned by the bank: #461, $8.22; #463,
$19.72; and #464, $33.91. A deposit of $52.50
was not shown on the bank statement. The bank
deducted $2.25 for a service charge. Find the
correct available checkbook and bank balance.

12. Jane Reynolds found that her bank balance on
[153] March 4 was $461.63. Her last check stub
showed a balance of $365.09. She found that
the following checks had not been cashed and
returned by the bank: #312, $119.49; #314,
$44.95; and #316, $10.00. A deposit of $75.00
was not shown on the bank statement. The bank
deducted $2.90 for a service charge. Find the
correct available checkbook and bank balance.

Career/INSURANCE

Insurance specialists are employed by more than 1,800 companies in the United States. The idea of life and health insurance has changed from one of financial protection to one of promise for enjoyment of life.

Job Descriptions

- Actuary—gathers and interprets information about people; makes predictions involving long term financial planning using mathematical formulas.

- Insurance agent—convinces the public that insurance coverage is a product that can provide financial security and peace of mind; may require long and unusual hours of work.

- Investment counselor—decides on how premium money can be invested to pay the beneficiaries when policies come due; investigates real estate, business ventures, bonds, mortgages, and stocks as sources of investments.

- Claims adjustor—examines proof of loss; determines the amount of settlement to be made by the insurance company.

Training

Entry-level jobs are available in field and home offices to high school graduates. These are primarily clerical skills jobs. Many two- and four-year colleges prepare insurance specialists in business administration mathematics.

Further Investigation

Arrange an interview with an insurance agent. Ask about job qualifications, working conditions, possibilities for advancement, entry-level jobs.

Consult your guidance department about the possibilities of work experience programs offered in your business education department. Also inquire about post-high-school programs available in your area.

Cash Discounts

cash discount A cash discount is a deduction allowed in an invoice for early payment.

invoice terms The invoice terms refer to the percent cash discount allowed if payment is made within a specific time from the invoice date.

net profit (net income) The net profit or net income is found by deducting the operating expenses of a business from its gross profit or margin.

For Discussion

- What encouragement does one business person give another to pay invoices promptly?
- How does a cash discount affect the net profit of a business?
- How can taking a cash discount give the seller an advantage in pricing goods?

Reading

Ms. Helen Bergman, the owner of a neighborhood business, was speaking to Mr. Cole's distributive education class. She was explaining how a small business could compete with a large one in a major shopping center.

"I realize I must make every dollar work for me and my customers," she told the class. "I must be sure my prices are fair; I can't charge more than my competitors, otherwise I'll lose my customers. One thing I insist on is paying my invoices promptly. Most of our suppliers offer cash discounts. In most cases, our invoice terms allow a 3% cash discount if payment is made within 10 days of the invoice date."

"What happens if you are short of cash and unable to pay within 10 days?" Gail Wheeler, a student in that class, asked.

"The terms usually allow up to 30 days to pay the total invoice price," she replied.

She wrote 3/10 n/30 on the chalkboard and said, "3% discount if paid within 10 days, otherwise the full amount of the invoice is due within 30 days, no discount. Every time I save money on the cost of my purchases I can reduce the selling price charged to my customers. If I can increase my sales and reduce the cost of my purchases, I will end up with more gross profit. And most important to my success, if I can keep my operating expenses down, my final net profit will be higher, too."

DEVELOPING SKILLS

What is the meaning of the invoice terms?

MODEL   2/10, n/30

2/10,   n/30

2%   in   10 days   Amount or net in 30 days

So, 2/10, n/30 means 2% discount if paid within 10 days; otherwise, the full
amount of the invoice is due within 30 days.

1. 3/10, n/30   **2.** 2/15, n/30   **3.** 3/10, 2/20, n/30   **4.** 5/10, 3/30, n/60

Find the last date of payment within the discount period.

MODEL   Date of invoice: May 22   Terms: 2/10, n/30

31 ⟵——— Number of days in May   10 ⟵——— Number of days in period

− 22 ⟵——— Invoice date   − 9

9 ⟵——— Number of days left in May   1 ⟵——— Number of days in June

So, the last date of payment within the discount period is June 1.

Date of Invoice	Terms	Date of Invoice	Terms
5. March 21	2/10, n/30	**6.** April 24	2/15, n/45
7. September 16	1/20, n/30	**8.** January 6	3/10, n/25
9. May 4	3/10, 2/15, n/30	**10.** June 15	5/10, 3/30, n/60

Complete the chart.

	Invoice Price	Terms	Date of Invoice	Date Paid	Number of Days	Cash Discount	Amount Due
	$250	2/10, n/30	May 24	May 31	7	$5	$245
	$250	3/10, n/30	May 2	May 15	13	None	$250
11.	$150	2/10, n/30	August 1	August 6			
12.	$500	1/10, n/30	October 3	October 10			
13.	$300	2/10, n/30	May 1	May 22			
14.	$700	3/10, n/30	June 6	June 20			

APPLYING SKILLS

1. An invoice with terms 2/10, *n*/30 is dated October 30. What is the last date for payment in order to take advantage of the cash discount?

   What is the last date for payment of the full invoice?

2. An invoice with terms 3/15, *n*/60 is dated September 16. What is the last date for payment in order to take advantage of the cash discount?

   What is the last date for payment of the full invoice?

3. An invoice with terms 2/10, 1/20, *n*/30 is dated May 25. What is the last date for payment in order to take advantage of the 2% discount?

   What is the last date for payment in order to take advantage of the 1% discount?

   What is the last date for payment of the full invoice?

4. An invoice with terms 3/10, 1/20, *n*/45 is dated May 28. What is the last date for payment in order to take advantage of the 3% discount?

   What is the last date for payment in order to take advantage of the 1% discount?

   What is the last date for payment of the full invoice?

5. Mitzi Wentz received a bill for $250 with terms 2/10, 1/20, *n*/30. What amount will be due if Mitzi pays on the 10th day? on the 19th day? on the 21st day?

6. Miguel Diaz received a bill for $225 with terms 3/10, 1/20, *n*/60. What amount will be due if Miguel pays on the 5th day? on the 20th day? on the 30th day?

7. Dr. Yelloweyes received an invoice for $176.54 with terms 3/10, *n*/30. The invoice was dated May 22. He paid on June 1. How much did he pay?

8. Dr. Stengel received an invoice for $201.66 with terms 2/15, *n*/45. The invoice was dated March 23. She paid on April 7. How much did she pay?

9. Sharon Toomey received an invoice for $126.44 with terms 1/10, *n*/30. The invoice was dated June 15. She paid on June 27. How much did she pay?

10. Victor Barto received an invoice for $197.38 with terms 3/10, *n*/30. The invoice was dated July 12. He paid on July 24. How much did he pay?

11. Ed Speers received an invoice for $695 with terms 3/10, 1/20, *n*/45. The invoice was dated April 28. He paid on May 9. How much was due?

12. Iris Kline received an invoice for $750 with terms 4/10, 2/20, *n*/30. The invoice was dated May 22. She paid on June 3. How much was due?

MAINTAINING SKILLS

Compute. [119]

1. 40% of 80

2. 13% of 36

3. 36 is what percent of 48?

4. 50 is what percent of 250?

5. 14 is 5% of what number?

6. 90 is 20% of what number?

Find the cost of goods sold and the gross profit. [229]

7. Starting inventory: $7,500
Purchases: $14,000
Final inventory: $6,500
Total retail sales: $24,000

8. Starting inventory: $4,000
Purchases: $12,000
Final inventory: $3,800
Total retail sales: $19,000

Find the amount of money on deposit in each of the following accounts. Use the compound interest table on page 329. [164]

9. $600 for 3 years @ 5% interest compounded semiannually

10. $1,000 for 2 years @ 6% interest compounded quarterly

11. $1,200 for 5 years @ 6% interest compounded semiannually

12. $800 for 6 years @ 5% interest compounded annually

Solve these problems.

13. Which earns the higher interest after 4 years:
[164] $500 @ 4% compounded semiannually, or $500 @ 5% compounded annually?

14. Which earns the higher interest after 6 years:
[164] $1,500 @ 6% compounded semiannually, or $1,500 @ 5% compounded quarterly?

15. Margaret Garcia wanted to determine how suc-
[229] cessfully her business had been operating. She obtained this information: final inventory, $12,146; merchandise purchased, $45,961; beginning inventory, $13,495; retail sales to date, $68,428. Find the cost of goods sold. What was the gross profit?

16. Jim Chan wanted to determine how success-
[229] fully his ice cream store had been operating. He obtained this information: final inventory, $40,500; merchandise purchased, $180,900; beginning inventory $42,000; retail sales to date, $301,500. Find the cost of goods sold. What was the store's gross profit?

Self-Test: Chapter 9

Find the single discount that is equivalent to the chain of discounts. [224]

1. 35% and 10%

2. 30% and 15%

Find the cost of goods sold. [229]

3. Starting inventory: $3,500
Purchases: $36,000
Final inventory: $3,200

4. Starting inventory: $1,500
Purchases: $29,500
Final inventory: $1,650

Find the last date of payment within the discount period. [235]

5. Date of invoice: March 10
Terms: 3/10, *n*/30

6. Date of invoice: July 25
Terms: 4/15, *n*/45

Solve these problems.

7. [224] The list price for a blouse is $9.50 each. A retailer purchased 15 of these blouses. The trade discount was 40%. What was the invoice price?

8. [224] The Sunshine Florist buys plants at 35% less 20%. The florist bought $600 worth of plants. What was the total discount? What was the invoice price?

9. [229] Max Miller wishes to see how successful his business has been operating this year. He obtained this information:

Beginning inventory	$20,000
Merchandise purchased	$60,000
Inventory at present	$21,000
Retail sales to date	$81,000

What was the gross profit?

10. [229] Mary Wang wishes to see how successful her store has been operating this year. She obtained this information:

Beginning inventory	$2,500
Merchandise purchased	$18,000
Inventory at present	$4,000
Retail sales to date	$24,000

What was the gross profit?

Copy and complete. [235]

	Invoice Price	Terms	Date of Invoice	Date Paid	Number of Days	Cash Discount	Amount Due
11.	$400	3/10, *n*/30	May 6	May 18			
12.	$550	4/15, *n*/45	July 8	July 18			

Test: Chapter 9

Find the single discount that is equivalent to the chain of discounts.

1. 30% and 10%

2. 40% and 20%

Find the cost of goods sold.

3. Starting inventory: $4,500
Purchases: $40,000
Final inventory: $4,200

4. Starting inventory: $16,400
Purchases: $180,000
Final inventory: $17,000

Find the last date of payment within the discount period.

5. Date of invoice: April 17
Terms: 5/10, *n*/30

6. Date of invoice: August 18
Terms: 4/15, *n*/45

Solve these problems.

7. The list price for a jar of grape jelly is $.35 a jar. A grocer purchased 30 jars. The trade discount was 35%. What was the invoice price?

8. The Casual Shoe Shop buys shoes at 30% less 15%. The owner bought $1,200 worth of shoes. What was the total discount? What was the invoice price?

9. Sue Thompson wishes to see how successful her business has been operating this year. She obtained this information:

Beginning inventory	$3,000
Merchandise purchased	$30,000
Inventory at present	$3,500
Retail sales to date	$40,500

What was the gross profit?

10. Jack Harris wishes to see how successful his store has been operating this year. He obtained this information:

Beginning inventory	$16,000
Merchandise purchased	$200,000
Inventory at present	$22,000
Retail sales to date	$280,000

What was the gross profit?

Copy and complete.

	Invoice Price	Terms	Date of Invoice	Date Paid	Number of Days	Cash Discount	Amount Due
11.	$600	3/10, *n*/30	Jan. 16	Jan. 21			
12.	$800	4/15, *n*/45	Sept. 8	Sept. 28			

Form 1040A: Using Tax Tables

The Fargo's had an adjusted gross income of less than $10,000. Use their completed tax return as a guide for solving similar problems on pages 265–266.

Short Form 1040A — **U.S. Individual Income Tax Return** — Department of the Treasury Internal Revenue Service — **1974**

Name (If joint return, give first names and initials of both) — JAMES T. & RUTH M. — Last name — FARGO

COUNTY OF RESIDENCE — ALLEN

Your social security number — 136 10 2029

Spouse's social security no. — 135 06 3154

Present home address (Number and street, including apartment number, or rural route) — 147 AVENUE B

City, town or post office, State and ZIP code — OWNTOWN, YOURSTATE — 07646

Occu-pation — Yours ► MAILMAN — Spouse's ► HOMEMAKER

Filing Status (check only one)
1 ☐ Single
2 ☒ Married filing joint return (even if only one had income)
3 ☐ Married filing separately. If spouse is also filing, give spouse's social security number in designated space above and enter full name here ►
4 ☐ Unmarried Head of Household (See instructions on page 5)
5 ☐ Widow(er) with dependent child (Year spouse died ► 19   )

Exemptions — Regular / 65 or over / Blind
6a Yourself . . ☒ ☐ ☐ — Enter number of boxes checked ► 2
b Spouse . . ☒ ☐ ☐
c First names of your dependent children who lived with you — SALLY WILLIAM — Enter number ► 2
d Number of other dependents (from line 26) . . ► 0
7 Total exemptions claimed . . . . ► 4

8 Presidential Election Campaign Fund . . . — Do you wish to designate $1 of your taxes for this fund? . . ☒ Yes / ☐ No — If joint return, does your spouse wish to designate $1? . . ☒ Yes / ☐ No — Note: If you check the "Yes" box(es) it will not increase your tax or reduce your refund.

9 Wages, salaries, tips, and other employee compensation. (Attach Forms W-2. If unavailable, see Instructions on page 3.) . . . — 9 — $9,620 00 ◄ Total earnings from W – 2
10a Dividends (if over $400, use Form 1040—see instructions) $.............. 10b Less Exclusion $............ Balance ► — 10c — -0-
11 Interest income (if over $400, use Form 1040) . . . . — 11 — 270 00 ◄ Interest income
12 Total (add lines 9, 10c, and 11) (Adjusted Gross Income) . . . . . . — 12 — $9,890 00 ◄ Total taxable income

● If you want IRS to figure your tax, skip the rest of this page and see instructions on page 3.
● If line 12 is under $10,000, find tax in Tables 1–12 and enter on line 17, on back. Skip lines 13, 14, 15, and 16.

13 If line 12 is $10,000 or more, enter 15% of line 12 but not more than $2,000 ($1,000 if line 3 checked) . — 13
14 Subtract line 13 from line 12 . . . . — 14
15 Multiply total number of exemptions claimed on line 7 by $750 . . — 15
16 Taxable income (subtract line 15 from line 14) (Figure tax on amount on line 16 using Tax Rate Schedule X, Y, or Z, and enter on line 17, on back.) — 16

Form 1040A (1974) — Page 2

17 Tax, check if from: ☒ Tax Tables 1–12 — OR — ☐ Tax Rate Schedule X, Y, or Z . . — 17 — $885 00 ◄ From tax table
18 Credit for contributions to candidates for public office (see instructions on page 4) . . . . . — 18 — -0-
19 Income tax (subtract line 18 from line 17). If less than zero, enter zero . . — 19 — $885 00
20a Total Federal income tax withheld (attach Forms W-2 to front) . . — 20a — 941 20
b Excess FICA tax withheld (two or more employers—see instructions on page 4) — 20b
c 1974 estimated tax payments (include amount allowed as credit from 1973 return) — 20c

21 Total (add lines 20a, b, and c) . . . . — 21 — $941 20 ◄ Tax withheld from wages
22 If line 19 is larger than line 21, enter BALANCE DUE IRS — Pay in full with return. Write social security number on check or money order and make payable to Internal Revenue Service ► — 22
23 If line 21 is larger than line 19, enter amount OVERPAID . . . . . ► — 23 — 56 20
24 Amount of line 23 to be REFUNDED TO YOU . . . . ► — 24 — $ 56 20
25 Amount of line 23 to be cred-ited on 1975 estimated tax . ► 25 — If all of overpayment (line 23) is to be refunded (line 24), make no entry on line 25.

Other Dependents

(a) NAME	(b) Relationship	(c) Months lived in your home. If born or died during year, write B or D.	(d) Did dependent have income of $750 or more?	(e) Amount YOU furnished for dependent's support. If 100% write ALL.	(f) Amount furnished by OTHERS including dependent.
				$	$

26 Total number of dependents listed in column (a). Enter here and on line 6d . . . . ► 0

Under penalties of perjury, I declare that I have examined this return, including accompanying schedules and statements, and to the best of my knowledge and belief it is true, correct and complete. Declaration of preparer (other than taxpayer) is based on all information of which he has any knowledge.

Sign here ► Your signature — James T. Fargo — Date 3/20/75 — Preparer's signature (other than taxpayer) — Date
► Spouse's signature (if filing jointly, BOTH must sign even if only one had income) — Ruth M. Fargo 3/20/75 — Address (and ZIP Code) — Preparer's Emp. Ident. or Soc. Sec. No.

☆ U.S. GOVERNMENT PRINTING OFFICE : 1974—O-548-290 — 52-07-33-972

Cumulative Review

Find the amount of money on deposit in this account. Use the table on page 329. [164]

1. $600 for 6 yr @ 6% compounded semiannually.

Find the price including a 5% sales tax. [211]

3. A coat at $54.40

Find the total installment price and the carrying charge. [205]

5. A television $350 or $50 down and $33.50 for 10 months.

Make true sentences.

7. 36 km = _____ cm
[53]

8. 64 kl = _____ ℓ
[57]

9. 4.6 g = _____ kg
[63]

Find the last date of payment within discount period. [235]

10. Date of invoice: April 19
Terms: 3/15, n/45

Find the total amount of this deposit. [149]

12.
4 twenty-dollar bills	30 quarters
25 ten-dollar bills	45 dimes
15 five-dollar bills	80 nickels
Checks: $16.80, $152.75, $18.40	

Solve these problems.

14. Jack Brown purchased 10 shares of stock at 42.
[179] The stock pays a semiannual dividends of $2 per share. What is the annual rate of return?

16. Last year Buy Right Food Store had a net profit
[125] of $20,000. This year the profit was $16,000. What was the percent decrease?

Find the selling price and annual interest on these bonds. Par value is $1,000. [169]

2. PAA $5\frac{1}{2}$s, 89

Find the unit price to the nearest tenth of a cent. [201]

4. 12 oz for 65¢

Find the gross profit and the net profit. [196]

6. Selling price: $16,000   Cost: $11,500
Expenses: $2,500

Find the invoice price. [224]

11. List price: $460
Discounts: 20% and 10%

Find the new balance. There is a $1\frac{1}{2}$% interest charge on the unpaid balance. [215]

13.
April balance	$89.50
May 2, payment	$25.00
May 5, coat	$56.40
May 10, sheets	$14.20

15. Janet Kapp's hospital board and room bill is
[187] listed as 45 days at $70 a day. Her insurance provides coverage for 60 days at $50 a day. How much does Janet have to pay?

17. A 60-day note for $550 was signed on Septem-
[138] ber 4. The interest rate was 6%. When is the note due? Find the amount due.

Using Tax Rate Schedules

Ms. Gray Eagle had an adjusted gross income of more than $10,000. Use her completed tax return as a guide for solving similar problems on pages 265–266.

Short Form 1040A **U.S. Individual Income Tax Return** Department of the Treasury Internal Revenue Service **1974**

Name (If joint return, give first names and initials of both)
ELEANOR R.   Last name GRAY EAGLE

COUNTY OF RESIDENCE   WAKE

Your social security number 543 01 1206

Spouse's social security no.

Present home address (Number and street, including apartment number, or rural route)
45 LOUIS STREET

City, town or post office, State and ZIP code
HERTOWN, YOURSTATE   07606

Occupation Yours ► TEACHER   Spouse's ►

Filing Status (check only one)
1 ☒ Single
2 ☐ Married filing joint return (even if only one had income)
3 ☐ Married filing separately. If spouse is also filing, give spouse's social security number in designated space above and enter full name here ►
4 ☐ Unmarried Head of Household (See instructions on page 5)
►
5 ☐ Widow(er) with dependent child (Year spouse died ► 19)

Exemptions Regular / 65 or over / Blind
6a Yourself . . ☒ ☐ ☐   Enter number of boxes checked ► 1
b Spouse . . ☐ ☐ ☐
c First names of your dependent children who lived with you_____
Enter number ► 0
d Number of other dependents (from line 26) . . ► 1
7 Total exemptions claimed . . . . ► 2

8 Presidential Election Campaign Fund . . Do you wish to designate $1 of your taxes for this fund? . . Yes ☐ / No ☒
If joint return, does your spouse wish to designate $1? . . Yes ☐ / No ☐
Note: If you check the "Yes" box(es) it will not increase your tax or reduce your refund.

9 Wages, salaries, tips, and other employee compensation. (Attach Forms W-2. If unavailable, see Form on page 3.) . . . . 9 | $12,800 | 00
10a Dividends (if over $400, use Form 1040—see instructions) $ 275.00 . 10b Less Exclusion $ 100.00 Balance ► 10c | 175 | 00
11 Interest income (if over $400, use Form 1040) . . . . 11 | 400 | 00
12 Total (add lines 9, 10c, and 11) (Adjusted Gross Income) . . . 12 | $13,375 | 00

● If you want IRS to figure your tax, skip the rest of this page and see instructions on page 3.
● If line 12 is under $10,000, find tax in Tables 1–12 and enter on line 17, on back. Skip lines 13, 14, 15, and 16.

13 If line 12 is $10,000 or more, enter 15% of line 12 but not more than $2,000 ($1,000 if line 3 checked) . 13 | $ 2,000 | 00   *◄ 15% of $13,375 is $2,006, so use $2,000*
14 Subtract line 13 from line 12 . . . . 14 | 11,375 | 00
15 Multiply total number of exemptions claimed on line 7 by $750 . . 15 | 1,500 | 00
16 Taxable income (subtract line 15 from line 14) (Figure tax on amount on line 16 using Tax Rate Schedule X, Y, or Z, and enter on line 17, on back.) 16 | 9,875 | 00

Form 1040A (1974)   Page **2**

17 Tax, check if from: ☐ Tax Tables 1–12 OR ☒ Tax Rate Schedule X, Y, or Z . . 17 | $2,059 | 00   *◄ $1,590 + 25% of $1,875*
18 Credit for contributions to candidates for public office (see instructions on page 4) . . . . . 18 | –0–
19 Income tax (subtract line 18 from line 17). If less than zero, enter zero . . . . . 19 | $2,059 | 00
20a Total Federal income tax withheld (attach Forms W-2 to front) . 20a | $1,808 | 00
b Excess FICA tax withheld (two or more employers—see instructions on page 4) . b
c 1974 estimated tax payments (include amount allowed as credit from 1973 return) . c

21 Total (add lines 20a, b, and c) . . . . 21 | $1,808 | 00
22 If line 19 is larger than line 21, enter **BALANCE DUE IRS** Pay in full with return. Write social security number on check or money order and make payable to Internal Revenue Service ► 22 | 251 | 00
23 If line 21 is larger than line 19, enter amount **OVERPAID** . . . . ► 23
24 Amount of line 23 to be **REFUNDED TO YOU** . . . . ► 24
25 Amount of line 23 to be credited on 1975 estimated tax . ► 25   If all of overpayment (line 23) is to be refunded (line 24), make no entry on line 25.

Other Dependents

(a) NAME	(b) Relationship	(c) Months lived in your home. If born or died during year, write B or D.	(d) Did dependent have income of $750 or more?	(e) Amount YOU furnished for dependent's support. If 100% write ALL.	(f) Amount furnished by OTHERS including dependent.
ENID GRAY EAGLE	MOTHER			$ ALL.	$

26 Total number of dependents listed in column (a). Enter here and on line 6d . . . . ► 1

Under penalties of perjury, I declare that I have examined this return, including accompanying schedules and statements, and to the best of my knowledge and belief it is true, correct and complete. Declaration of preparer (other than taxpayer) is based on all information of which he has any knowledge.

Sign here ► *Eleanor R. Gray Eagle 2/21/75*
Your signature   Date

Preparer's signature (other than taxpayer)   Date

Spouse's signature (if filing jointly, BOTH must sign even if only one had income)
☆ U.S. GOVERNMENT PRINTING OFFICE : 1974—O-548-290   52-07-33-972

Address (and ZIP Code)   Preparer's Emp. Ident. or Soc. Sec. No.

INCOME
AND
TAXES

A trucker maneuvering
his load into a depot
loading platform

Activities

You and your friend have jobs that pay $3.00 per hour. Your friend works for a firm which pays time-and-a-half for overtime beyond 40 hours per week. You receive time-and-a-half for overtime beyond 8 hours per day. Last week each of you worked the following hours:

Monday	8 hours	Thursday	9 hours
Tuesday	8 hours	Friday	9 hours
Wednesday	7 hours		

Who earned more? What was the difference in the total wages earned?

Prepare a bulletin-board display on the federal government's income and expenditures. Prepare two circle graphs to show the information. Label the first graph, "Where the Tax Dollar Comes From," and the second graph, "How the Tax Dollar Is Spent."

Form a Personnel Department in your classroom:
1) Set up a committee to act as personnel representatives. This committee will post 3 to 5 ads from firms looking for applicants. The ads should come from your local newspaper want ads and should include the firm name, the salary offered and any other important information.
2) Select one job that interests you as a career. Write a resume to present to the personnel department for an oral interview.
3) Personnel representatives should first review all resumes and then arrange an interview with at least 3 or 4 applicants for a particular job.
4) When an applicant is selected, the interviewer (personnel representative) will prepare an oral report to the class stating the reasons the applicant was or was not chosen for the job.

Hourly Wages

minimum wage   A minimum wage is set by the federal and state governments. It is the lowest legal amount of hourly pay.

regular time   Regular time is the normal working time set by the employer and accepted by the union representing the employees. It is usually expressed as time per day or per week.

overtime   Overtime, or time worked beyond the regular hours, usually results in an employee receiving extra pay, or a bonus.

For Discussion

- What hours will Carol be required to work for her regular time?
- What is the minimum wage in Carol's state?
- How is an overtime rate for an hourly employee calculated?

Reading

"Mr. Reiner, the owner of the local drugstore, has asked me to start working for him next Monday," said Carol Sandman. "He wants me to work from 3 p.m. to 6 p.m. on Mondays, Wednesdays, and Fridays, and from 1 p.m. to 6 p.m. on Saturdays."

"This could turn out to be a full-time or regular 40-hour-week job during the summer," she continued. "A new state law has just increased the minimum wage to $2.20 per hour. My boss pays extra for overtime beyond 40 hours per week. Since other employees will be taking vacations in the summer, I should be able to earn some extra money."

"How can you turn down a job when it sounds as though you'll be getting a raise even before you start working?" her mother asked.

Her brother David asked, "If you work overtime, Carol, how will Mr. Reiner figure the amount of bonus you should receive?"

She explained that the usual overtime rate is time-and-a-half, or one and one-half times the regular hourly wage, for each hour of overtime worked.

Mr. Sandman said, "When I work 42 hours, I am paid for 40 hours at the regular rate and for 2 hours at the overtime rate."

Mrs. Sandman said, "My firm pays overtime beyond 8 hours per day. If I work 10 hours one day, I am paid for 8 hours at the regular rate and for 2 hours at the overtime rate."

DEVELOPING SKILLS

Find the overtime hourly rate at time-and-a-half.

MODELS

Regular rate: $1.80

$1.80

$\times 1\frac{1}{2}$

.90

1.80

$2.70 Overtime rate

Regular rate: $2.25

$2.25

$\times 1\frac{1}{2}$

$1.12\frac{1}{2}$

2.25

3.37\frac{1}{2}$ Overtime rate

1. $2.20   **2.** $2.10   **3.** $2.40   **4.** $1.90

5. $2.55   **6.** $2.85   **7.** $1.75   **8.** $3.15

Find the total wages earned. Each employee is paid on a 40-hour week basis, with time-and-a-half for overtime.

MODEL

J. Brown: 43 hours @ $2.60

Regular: $40 \times \$2.60 = \$104.00$

Overtime: $3 \times \$3.90 = +\ 11.70$

$115.70 Total earnings

9. C. Karoly: 44 hours @ $2.30   **10.** R. Russo: 41 hours @ $2.05

11. O. Marks: 42 hours @ $2.90   **12.** L. Stiles: 45 hours @ $2.75

Copy and complete the chart. Each employee is paid on an 8-hour day basis, with time-and-a-half for overtime.

MODEL

R. Topp: Regular Time, $8 + 8 + 8 + 7 + 8 = 39$ hours

Overtime, 2 hours

Regular pay, $39 \times \$2.90 = \$113.10$

Overtime pay, $2 \times \$4.35 = +\ 8.70$

$121.80 Total earnings

	Name	Hours Worked					Rate	Wages Earned		
		M	T	W	T	F		Regular	Overtime	Total
	R. Topp	8	8	9	7	9	$2.90	$113.10	$8.70	$121.80
13.	L. Levi	7	7	9	9	9	2.56			
14.	T. Ring	6	8	8	9	8	2.24			
15.	V. Nabb	9	9	9	4	9	3.30			
16.	F. Carr	10	8	8	7	9	2.70			

APPLYING SKILLS

1. Max Hartley worked 43 hours last week. He earns $2.90 per hour for a 40-hour week, with time-and-a-half for overtime. Find his total earnings for last week.

2. June Foley worked 47 hours last week. She earns $2.70 per hour for a 40-hour week, with time-and-a-half for overtime. Find her total earnings for last week.

3. The employees of Small and Butterfield, Inc., work on a 40-hour week basis, with time-and-a-half for overtime. For the week ending May 29, Alice Simpson worked 42 hours; Gregg Case worked 45 hours. Find the total wages earned by each employee if their hourly rates are $3.70 and $3.40 respectively.

4. The employees of Artistic Lighting, Inc., work on a 40-hour week basis, with time-and-a-half for overtime. For the week ending January 4, Eve Newton worked 43 hours; Jack Camden worked 42 hours. Find the total wages earned by each employee if their hourly rates are $4.20 and $4.50 respectively.

5. The waitresses at the Holsum Diner work an 8-hour day, with time-and-a-half for overtime. One week, Mary Cortina worked the following hours: Monday, $8\frac{1}{2}$; Tuesday, 9; Wednesday, 7; Thursday, 10; Saturday, 9. Find her total wages if she earns $2.70 per hour.

6. The waiters at the Waverly Road Inn work an 8-hour day, with time-and-a-half for overtime. One week, Jerry Silver worked the following hours: Monday, 7; Tuesday, $7\frac{1}{2}$; Wednesday, 9; Thursday, 9; Friday, 10. Find his total wages if he earns $2.50 per hour.

7. Joe Black Feather worked the following hours last week: Monday, 8; Tuesday, $8\frac{1}{2}$; Wednesday, $9\frac{1}{2}$; Thursday, 9; Friday, 8. He earns $2.85 per hour for an 8-hour day, with time-and-a-half for overtime. Find his gross earnings for the week.

8. Sharon Jeffries worked the following hours last week: Monday, 9; Tuesday, $8\frac{1}{2}$; Wednesday, $7\frac{1}{2}$; Thursday, 10; Friday, 10. She earns $2.75 per hour for an 8-hour day, with time-and-a-half for overtime. Find her gross pay for the week.

9. Mario Spinelli worked 7 hours on Monday, 9 hours on Tuesday, 8 hours on Wednesday, 9 hours on Thursday, and $7\frac{1}{2}$ hours on Friday. He earns $5.20 per hour for an 8-hour day, with time-and-a-half for overtime. Find his total earnings.

10. Diane Robinson worked 8 hours on Monday, 7 hours on Tuesday, 9 hours on Wednesday, 8 hours on Thursday, and $9\frac{1}{2}$ hours on Friday. She earns $5.00 an hour for an 8-hour day, with time-and-a-half for overtime. Find her total earnings.

MAINTAINING SKILLS

Find the last date of payment within the discount period. [235]

	Date of Invoice	Terms		Date of Invoice	Terms
1.	February 13	4/10, *n*/30	**2.**	May 8	3/15, *n*/30
3.	April 20	3/15, *n*/45	**4.**	November 15	2/20, *n*/45

Find the selling price and annual interest on these bonds. Par value is $1,000. [169]

5. Am Co 7s, 115

6. Ex Con 4s, 92

7. Nat Con 8s, 87

8. Stan Am 6s, 78

Solve these problems.

9. During one month, the Walker Equipment Co. [125] had 1,400 employees. The following month it had 1,540 employees. Find the percent increase.

10. The average salary of employees at Harris [125] and William Tool, Inc., went from $9,500 to $10,260. Find the percent increase.

11. The cost of a new family size car in January was [125] $3,500. In September, the same car cost $3,150. What was the percent decrease in cost?

12. In 1974 the Goldberg Employment Agency had [125] a profit of $12,000. In 1975 the profit was $11,400. What was the percent decrease in profit?

13. Doris Williams received an invoice for $250 [235] with terms 2/10, *n*/45. The invoice was dated August 27. She paid on Sept. 8. How much did she pay?

14. Earl Jones received an invoice for $130.00 with [235] terms 4/10, *n*/60. The invoice was dated July 8. He paid on July 16. How much did he pay?

15. Ruth White received a bill for $300 with terms [235] 3/10, 2/30, *n*/60. What amount will be due if she pays on the 9th day? on the 29th day? on the 60th day?

16. John Wilson received a bill for $750 with terms [235] 4/10, 1/30, *n*/45. What amount will be due if he pays on the 5th day? on the 15th day? on the 31st day?

17. Ms. Chin wishes to purchase three $500 Stan [169] Li bonds. They are quoted at $94\frac{1}{2}$. Find the market price of these bonds.

18. Mr. Lopez wishes to buy six $1,000 Am Con [169] bonds. They are quoted at $77\frac{1}{4}$. Find the market value.

Consumer Tips____

SOCIAL SECURITY

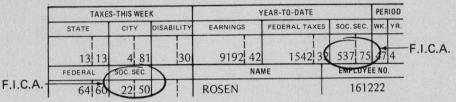

TAXES-THIS WEEK			YEAR-TO-DATE			PERIOD	
STATE	CITY	DISABILITY	EARNINGS	FEDERAL TAXES	SOC. SEC.	WK.	YR.
13 13	4 81	30	9192 42	1542 39	537 75	27 4

F.I.C.A.

FEDERAL	SOC. SEC.		NAME	EMPLOYEE NO.
64 60	22 50		ROSEN	161222

F.I.C.A.

You may be interested in reading the pamphlet, "Social Security Information for Young Families." This may be obtained from your local social security office. (See your telephone directory.)

Social security is financed through equal contributions by you and your employer. The deduction is noted in your salary check as F.I.C.A. (Federal Insurance Contributions Act). It is more commonly known as social security tax. The base on which employers and employees contribute has a maximum. For each year that you earn the maximum credited to social security, you receive a full year of social security credit. The number of credits earned is very important in determining eligibility for benefits.

There are 3 types of benefits paid by social security:

- retirement – available, if eligible, to men at age 65 and women at age 62. Men may retire at 62 with reduced benefits.

- disability insurance – available, if eligible, to a worker and family if his or her physical or mental condition does not allow a substantial work load.

- survivors – available, if eligible, to the widow or widower, and certain family members.

There is also health insurance paid under Medicare for persons 65 or older. All the benefits depend upon two types of eligibility, fully insured and currently insured. A person may learn his or her eligibility by visiting the local social security office. The amount of benefit is based on a person's average earnings covered by social security.

Piece-rate Wages and Commissions

piece-rate   An employee who is paid according to the number of units of work produced is paid on a piece-rate basis.

incentive   Any employee who produces more may be paid more per piece as an incentive to increase input.

commission   Many employees, particularly salespeople, are paid a certain percent of the dollar value of sales as their commission. The commission might also be a certain amount for each item sold.

For Discussion

- If an employee is paid on a piece-rate basis, what incentive does the employee have?

- If an employee is paid on a piece-rate or a commission basis, does the number of hours worked determine in any way the amount of income earned?

- How might a salesperson increase his or her total weekly or monthly income?

Demetria Pappas was discussing her new job at the Jessup Shirt Company. She sews cuffs on shirts.

"The job gets a bit boring, but we do have music, and we do a lot of talking to make it more interesting. However, the more shirts that I complete the more I can earn."

Her husband, George, asked, "What is your pay setup?"

She answered, "I get 7.5 cents for each shirt that is accepted by the inspector. I completed 220 shirts yesterday, and once I get used to the work, I should be able to complete 250 or 275 shirts per day. My supervisor says that the union is discussing an incentive plan. It is proposing 8 cents per piece if an employee completes 250 acceptable shirts per day and 9 cents for 300 per day."

George said, "That plan would be similar to the way I am paid as a salesman. I receive a regular salary plus a commission. The more I sell, the higher my weekly salary. My base salary is $100 per week. In addition to this, I get 3% on all sales and 4% on all sales over $2,000."

DEVELOPING SKILLS

Copy and complete the charts. Each employee is paid on a piece-rate basis.

MODEL   F. Jackson: 18 units @ $1.25

$1.25 \times 18 = $22.50 \longleftarrow$ Total wages

	Name	Units Completed	Rate Per Unit	Total Wages
	F. Jackson	18	$1.25	$22.50
1.	L. Taylor	44	1.50	
2.	S. Clark	36	2.25	
3.	J. Martino	27	3.50	
4.	M. Forest	28	2.75	

	Name	Units Completed Each Day					Total Units Completed Each Week	Rate Per Unit	Total Wages
		M	T	W	T	F			
5.	T. Mudd	8	7	9	8	6		$1.50	
6.	G. Webb	9	9	10	9	7		1.75	
7.	J. Ness	8	10	11	9	8		1.60	
8.	V. Giles	9	9	6	12	10		1.85	

Copy and complete the chart. Each employee is paid on a commission basis.

MODEL   N. Tucker: $500 sales, $50 weekly salary, 5% commission

$500 \times .05 = 25 Commission

$\underline{+ 50}$ Salary

$75 Total wages

	Name	Weekly Sales	Weekly Salary	Rate of Commission	Total Wages
	N. Tucker	$ 500	$50	5%	$75
9.	H. Kriss	1,200	100	2%	
10.	M. Soong	1,400	65	3%	
11.	R. Morgan	7,500	70	4%	
12.	M. Tyler	1,800	80	8%	

APPLYING SKILLS

Find the total weekly or monthly wages for each of the following salespersons.

MODEL   Paula Cravins receives a $75 weekly salary plus a 2% commission on all sales. In addition, she is paid a 3% commission on sales in excess of $2,500. Last week she sold $3,000 worth of merchandise.

$$\$3,000 \times .02 = \$60$$
$$(3,000 - 2,500) \longrightarrow 500 \times .03 = \underline{+15}$$
$$\$75 \text{ Commission}$$
$$\underline{+75} \text{ Salary}$$
$$\$150 \text{ Total wages}$$

1. Kenneth Lee earns a $50 weekly salary, plus 3% commission on all sales, plus a 4% commission on sales in excess of $2,000. Last week, his sales amounted to $2,500.

2. Kim Wong earns a $60 weekly salary, plus 2% commission on all sales, plus a 3% commission on sales in excess of $2,000. Last week, her sales amounted to $3,000.

3. Carol Scheiber earns a $65 weekly salary plus a 3% commission on sales in excess of $5,000. Last week, her sales amounted to $6,782.30.

4. Ross Mancini earns a $75 weekly salary plus a 4% commission on sales in excess of $3,000. Last week, his sales amounted to $4,445.90.

5. Molly Taylor receives a $70 weekly salary plus a $2\frac{1}{2}\%$ commission on sales in excess of $2,750. Last week, her sales amounted to $4,000.

6. Robert Shaw receives an $80 weekly salary plus a $3\frac{1}{2}\%$ commission on sales in excess of $3,250. Last week, his sales amounted to $5,000.

7. Jack Kutcher is paid a $350 monthly salary, plus a 3% commission on all sales, plus a 4% commission on sales in excess of $7,500. Last month, his sales amounted to $9,000.

8. Marilyn Smith is paid a $300 monthly salary, plus a 4% commission on all sales, plus a 5% commission on sales in excess of $6,000. Last month, her sales amounted to $7,600.

9. Bill Maris is paid the following commissions:
    2% on sales up to $3,000
    3% on sales over $3,000 up to $5,000
    4% on sales over $5,000
Last month, his sales amounted to $6,800.

10. Marion Roth is paid the following commissions:
    3% on sales up to $2,000
    4% on sales over $2,000 up to $4,000
    5% on sales over $4,000
Last month, her sales amounted to $5,200.

11. Jane Price is paid $.40 per unit of completed work on the first 200 units and $.50 on each additional unit of work. Last week, she completed 248 units.

12. Tom Long Arrow is paid $.50 per unit of completed work on the first 250 units and $.60 on each additional unit of work. Last week, he completed 316 units.

MAINTAINING SKILLS

Copy and complete this chart. Each employee is paid on an 8-hour day basis, with time-and-a-half for overtime.   [246]

	Employee Number	Hours Worked					Rate	Wages Earned		
		M	T	W	T	F		Regular	Overtime	Total
1.	8461	$8\frac{1}{2}$	9	8	$8\frac{1}{2}$	8	$2.70			
2.	8732	9	8	$8\frac{1}{2}$	$9\frac{1}{2}$	8	2.90			
3.	6812	8	$7\frac{1}{2}$	8	$9\frac{1}{2}$	9	3.00			
4.	8312	8	—	$9\frac{1}{2}$	$9\frac{1}{2}$	10	2.40			

Find the amount spent on each item.   [129]

5. Yearly net income: $9,500

Item	Percent
Food	20%
Housing	25%
Clothing	18%
Transportation	12%
Insurance and savings	15%
Recreation	10%

6. Monthly net income: $600

Item	Percent
Food	25%
Housing	30%
Clothing	18%
Transportation	10%
Insurance and savings	10%
Recreation	7%

Find the cost of these stocks, including brokerage fee.   [173]

7. 40 shares of Telex Co. @ $2\frac{7}{8}$
Brokerage fee: $7.96

8. 100 shares Reed Tool @ $17\frac{5}{8}$
Brokerage fee: $41.47

9. 75 shares SherryR @ $28\frac{1}{8}$
Brokerage fee: $44.45

10. 50 shares TexasInd @ $9\frac{3}{4}$
Brokerage fee: $16.81

Find the dividends earned on the following stock holdings.   [173]

No. of Shares	Stocks and Dividends in Dollars		No. of Shares	Stocks and Dividends in Dollars
11. 50	ReyInd 2.88		**12.** 200	Telcor .25
13. 150	TexETr 1.70		**14.** 75	Walgreen 1

Social Security Taxes and Benefits

workmen's compensation Workmen's compensation laws require employers to carry insurance for their employees to provide payments in case of accident or death as a result of their employment.

disability benefits Disability benefits are payable if a worker has a physical or mental condition which prevents the worker from earning a living. Such condition may be expected to last at least 12 months or result in death.

F.I.C.A. The initials F.I.C.A. stand for Federal Insurance Contributions Act, more commonly known as *social security*.

unemployment compensation Unemployment compensation is required by federal and state laws. In most states this is paid by the employers only. Payments are made to eligible employees who have lost their jobs.

For Discussion

- May a student be eligible for any benefits?

- What is the age limitation for a student who may be receiving social security benefits?

Kim and Hiro Tekagi live with their widowed mother. Kim attends the local high school. Hiro, who is 20 years old, is a full-time student at a local college. Mr. Tekagi died last year as a result of an accident on the job.

Mrs. Tekagi is grateful that her husband's firm was covered by workmen's compensation laws. These laws required the firm to carry insurance to pay employee disability benefits in such cases. Because her husband was fully covered, she and the children received weekly checks while her husband was hospitalized. Since his death, they have collected monthly social security benefit checks.

"Even though I am working part time now," she explained to her children, "I will continue to receive these checks until Kim has completed all of her schooling or until she is 22 years old."

"What happens after that?" Hiro asked.

"By then I should be able to take care of myself. When I reach the age of 60, I will be eligible for a widow's pension again. If I lose my present job, I will be eligible for unemployment compensation. This could last several weeks or until I can find another job."

DEVELOPING SKILLS

Find the annual amount of the F.I.C.A. payment. The F.I.C.A. rate is 5.85% on a $14,100 base maximum.

MODEL

$13,600		$15,500	
↓		↓	
$13,600	Wages	$14,100	Maximum base wage
×.0585		×.0585	
$795.60	F.I.C.A. deduction	$824.85	F.I.C.A. deduction

1. $14,050   **2.** $12,500   **3.** $11,050   **4.** $9,720   **5.** $15,480

6. $12,300   **7.** $13,800   **8.** $10,040   **9.** $8,550   **10.** $16,020

Find the weekly deduction for F.I.C.A. Use the table on page 332.

MODEL $161.23
$161.23 is at least $161.12 but less than $161.29
So, tax to be withheld is $9.43

11. $94.70   **12.** $105.65   **13.** $139.00   **14.** $204.10   **15.** $249.42

Find the monthly cash benefit payment for each of the following cases. Use the table on page 333.

MODEL   Widowed mother and one child; husband's average yearly income was
$8,600 at the time of death.

$8,600 is between $8,000 and $9,000
$590.40 $9,000 entry in table
−558.40 $8,000 entry in table
$ 32.00
× .6 $600 / $1,000
$ 19.20
+558.40 $8,000 entry
$577.60 Monthly cash benefit

16. Disabled worker, average yearly income was $7,500.

17. Disabled worker, average yearly income was was $5,700.

APPLYING SKILLS

Solve these problems. Use 5.85% as the F.I.C.A. rate on a $14,100 annual base maximum.

1. Maude Driscoll earned $9,200 last year, $8,500 the year before, and $7,900 the year before that. What was her F.I.C.A. contribution for those three years?

2. Ed Roberts earned $8,900 last year, $8,450 the year before, and $8,000 the year before that. What was his F.I.C.A. contribution for those three years?

3. Jim Baumgartner's earnings for the last three years were $15,800, $14,500, and $13,200. Find his total F.I.C.A. contribution.

4. Emily Clifford's earnings for the last three years were $15,500, $15,000, and $14,500. Find her total F.I.C.A. contribution.

Solve these problems. Use the F.I.C.A. weekly deduction schedule on page 332.

5. Marie Vitale's weekly salary was $192.52. Last week, she received a salary increase. Her gross pay is now $216.14. Find the increase in her F.I.C.A. deduction.

6. Don Morton's weekly salary was $215.32. Last week, he received a salary increase. His gross pay is now $248.73. Find the increase in his F.I.C.A. deduction.

Solve these problems. Use the social security monthly cash benefit schedule on page 333.

MODEL — Disabled worker with one child, average yearly income was $6,800. Find the total family payment.

For $6,000:
$299.40 Disabled worker
+ 149.70 One child
$449.10 Total cash benefit

For $7,000:
$335.50 Disabled worker
+ 167.80 One child
$503.30 Total cash benefit

$503.30 Cash benefit for $7,000
− 449.10 Cash benefit for $6,000
$ 54.20

$ 54.20 × .8 $\frac{\$800}{\$1,000}$
$ 43.36
+ 449.10
$492.46 Cash benefit for $6,800

7. Harold Gray, age 52, is disabled. His wife is under 65 and they have one child, age 17. Mr. Gray's average yearly earnings were $7,600. What is their total monthly benefit payment?

8. Bert Kulik, age 60, is disabled. His wife is under 65 and they have two children, ages 16 and 24. Mr. Kulik's average yearly earnings were $8,100. What is their total monthly benefit payment?

MAINTAINING SKILLS

Add. [33]

1.	4.873	**2.**	9.67	**3.**	146.832	**4.**	42.46
	57.82		21.872		4.896		188.42
	+ 56.837		+ 3.891		+ 51.832		+ 19.672

Find the annual rate of return. Round answers to the nearest .1%. [179]

5. A 6s, $500 bond @ 88

6. A 7s, $1,000 bond @ 79

7. A 7s, $1,000 bond @ 85

8. A 5s, $500 bond @ 92

Solve these problems. [251]

9. Walt Little Crow earns $60 a week plus commission. He earns a 5% commission on all sales. Last week his sales totaled $2,800. How much did he earn last week?

10. Eiko Inoue earns $30 a week plus commission. She earns an 8% commission on all sales. Her sales totaled $1,875 for one week. How much did she earn that week?

11. Linda Kerns is paid $.40 per unit of completed work. For each additional unit over 220, she earns $.50 per unit. Last week she completed 350 units. How much did she earn?

12. David Hines is paid $.60 per unit of completed work. He earns $.80 per unit for each additional unit over 175. Last week he completed 255 units. How much did he earn?

13. Akira Togo is paid the following commissions:
  3% on sales up to $3,000
  4% on sales over $3,000 up to $5,000
  5% on sales over $5,000
Last week his sales amounted to $4,870. How much did he earn?

14. Sally White Eagle is paid the following commissions:
  2% on sales up to $2,000
  3% on sales over $2,000 up to $4,000
  5% on sales over $4,000
Last week her sales amounted to $4,020. How much did she earn?

Solve these problems. Disregard brokerage fees. [179]

15. Miss Olsen purchased a share of stock at 24. The stock pays a semiannual dividend of $2 per share. What is the annual rate of return on this stock?

16. Mr. Crawford purchased a share of stock at 21. The stock pays a semiannual dividend of $1.40 per share. What is the annual rate of return on this stock?

Career/FOOD PRODUCTION

Food production specialists help in the production, processing, and marketing of farm products. Their role is a major occupation in a world where population growth places an ever-increasing demand for food production. Even in the United States, where the number of farms has decreased, the demand for agriculture specialists continues to increase.

Job Descriptions

- Service and supply technician—produces and sells products needed for food production as seed, fertilizer, pesticides, machinery, fuels; assists in research to develop new products and techniques.

- Crop production technician—tests soil, machinery, techniques, to determine efficiency of production programs.

- Farm owner or operator—combines the talents of the technician, manager, and foreman in the operation of the total farm program.

- Processor and distributor—tests, grades, packages, and transports food produced, whether on the farm or in the laboratory.

Training

Entry-level jobs are available to high school students in canneries, freezing plants, packing plants, and farms. Higher level opportunities are open to those who have completed two or four year agriculture programs available in most state universities.

Further Investigation

Arrange a visit to a food production specialist. Ask about job qualifications, working conditions, possibilities for advancement, entry-level jobs.

Consult your guidance department about the agriculture programs in your school, county, or state. Ask about post-high-school programs available in your state university system.

Withholding Taxes and Preparing Payrolls

working papers In most states working papers must be obtained by minors who want jobs.

W-4 form A W-4 form is an employee's withholding certificate indicating how many dependents the employee is claiming.

social security number A social security number, which serves as an identification number, is issued to each worker covered by the F.I.C.A.

withholding taxes Withholding taxes are deductions made by an employer from an employee's wages. They include federal as well as state and local income taxes.

gross income Gross income is the total income earned.

net income Net income is the amount of take-home pay, after all deductions have been made.

For Discussion

- Are all employees covered by the F.I.C.A.?
- What information is shown on a paycheck stub or voucher?
- How may one check the accuracy of one's pay?

Hank Dombrowski started to work after school at S. Lyon's Department Store. He earns $2.25 per hour and works a total of 22 hours each week. Because he was only 17 years old, his employer required that Hank obtain working papers.

"My total wages were $49.50, but my paycheck was made out for only $41.60," Hank told his friend Stanley. "I claimed only one dependent, myself, on the W-4 form that I signed."

"Did you look at your paycheck stub?" Stanley asked. "That should show all of the deductions that were made."

Hank found his check stub and together they looked it over.

Stan explained, "The F.I.C.A. tax is 5.85% of your gross income, up to a maximum of $14,100 this year. The other deductions are for withholding taxes and medical insurance. If you subtract the total deductions from your gross income, you should get $41.60 for your net income."

DEVELOPING SKILLS

OBJECTIVES To determine amounts to be withheld for federal income tax
To find the amount of net income

Find the amount to be withheld for federal income tax. Use the tables on pages 330–331.

MODEL   Single person earning $248.50, claiming one exemption
$248.50 is between $240 and $250 in the table.
The entry in the table for 1 exemption is $43.90.
So, the federal income tax to be withheld is $43.90.

1. Single person earning $208.78, claiming 2 exemptions

2. Married person earning $241.32, claiming 3 exemptions

3. Married person earning $305.10, claiming 1 exemption

4. Single person earning $341.90, claiming no exemptions

5. Single person earning $299.90, claiming 3 exemptions

6. Married person earning $232.48, claiming 6 exemptions

Find the amount of net income. Use the tables on pages 330–332 for federal income tax and F.I.C.A. The state income tax is 1% of the gross income. The medical insurance premium is $1.75 per employee.

MODEL   D. Johnson: $272.48, married, 2 exemptions
$41.80 Federal income tax (from table)
$15.94 F.I.C.A. (from table)

$272.48 Gross income
$\times .01$ State income tax rate
$2.7248 State income tax

$41.80 Federal income tax deduction
15.94 F.I.C.A.
2.72 State income tax deduction
+ 1.75 Medical insurance premium
$62.21 Total deductions
$272.48 − $62.21 = $210.27 Net income

	Employee	Gross Income	Marital Status	Exemptions	Federal Income Tax Deduction	F.I.C.A.	State Income Tax Deduction	Medical Insurance	Net Income
	D. Johnson	$272.48	M	2	$41.80	$15.94	$2.72	$1.75	$210.27
7.	A. Faughey	$137.69	S	1					
8.	C. Vine	$282.35	M	5					
9.	G. Zeller	$116.40	S	3					
10.	M. Evans	$248.70	M	4					

APPLYING SKILLS

**Find the tables on pages 330–332 to determine the federal income tax and
F.I.C.A. deductions. For each problem, also include the taxpayer as a
dependent deduction.**

1. Gary Montemarano, married with 2 dependent children, earned $238.60 last week. His deductions include $2.00 for union dues and $2.40 for medical insurance. His state income tax deduction is 10% of his federal income tax deduction. What is his take-home pay?

2. June McNamara, married with a dependent child, earned $250.00 last week. Her deductions include $10 for U.S. savings bonds and $3.00 for medical insurance. Her state income tax deduction is 7% of her federal income tax deduction. What is her take-home pay?

3. Wilma DeJesu, single with a dependent father, earned $270.99 last week. Her deductions include $6.25 for U.S. savings bonds, union dues of $2.20, and a medical insurance premium of $2.00. Her state income tax deduction is 2% of her gross income. Find her net income.

4. Elmer Harris, single with no dependents, earned $271.35 last week. His deductions include $8.00 for bonds, $5.40 for extended disability coverage, and $3.00 for medical insurance. His state income tax deduction is 1.5% of his gross income. Find his net income.

5. Joe Drake, married with 4 dependents, earned $181.53 last week. His deductions include 5% of his gross income for the employee investment fund and $3.50 for medical insurance. His state does not levy an income tax. Find his net income.

6. Jean Ford, married with 2 dependents, earned $215.41 last week. Her deductions include 4% of her gross income for the employee investment plan and $1.75 for medical insurance. Her state does not levy an income tax. Find her net income.

7. Delia Bunker, married with no dependents, earned $171.48 last week. Her deductions include $5 for the credit union, $1.80 for extended disability coverage, and 3% of her gross pay for state taxes. What was her take-home pay?

8. John Forsythe, married with 5 dependents, earned $182.11 last week. His deductions include $4 in union dues, $2.25 for disability insurance, and 2.5% of his gross pay for state taxes. What was his take-home pay?

Solve these problems.

9. Jerry Fontini, single with no dependents, earns $150.12. How much will his take-home pay be if he claims no exemptions on his W-4 form? How much will his take-home pay be if he declares one exemption?

10. Ellen Chu, married with no dependents, earns $203.89. How much will her take-home pay be if she claims no exemptions on her W-4 form? How much will her take-home pay be if she declares one exemption?

MAINTAINING SKILLS

Subtract. [33]

1. 4.8783
  − .8136

2. 14.7873
  − 8.6491

3. 14.2
  − 1.43

4. 81.5
  − 3.461

Find the annual premium for each policy.
Use the table on page 183. [183]

5. Ten-year term policy for $5,000 issued at age 25

6. Straight-life policy for $12,000 issued at age 30

7. Twenty-year limited payment for $10,000 issued at age 20

8. Thirty-year endowment policy for $8,000 issued at age 40

Find the annual amount of the F.I.C.A. payment. The F.I.C.A. rate is
5.85% on a $14,000 base maximum. [255]

9. $10,110

10. $8,460

11. $11,480

12. $9,550

Find the monthly cash benefit payment for each of the following cases.
Use the table on page 333. [255]

13. Widowed mother and one child, husband's average yearly income was $9,100.

14. Worker disabled at age 55, average yearly income was $8,750.

Solve these problems. Use both tables on page 183. [183]

15. Mrs. Olson took out a $15,000 straight-life insurance policy at age 25. She agreed to pay semiannual premiums. How much were her premiums?

16. Mr. Alexander took out a 30-year endowment policy for $12,000 at age 30. He agreed to pay quarterly premiums. How much were his premiums?

Solve these problems. Use the F.I.C.A. weekly deduction schedule on
page 332. [261]

17. Jan Morgan's weekly salary was $172.50. Last week she received a salary increase. Her gross pay is now $182.64. Find the increase in her F.I.C.A. deduction.

18. Tom Mayer's weekly salary was $181.20. Last week he received a salary increase. His gross pay is now $192.48. Find the increase in his F.I.C.A. deduction.

Federal Income Tax: Standard Deduction

W-2 form   The tax withholding statement, or W-2 form, is completed by an employer to inform an employee of his or her total annual earnings and all taxes withheld for the past year.

income tax return   An income tax return is an official form used by a taxpayer to report all information relating to the computation of the taxpayer's income tax.

standard deduction   A standard deduction provides a reasonable deduction for taxes, medical expenses, interest payments, and charities, and allows taxpayers to use the short form of the income tax return.

exemption   A taxpayer may claim an exemption of $750 for each family member who is legally dependent upon the taxpayer. There are certain limits as to age and degree of relationship to permit the deduction allowed.

taxable income   Taxable income is the amount on which income tax is calculated.

For Discussion

- Is any legal dependent an exemption?
- When does an employee receive a W-2 form?

Alicia Kaplan looked at the W-2 form which she found in her January paycheck envelope. She asked her supervisor, Indira Layne "Do I need to use this form when I make out my income tax returns?"

"Yes," Ms. Layne answered. "You should obtain the proper forms to complete a federal and state income tax returns. One copy of your W-2 form must be attached to each signed tax return. The tax returns should then be mailed to the proper governmental unit."

"Income taxes sound very complicated," Alicia said.

"Actually for a single person such as yourself, all you need to complete is the short form, 1040A, since you have few allowable deductions," said Ms. Layne. "As a matter of fact, the short form allows a standard deduction that might be even more than your itemized amounts. You can use tax tables to find the amount of tax, making it easier to complete this form. The five basic parts of the short form are (1) gross income, (2) exemptions, (3) deductions, (4) taxable income, and (5) income tax. Most state income tax returns are based upon the federal return."

DEVELOPING SKILLS

> **OBJECTIVE** To compute federal income tax, or refund, due using the standard deduction (Form 1040A)

For these taxpayers who earned under $10,000, find the tax due. Use Tables 1–6 on pages 334–335.

MODEL   D. Banks: wages, salaries, and tips, $5,028; dividends, $3 (after the exclusion); interest income, $12; married, filing joint return, claiming 3 exemptions

$5,028 Wages, salaries, tips etc
       3 Dividends
+   12 Interest
$5,043 Adjusted gross income

From Table 3, the tax due is $211.

1. J. Marshall: wages, salaries, tips, $6,942; dividends, $2.10 (after the exclusion); interest income, $6; single, not head of household, claiming 1 exemption

2. E. Thornton: wages, salaries, tips, $9,225; dividends, $5 (after the exclusion); interest income, $20; married, filing joint return, claiming 5 exemptions

3. W. Campbell: wages, salaries, tips, $9,100; dividends, $6.50 (after the exclusion); interest income, $11; married, filing joint return, claiming 2 exemptions

4. T. Clark: wages, salaries, tips, $7,235; dividends, $2 (after the exclusion); interest income, $7.13; single, head of household, claiming 3 exemptions

For these taxpayers who earned $10,000 or over, find the tax due. Use tax rate schedules X, Y, or Z on page 336.

MODEL   V. Lazlow: wages, salaries, tips, $12,500; dividends, $100 (after the exclusion); interest, $150; married, filing joint return, claiming 2 exemptions

$12,500 + $100 + $150 = $12,750   Adjusted gross income (line 12, Form 1040A)
                          $\times$ .15
                        $1,912.50 Standard deduction (line 13, Form 1040A)
$750 $\times$ 2 =   + 1,500   Exemption deduction (line 15, Form 1040A)
                        $3,412.50 Total deductions
$12,750 − $3,412.50 = $9,337.50 Taxable income

From Table Y, tax due = $1,380 + [($9,337.50 − $8,000) $\times$ .22]
                      = $1,380 + ($1,337.50 $\times$ .22)
                      = $1,380 + $294.25
                      = $1,674.25

5. P. Berger: wages, salaries, tips, $11,523; dividends, $15 (after the exclusion); interest income, $40.30; single, not head of household, claiming 1 exemption

6. S. Brown: wages, salaries, tips, $12,500; dividends, $20 (after the exclusion); interest income, $37.05; married, filing joint return, claiming 2 exemptions

APPLYING SKILLS

Solve these problems for taxpayers who earned under $10,000. (Use Tables 1–6 on pages 334–335.)

MODEL   K. Bickel, wages, salaries, tips, $2,875.
interest income, $55.21; single, not head of household, claiming 1
exemption; taxes withheld, $234.50

$2,875.00 ⟵——— Wages
$+$ 55.21 ⟵——— Interest
$2,930.21 ⟵——— Adjusted gross income
From Table 1 on page 334, the tax due is $128.
$234.50 ⟵——— Taxes withheld
$-$ 128.00 ⟵——— Tax due
$106.50 ⟵——— Refund due to K. Bickel

1. James Birch, single, head of household, claims 4 exemptions. He earned $9,050 last year. He received dividends (after the exclusion) amounting to $154. Interest on savings amounted to $58. His W-2 form listed tax withheld of $872.40. What balance is due on his tax, or is he entitled to a refund? If so, how much?

2. Lois Bredhoff, single, not head of household, claims 1 exemption. Her wages amounted to $8,905, and the tax withheld amounted to $1,300. She earned dividends (after the exclusion) of $145, and interest on savings amounted to $52.70. What balance is due on her tax, or is she entitled to a refund? If so, how much?

3. The Smiths, married and filing a joint return, are claiming 3 exemptions. Their income was $9,321. Taxes withheld amounted to $954.20. Find the balance due or the amount of their refund.

4. The Clarks, married and filing a joint return, are claiming 2 exemptions. Their income was $7,297. Taxes withheld amounted to $743.10. Find the balance due or the amount of their refund.

Solve these problems for taxpayers who earned $10,000 or more. (Use tax rate schedules X, Y, or Z on page 336.)

5. Jane and Bob Reilly, married and filing a joint return, are claiming 2 exemptions. Their combined wages were $10,050. They received dividends (after the exclusion) amounting to $154, and $58 in interest on a savings account. Their combined taxes withheld amounted to $1,372.40. What balance is due on their tax, or are they entitled to a refund?

6. Marcia Clayton, single, head of household, is claiming 3 exemptions. Her total wages were $11,500. She received $16.75 in dividends (after the exclusion). One of her savings accounts earned $35 in interest, another earned $12. Her taxes withheld amounted to $1,850.30. What balance is due on her tax, or is she entitled to a refund?

MAINTAINING SKILLS

Multiply. [39]

1. 4.367
×.04

2. 52.03
×.045

3. 587.1
×.081

4. 361.4
×.025

Find the amount to be withheld for federal income tax. Use the table on pages 330–331. [261]

5. Married person earning $305.16, claiming 2 exemptions

6. Single person earning $250.18, claiming 1 exemption

7. Single person earning $238.92, claiming 2 exemptions

8. Married person earning $285.50, claiming 1 exemption

Solve these problems. [187]

9. Jack Arnold's hospital room and board bill is listed as 30 days at $70 per day. His medical insurance provides coverage for 90 days at $60 per day. How much did it cost the insurance company? Jack?

10. Sue Donaldson's hospital room and board bill is listed as 15 days at $75 per day. Her medical insurance provides coverage for 60 days at $65 per day. How much did it cost the insurance company? Sue?

11. Mrs. Howe's hospital bill is $8,900. She has a major medical insurance policy. After she pays a deductible amount of $750, the insurance company pays 80% of the first $5,000, and Mrs. Howe pays 20%. Thereafter, the insurance company pays 100% of the remaining balance. How much does the insurance company pay? Mrs. Howe?

12. Mr. Douglas' hospital bill is $12,500. He has a major medical insurance policy. After he pays a deductible amount of $1,000, the insurance company pays 80% of the first $5,000, and Mr. Douglas pays 20%. Thereafter, the insurance company pays 100% of the remaining balance. How much does the insurance company pay? Mr. Douglas?

Copy and complete this table. Use the tables on pages 330–332 for federal income tax and F.I.C.A. deductions. The state income tax is 1% of gross income. [261]

	Employee	Gross Income	Marital Status	Exemptions	Federal Income Tax Deduction	F.I.C.A.	State Income Tax Deduction	Medical Insurance	Net Income
13.	Caine, R.	$193.42	M	1				$2.75	
14.	Jones, H.	$304.92	M	2				$2.75	
15.	Stone, E.	$215.91	S	2				$1.75	
16.	Wilson, H.	$271.81	S	1				$1.75	

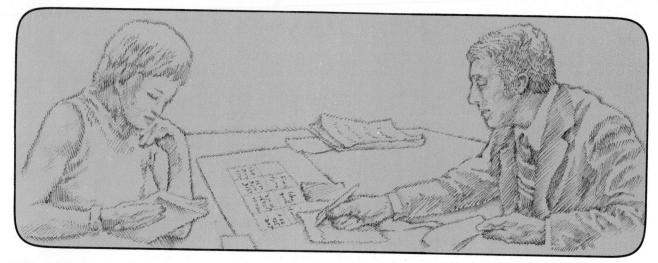

Federal Income Tax: Itemized Deductions

joint tax return A joint tax return may be completed by husband and wife, whether one or both have earned income.

itemized deductions A taxpayer who itemizes deductions to find his or her taxable income must complete income tax form 1040.

tax refund A tax refund is the amount of overpayment, of income taxes in a given year, to which the taxpayer is entitled. The refund may be applied to the payment of the following year's tax.

For Discussion

- What types of expenses may be claimed as deductions by a taxpayer?

- How do large amounts of deductions affect the amount of income tax due?

- Why might a taxpayer claim 0 exemptions when filling out a W-4 form?

Reading

The Walls were getting ready to make out a joint income tax return. They used their W-2 forms to combine similar items.

	Federal Income Tax	Wages Paid	F.I.C.A. Tax	State Income Tax
Mike Marsha	$1,850 1,205	$12,500 8,200	$731.25 479.70	$125 82
TOTAL	$3,055	$20,700	$1,210.95	$207

On their W-4 forms, Mike had claimed two exemptions and Marsha had claimed no exemptions. By doing this, they hoped to cut down the amount of any additional tax which might be due when they made out their tax return. Marsha's mother lives with them and is a dependent of the Walls.

Referring to the instruction booklet, the Walls itemized their allowable deductions:

Medical and dental	$ 245
Taxes (real estate, sales, etc.)	1,807
Interest (mortgage, loans, etc.)	825
Contributions	460
Miscellaneous (union dues, business expenses not reimbursed)	165

DEVELOPING SKILLS

In each case, determine whether the taxpayer should itemize deductions.

MODEL

Greta and Bernard Hausmann have a combined taxable income of $11,630. Their itemized deductions are:

$ 706.12	Medical and dental
1,005.71	Taxes
113.10	Interest expense
150.00	Contributions
+ 50.00	Miscellaneous deductions
$2,024.93	Total itemized deductions

$11,630
× .15
$1,744.50 15% of income

Since the total itemized deductions are greater than 15% of the combined income, the Hausmann's should itemize.

1. Rose and Alex Klein have a total income of $8,750. Their itemized deductions are:

Medical and dental	$365
Taxes	450
Interest expense	432
Contributions	190
Miscellaneous	75

2. Louise and Charles Petraglia have a total income of $9,925. Their itemized deductions are:

Medical and dental	$250
Taxes	175
Interest expense	335
Contributions	265
Miscellaneous	195

For each of these taxpayers who are itemizing deductions, find the total taxable income.

MODEL

J. Callahan: claiming 2 exemptions;

$12,000	Wages
175	Dividends
+ 75	Interest income
$12,250	Total income
− 2,080	
$10,170	
− 1,500	For 2 exemptions (2 × $750)
$ 8,670	Total taxable income

$ 375	Medical and dental expenses
1,280	Taxes paid
245	Interest expense
130	Contributions
+ 50	Miscellaneous
$2,080	Total itemized deductions

	Taxpayer	Exemptions	Wages	Dividends (after exclusion)	Interest income	Medical and dental	Taxes paid	Interest expense	Contri.	Misc. Ded.
3.	S. Paul	3	$13,450	$200	$100	$300	$1,850	$195	$275	$85
4.	P. Roth	2	$14,400	$75	$150	$750	$650	$275	$250	$145

APPLYING SKILLS

Determine whether these taxpayers should itemize their deductions.

1. Joseph Mahoney has a total income of $8,000.
   His allowable deductions are:

Medical & dental	$446
Taxes	223
Interest expense	388
Contributions	229
Miscellaneous	108

2. Belle Jankowitz has a total income of $5,660.
   Her allowable deductions are:

Medical & dental	$295
Taxes	125
Interest expense	95
Contributions	135
Miscellaneous	65

3. Mary Wilson has a total income of $11,700.
   Her allowable deductions are:

Medical & dental	$435
Taxes	115
Interest expense	105
Contributions	235
Miscellaneous	80

4. Jake Matthews has a total income of $7,300.
   His allowable deductions are:

Medical & dental	$525
Taxes	105
Interest expense	150
Contributions	300
Miscellaneous	100

For each of these taxpayers who are itemizing deductions, find the total taxable income.

5. Walter Baines earned $15,600 last year. He received dividend income of $130 and interest income of $57. His allowable deductions were:

Medical & dental	$815
Taxes	1,005
Interest expense	95
Contributions	100
Miscellaneous	50

   For this period, he claimed 4 exemptions.

6. Ellen Dwight earned $14,500 last year. She received dividend income of $250 and interest income of $100. Her allowable deductions were:

Medical & dental	$785
Taxes	640
Interest expense	220
Contributions	260
Miscellaneous	115

   For this period, she claimed 2 exemptions.

7. Laura Williams earned $6,400 last year. Her allowable deductions were:

Medical & dental	$500
Taxes	290
Interest expense	25
Contributions	115
Miscellaneous	175

   For this period, she claimed 1 exemption.

8. Frank Brown earned $7,700 last year. His allowable deductions were:

Medical & dental	$620
Taxes	325
Interest expense	54
Contributions	105
Miscellaneous	85

   For this period, he claimed 1 exemption.

MAINTAINING SKILLS

Divide. [43]

1. $2.3\overline{)2.392}$

2. $4.1\overline{)11.931}$

3. $.42\overline{)1.3188}$

4. $.14\overline{)5.964}$

Find the selling price. [196]

5. Cost: $46.00   Markup: 45%

6. Cost: $150.00   Markup: 46%

Find the net profit. [196]

	Selling Price	Cost	Expenses		Selling Price	Cost	Expenses
7.	$14,500	$10,250	$2,900	**8.**	$22,000	$14,500	$5,500
9.	$15.00	$10.00	$3.00	**10.**	$25.00	$18.00	$4.80

For these taxpayers who earned under $10,000, find the tax due. Use Tables 1–6 on pages 334–335. [265]

11. R. Harris: wages, salaries, tips, $9,162; interest income, $4.50; married, filing joint return, claiming 2 exemptions

12. B. White: wages, salary, tips, $6,965; interest income, $14.00; single, not head of household, claiming 1 exemption

Solve these problems for taxpayers who earned $10,000 or more. Use tax rate schedules X, Y, or Z on page 336. [265]

13. Mr. and Mrs. Johnson, married and filing a joint return, are claiming 3 exemptions. Their combined income last year was $12,052. They received $47 in interest on a savings account. Their combined taxes withheld amounted to $1,356.52. What balance is due on their taxes, or are they entitled to a refund?

14. Mr. and Mrs. Morrison, married and filing a joint return, are claiming 4 exemptions. Their combined income last year was $13,106. They received $12.35 in dividends (after the exclusion). Their combined taxes withheld amounted to $1,587.46. What balance is due on their taxes, or are they entitled to a refund?

Solve these problems. [196]

15. A gallon of paint cost a retailer, Ms. Johnson, $6.00. She sold it for $10. Her expenses were 35% of the cost. What was her gross profit? What was her net profit?

16. A typewriter cost a retailer, Mr. Welsh, $95. He sold it for $135. His expenses were 40% of the cost. What was his gross profit? What was his net profit?

Self-Test: Chapter 10

Solve these problems.

1. George worked 44 hours at $2.56 an hour. His
[246] pay is based on a 40-hour week, with time-and-
a-half for overtime. How much did he earn?

2. Linda expects to earn $11,500 this year. What
[255] will be her annual F.I.C.A. payment? The
F.I.C.A. rate is 5.85% on a $14,100 base max-
imum.

3. What is the total monthly cash benefit payment
[255] for a disabled worker and his small child? His
average yearly income was $8,900. Use the
table on page 333.

4. What is the amount withheld for federal income
[261] tax for a married person earning $364.49,
claiming 4 exemptions. Use the tables on pages
330 and 331.

5. Barry Mills, single with a dependent uncle,
[261] earns $249 a week. His deductions include
$10.00 for U.S. savings bonds and 2% of his
gross income for state income tax. Use the
tables on pages 330–332 for federal income tax
and F.I.C.A. deductions. Find his net income.

6. Donna Blake worked 7 hours on Monday, 9
[246] hours on Tuesday, 8 hours on Wednesday, 9
hours on Thursday, and 8 hours on Friday. She
earns $3.50 per hour for a 8-hour day, with
time-and-a-half for overtime. Find her total
earnings.

7. John Chu earns a 5% commission on all sales.
[251] Last week, his sales amounted to $5,432. How
much did he earn?

8. Betty Smith is paid $.50 per unit of completed
[251] work. Last week, she completed 575 units.
How much did she earn?

9. Mr. and Mrs. Williams have a total income of
[269] $11,462. Their itemized deductions are:

Medical and dental	$250
Taxes	875
Interest expenses	152
Contributions	175
Misc. deductions	80

Should they itemize their deductions when they
file their federal income tax?

10. Jo and Bill Martin have a total income of
[269] $12,046. Their itemized deductions are:

Medical and dental	$ 210
Taxes	1,260
Interest expenses	452
Contributions	125
Misc. deductions	75

They claim 2 exemptions. What is their taxable
income? (Use itemized deductions.)

**For this taxpayer who earned under $10,000, find
the tax due. Use Tables 1–6 on pages 334–335.**
[265]

11. B. Wilson: wages, salary, tips, $7,260; interest
income, $14; single, not head of household,
claiming 1 exemption.

**For this taxpayer who earned over $10,000, find
the tax due. Use schedules X, Y, or Z, on page
336.** [265]

12. S. Gatto: wages, salary, tips, $11,423; divi-
dends (after exclusion), $120; married, filing
joint return, claiming 2 exemptions.

Test: Chapter 10

Solve these problems.

1. Betty worked 45 hours at $2.42 an hour. Her pay is based on a 40-hour week, with time-and-a-half for overtime. How much did she earn?

2. Louis expects to earn $11,200 this year. What will be his annual F.I.C.A. payment? The F.I.C.A. rate is 5.85% on a $14,100 base maximum.

3. What is the total monthly cash benefit payment for a disabled worker and his small child? His average yearly income was $7,800. Use the table on page 333.

4. What is the amount withheld for federal income tax for a married person earning $364.49, claiming 4 exemptions. Use the tables on pages 330 and 331.

5. Ruth Sills, single with 2 dependent nieces, earns $227 a week. Her deductions include 1% of her gross income for state income tax and $3.50 for union dues. Use the tables on pages 330–332 for federal income tax and F.I.C.A. deductions. Find her net income.

6. Curt Pool, worked 8 hours Monday, 9 hours Tuesday, 10 hours Wednesday, 9 hours Thursday, and 8 hours on Friday. He earns $2.70 per hour for an 8-hour day, with time-and-a-half for overtime. Find his total earnings.

7. Sue Gray Eagle earns a 4% commission on all sales. Last week, her sales amounted to $6,425. How much did she earn?

8. Glen Stuart is paid $.60 per unit of completed work. Last week, he completed 490 units. How much did he earn?

9. Mr. and Mrs. Smith have a total income of $10,468. Their itemized deductions are:

Medical and dental	$175
Taxes	750
Interest expenses	94
Contributions	145
Misc. deductions	10

Should they itemize their deductions when they file their federal income tax?

10. Ruby and Joe Harris have a total income of $12,942. Their itemized deductions are:

Medical and dental	$310
Taxes	942
Interest expenses	740
Contributions	210
Misc. deductions	85

They claim 2 exemptions. What is their taxable income? (Use itemized deductions.)

For this taxpayer who earned under $10,000, find the tax due. Use Tables 1–6 on pages 334–335.

11. J. Stein: wages, salary, tips, $8,980; interest income, $140; single not head of household, claiming 2 exemptions.

For this taxpayer who earned over $10,000, find the tax due. Use schedules X, Y, or Z, on page 336.

12. A. Anderson: wages, salary, tips, $10,450; dividends (after exclusion), $110; married, filing joint return, claiming 2 exemptions.

Mode and Median

Find the mode(s) if any.

The mode is the number which occurs most often in a set of data.

MODELS

$1,500			$100		$2,000 ⎫ Occurs
$1,000 ⎫ Occurs		$700	Each	$2,000 ⎭ twice
$1,000 ⎭ twice		$750	occurs	$1,500 ⎫ Occurs
$500 ⎫ Occurs		$800	only	$1,500 ⎭ twice
$500 ⎬ 3		$900	once.	$1,000
$500 ⎭ times		$1,000		$500
Mode: 500		Mode: none		Modes: $2,000 and $1,500

1. $1,800, $1,500, $1,800, $2,400, $1,800, $1,600

2. $800, $900, $10,000, $150, $890, $400

3. $25, $30, $25, $35, $30, $25, $30, $20

4. $6,500, $7,800 $8,100, $7,800, $9,500 $7,800

Find the median salary.

The median is the middle number in a set of data.

MODEL $6,800, $9,300, $10,000, $8,500, $7,200, $6,800, $9,300

$6,800, $6,800
$7,200
$8,500 ⟵ **Middle number, or median**
$9,300, $9,300
$10,000

5. $8,500, $7,800, $7,500, $9,100, $7,900

6. $125, $140, $145, $125, $150, $135, $120

Find the median price.

MODEL   68¢, 93¢, 78¢, 68¢, 72¢, 68¢, 93¢, 80¢

68¢, 68¢, 68¢
2 middle → 72¢
numbers → 78¢
80¢
93¢, 93¢

$$\begin{array}{r} 72 \\ +78 \\ \hline 150 \end{array} \qquad \begin{array}{r} 75 \\ 2\overline{)150} \end{array} \longleftarrow \left\{ \begin{array}{l} \text{Average of middle} \\ \text{numbers} \end{array}\right.$$

So, the median price is 75¢.

7. 80¢, 90¢, 70¢, 80¢, 65¢, 75¢, 60¢, 50¢

8. 32¢, 40¢, 36¢, 35¢, 37¢, 38¢, 39¢, 39¢

9. $100, $200, $500, $600, $300, $100, $400, $600

10. $7,500, $6,500, $6,000, $5,500, $7,500, $5,500

A telephone company
technician working at
a circuit frame

Activities

A large wooden cube, 3 feet on each edge, is first painted red. Then it is sawed into 27 cubes with 1 foot on each edge. How many cubes have 0 red sides? 1 red side? 2 red sides? 3 red sides? 4 red sides? 5 red sides? 6 red sides?

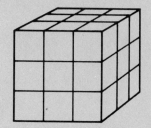

Choose a classmate to make a joint report to the class on the catalytic converter placed on all new cars. Make an enlarged drawing to explain how the converter works. Discuss the advantages and disadvantages of the converter in terms of pollution, burning of gasoline, mileage, etc. Consult automobile consumer and mechanics magazines in your school or local library.

Make a report on the advantages and disadvantages of leasing a car instead of buying. Visit or call local leasing companies to obtain information about this method. Arrange to visit the showrooms of several automobile agencies, different banks, credit unions, etc., and request information on types of car financing.

Make a bulletin board display of the various types of tires—radial, belted, studded, etc.—used on all types of cars. Use newspaper advertisements to illustrate costs. Discuss the various advantages and disadvantages of the tires. Consult automobile, consumer, and mechanics magazines in your school or local library. A catalogue listing the various consumer pamphlets may be obtained from the U.S. Post Office or by writing to Consumer Information, Public Documents Distribution Center, Pueblo, Colorado 81009.

Buying and Financing

end-of-year model End-of-year model refers to a car that has not been sold by the time that the new model cars are coming on the market. For example, a 1976 comes on the market in September 1975 and is an end-of-year model in August 1976.

depreciation Depreciation is the amount of decrease in the value of an article caused by age and wear.

acceleration Acceleration means an increase in speed. For cars, it refers to "pickup."

financing a car Financing a car means a method of paying for a car through installments after a suitable down payment.

For Discussion

- Why did Marta suggest that Karen buy a new car if she planned to keep it a few years?

- What did Marta suggest that Karen do before she buys a car?

"You should consider several things before you buy a new car," said Ms. Marta Griffin to her niece, Karen Wills.

"Aunt Marta, should I buy a new car or an end-of-year model?" Karen asked.

"Well, if you plan to keep a car for a few years, you should buy the new model as soon as it comes out because of the rapid depreciation involved," Marta replied. "Otherwise, buy an end-of-year model."

"What should I do first?" Karen asked.

"Well, Karen, first you should study some automobile and consumer magazines to find out about dimensions, weight and tires, engine and performance, acceleration, braking, and interior noise. You should always test-drive a car before buying."

"And what about financing?"

"There are several ways," Marta replied. "Some dealers will arrange a contract for you with a finance company. However, you can shop around for the best financing. Banks are now offering $10\frac{3}{4}\%$ loans for new cars with a maximum of 36 months if you make a one-third down payment."

DEVELOPING SKILLS

Find the actual cost of the car and the interest charged.

MODEL   Showroom price, $3,000; down payment, $1,000;
36 monthly payments of $73.89

Actual cost = total of payments + down payment
$$= 36 \times \$73.89 \quad + \$1,000$$
$$= \$2,660.04 \quad + \$1,000 = \$3,660.04$$

Interest = actual cost − showroom price
$$= \$3,660.04 - \$3,000 \quad = \$660.04$$

1. Showroom price: $3,300
Down payment: $1,100
24 monthly payments of $119.17

2. Showroom price: $2,000
Down payment: $500
30 monthly payments of $65.00

3. Showroom price: $2,600
Down payment: $400
36 monthly payments of $75.04

4. Showroom price: $5,400
Down payment: $1,500
36 monthly payments of $168.00

Find the amount of each monthly payment.

MODEL   Showroom price, $2,700; down payment, one third of showroom
price; rate of interest, 10%; number of monthly payments, 36

$2,700 ÷ 3 = $900   Amount of down payment

$2,700 − $900 = $1,800   Amount to be financed

$I = p \times r \times t$
$\quad = \$1,800 \times .1 \times 3 = \$540$ Amount of interest

$1,800 + $540 = $2,340   Amount to be repaid

$2,340 ÷ 36 = $65.00   Amount of monthly payment

5. Price, $2,400; $\frac{1}{3}$ down payment;
10% interest; 36 monthly payments

6. Price, $1,500; $\frac{1}{5}$ down payment;
12% interest; 30 monthly payments

7. Price, $3,000; 25% down payment;
9% interest; 24 monthly payments

8. Price, $4,000; 30% down payment;
10% interest; 36 monthly payments

APPLYING SKILLS

1. The price of a subcompact car with accessories is listed as follows: basic car, $2,418; air conditioning, $331; power brakes, $43; tinted glass (all), $36; AM-FM radio, $110; wheel covers, $43; steel belted radial tires, $55. What is the total cost?

2. The price of a compact car with accessories is listed as follows: basic car, $2,805; air conditioning, $341; AM radio, $54; power brakes front disc, $61; power steering, $100; tinted glass (all), $49; wheel covers, forged aluminum, $131. What is the total cost?

3. John learned that an end-of-year model car is now priced at $2,299. It was originally listed at $2,975. How much had the price been reduced?

4. Susan learned that an end-of-year model car is now selling for $1,999. It was originally listed at $2,518. How much had the price been reduced?

5. Jerry bought a car selling for $3,600. After making a $1,200 down payment, he paid off the loan in 36 payments of $86.67 each. How much did the car really cost Jerry?

6. Karen bought a car selling for $2,400. After making an $800 down payment, she paid the loan in 30 payments of $66.67 each. How much did the car really cost Karen?

7. The Fidelity Trust Co. agreed to finance Pedro's new car. The showroom price of the car was $2,658. He had to pay $\frac{1}{3}$ down, 11% interest, and make 36 monthly payments. How much was each monthly payment?

8. The National Bank agreed to finance Karen's new car. The showroom price of the car was $3,144. She had to pay $\frac{1}{3}$ down, 10% interest, and make 30 monthly payments. How much was each monthly payment?

9. Jimmy wants to buy a 5-year-old used car selling for $1,440. For used car financing, he has to pay 20% down, 12% interest, and make 18 monthly payments. How much does Jimmy have to pay down? How much is each monthly payment?

10. Diane wants to buy a 3-year-old used car selling for $2,150. For used car financing, she has to pay 20% down, 12% interest, and make 30 monthly payments. How much does Diane have to pay down? How much is each monthly payment?

11. Henry needs to finance $1,840 after making a suitable down payment on a car. Bank A offered a loan for 36 months at 10%. Bank B offered a loan for 24 months at 12%. Should Henry choose the bank with the lower rate of interest? Prove your answer is correct by showing your calculations.

12. Irma wants to finance $1,600 after making a suitable down payment on a car. Bank X offered a loan for 30 months at 10%. Bank Y offered a loan for 36 months at 11%. Should Irma choose the bank with the lower rate of interest? Prove your answer is correct by showing your calculations.

MAINTAINING SKILLS

Which is the better buy? [201]

1. Cookies: 350-g box for 73¢
or 500-g box for 99¢

2. Shampoo: 10 oz for $.79
or 16 oz for $1.15

3. Apples: 3 for $.59
or 10 for $1.79

4. Soup: 8-oz can for $.25
or 12-oz can for $.39

In each case, determine whether or not the taxpayer should itemize deductions. [269]

5. Bob and Jane Bower have a combined income of $11,468. Their allowable deductions are:

Medical and dental	$246
Taxes	987
Interest expense	552
Contributions	175
Miscellaneous	105

6. Charlotte and Antony Richards have a combined income of $12,495. Their allowable deductions are:

Medical and dental	$ 175
Taxes	1,115
Interest expense	126
Contributions	250
Miscellaneous	75

Solve these problems.

7. [269] Sara and Paul Newburg received wages totaling $15,450, dividend earnings of $210, and interest income of $153. They claim 3 exemptions. Their allowable deductions include: medical and dental expenses, $215; taxes paid, $1,105; interest expense, $583; contributions, $265; and miscellaneous deductions, $80. What is their total taxable income?

8. [269] Irene and Earl Harris received wages totaling $14,875, dividend earnings of $310, and interest income of $115. They claim 4 exemptions. Their allowable deductions include: medical and dental expenses, $295; taxes paid, $935; interest expense, $648; contributions, $250; and miscellaneous deductions, $150. What is their total taxable income?

9. [201] Walter bought an 8-pack of soda for $1.49. Ron bought a 6-pack of the same soda for $1.19. Which purchase was the better buy?

10. [201] Dorothy bought three 6-oz cans of frozen juice for $.68. Shirley bought two 12-oz cans of the same juice for $1.16. Which purchase was the better buy?

11. [201] Barbara found that a store sold pencils 3 for 25¢ or a box of 10 for $1.00. Which was the better buy?

12. [201] Don found that a store sold carbon paper 10 sheets for 15¢ or a pad of 100 for $1.55. Which was the better buy?

Consumer Tips——

CONSERVING GASOLINE

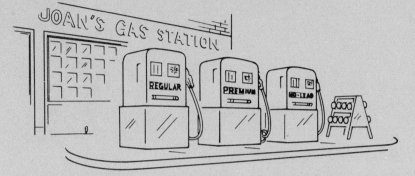

- Have engine tune-ups every 10,000 miles. (An untuned engine loses about 2% to 5% in gas mileage.)

- Don't warm up a cold engine by idling the engine for a long time. (Combustion chambers become loaded with engine deposits, causing misfires and uneven running.) Let a cold engine idle fast for about 10 to 30 sec. Then drive for a few miles at 20 to 30 mph.

- Use gas with the octane rating recommended for your car. Higher octane is wasteful. Lower octane causes engine knock. Continued knocking damages the engine.

- Drive smoothly and at moderate speeds. Drive in the 30-to-40-miles-per-hour range for best gas mileage. Good fuel economy for highway driving can be had by steady driving at 50 miles per hour.

- Avoid excessive speeds, gunning the motor, jiggling the accelerator.

- Don't make ''jack-rabbit'' starts and sudden stops.

- Use radial tires. They save about 5% to 10% on gas mileage.

- Use your air conditioner only when needed.

- Try gas at ''non-brand'' gas stations or at ''gas-and-go'' stations.

- Buy the smallest car that will meet your business and personal needs.

Operating Costs

maintaining a car   Maintaining a car means keeping a car in good repair.

compact car   A compact car is smaller than a full or standard size car, but holds four people in reasonable comfort.

subcompact car   A subcompact car is smaller than a compact car. It usually has two bucket seats and can hold two people in fair comfort.

octane rating   An octane rating is a number that shows the antiknock qualities of the gas. Higher octane ratings show greater antiknock properties.

For Discussion

- Why do you think that a smaller car would be less expensive to maintain?

- What costs were included in the U.S. study of average operating costs per mile?

- What does the U.S. study suggest as a way of saving money?

- Why should Henry avoid rapid acceleration?

''The cost of maintaining a car should be a factor in choosing a car,'' Mr. Thomas said to his son, Henry. ''This latest government report says that the subcompact car has a lower operating cost per mile than the compact or full-sized car. These figures are based on the costs of gas, oil, insurance, depreciation, taxes, and repairs. It also says that you save more by buying the smallest car which is big enough for your needs.''

''That makes sense, Dad. Do you have other tips about cutting down costs?''

''Let's make a list,'' suggested his father.

1. Don't buy gas having an octane rating higher than is needed in your car.
2. Try the gas at independent gas stations where gas is usually cheaper.
3. Drive at moderate speeds to save gas.
4. Avoid ''jack-rabbit'' starts and racing your motor.
5. Brake gradually to save wear on tires.
6. Get written, detailed estimates for repair work to be done at a garage.
7. Learn how to change oil and filters and to replace spark plugs and points.
8. Follow your owner's manual carefully.

DEVELOPING SKILLS

Find the annual operating costs and the cost per mile or kilometer.

MODEL   Pam drove 12,000 miles during the past year. Her operating expenses were: gasoline, oil, and lubrication, $735; repairs and parts, $375; insurance and license, $270; depreciation, $600.

$$\text{Total operating cost} = \$735 + \$375 + \$270 + \$600$$
$$= \$1,980$$

$$\text{Operating costs per mile} = \frac{\$1,980}{12,000 \text{ mi}} = \$.165 \text{ per mile, or } 16.5\text{¢ per mile}$$

	Distance Traveled	Gasoline, Oil and Lubrication	Repairs or Parts	Insurance License	Depreciation
1.	10,600 mi	$460	$ 75	$215	$800
2.	19,200 km	$625	$180	$265	$700
3.	11,500 mi	$574	$176	$240	$700
4.	20,500 km	$525	$167	$228	$750

Find the number of kilometers per liter $\left(\frac{km}{\ell}\right)$ or miles per gallon $\left(\frac{mi}{gal}\right)$.
Then find the cost in cents per kilometer or cents per mile.

MODEL   Bill took a trip of 1,152 km. He used 151.6 liters of gas @ 14¢ per liter.

$$\text{Kilometers per liter} = \frac{1,152 \text{ km}}{151.6 \ \ell} = 7.6 \ \frac{km}{\ell}$$

$$\text{Cost per kilometer} = \frac{\text{cost of entire trip}}{\text{number of kilometers}}$$

$$= \frac{151.6 \times \$.14}{1,152}$$

$$= \frac{\$21.22}{1,152} = \$.018 \text{ per kilometer, or } 1.8\text{¢ per kilometer}$$

5. Ruth took a trip of 1,176 km. She used 132.5 liters of gas @ $.15 per ℓ.

6. Sam takes a trip of 2,400 miles. He uses 125 gallons of gas @ $.53 per gal.

7. Jim took a trip of 600 mi. He used 25 gal of gas @ $.45 per gal.

8. June took a trip of 250 km. She used 40ℓ of gas @ $.16 per ℓ.

APPLYING SKILLS

1. Aaron's car averages 18.6 miles per gallon of gas. His gas tank holds 16 gallons. How far can he expect to go on a full tank of gas?

2. Melinda's car averages 9.8 kilometers per liter of gas. Her gas tank holds 79.5 liters. How far can she expect to go on a full tank of gas?

3. Ann Moss drove her car 12,096 miles last year. She averaged 18 miles per gallon. She paid 52¢ a gallon for gas. How much did she spend on gas last year?

4. Dick Mills drove his car 28,776 kilometers last year. He averaged 6.6 km per liter. He paid 14.3¢ per liter of gas. How much did he spend on gas last year?

5. Terry bought 2 radial tires. Each tire cost $71.95 with a federal tax of $2.97. The cost of aligning the front wheels was $12.95. A 4% state sales tax was figured on the total bill. How much did Terry pay?

6. Grace bought 2 snow tires. Each tire cost $41.50 with a federal tax of $2.25. The cost for aligning the front wheels was $13.95. A 5% sales tax was figured on the total bill. How much did Grace pay?

7. Ellen Jackson drove her car 15,090 miles last year. Her operating expenses were:

1,006 gal of gas @ 52¢ per gal	$523.12
Oil and lubrication	35.50
Repairs and parts	160.00
Insurance, license	190.00
Depreciation	650.00

What were the total operating costs?

Find the operating cost in cents per mile.

8. Gene Kramer drove his car 27,840 km last year. His operating expenses were:

3,572 liters of gas @ 14¢ per liter	$500.08
Oil and lubrication	40.25
Repairs and parts	210.00
Insurance, license	235.00
Depreciation	800.00

What were the total operating costs?

Find the operating cost in cents per km.

9. Charles used 1,152 gallons of gas last year. He is allowed an income tax deduction of 11¢ per gal. How much may he deduct?

10. Mary used 3,274.4 liters of gas last year. She is allowed an income tax deduction of 3.2¢ per liter. How much may she deduct?

11. The odometer before a trip read 27,792 miles. It read 28,636 miles after the trip. 49 gallons of gas were used. Find, to the nearest tenth, the number of miles per gallon.

12. The odometer before a trip read 31,132 km. After the trip it read 31,948 km. 102 liters of gas were used. Find, to the nearest tenth, the number of kilometers per liter.

MAINTAINING SKILLS

Find the amount of each payment (installment). [205]

1. Electric range
   Cash price: $365   Down payment: $40
   Carrying charge: $45   No. of payments: 10

2. Television
   Cash price: $525   Down payment: $75
   Carrying charges: $80   No. of payments: 15

Find the total installment price and the carrying charge. [205]

3. A camera for $86 cash or $10.00 down and $12 for 7 months

4. A piano for $600 cash or $75 down and $34 for 18 months

Find the actual cost of the car and the interest charged. [278]

5. Showroom price: $2,500
   Down payment: $400
   36 monthly payments of $75.83

6. Showroom price: $3,400
   Down payment: $700
   36 monthly payments of $97.50

Solve these problems.

7. The City Savings Bank agreed to finance Mrs. [278] Garcia's new car. The showroom price of the car was $3,600. She had to pay $\frac{1}{3}$ down, 10% interest, and make 30 payments. How much was each monthly payment?

8. The County Trust Co. agreed to finance Mr. [278] Gray Eagle's new car. The showroom price of the car was $3,400. He had to pay $\frac{1}{5}$ down, 10% interest, and make 24 payments. How much was each monthly payment?

9. Sam Small works on a 40-hour week basis, [246] with time-and-a-half for overtime. For the week ending March 16, he worked 47 hours. He earns $2.55 an hour. Find his total wages for the week.

10. Ruth Barnet works on a 40-hour week basis, [246] with time-and-a-half for overtime. For the week ending September 5, she worked 45 hours. She earns $2.60 an hour. Find her total wages for the week.

Copy and complete the chart. Each employee is paid on an 8-hour day basis, with time-and-a-half for overtime. [246]

	Name	HOURS WORKED M	T	W	T	F	Rate	WAGES EARNED Regular	Overtime	Total
11.	Bell, E.	8	8	9	9	10	$3.10			
12.	Evans, D.	9	9	8	8	10	$2.40			
13.	Spencer, R.	10	8	10	8	10	$2.75			
14.	Wong, T.	8	8	8	8	8	$2.55			

Career/AUTO TECHNOLOGY

The work of the automotive technician directly affects every industrial activity. The ever-increasing demand for more and greater power has created a need for technicians. They must be able to produce the equipment designed by the scientist and engineer.

Job Descriptions

- Utility technician—compares fuels on test engines; determines knock characteristics of fuels.

- Service manager—plans the auto service department; selects equipment; organizes and manages shop; assists in diagnosing automotive problems.

- High performance engine technician—designs, tests, analyzes, and maintains engines now available in the automotive industry.

- Engine test cell technician—prepares gas turbine and jet engines for operation; installs test instruments to record information.

Training

Entry-level jobs are available to high school graduates. It is helpful to have studied automotive mechanics. Higher level jobs are open to those who are graduates of technical programs. These are available in many two- and four-year colleges or technical institutes.

Further Investigation

Arrange an interview with an automotive technician. Ask about job qualifications, working conditions, possibilities for advancement, entry-level jobs.

Consult your guidance department about automotive mechanic programs available in high schools. Also ask about post-high-school programs in this area.

Depreciation

depreciation   Depreciation is the amount of decrease in the value of an article due to age and wear.

estimated life   The estimated life of an article is the length of time it probably will last under normal use.

straight-line method   The straight-line method assumes that the amount of depreciation will be the same each year during an article's estimated life.

$$\text{Annual depreciation} = \frac{\text{cost—trade-in}}{\text{estimated life}}$$

trade-in value   The trade-in value of an article is its worth at the end of a certain period of time.

For Discussion

- In what way is the depreciation for a car different from straight-line depreciation?

"Sylvia's father is trading in his two-year old Spartan for a new model," Sandra Cohen told her mother, who was an accountant. "The dealer said I could have it for $1,500."

"Is it a good buy, Sandy?" her mother asked.

"It really is," answered Sandy. "The dealer said the depreciation is about $1,000 in the first two years of a Spartan's estimated life. I learned how to find depreciation. Here's an example." She wrote:

Cost of a car	$3,000
Less trade-in	− 600
Total depreciation	$2,400

Estimated life: 8 years

Annual depreciation $= \frac{\$2,400}{8}$, or $300

Her mother interrupted, "But Sandy, that is the *straight-line method* which assumes that the machine depreciates the same amount each year. Cars depreciate more the first years they are used. The depreciation for the first year is much larger than it is for the second. Remember that."

DEVELOPING SKILLS

Calculate the amount of annual depreciation by the straight-line method.

MODEL   Cost, $4,000
             Trade-in value, $600
             Useful life, 5 years
                    $4,000
                 −   600
                 _____
                    $3,400 Cost less trade-in value

        $3,400 ÷ 5 = $680 Annual depreciation

1. Cost, $7,500
    Trade-in value, $900
    Useful life, 8 yr

2. Cost, $11,000
    Trade-in value, $800
    Useful life, 6 yr

3. Cost, $2,500
    Trade-in value, $50
    Useful life, 9 yr

4. Cost, $18,700
    Trade-in value, $3,500
    Useful life, 12 yr

5. Cost, $236
    Trade-in value, $10
    Useful life, 6 yr

6. Cost, $1,335
    Trade-in value, $200
    Useful life, 8 yr

7. Cost, $2,750
    Trade-in value, $350
    Useful life, 4 yr

8. Cost, $20,000
    Trade-in value, $1,200
    Useful life, 10 yr

9. Cost, $4,100
    Trade-in value, $650
    Useful life, 7 yr

Calculate the total amount of depreciation according to the schedule shown in the chart.

MODEL   Cost, $3,200
             1st year, $3,200 × .20 = $640
             2nd year, $2,560 × .15 = $384
             3rd year, $2,176 × .10 = $217.60
             4th year, $1,958.40 × .08 = $156.67
             5th year, $1,801.73 × .07 = $126.12
                              _____
                              $1,524.39 Total depreciation

Year	Percent of Depreciation
1st	20
2nd	15
3rd	10
4th	8
5th	7

10. Cost, $5,600

11. Cost, $4,650

12. Cost, $75

13. Cost, $8,900

14. Cost, $11,500

15. Cost, $525

16. Cost, $100.75

17. Cost, $87.50

18. Cost, $62.25

APPLYING SKILLS

1. Karen Levine bought a new car for $3,253.87. Three years later, she sold it for $725. What was the amount of annual depreciation?

2. Jim Larsen bought a new car for $4,500. Five years later, he sold it for $500. What was the amount of annual depreciation?

3. The Behrman family bought a new car in 1969 for $2,953. They sold it in 1971 for $1,095. What was the average yearly depreciation?

4. The Keller family bought a new car in 1972 for $3,761. They sold it in 1976 for $700. What was the average yearly depreciation?

5. Tom Sullivan bought a new bicycle for $65. After $4\frac{1}{2}$ years of use, he sold it to a second-hand dealer for $15. What was the annual depreciation on the bicycle?

6. Mary Foster bought a new television set for $400. After $6\frac{1}{2}$ years of use, she sold it to a second-hand dealer for $150. What was the annual depreciation on the set?

7. A factory acquired a certain machine for $50,000. The machine is expected to have a useful life of 20 years. It can then be sold for scrap metal for $2,000. How much is the annual depreciation?

8. A farm co-op acquired new machinery for $20,000. The equipment is expected to have a useful life of 15 years. The machinery can then be traded in for $2,000. How much is the annual depreciation?

9. A truck cost $4,500 when new. It was estimated to have a trade-in value of $500 in 5 years. Find the estimated value after 3 years of use.

10. A tractor cost $8,000 when new. It was estimated to have a trade-in value of $1,200 in 7 years. Find the estimated value after 4 years of use.

11. Ellen Robinson bought a car for $4,200. The dealer told her that the car could be expected to have a useful life of 8 years. The trade-in value after that time was estimated to be $150. Ellen decided to trade the car in after 5 years. Find the estimated value.

12. Joe Girardi bought a car for $3,800. The dealer told him that the car could be expected to have a useful life of 6 years. The trade-in value after that time was estimated to be $200. Joe decided to trade the car in after 3 years. Find the estimated value.

13. A machine costs $2,600. Find the total depreciation after 5 years. Use the chart on page 289.

14. A typewriter costs $180. Find the total depreciation after 5 years. Use the chart on page 289.

MAINTAINING SKILLS

Find the price including a 4% sales tax and a 5% excise tax. [211]

1. Chair @ $59.49

2. Air conditioner @ $214.50

3. Refrigerator @ $589.60

4. Television @ $446.87

5. Sofa @ $214.93

6. Washing machine @ $189.65

Solve these problems.

7. James Harris is paid $.35 per unit of completed
[251] work on the first 250 units. For each additional
unit he is paid $.45. Last week he completed
305 units. How much did he earn?

8. Barbara Williams is paid $.75 per unit of com-
[251] pleted work on the first 100 units. For each additional unit she is paid $.90. Last week she com-
pleted 135 units. How much did she earn?

9. Lee Wong earns a $45 weekly salary plus a 5%
[251] commission on all sales in excess of $2,000.
Last week his sales amounted to $4,240. How
much did he earn?

10. Susan White Eagle earns a $65 weekly salary
[251] plus a 2% commission on all sales in excess of
$1,000. Last week her sales amounted to
$5,560. How much did she earn?

11. Martha Reynolds drove her car 14,091 miles
[283] last year. Her operating expenses were:

991 gal of gas at 51¢ per gal	$505.41
Oil and lubrication	34.81
Repairs and parts	181.30
Insurance, license	210.45
Depreciation	655.00

What were the total operating costs? Find the
operating cost per mile.

12. Karl Rockwell drove his car 28,016 km last
[283] year. His operating expenses were:

3,601 liters of gas at 15¢ per liter	$540.15
Oil and lubrication	50.87
Repairs and parts	246.93
Insurance, license	256.95
Depreciation	810.00

What were the total operating costs? Find the
operating cost per kilometer.

13. The odometer before a trip read 41,873 km.
[283] After the trip it read 42,689 km. 103 liters of
gas were used. Find, to the nearest tenth, the
number of kilometers per liter.

14. The odometer before a trip read 48,467 miles.
[283] It read 49,311 miles after the trip. 48 gallons of
gas were used. Find, to the nearest tenth, the
number of miles per gallon.

Automobile Insurance

public liability   Public liability refers to the combination policy containing coverages for both bodily injury insurance and property damage insurance.

collision insurance   Collision insurance covers damage to a driver's automobile in case of an accident.

bodily injury insurance   Bodily injury insurance gives financial protection to the automobile owner for injuries to other people.

property damage insurance   Property damage insurance gives financial protection to the automobile owner for damages to property, including automobiles, which belongs to others.

medical payments insurance   Medical payments insurance provides payments for treatment of injuries to the driver or to the driver's passengers.

deductible clause   A $50 or $100 deductible clause provided for in a collision insurance policy means that the insured party pays the first $50 or $100 of damages.

For Discussion

● What is *they* insurance? *we* insurance?

Mike O'Hara told his father about the insurance agent who spoke to his driver's education class that day.

"What did she say?" his father asked.

"A driver as well as the public needs protection against financial losses due to accidents. Many states require two types of insurance: public liability, which she called *they* insurance, and collision, which she called *we* insurance."

"Mike, why did she use *they* and *we*?"

"Dad, public liability insurance is carried by a car owner to pay for losses caused to other people and their property; in other words, *they* insurance."

Mike continued, "The second type, collision insurance, along with medical payments insurance, protects the car owner, the owner's property, and any passengers in the owner's car; in other words, *we* insurance. Taking a $50 or $100 deductible clause in collision insurance reduces the premium. Another type of *we* insurance called *comprehensive* insurance, provides protection in case of fire, theft, and similar causes."

DEVELOPING SKILLS

OBJECTIVE   To find annual premiums for automobile insurance

Class	Remarks	Territory		
		#7	#23	#46
A-1	Not for business; no male driver under 25	$19.50	$27.00	$43.52
A-2	Not for business	27.10	35.84	52.17
B	Used for business	28.90	38.27	53.88

TABLE 1 PREMIUM RATES
Bodily Injury Insurance—Limits, $5,000 & $10,000 (5/10)

Premium rates for larger amounts:
Limits, $10,000 & $20,000 : 1.5 × basic rate
Limits, $20,000 & $40,000 : 1.8 × basic rate
Limits, $25,000 & $50,000 : 2 × basic rate

Class	Territory		
	#7	#23	#46
A-1	$ 8.78	$14.74	$17.22
A-2	12.85	19.75	24.32
B	14.13	22.00	25.90

TABLE 2 PREMIUM RATES
Property Damage Insurance Limit, $5,000

Premium rates for larger amounts:
Limit, $10,000 1.5 × base rate
Limit, $15,000 2 × basic rate
Limit, $20,000 2.3 × basic rate

Calculate the premium for one year's bodily injury insurance. Use Table 1.

MODEL $10,000/$20,000 coverage, Class A-1, Territory 7

$10,000 for injury to 1 person, $20,000 maximum for injury to 2 or more persons

Premium rate for 5/10 = $19.50
Rate for 10/20 ⟶ × 1.5
$29.25

1. $5,000/$10,000 coverage, Class B, Territory 23

2. $5,000/$10,000 coverage, Class A-1, Territory 23

3. 10/20, Class A-1, Territory 46

4. 20/40, Class A-2, Territory 46

5. 25/50, Class B, Territory 7

6. 25/50, Class A-2, Territory 7

Calculate the premium for one year's property damage insurance. Use Table 2.

7. $5,000 coverage, Class B, Territory 46

8. $5,000 coverage, Class A-1, Territory 23

9. $10,000, Class A-2, Territory 7

10. $15,000, Class B, Territory 7

11. $15,000, Class A-2, Territory 23

12. $20,000, Class A-1, Territory 46

APPLYING SKILLS

Find the premium for each of the following policies.
Use Tables 1 and 2 on page 293.

MODEL   A 10/20/15 policy, Territory 7, Class A-2

$$10/20 \text{ Bodily Injury Insurance: } \$27.10 \times 1.5 = \quad \$40.65$$
$$\$15,000 \text{ Property Damage Insurance: } 12.85 \times 2 = \underline{+ 25.70}$$
$$\$66.35 \text{ Total premium}$$

1. 10/20/10, Territory 23, Class B

2. 20/40/15, Territory 46, Class A-1

3. 20/40/20, Territory 23, Class A-2

4. 25/50/20, Territory 7, Class B

Copy and complete the chart. Use Tables 1 and 2.

	Coverage			Annual Premium
	Public Liability	Collision	Comprehensive	
	5/10/5, Class A-1, Territory 7	$135 ($50 ded.)	$65	$228.28
5.	10/20/10, Class A-2, Territory 23	$110 ($100 ded.)	$75	
6.	25/50/15, Class B, Territory 46	$185 (No ded.)	$85	
7.	20/40/10, Class A-1, Territory 23	$124 ($50 ded.)	$68	
8.	20/40/20, Class A-2, Territory 7	$120 ($100 ded.)	$72	

Solve these problems. None of these accidents involve no-fault insurance.

9. A man caused an accident resulting in $280 in damages to his car and $320 in damages to the other car. He has a policy with coverage of 5/10/5, and a $50 deductible collision. Who pays for all the losses and how much?

10. A woman caused an automobile accident resulting in $510 damages to her car and completely wrecked a parked car valued at $1,150. She has a 10/20/10 policy and $100 deductible collision. Who pays for all the losses, and how much?

11. Sara Kassel carries bodily injury insurance with limits of $5,000 and $10,000. One day, she injured a pedestrian crossing a street. The court awarded the injured party $8,500. How much of this expense will be paid by the insurance company? How much will Ms. Kassel pay?

12. Mike Gale, carrying 5/10/10 coverage, causes an accident in which 4 people were injured and 2 cars were demolished. The injured people were awarded damages totaling $10,665. The car owners were awarded $4,450. How much of this expense did the insurance company pay? How much will Mr. Gale pay?

MAINTAINING SKILLS

Solve these problems about charge accounts. There is a $1\frac{1}{2}$% monthly interest charge on unpaid balances. [215]

1. Mary Stuart's March balance was $86.42. On April 5, she made a payment of $25.00. During April she charged these items:

   April 2, records, $12.79
   April 5, lamp, $54.63
   April 15, shoes, $39.41

   On April 17, she returned one pair of shoes for a credit of $19.46. Find her new balance.

2. Vernon Seaton's September balance was $46.75. On Oct. 6, he made a payment of $20. During Oct. he charged these items:

   Oct. 7, coat, $89.96
   Oct. 10, towels, $17.49
   Oct. 15, shirts, $14.62

   On Oct. 15, he returned 2 of the towels for a credit of $8.24. Find his new balance.

Solve these problems. Use 5.85% as the F.I.C.A. rate on a $14,100 base maximum. [255]

3. Helen Clines' earnings for the last three years were $9,846, $11,746, and $14,636. What was the total F.I.C.A. contribution?

4. Roger Henry's earnings for the last three years were $8,567, $10,964, and $14,146. What was his total F.I.C.A. contribution?

Solve these problems. Use the social security monthly cash benefit schedule on page 333. [255]

5. Harry Robinson, age 43, is disabled. His wife is under 65 and they have one child age 12. Mr. Robinson's average earnings were $9,600. What is their monthly family benefit payment?

6. Edith Thomas, age 31, is a widow. She has two children, ages 10 and 6. Her husband's average yearly earnings were $8,500. What is the amount of her monthly benefit payment?

Solve these problems. Use the straight-line method to find annual depreciation. [289]

7. Lisa bought a new car in 1974 for $3,100. She sold it in 1976 for $1,400. What was the average yearly depreciation?

8. John bought a new car in 1974 for $3,200. He sold it 3 years later for $700. What was the average yearly depreciation?

9. A truck cost $8,500 when new. It was estimated to have a trade-in value of $500 in 5 years. What was the estimated value after 3 years of use?

10. A tractor cost $10,350 when new. It was estimated to have a trade-in value of $2,000 in 10 years. What was the estimated value after 6 years of use?

Self-Test: Chapter 11

Find the actual cost of each car and the interest charged. [278]

1. Showroom price: $3,760
   Down payment: $800
   36 monthly payments of $110

2. Showroom price: $4,000
   Down payment: $800
   24 monthly payments of $160

Calculate the amount of annual depreciation by the straight-line method.
[289]

3. Cost: $18,000
   Trade-in value: $4,000
   Useful life: 10 years

4. Cost: $3,500
   Trade-in value: $500
   Useful life: 4 years

Copy and complete. [283]

	Distance Traveled	Gasoline, Oil, Lubrication	Repairs, Parts	Insurance, License	Depreciation	Annual Costs	Cost Per Km or Mi
5.	18,000 km	$570	$75	$225	$750		
6.	12,000 mi	$600	$160	$240	$500		

Solve these problems.

7. Henry took a trip of 1,800 km. He used 143.5
[283] liters of gas, costing $.16 per liter. Find the distance per liter, to the nearest tenth kilometer. Find the cost of gas per kilometer.

8. Julie wants to buy a used car that costs $2,700.
[278] She can finance by paying one-third down, 9% interest and 24 monthly payments. Find the amount of each payment.

9. Mr. Roberts wants to buy automobile insurance.
[293] He wants 10/20/15 coverage for a Class A-1 policy in territory #23. The rates were:
   Bodily injury   5/10–$27
                         10/20–1.5 × basic rate
   Property damage $5,000–$14.74
                         $15,000–2 × basic rate
   What will be the amount of his annual premium?

10. Ms. Jones wants to buy automobile insurance.
[293] She wants a 10/20/5 policy, plus collision and comprehensive coverage. The rates were:
   Bodily injury   5/10–$28.90
                         10/20–1.5 × basic rate
   Property damage $5,000–$14.13
   Collision $120 ($100 deductible)
   Comprehensive $80
   Find her annual premium.

Test: Chapter 11

Find the actual cost of each car and the interest charged.

1. Showroom price: $4,400
   Down payment: $800
   24 monthly payments of $185

2. Showroom price: $3,500
   Down payment: $650
   36 monthly payments of $100

Calculate the amount of annual depreciation by the straight-line method.

3. Cost: $20,000
   Trade-in value: $4,500
   Useful life: 11 years

4. Cost: $3,200
   Trade-in value: $350
   Useful life: 5 years

Copy and complete.

	Distance Traveled	Gasoline, Oil, Lubrication	Repairs, Parts	Insurance, License	Depreciation	Annual Costs	Cost Per Km or Mi
5.	16,000 km	$525	$50	$230	$800		
6.	10,000 mi	$440	$125	$200	$600		

Solve these problems.

7. Marsha took a trip of 900 km. She used 80 liters of gas, costing $.15 per liter. Find the distance per liter, to the nearest tenth kilometer. Find the cost of gas per kilometer.

8. Uvaldo wants to buy a used car that cost $2,600. He can finance it by paying 20% down, 10% interest and 24 payments. Find the amount of each payment.

9. Mrs. Stonewell wants to buy automobile insurance. She wants 20/40/15 coverage for a Class A-2 policy in territory #7. The rates were:
   Bodily injury   5/10–$27.10
                                  20/40–1.8 × basic rate
   Property damage $5,000–$14.13
                              $15,000–2 × basic rate
   What will be the amount of her annual premium?

10. Mr. Nelson wants to buy automobile insurance. He wants a 25/50/5 policy, plus collision and comprehensive coverage. The rates were:
    Bodily injury   5/10–$43.52
                                 25/50–2 × basic rate
    Property damage $5,000–$17.22
    Collision $160–($100 deductible)
    Comprehensive $85
    Find his annual premium.

Mean

Find the mean.

The mean is the average.

MODEL   Sales: $1,500, $1,700, $1,500, $1,900, $1,600,
     $1,500, $1,600, $1,800, $1,900, $1,600

Make a frequency chart.

Sales (S)	Tally	Frequency (F)	F × S
$1,900	//	2	$3,800
1,800	/	1	1,800
1,700	/	1	1,700
1,600	///	3	4,800
1,500	///	3	4,500
	TOTALS	10	$16,600

Mean = $16,600 ÷ 10, or $1,660

1. Sales: $800, $850, $900, $800, $900, $850, $800, $850, $900, $850

2. Sales: $450, $500, $450, $600, $550, $500, $450, $600, $500, $400

3. Height in cm: 176, 180, 165, 175, 160, 172, 165, 158, 165, 168, 175

4. Height in cm: 190, 185, 180, 175, 177, 177, 187, 195, 178, 182, 187

5. Yards: $6\frac{1}{2}$, $7\frac{2}{3}$, $6\frac{1}{2}$, $3\frac{1}{3}$, $3\frac{1}{3}$, $6\frac{2}{3}$

6. Yards: $5\frac{3}{4}$, $1\frac{1}{2}$, $8\frac{1}{4}$, $9\frac{1}{2}$, $5\frac{3}{4}$, $8\frac{1}{4}$

7. Liters: 14, 2, 15, 1, 14.2, 16.3, 8.5, 14.2, 15.1, 16.3, 8.5

8. Liters: 12.6, 14.3, 12.6, 13.6, 9.4, 12.6, 14.3, 13.6, 9.5

9. Charges: $195.99, $200, $195.95, $200, $150.95, $300, $195.99, $200

10. Charges: $225.95, $275, $225.95, $275, $399.92, $225.95, $399.99, $250

11.
Name	Salary	Name	Salary
J. Beck	$10,800	C. Kane	$12,000
R. Carr	12,000	M. Lunt	10,800
L. Diaz	10,800	R. Ono	12,500
S. Hu	12,500	N. Polk	10,850
A. Jones	12,000	J. York	12,000

12.
Name	Salary	Name	Salary
T. Ames	$10,500	P. North	$10,800
F. Epp	10,400	J. Roth	11,000
B. Gomez	11,000	G. Shea	10,400
M. Ito	11,500	K. Troy	11,000
F. Marks	10,400	L. Wang	11,500

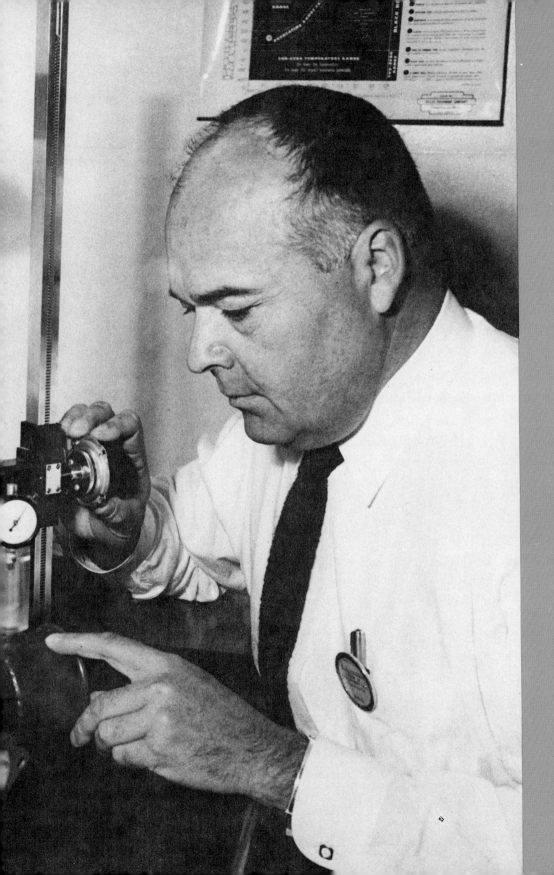

12

OWNING A HOME

An inspector checking
a porcelain motor part
for glass coverage

Activities

How many triangles are there in Figure A? in Figure B?

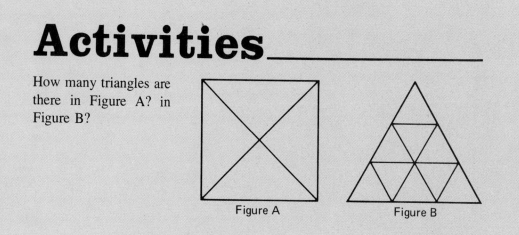

Figure A   Figure B

Form a committee to investigate the various types of house financing offered by local savings banks, savings and loan associations, credit unions, and other lending institutions. Be sure to contact the local FHA (Federal Housing Administration) for information on the types of government guaranteed loans for housing. Obtain materials and pamphlets to make a bulletin-board display.

Visit local real estate agencies to obtain knowledge of their operations. Find out the nature of a real estate sales representatives job. Make a report to your class on the information you have collected.

Arrange for a debate on ''Owning a Home vs. Renting an Apartment—Which Is Better?'' Be sure that you know the advantages and disadvantages of both sides of the question. Consult consumer magazines in your school or local library. Also call on real estate sales representatives who handle rental of apartments to give you their ideas.

Give a report on the steps necessary to build a house—the materials needed and cost, labor, plumbing, lumber, heating, etc. Visit your school or local library for this information. Your industrial arts teacher can also be very helpful.

Buying and Mortgaging

mortgage   A mortgage is a large loan used for paying for a house over a long period of time.

conventional loan   A conventional loan may be obtained from savings and loan associations. It usually has a high rate of interest.

FHA loan   An FHA (Federal Housing Administration) loan is a loan obtained from a bank, but approved and insured by the U.S.

amortized   An amortized mortgage is a scheduled repayment of a mortgage in which some of each succeeding monthly payment is used to reduce the debt. The interest each month also decreases.

closing costs   Closing costs include attorney's fees, title search, appraiser's fee, recording fee, federal stamps, insurance, and a part of the property tax for the year.

For Discussion

- What kinds of loans did Martha describe?

- What is an amortized mortgage?

Real estate agent Martha Becker was explaining how to buy and finance a new home to her newlywed friends, Cesar and Christine Outler.

"You need a mortgage since you can't pay cash. A mortgage is a long-term loan from a lending institution. This loan will not pay the entire cost of the house. You will have to make a down payment."

"How much?" Christine asked.

"The down payment depends on the kind of loan you get and the cost of the house," Martha replied. "One type of loan is called a conventional loan. A bank may lend you up to 75% of the cost; your down payment would be 25% or more of the cost of the house."

Martha continued, "Another type of loan is a government insured loan, like FHA loans. You can borrow a higher percentage of the cost than on a conventional loan. The down payment and the interest are also lower. The conventional and FHA mortgages are said to be amortized. This means that more of each succeeding monthly payment is used to reduce the loan. The interest decreases also each month. Finally, you will also need $500 to $1,000 for closing costs."

DEVELOPING SKILLS

OBJECTIVE   To find the cost of buying a house

Amount of Loan	MONTHLY PAYMENTS TO AMORTIZE A 9% LOAN						
	Length of Loan						
	1 Yr	5 Yr	10 Yr	15 Yr	20 Yr	25 Yr	30 Yr
$ 5,000	$ 437.26	$103.80	$ 63.34	$ 50.72	$ 44.99	$ 41.96	$ 40.24
10,000	874.52	207.59	126.68	101.43	89.98	83.92	80.47
20,000	1,749.03	415.17	253.36	202.86	179.95	167.84	160.93
30,000	2,623.55	622.76	380.03	304.38	269.92	251.76	241.39

Find the total interest charged.

MODEL   A loan of $20,000 at 9% for 15 years
Find the monthly payment: $202.86 (Use the table.)
Find the number of months: 180 (15×12)
Find the total amount paid: $36,514.80 ($202.86 \times 180$)
Subtract the amount of the loan to
find the amount of interest charged: $16,514.80 ($36,514.80 - $20,000$)

	Loan	Time	Rate		Loan	Time	Rate
1.	$20,000	20 yr	9%	**2.**	$10,000	15 yr	9%
3.	$30,000	25 yr	9%	**4.**	$ 5,000	10 yr	9%
5.	$20,000	30 yr	9%	**6.**	$30,000	20 yr	9%

Prepare an amortization schedule for the first 2 payments of each loan.

MODEL $20,000 loan at 9% for 25 years

Payment Number	Monthly Payment	Interest Paid	Principal Paid	Remaining Balance
1	$167.84 (from the table)	$20,000 \times .09 \times \frac{1}{12} =$ $150.00	$167.84 - $150 =$ $17.84	$20,000 - $17.84 =$ $19,982.16
2	167.84	$19,982.16 \times .09 \times \frac{1}{12} =$ $149.87	$167.84 - $149.87 =$ $17.97	$19,982.16 - $17.97 =$ $19,964.19

7. $30,000 loan at 9% for 25 years.

8. $10,000 loan at 9% for 15 years.

APPLYING SKILLS

1. Marie Hancock arranged a 9% loan of $20,000 for 20 years to buy a condominium. Use the table on page 302 to find her monthly payment on the loan.

2. Ralph Garcia arranged a 9% loan of $30,000 for 15 years to buy a house. Use the table on page 302 to find his monthly payment on the loan.

MODEL   Tim Anderson's monthly payment on his home loan is $164.04. His yearly real estate tax is $720. His yearly fire insurance premium is $156. Find Tim's total monthly payment, including taxes and insurance.

$$\text{Total monthly payment} = \$164.04 + \tfrac{1}{12} \times 720 + \tfrac{1}{12} \times 156$$
$$= 164.04 + 60 + 13$$
$$= \$237.04$$

3. Jane Starr's monthly payment on her home loan is $185.25. Her yearly real estate tax is $750.12. Her yearly fire insurance premium is $164.28. Find her total monthly payment, including taxes and insurance.

4. Mr. Williams' monthly payment on his home loan is $203.42. His yearly real estate tax is $843.60. His yearly fire insurance premium is $180.00. Find his total monthly payment, including taxes and insurance.

5. Iris Kleinman arranged a 9% loan of $30,000 for 20 years to buy a condominium. Her yearly real estate taxes are $672. Her yearly fire insurance premium is $120. Find her total monthly payment, including taxes and insurance. Use the 9% table on page 302 to find the monthly payment on the loan.

6. Henry Schmidt purchased a house using a $20,000 loan at 9% for 20 years. His yearly real estate taxes are $544.32. His yearly fire insurance premium is $162.24. Find his total monthly payment, including taxes and insurance. Use the 9% table on page 302 to find the monthly payment on the loan.

7. Mr. Chang made a house loan of $15,000 at 10% for 20 years. His monthly payment on the loan was $144.76. Prepare an amortization schedule for the first 4 monthly payments.

8. Ms. Harrison borrowed $20,000 at 10% for 15 years. Her monthly payment on the loan is $214.93. Prepare an amortization schedule for the first 4 monthly payments.

MAINTAINING SKILLS

Find the premium for each of the following policies. Use Tables 1 and 2 on page 293. [293]

1. 5/10/10, Territory 23, Class A-2

2. 5/10/5, Territory 46, Class B

3. 20/40/15, Territory 7, Class A-1

4. 25/50/20, Territory 23, Class A-2

Find the amount to be withheld for federal income tax. Use the table on pages 330–331. [261]

5. Single person earning $246.68, claiming 2 exemptions

6. Married person earning $236.48, claiming 4 exemptions

Find the single discount that is equivalent to the chain of discounts. [224]

7. 30% and 10%

8. 25% and 10%

9. 30%, 20%, and 5%

Solve these problems.

10. [224] Sue's Candy Palace buys candy at 30% less 15%. Sue purchased $12,000 worth of candy. What was the total discount? What was the invoice price?

11. [224] George's Art Shop buys canvas at 35% less 20%. George purchased $6,000 worth of canvas. What was the total discount? What was the invoice price?

12. [293] A woman had an accident resulting in $640 damages to her car and $1,200 damages to the car she hit. She had a 25/50/15 policy and $100 deductible collision. How much did her insurance company pay?

13. [293] A man had an accident resulting in $1,050 damages to his car and $2,400 damages to the car he hit. He had a 5/10/5 policy and $50 deductible collision. How much did his insurance company pay?

Copy and complete. Use the tables on pages 330–332 for federal income tax and F.I.C.A. The state income tax is 1.5% of the gross income. [261]

	Employee	Gross Income	Marital Status	Exemptions	Federal Income Tax Deductions	F.I.C.A.	State Income Tax Deductions	Net Income
14.	Adams, H.	$215.26	M	3				
15.	Harris, A.	$249.36	S	1				
16.	Smith, R.	$226.42	S	2				

Consumer Tips———

USING THE TELEPHONE

STATION-TO-STATION   Charges for calls   COMPLAINTS   Area Codes

How to Dial   Collect Calls   EMERGENCY NUMBERS   *Annoyance Calls*

PAYMENTS   Telephone Tips

- Use the front of your directory to locate rates on station-to-station, person-to-person, and collect calls.

- Keep emergency telephone numbers such as police, fire, ambulance, doctor, poison control center, close to the phone.

- Use the yellow pages to locate local industries, businesses, and services. First look under general subject headings.

- Cut telephone costs:

    Use the limited service plan. It allows fewer calls but charges a lower basic rate.

    Select an unlimited plan with a smaller geographical area.

    Use dial-it-yourself, station-to-station calls when possible.

    Call long distance at cheaper rates and times by a dial-it-yourself, station-to-station call. The cheapest long distance call can be made from 11 p.m. to 8 a.m. daily. Other reduced rates are the Weekend Rate and the Evening Rate.

    Use a black dial phone for the lowest equipment cost.

A "beep" signal on your telephone every 15 seconds means that you are being recorded. If you do not wish this, tell the other party to shut off the recording. The "beep" should stop.

Real Estate Taxes

real estate   Real estate refers to land and buildings.

assessed value   The assessed value is the taxable value of real property, usually given as a percent of its original cost or market value.

taxes   Taxes are levied to raise the amount of money needed to pay for items in a community's budget for schools, parks, roads, police and fire protection, and so on.

mills   Property taxes may be stated in terms of mills. One mill has a value of .1 cent, or $.001.

For Discussion

- For what are local property taxes used?

- What determines a local community's tax rate?

- How are tax rates expressed in different communities?

"Our new real estate tax rate is $3.60 per $100 of assessed valuation," said Mrs. Schultz.

"How much do we pay?" Bill asked.

"Our house has a market value of $30,000. Our town assesses each owner at 50% of market value. This makes our assessed value, $15,000. There are 150, $100 units in $15,000. Multiply 150 by $3.60, the tax rate per $100. This gives us our taxes, $540."

"That seems high," said Bill.

"Services such as schools, parks, roads, police, fire protection all cost money."

"How is the tax rate figured?" Bill asked.

"Tax rate is a ratio, Bill." She wrote:

$$\text{Tax rate} = \frac{\text{budget needs for town services}}{\text{total town assessed valuation}}$$

$$\frac{\text{compared number} \longrightarrow \$1,800,000}{\text{compared-to number} \longrightarrow \$50,000,000} = .036$$

Mrs. Schultz continued, "This tax rate could be expressed as:

$.036 per $1 of assessed valuation
3.6% per $1 of assessed valuation
$3.60 per $100 of assessed valuation
$36.00 per $1,000 of assessed valuation
36 mills per $1 of assessed valuation."

DEVELOPING SKILLS

OBJECTIVE   To compute the tax rate and to find tax on property

Find the tax rate per $1 of assessed valuation.

MODEL   Budget proposal: $2,000,000
Total assessed valuation: $80,000,000

$$\text{Tax rate per } \$1 = \frac{\text{budget proposal}}{\text{total assessed valuation}}$$

$$= \frac{\$2,000,000}{\$80,000,000}$$

$$= \frac{1}{40}$$

$$= .025, \text{ or } 2.5\%$$

1. Budget proposal: $3,000,000
Total assessed valuation: $96,000,000

2. Budget proposal: $1,600,000
Total assessed valuation: $48,000,000

Find the tax rate per $100 of assessed valuation.

MODEL   Budget proposal: $9,200,000
Total assessed valuation: $184,000,000

$$\text{Tax rate per } \$1 = \frac{\$9,200,000}{\$184,000,000}$$

$$= \frac{1}{20}$$

$$= .05$$

Tax rate per $100 = $.05 \times 100$, or $5.00

3. Budget proposal: $1,500,000
Total assessed valuation: $70,000,000

4. Budget proposal: $8,000,000
Total assessed valuation: $100,000,000

Find the tax rate per $1,000 of assessed valuation.

5. Budget proposal: $700,000
Total assessed valuation: $2,450,000

6. Budget proposal: $2,500,000
Total assessed valuation: $60,000,000

Find the tax due on the assessed valuation of these lots.

MODEL   Lot #385: cost $12,000; assessed valuation, 40%;
tax rate, $48.20 per $1,000
Assessed value: $12,000 \times .40 = $4,800$, or 4.8 thousand dollars
Tax: $48.20 \times 4.8 = 231.36

7. Lot #227: cost, $15,000;
assessed valuation, 45%
tax rate, .035 per $1

8. Lot #357: cost, $9,500;
assessed valuation, 40%
tax rate, $4.10 per $100

APPLYING SKILLS

1. Madison's town park budget is $240,000. The assessed valuation is $40,000,000. What is the tax rate per $1?

2. Valley Park's school budget is $5,800,000. The assessed valuation is $102,500,000. What is the tax rate per $1?

3. Green Lake City's local services budget is $4,590,000. The total taxable property is $90,000,000. Find the tax rate per $100.

4. Thomasville's local services budget is $6,700,000. The total taxable property is $145,000,000. Find the tax rate per $100.

5. The proposed budget for Cariville is $1,072,000. The total assessed valuation is $32,000,000. Find the tax rate per $1,000.

6. The proposed budget for Danton is $2,371,500. The total assessed valuation is $51,000,000. Find the tax rate per $1,000.

7. Galeton has a tax rate of 3.2% per $1. Property is assessed at 50% of cost. Find the tax on property which cost $23,000,000.

8. Ocean City has a tax rate of 4.3% per $1. Property is assessed at 70% of cost. Find the tax on property which cost $18,000,000.

9. Jamesville has a tax rate of $.0425 per $1. Property in this area is assessed at 45% of cost. Find the tax on property which cost $15,000.

10. Freetown Center has a tax rate of $.0375 per $1. Property in this area is assessed at 55% of cost. Find the tax on property which cost $25,000.

11. Bolling has a tax rate of $.51 per $100. Property is assessed at 60% of cost. Find the tax on property which cost $35,000.

12. Grover Lakes has a tax rate of $.46 per $100. Property is assessed at 75% of cost. Find the tax on property which cost $22,000.

13. Cortland has set a tax of $5.42 per $100. Property is assessed at $33\frac{1}{3}$% of cost. Find the tax on a building which cost $48,000.

14. Ashton has set a tax of $4.25 per $100. Property is assessed at 80% of cost. Find the tax on a lot which cost $16,000.

15. Statesboro, which has a tax rate of 42.6 mills on the dollar, has set a 40% assessment. Find the tax due on a $130,000 building and lot.

16. Elderville, which has a tax rate of 27.9 mills on the dollar, has set a 52% assessment. Find the tax due on a $60,000 home and lot.

MAINTAINING SKILLS

Find the cost of goods sold and the gross profit. [229]

1. Starting inventory: $4,000
Purchases: $16,000
Final inventory: $2,500
Total retail sales: $25,000

2. Starting inventory: $12,000
Purchases: $120,000
Final inventory: $10,500
Total retail sales: $210,000

Find the actual cost of the car and the interest charged. [278]

3. Showroom price: $4,100
Down payment: $600
36 monthly payments of $109.85

4. Showroom price: $3,200
Down payment: $500
36 monthly payments of $82.50

Solve these problems.

5. [302] Mr. and Mrs. Wright bought a new house with a loan of $30,000 at 9% for 25 years. Their monthly payment was $251.76. Find the total interest charged.

6. [302] Mr. and Mrs. Yoshida bought a new house with a loan of $20,000 at 9% for 30 years. Their monthly payment was $160.93. Find the total interest charged.

7. [302] Mrs. Dower's monthly payment on her home loan is $215.87. Her yearly fire insurance premium is $174.46. Her real estate tax is $864.82. Find her total monthly payment, including taxes and insurance.

8. [302] Mr. Edward's monthly payment on his home loan is $196.42. His real estate tax is $786.92. His real estate tax is $786.92. His fire insurance premium is $181.45. Find his total monthly payment, including taxes and insurance.

9. [278] Joyce needs to finance $1,540 after making a suitable down payment on a car. Bank A offers her a loan for 36 months at 10%. Bank B offers her a loan for 24 months at 12%. Should Joyce choose the bank with the lower rate of interest? Prove that your answer is correct by showing your calculations.

10. [278] Ivan wants to finance $1,850 after making a suitable down payment on a car. Bank X offers him a loan for 30 months at 10%. Bank Y offers him a loan for 24 months at 11%. Should Ivan choose the bank with the lower rate of interest? Prove that your answer is correct by showing your calculations.

11. [229] Maria Contreras wanted to determine how successfully her business had been operating this year. She obtained the following information: beginning inventory, $12,000; purchases, $28,000; inventory at present, $16,000; sales to date, $35,400. What was the gross profit?

12. [229] John Black Hawk wanted to determine how successfully his business had been operating this year. He obtained the following information: beginning inventory, $6,000; purchases, $18,000; inventory at present, $8,500; sales to date, $23,100. What was the gross profit?

Cost of Utilities

public utilities   Public utilities are essential services to the public such as electricity, gas, water, and telephone.

state public utilities commission   A state public utilities commission is a special group of appointed citizens. They regulate the public utility companies by checking their operating costs and by determining a fair rate of return to the utilities.

users of public utilities   The chief users of public utilities fall into three groups: industrial, commercial, and residential.

kilowatt hour   A kilowatt hour (kwh) = 1,000 watts and is the amount of electricity used by a 50-watt bulb that burns for 20 hours.

For Discussion

- What affects the price of electricity?

- Why do you think that a sliding scale of rates is used for homeowners?

"This electric and gas bill is terribly high," said Mrs. Gavin to her daughter, Nancy. "But this letter explains the reason. It is due to the high price of fuel oil and coal, higher operating costs, and increased demand."

"Who sets the rates?" asked Nancy.

"This is done by our state public utilities commission. It has the responsibility to check operating costs and determine a fair rate of return to the four types of public utilities: electricity, gas, water, and telephone. The more electricity you use up to a certain step, the less it costs you for the next step. Our meter is read monthly to see how many kilowatt hours were used. The basic unit, kilowatt hour (kwh) = 1,000 watts and is the amount of electricity used by a 50-watt bulb that burns for 20 hours. If you use 40 kwh, the rate is 6.3¢ per kwh. If you use 150 kwh, the rate is 4.2¢ per kwh after the first 40 kwh. The less electricity you use, the higher the rate per kwh. Let me show you how our electric bill is calculated, Nancy. It's easy."

DEVELOPING SKILLS

OBJECTIVES   To compute operating costs of electrical appliances
To compute monthly electric bills

Compute the operating costs of these electrical appliances.

MODEL   Vacuum cleaner, 630 watts, used 2 hours a day for 7 days at 4¢/kwh

                                                     └Read: per

               └Wattage rate is the number of watts
of electricity used per hour.

Watts used	Kilowatts used	Cost
$630 \times 2 \times 7 = 8{,}820$	$8{,}820 \div 1{,}000 = 8.82$	$8.82 \times .04 = .3528$ or 35¢

1. Color TV, 200 watts, used 4 hr a day for 7 days at 5¢/kwh

2. Radio, 71 watts, used 8 hours a day for 30 days at 4¢/kwh

3. Toaster, 1,146 watts used 15 min a day for 30 days at 3.5¢/kwh

4. Clothes dryer, 4,856 watts, used 45 min a day for 15 days at 4.5¢/kwh

Use the rates in the table to compute these monthly electric bills.

First 50 kwh	→ 6.4¢/kwh
Next 100 kwh	→ 4.3¢/kwh
Next 150 kwh	→ 3.2¢/kwh
Next 200 kwh	→ 2.5¢/kwh
All over 500 kwh	→ 1.5¢/kwh
Fuel rate adjustment	→ 1.3¢/kwh
State sales tax rate	→ 5%

MODEL   756 kwh

                         $50 \times .064 =$ \$3.20

500 kwh $100 \times .043 =$ 4.30

                         $150 \times .032 =$ 4.80

                         $200 \times .025 =$ 5.00

                         $256 \times .015 =$ 3.84

Fuel rate adjustment $756 \times .013 =$ $+9.83$

                                            30.97

          Tax $(5\% \times 30.97) =$ $+1.55$

                             \$32.52   So, the monthly bill for 756 kwh is \$32.52.

5. 50 kwh   **6.** 150 kwh   **7.** 300 kwh   **8.** 500 kwh

9. 78 kwh   **10.** 180 kwh   **11.** 1,465 kwh   **12.** 2,316 kwh

APPLYING SKILLS

1. Find the operating cost of a $\frac{1}{2}$-horsepower electric motor for a furnace blower. It is running 6 hours a day for 30 days at 4.5¢/kwh. One horsepower equals 746 watts in 1 hour.

2. Find the operating cost of a $\frac{1}{3}$-horsepower electric motor for a washing machine. It is used 2.5 hours a day for 15 days at 4¢/kwh. One horsepower equals 746 watts in 1 hour.

3. Jack uses his 700-watt hair blower for 10 minutes each day. The cost of electricity is 4.5¢/kwh. What does it cost to use the hair blower for 30 days?

4. Barbara found that her family uses seven 75-watt light bulbs for 5 hours each day. The cost of electricity is 5¢/kwh. What did it cost to use the lights each week?

5. On November 1 the reading of Audrey Finch's electric meter was 8,465 kwh. One month later the meter read 8,889 kwh. How many kwh of electricity did Audrey use that month?

6. On October 1 the reading of Leonard Robinson's electric meter was 22,645 kwh. One month later the meter read 24,132 kwh. How many kwh of electricity did Leonard use that month?

7. The reading of Harry Conner's electric meter on June 24 was 46,875 kwh. On July 24 his electric meter read 48,109 kwh. Find the amount of Harry's electric bill for the past month. Use the table on page 311.

8. The reading of Maria Diaz's electric meter on September 10 was 78,965 kwh. On October 10 the electric meter read 79,791 kwh. Find the amount of Maria's electric bill for the past month. Use the table on page 311.

9. The reading of Eiko Sato's gas meter on April 1 was 8,123 units of gas. A month later his meter read 8,246 units of gas. The gas rates are:

The first 2 units, 66.3¢/unit
For the next 8 units, 21.4¢/unit
For all over 10 units, 14.4¢/unit
Rate adjustment, 3.2¢/unit (total units)

Find the amount of Eiko's bill if a state sales tax of 5% is computed on the total cost of gas used.

10. The reading on Mary White Feather's gas meter on May 1 was 52,656 units of gas. A month later the meter read 52,824 units of gas. The gas rates are:

The first 3 units, 62.7¢/unit
For the next 7 units, 21.5¢/unit
For all over 10 units, 14.7¢/unit
Rate adjustment, 3.3¢/unit (total units)

Find the amount of Mary's bill if a state sales tax of 4% is computed on the total cost of gas used.

MAINTAINING SKILLS

Find the last date of payment within the discount period. [235]

1. Date of invoice: March 8
Terms: 4/10, n/45

2. Date of invoice: Sept. 10
Terms: 3/15, n/30

Find the tax due on the assessed valuation of these lots. [307]

3. Lot #314
Cost: $12,000
Assessed valuation: 45%
Tax rate: $.044 per $1

4. Lot #816
Cost: $37,000
Assessed valuation: 40%
Tax rate: $.051 per $1

Find the number of kilometers per liter and the cost in cents per kilometer.
[283]

5. Gordon took a trip of 300 km. He used 48 liters of gas @ $.15 per liter.

6. Colleen took a trip of 1,200 km. She used 132 liters of gas @ $.14 per liter.

Solve these problems.

7. Ernesto drove 14,000 miles during the past
[283] year. His operating expenses were: gasoline, oil and lubrication, $755; repairs and parts, $370; insurance and license, $290; and depreciation, $650. Find the total operating costs and the cost per mile.

8. Taeko drove 12,000 miles during the past year.
[283] Her operating expenses were: gasoline, oil, and lubrication, $612; repairs and parts, $187; insurance and license, $245; and depreciation, $700. Find the total operating costs and cost per mile.

9. Youngton's school budget is $160,000. The
[307] assessed valuation is $25,000,000. What is the tax rate per $1?

10. Springville's school budget is $2,800,000. The
[307] assessed valuation is $50,000,000. What is the tax rate per $1?

Copy and complete. [235]

	Invoice Price	Term	Date of Invoice	Date Paid	Number of Days	Cash Discount	Amount Due
11.	$480	2/10, n/30	May 8	May 20			
12.	$780	4/10, n/45	July 8	Sept. 1			
13.	$546	3/10, n/30	Oct. 3	Oct. 10			
14.	$810	5/10, n/45	Jan. 5	Jan. 12			

Career/FOOD SERVICES

Food service specialists purchase, prepare, and serve food in cafeterias, restaurants, hospitals, and so on. One of the more recent needs for such services is by airlines. Food service ranks among the first five largest industries in the United States. Purchasing, preparing, and servicing of food are key jobs in this industry.

Job Descriptions

- Restaurant manager—deals with staff and employees; maintains efficiency and quality in service.

- Flight kitchen manager—supervises airline food service; schedules employees and delivery of food and supplies.

- Kitchen supervisor—coordinates kitchen and stores; purchases food and supplies; recommends menu to management.

- Kitchen steward—supervises dishwashing, workrooms; keeps inventory; requisitions replacement of flatware, glassware, and china.

Training

Food service specialists often receive on-the-job training. Some vocational schools offer preparatory courses in this area. One-year courses in technical training are offered in some post high school programs. Two-year programs are offered by junior and community colleges. Four-year college food service administration programs are also available.

Further Investigation

Arrange an interview with a food service specialist. Ask about job qualifications, working conditions, possibilities for advancement, entry-level jobs.

Consult your guidance department about vocational training. Also ask about post-high-school technical courses in this area.

Fire Insurance

fire insurance   Fire insurance is financial protection against loss of property due to fire.

fully covered   To be fully covered means to be completely insured for all possible losses.

fire hazard   A fire hazard is a dangerous situation which might result in a fire.

coinsurance clause   A coinsurance clause in a fire insurance policy provides that a property owner agrees to share any loss with the insurance company if the amount of insurance carried is less than the percent required, usually 80% of value.

For Discussion

- Why should the average homeowner's insurance be examined every few years?

- What factors determine fire insurance premium rates?

- How are premiums for fire insurance quoted?

- What is the rule for company liability?

Ms. Gray had invited Mr. Hague, her insurance agent, to her home to discuss the renewal of her fire insurance policy.

Mr. Hague said, "Rising prices and property values along with the new furniture and rugs you bought mean that you are not fully covered under the old policy."

"Well, I want to be fully insured," Ms. Gray said. "What are the rates?"

Mr. Hague answered, "Premium rates depend on the fire hazard; that is, the type of building and available fire protection. The rate for 1 year is \$.25 per \$100 of insurance. This is reduced if the policy is taken for 3 or 5 years. To be fully insured, you should carry insurance equal to 80% of the value of your home. Should your home be completely destroyed, you would collect 80% of the loss. Since many homeowners do not fully insure their property, they actually become coinsurers, and share part of the loss. The limit of company liability is given by this rule." He wrote:

$$\text{Company liability} = \frac{\text{policy carried}}{80\% \text{ of full value}} \times \text{loss}$$

DEVELOPING SKILLS

Find the annual premium for each policy.

MODEL   Amount of insurance: $9,000
             Cost per $100: $.26
                  90 (number of 100's in 9,000)
             × $.26
             ‾‾‾‾‾‾
             $23.40 Annual premium

1. Amount of insurance: $12,000
   Cost per $100: $.24

2. Amount of insurance: $17,500
   Cost per $100: $.19

Find the total premium due. Use the table at the right.

Term	Special Premium Rate
3 years	2.7 × 1 year's cost
5 years	4.4 × 1 year's cost

MODEL   Amount of insurance: $12,500
             Cost per $100, $.21; Term 3 yr
                  125
             × $.21
             ‾‾‾‾‾
             $26.25 Cost for 1 yr
             × 2.7
             ‾‾‾‾‾
             $70.88 Cost for 3 yr

3. Amount of insurance: $14,000
   Cost per $100, $.26   Term: 5 yr

4. Amount of insurance: $25,000
   Cost per $100: $.22   Term: 3 yr

Find the fire insurance company's liability.

MODEL   Property value: $20,000
             Value of policy carried: $10,000
             Amount of loss: $12,000

$$\text{Company liability} = \frac{\text{Value of policy carried}}{80\% \text{ of property value}} \times \text{Loss}$$

$$= \frac{\$10,000}{\$16,000} \times \$12,000 \quad (80\% \text{ of } \$20,000)$$

$$= \frac{5}{8} \times \$12,000$$

$$= \$7,500$$

5. Property value: $100,000
   Value of policy: $75,000
   Amount of loss: $60,000

6. Property value: $50,000
   Value of policy: $30,000
   Amount of loss: $40,000

APPLYING SKILLS

Solve these problems. Use the special premium rate table on page 317.

1. Anne Newman purchased $13,000 worth of fire insurance for her apartment. The cost of this policy is $.28 per $100 for 1 year. What is her annual premium?

2. Rich Vallario purchased $9,000 worth of fire insurance for his boat. The cost of this policy is $.26 per $100 for 1 year. What is his annual premium?

3. Mr. Stanford insured his home for $40,000. The cost per $100 is $.30. He purchased the policy for a 3-year term so as to take advantage of the special premium rate. What was the total premium due?

4. Ms. Whiting insured her home for $50,000. The cost per $100 is $.27. She purchased the policy for a 3-year term so as to take advantage of the special premium rate. What was the total premium due?

5. The Bental Corporation insured its factory for $200,000. The cost per $100 is $.19. The policy was purchased for a 5-year term. What was the total premium due?

6. The Thompson Company insured its warehouse for $850,000. The cost per $100 is $.21. The policy was purchased for a 5-year term. What was the total premium due?

7. A factory valued at $120,000 was insured for $70,000. The policy had a 80% coinsurance clause. A fire resulted in $48,000 worth of damages. How much will the insurance company pay?

8. A home valued at $40,000 is insured for $32,000. The policy has a 80% coinsurance clause. A fire resulted in $9,000 worth of damages. How much will the insurance company pay?

9. A building valued at $60,000 is insured for $40,000 under a policy with an 80% coinsurance clause. A fire causes $30,000 worth of damages. How much can the owner of the building expect to collect?

10. A store valued at $150,000 is insured for $100,000 under a policy with an 80% coinsurance clause. A fire causes $80,000 worth of damages. How much can the owner of the store expect to collect?

11. A home valued at $35,000 is insured for 75% of its value. The policy contains an 80% coinsurance clause. Damages resulting from a fire total $10,000. How much can the owner expect to receive from the insurance company?

12. A condominium valued at $50,000 is insured for 75% of its value. The policy contains an 80% coinsurance clause. Damages resulting from a fire total $25,000. How much can the owner expect to receive from the insurance company?

MAINTAINING SKILLS

Use the rates in the table to compute these monthly electric bills. [311]

First 50 kwh ———————→ 6.5¢/kwh	
Next 100 kwh ———————→ 4.4¢/kwh	
Next 150 kwh ———————→ 3.3¢/kwh	
Next 200 kwh ———————→ 2.2¢/kwh	
All over 500 kwh ——————→ 1.6¢/kwh	
Fuel rate adjustment ————→ 1.4¢/kwh	
State sales tax rate ————————→ 4%	

1. 465 kwh

2. 583 kwh

3. 1,462 kwh

4. 1,387 kwh

Compute the operating cost of these electrical appliances. [311]

5. Radio, 75 watts, used 4 hours a day for 30 days at 4.5¢/kwh

6. Toaster, 1,200 watts used 6 minutes a day for 20 days, at 5¢/kwh

Calculate the amount of depreciation by the straight-line method. [289]

7. Cost: $8,500
   Trade-in value: $700
   Useful life: 6 years

8. Cost: $10,500
   Trade-in value: $2,500
   Useful life: 5 years

For these taxpayers who earned over $10,000, find the tax due. Use Schedules X, Y, and Z page 336. [265]

9. H. Jones: Wages, salaries, tips, $12,468; dividends, $17 (after exclusion); interest income, $105.42; married, filing joint return, claiming 3 exemptions

10. A. Wallace: wages, salaries, tips, $10,843; dividends, $68 (after exclusion); interest income, $138; single, head of household, claiming 2 exemptions

Solve these problems for taxpayers who earned under $10,000. Use Tables 1–6 on pages 334–335. [265]

11. Janet Green, single, not head of household, claims 1 exemption. She earned $8,981 last year. She received dividends amounting to $65 (after exclusion). Interest on savings amounted to $135. Her W-2 form listed tax withheld of $1,287. What balance is due on her tax, or is she entitled to a refund? If so, how much?

12. Mike Redford, single, head of a household, claims 2 exemptions. He earned $6,943 last year. He received dividends amounting to $95 (after exclusion). Interest on savings amounted to $175. His W-2 form listed tax withheld of $946. What balance is due on his tax, or is he entitled to a refund? If so, how much?

Homeowner's Coverages

homeowner's insurance policy A homeowner's insurance policy is usually divided into two parts. The first part concerns damage or loss of property; the second part includes personal liability.

extended coverage Extended coverage is insurance covering losses resulting from windstorms, hail, riot, explosion, and other similar causes.

personal liability Personal liability insurance covers the homeowner for damages to people who are injured on the homeowner's property.

theft insurance Theft insurance protects the homeowner from losses of personal property by theft. Most policies cover this kind of loss when away from home or on vacation. The policy may also cover losses of credit cards.

For Discussion

- What clause can be included in extended coverage?

Ms. Agnes Johnson, insurance agent and friend of the Williams family, said, ''Your present homeowner's insurance policy does protect you against damage to property and personal liability. However, I suggest that you now include extended coverage in your policy.''

''What does it offer?'' Sara Williams asked.

''This extra coverage protects you against damage to property due to windstorm, hail, explosions, riot, strikes, smoke, or falling aircraft,'' Agnes replied. ''Our policy carries a $50 deductible clause like the one in your automobile collision insurance.''

Mr. Williams said, ''That sounds good. It will improve our protection.''

Agnes continued, ''Since you carry the lowest amount of personal liability coverage in your homeowner's policy, you should increase the amount. Remember, if someone slips on ice on your walk or falls from your roof, you might be liable for damages because your coverage is low. Finally, you should also include theft insurance which will protect you against losses in your home while you are away.''

DEVELOPING SKILLS

OBJECTIVE	To determine policy premiums and company liabilities for homeowner's insurance

Copy and complete the chart.

MODEL   Property value, $45,500; insured for 80%; cost per $100 for fire insurance is $.27; cost for extended coverage, $32.90; cost for public liability, $25.70; cost for theft, $19.10

$45,500 Property value
$\times .80$
$36,400 Amount of insurance
    364 (number of hundreds in $36,400)
    $\times .27$
$ 98.28 Cost for fire insurance
   32.90 Cost for extended coverage
   25.70 Cost for public liability
+ 19.10 Cost for theft
$175.98 Total annual premium

	Property value	Percent Insured	Cost per $100	Fire	Extended Coverage	Public Liability	Theft	Total
	$45,500	80	$.27	$98.28	$32.90	$25.70	$19.10	$175.98
1.	$30,000	80	$.26		$42.50	$35.00	$18.60	
2.	$24,000	75	$.25		$36.20	$28.80	$14.50	
3.	$25,000	80	$.24		$37.30	$29.60	$15.30	
4.	$27,500	90	$.22		$38.40	$30.90	$16.00	
5.	$32,000	80	$.26		$44.00	$33.20	$17.50	

For what percent is each company liable?

MODEL   A building is insured by company A for $75,000 and company B for $25,000.

$75,000 Company A
  25,000 Company B
$100,000 Total insurance

$\frac{\$75,000}{\$100,000} = \frac{3}{4}$, or 75% Company A's share of liability

$\frac{\$25,000}{\$100,000} = \frac{1}{4}$, or 25% Company B's share of liability

6. Company A, $50,000
   Company B, $40,000

7. Company A, $12,000
   Company B, $18,000

8. Company A, $30,000
   Company B, $20,000

APPLYING SKILLS

1. The fire insurance premium on a store insured for $100,000 for one year is $.48 per $100. The cost for extended coverage is $72.50. The premium for public liability insurance is $63.40. The cost for theft insurance is $31.25. Find the total premium for this coverage.

2. The fire insurance premium on a farm insured for $80,000 for one year is $.42 per $100. The cost for extended coverage is $70.20. The premium for public liability insurance is $47.60. The cost for theft insurance is $24.80. Find the total premium for this coverage.

3. Mr. Peters bought an extended coverage policy with a $25 deductible clause included. Last year hailstones broke several windows which cost $45.50 to replace, and a severe windstorm damaged his roof to the extent of $485. How much did the insurance company pay him?

4. Ms. Landers bought an extended coverage policy with a $50 deductible clause included. Last year a gas explosion nearby broke windows which cost $112.40 to replace and ruined furnishings which were worth $240. How much did the insurance company pay her?

5. A building worth $30,000 was insured in the following manner: Newton Casualty, $10,000; Mutual Underwriters, $6,000; National Security, $14,000. For what percent is each company liable?

6. A home worth $54,000 was insured in the following manner: Bedford Mutual, $24,000; Leland Casualty, $11,000; Fortune Security, $19,000. For what percent is each company liable?

Solve these problems.

MODEL Carl Rosenberg bought two homeowner's coverage policies, one for $12,000 with the Mariner's Insurance Company and one for $8,000 with the Globe Insurance Company. A fire caused $6,300 worth of damage. What amount must each company pay?

$$\$12,000 + \$8,000 = \$20,000 \text{ Total insurance}$$

$$\frac{\$12,000}{\$20,000} = \tfrac{3}{5}, \text{ or } 60\% \quad \text{Mariner's percent}$$

$$\$6,300 \times .6 = \$3,780 \text{ Mariner's share}$$

$$\frac{\$\,8,000}{\$20,000} = \tfrac{2}{5}, \text{ or } 40\% \quad \text{Globe's percent}$$

$$\$6,300 \times .4 = \$2,520 \text{ Globe's share}$$

7. An office building is insured with the Hersey Insurance Company for $30,000 and with the Sanford Casualty Company for $50,000. A severe storm resulted in $32,000 worth of damages. How much must each company pay?

8. A summer home is insured with the Fidelity Insurance Company for $25,000 and the Shore Casualty Company for $15,000. In a public liability suit the injured party was awarded $10,000. How much of this must each company pay?

MAINTAINING SKILLS

Find the annual premiums for each of the following automobile insurance policies. Use Tables 1 and 2 on page 293. [293]

1. 10/20/15, Territory 46, Class B

2. 20/40/15, Territory 23, Class A-2

3. 5/10/5, Territory 7, Class A-1
Collision $115 ($50 ded.)
Comprehensive $65

4. 25/50/20, Territory 46, Class B
Collision $145 ($50 ded.)
Comprehensive $85

Find the annual premium for each fire insurance policy. [317]

5. Amount of insurance: $16,500
Cost per $100: $.22

6. Amount of insurance: $20,000
Cost per $100: $.24

Find the insurance company's liability in each of the following cases. [317]

7. Property value: $25,000
Value of policy: $15,000
Amount of loss: $18,000

8. Property value: $30,000
Value of policy: $18,000
Amount of loss: $18,000

For each of these taxpayers who are itemizing deductions, find the total taxable income. [269]

	Taxpayer	Exemptions	Wages	Dividends	Interest Income	Medical and Dental	Taxes Paid	Interest Expenses	Contri.	Misc. Ded.
9.	Randall, R.	3	$12,380	$1,500	$280	$455	$1,900	$856	$155	$75
10.	Stein, S.	4	$14,568	$ 85	$356	$380	$1,146	$648	$215	$92

In each case, determine whether the taxpayer should itemize deductions. [269]

11. Kichiko and Kaoni Saito have a combined income of $13,287. Their allowable deductions are:

Medical and dental	$ 258
Taxes	1,087
Interest expense	242
Contributions	110
Miscellaneous	50

12. Ruth and Charles Loftin have a combined income of $12,142. Their allowable deductions are:

Medical and dental	$ 456
Taxes	1,028
Interest expense	842
Contributions	175
Miscellaneous	85

Self-Test: Chapter 12

Find the total interest charged for these home loans. [302]

1. Loan: $30,000   Time: 25 yr
Payment: $251.76 per month

2. Loan: $20,000   Time: 20 yr
Payment: $179.95 per month

Find the rate per $1 of assessed valuation. [307]

3. Budget proposal: $3,000,000
Total assessed valuation: $50,000,000

4. Budget proposal: $1,500,000
Total assessed valuation: $60,000,000

Compute the operating costs of these electrical appliances. [311]

5. Color TV, 250 watts, 5 hr a day, 7 days, at
5¢/kwh

6. Toaster, 1,500 watts, 5 minutes a day, 28 days,
at 4¢/kwh

Find the annual premium for each policy. [317]

7. Amount of insurance: $14,000
Cost per $100: $.25

8. Amount of insurance: $20,000
Cost per $100: $.22

For what percent is each fire insurance company liable? [321]

9. Company A: $24,000
Company B: $36,000

10. Company A: $12,000
Company B: $24,000

Solve these problems.

11. Johnston has a tax note of $5.10 per $100. Prop-
[307] erty in this area is assessed at 50% of cost. Find
the tax on a new apartment house that cost
$75,000.

12. A building valued at $100,000 is insured for
[317] $75,000 under a policy with a 80% coinsurance
clause. A fire causes $40,000 worth of dam-
age. How much can the owner expect to collect?

13. Use the rates in this table to compute the
[311] monthly electric bill for 450 kwh.

First 100 kwh	6.5¢/kwh
Next 200 kwh	4.4¢/kwh
All over 300 kwh	1.8¢/kwh
Fuel rate adjustment	1.4¢/kwh
State sales tax rate	3%

14. Mrs. Morris' fire insurance premium on her
[321] store insured for $80,000 for one year is $.38
per $100. The cost for extended coverage is
$58.50. The premium for public liability insur-
ance is $51.45. The cost of theft insurance is
$35.50. Find the total premium for this cover-
age.

Test: Chapter 12

Find the total interest charged for these home loans.

1. Loan: $30,000   Time: 30 yr
   Payment: $241.39 per month

2. Loan: $10,000   Time: 10 yr
   Payment: $126.68 per month

Find the rate per $1 of assessed valuation.

3. Budget proposal: $4,000,000
   Total assessed valuation: $80,000,000

4. Budget proposal: $2,000,000
   Total assessed valuation: $50,000,000

Compute the operating costs for these electrical appliances.

5. Clothes dryer, 4,700 watts, 60 minutes a day,
   15 days, 4¢/kwh

6. Radio, 70 watts, 2 hours a day, 30 days, at
   5¢/kwh

Find the annual premium for each policy.

7. Amount of insurance: $25,000
   Cost per $100: $.30

8. Amount of insurance: $16,000
   Cost per $100: $.28

For what percent is each fire insurance company liable?

9. Company A: $30,000
   Company B: $70,000

10. Company A: $12,000
    Company B: $48,000

Solve these problems.

11. Wattson has a tax rate of $4.80 per $100. Property in this area is assessed at 45% of cost. Find the tax on a new building that cost $100,000.

12. A building valued at $150,000 is insured for $100,000 under a policy with an 80% coinsurance clause. A fire causes $40,000 worth of damage. How much can the owner expect to collect?

13. Use the rates in this table to find the monthly electric bill for 540 kwh.

First 100 kwh ⟶	7.5¢/kwh
Next 300 kwh ⟶	4.3¢/kwh
All over 400 kwh ⟶	1.9¢/kwh
Fuel adjustment rate ⟶	1.4¢/kwh
State sales tax ⟶	5%

14. Mr. Overman's fire insurance premium on his store insured for $90,000 for one year is $.32 per $100. The cost for extended coverage is $63.50. The premium for public liability insurance is $56.40. The cost of theft insurance is $39.25. Find the total premium for this coverage.

How Many Ways?

MODEL   Omari is tossing 3 coins. What is the total number of different ways that the coins can land?

Method A   Make a table.

Possibility	1st Coin	2nd Coin	3rd Coin	
3 Heads	H	H	H	→ 1 way
2 Heads	H	H	T	
	H	T	H	→ 3 ways
	T	H	H	
1 Head	H	T	T	
	T	H	T	→ 3 ways
	T	T	H	
0 Heads	T	T	T	→ 1 way

Total ⟶ 8 ways

Method B   Multiply the choices.

1st coin		2nd coin		3rd coin	
2	×	2	×	2	= 8
choices, H or T		choices, H or T		choices, H or T	

1. Lula is tossing 4 coins. What is the total number of different ways that the coins can land?

2. Paul is tossing 5 coins. What is the total number of different ways that the coins can land?

MODEL   Anita has 5 kinds of ice cream: vanilla, banana, pecan, raisin, and maple. She has 3 kinds of toppings: chocolate, walnut, and hot fudge. How many different sundaes, each with 1 ice cream and 1 topping, can she make?

	Vanilla (v)	Banana (b)	Pecan (p)	Raisin (r)	Maple (m)
Chocolate (c)	vc	bc	pc	rc	mc
Walnut (w)	vw	bw	pw	rw	mw
Hot fudge (f)	vf	bf	pf	rf	mf

There are 3 rows of 5 sundaes each. So, Anita can make 15 different sundaes.

3. Ms. Wang bought 4 pairs of slacks and 6 shirts which she could mix and match. How many different outfits can she make?

4. Mr. Kent Bergdoff can cook 4 kinds of meat and 7 desserts. How many different kinds of dinners can he serve?

Cumulative Review

Find the actual cost of this car and the interest charged. [278]

1. Showroom price: $3,500
   Down payment: $500
   24 monthly payments of $152.50

Find the total interest charged for this home loan. [302]

3. Loan: $20,000   Time: 25 yr
   Payment: $167.84 per month

Find the annual premium for this policy. [317]

5. Amount of fire insurance: $14,000
   Cost per $100: $.25

Find the unit price to the nearest tenth of a cent. [201]

7. 880 g for $1.10

Solve these problems.

9. What is the total monthly cash benefit payment [255] for a widow and two children? Her husband's average annual income was $7,800. Use the table on page 333.

11. Jake worked 48 hours this week. His pay is [246] based on $3.10 an hour for a 40-hour week, with time-and-a-half for overtime. How much did he earn?

13. Joe Williams, single, earns $182 a week. His [261] deductions include $2.10 for medical insurance and 1.5% of his gross income for state income tax. He claims 1 exemption. Use the tables on pages 330–332 for federal income tax and F.I.C.A. deductions. Find his net income.

Calculate the amount of annual depreciation by the straight-line method. [289]

2. Cost: $6,000
   Trade-in: $800
   Useful life: 5 years

Find the tax rate per $100 of assessed valuation. [307]

4. Budget proposal: $9,000,000
   Total assessed valuation: $180,000,000

For what percent is each company liable? [321]

6. Company A: $40,000
   Company B: $10,000

Find the interest and amount due on this loan. [138]

8. $1,200 @ 7% for 3 years

10. Sara is paid $.40 per unit of completed work on [251] the first 250 units, and $.60 on each additional unit. Last week she completed 475 units. How much did she earn?

12. Suzanne expects to earn $10,300 this year. [255] What will be her annual F.I.C.A. payment? The F.I.C.A. rate is 5.85% on a $14,100 base maximum.

14. Deborah Clark's in-hospital expenses were [187] $160 for blood, $190 for the operating room, $50 for medicine and X-rays, and $16 for a telephone in her room. Her medical insurance pays $450 maximum for in-hospital expenses. How much did the insurance company pay?

Probability

Solve these problems.

MODEL   Two nickels, 3 dimes, and 4 pennies are lying on a table. Without looking, Edith is to point to a coin. What is the probability that she will point to a nickel? a dime? a quarter? a penny? a nickel, a dime, or a penny?

Total number of coins: 9

2 of the 9 coins are nickels, so P (nickel) $= \frac{2}{9}$.

Read: the probability of pointing to a nickel⤴

3 of the 9 coins are dimes, so P (dime) $= \frac{3}{9}$, or $\frac{1}{3}$.

There are no quarters, so P (quarter) $= 0$.

4 of the 9 coins are pennies, so P (penny) $= \frac{4}{9}$.

P (nickel, dime, penny) $= \frac{2}{9} + \frac{3}{9} + \frac{4}{9} = \frac{9}{9}$, or 1.

1. Sheldon is rolling a die. What is $P(3)$? $P(5)$?

2. Sheila is tossing a dime. What is P(head)? P(tail)?

3. A jar contains 4 red marbles and 3 blue marbles. Without looking, Jose is to pick a marble from the jar. What is P(red)? P(blue)?

4. A bag contains 7 black beans and 2 white beans. Without looking, Lisa is to pick a bean from the bag. What is P(white)? P(black)?

5. Jack has four $1 bills and two $5 bills in his wallet. What is the probability that he will pull out a $5 bill?

6. June has six $1 bills and three $5 bills in her wallet. What is the probability that she will pull out a $5 bill?

7. Lou is rolling a die. What is the probability that he will roll a number greater than 6?

8. Meg is rolling a die. What is the probability that she will roll a number less than 8?

9. In rolling a die, what is the probability of rolling an even number?

10. In rolling a die, what is the probability of rolling a number less than 3?

11. Kaoni is tossing 3 coins. What is the probability that exactly 2 of the coins will land heads up? (Hint: Use the chart on page 326.)

12. Theresa is tossing 3 coins. What is the probability that exactly 2 of the coins will land tails up? (Hint: Use the chart on page 326.)

13. In tossing 3 coins, what is the probability 1 or more of the coins will land heads?

14. In tossing 3 coins, what is the probability that 2 or none of the coins will land heads?

COMPOUND AMOUNT OF $1 (FOR n INTERVALS)

n	1%	$1\frac{1}{4}$%	$1\frac{1}{2}$%	2%	$2\frac{1}{2}$%	3%	$3\frac{1}{2}$%	4%	$4\frac{1}{2}$%	5%	$5\frac{1}{2}$%	6%
1	1.0100	1.0125	1.0150	1.0200	1.0250	1.0300	1.0350	1.0400	1.0450	1.0500	1.0550	1.0600
2	1.0201	1.0252	1.0302	1.0400	1.0506	1.0609	1.0712	1.0816	1.0920	1.1025	1.1130	1.1236
3	1.0303	1.0380	1.0457	1.0612	1.0769	1.0927	1.1087	1.1249	1.1412	1.1576	1.1742	1.1910
4	1.0406	1.0509	1.0614	1.0824	1.1038	1.1255	1.1475	1.1699	1.1925	1.2155	1.2388	1.2625
5	1.0510	1.0641	1.0773	1.1041	1.1314	1.1593	1.1877	1.2167	1.2462	1.2763	1.3070	1.3382
6	1.0615	1.0774	1.0934	1.1262	1.1597	1.1941	1.2293	1.2653	1.3023	1.3401	1.3788	1.4185
7	1.0721	1.0909	1.1098	1.1487	1.1887	1.2299	1.2723	1.3159	1.3609	1.4071	1.4547	1.5036
8	1.0829	1.1045	1.1265	1.1717	1.2184	1.2668	1.3168	1.3686	1.4221	1.4775	1.5347	1.5938
9	1.0937	1.1183	1.1434	1.1951	1.2489	1.3048	1.3629	1.4233	1.4861	1.5513	1.6191	1.6895
10	1.1046	1.1323	1.1605	1.2190	1.2801	1.3439	1.4106	1.4802	1.5530	1.6289	1.7081	1.7908
11	1.1157	1.1464	1.1779	1.2434	1.3121	1.3842	1.4600	1.5395	1.6229	1.7103	1.8021	1.8983
12	1.1268	1.1608	1.1956	1.2682	1.3449	1.4258	1.5111	1.6010	1.6959	1.7959	1.9012	2.0122
13	1.1381	1.1753	1.2136	1.2936	1.3785	1.4685	1.5640	1.6651	1.7722	1.8856	2.0058	2.1329
14	1.1495	1.1900	1.2318	1.3195	1.4130	1.5126	1.6187	1.7317	1.8519	1.9799	2.1161	2.2609
15	1.1610	1.2048	1.2502	1.3459	1.4483	1.5580	1.6753	1.8009	1.9353	2.0789	2.2325	2.3966
16	1.1726	1.2199	1.2690	1.3728	1.4845	1.6047	1.7340	1.8730	2.0224	2.1829	2.3553	2.5404
17	1.1843	1.2351	1.2880	1.4002	1.5216	1.6528	1.7947	1.9479	2.1134	2.2920	2.4848	2.6928
18	1.1961	1.2506	1.3073	1.4282	1.5597	1.7024	1.8575	2.0258	2.2085	2.4066	2.6215	2.8543
19	1.2081	1.2662	1.3270	1.4568	1.5987	1.7535	1.9225	2.1068	2.3079	2.5270	2.7656	3.0256
20	1.2202	1.2820	1.3469	1.4859	1.6386	1.8061	1.9889	2.1911	2.4117	2.6533	2.9178	3.2071
21	1.2324	1.2981	1.3671	1.5157	1.6796	1.8603	2.0594	2.2788	2.5202	2.7860	3.0782	3.3996
22	1.2447	1.3143	1.3876	1.5460	1.7216	1.9161	2.1315	2.3699	2.6337	2.9253	3.2473	3.6035
23	1.2572	1.3307	1.4084	1.5769	1.7646	1.9736	2.2061	2.4647	2.7522	3.0715	3.4262	3.8198
24	1.2697	1.3474	1.4295	1.6084	1.8087	2.0328	2.2833	2.5633	2.8760	3.2251	3.6146	4.0489
25	1.2824	1.3642	1.4509	1.6406	1.8539	2.0938	2.3632	2.6658	3.0054	3.3864	3.8134	4.2919

To compute how much a certain number of dollars will be worth in a specified number of years, use the table to find the amount of $1 compounded annually. For semiannual rates, use $\frac{1}{2}$ of the annual rate and 2 times the number of years. (There are 2 interest periods annually if interest is figured semiannually.) For quarterly rates, use $\frac{1}{4}$ of the annual rate and 4 times the number of years.

MODEL

How much will $500 be worth at the end of 5 years at 4% interest compounded (a) annually, (b) semiannually, and (c) quarterly?

(a) $500 \times 1.2167 = \$608.35$

(b) $500 \times 1.2190 = \$609.50$

(c) $500 \times 1.2202 = \$610.10$

And the wages are—		And the number of withholding allowances claimed is—										
At least	But less than	0	1	2	3	4	5	6	7	8	9	10 or more
		The amount of income tax to be withheld shall be—										
$80	$82	$12.00	$9.10	$6.50	$3.90	$1.80	$0	$0	$0	$0	$0	$0
82	84	12.40	9.50	6.90	4.30	2.10	0	0	0	0	0	0
84	86	12.80	9.80	7.20	4.60	2.30	.30	0	0	0	0	0
86	88	13.20	10.20	7.60	5.00	2.60	.60	0	0	0	0	0
88	90	13.60	10.60	8.00	5.40	2.90	.90	0	0	0	0	0
90	92	14.10	11.00	8.30	5.70	3.20	1.20	0	0	0	0	0
92	94	14.50	11.40	8.70	6.10	3.50	1.40	0	0	0	0	0
94	96	14.90	11.90	9.00	6.40	3.90	1.70	0	0	0	0	0
96	98	15.30	12.30	9.40	6.80	4.20	2.00	0	0	0	0	0
98	100	15.70	12.70	9.80	7.20	4.60	2.30	.30	0	0	0	0
100	105	16.50	13.40	10.40	7.80	5.20	2.80	.80	0	0	0	0
105	110	17.50	14.50	11.50	8.70	6.10	3.50	1.50	0	0	0	0
110	115	18.60	15.50	12.50	9.60	7.00	4.40	2.20	.10	0	0	0
115	120	19.60	16.60	13.60	10.50	7.90	5.30	2.90	.80	0	0	0
120	125	20.70	17.60	14.60	11.60	8.80	6.20	3.60	1.50	0	0	0
125	130	21.70	18.70	15.70	12.60	9.70	7.10	4.50	2.20	.20	0	0
130	135	22.80	19.70	16.70	13.70	10.70	8.00	5.40	2.90	.90	0	0
135	140	23.80	20.80	17.80	14.70	11.70	8.90	6.30	3.70	1.60	0	0
140	145	24.90	21.80	18.80	15.80	12.80	9.80	7.20	4.60	2.30	.30	0
145	150	25.90	22.90	19.90	16.80	13.80	10.80	8.10	5.50	3.00	1.00	0
150	160	27.50	24.50	21.40	18.40	15.40	12.30	9.50	6.90	4.30	2.00	0
160	170	29.60	26.60	23.50	20.50	17.50	14.40	11.40	8.70	6.10	3.50	1.40
170	180	31.70	28.70	25.60	22.60	19.60	16.50	13.50	10.50	7.90	5.30	2.80
180	190	33.80	30.80	27.70	24.70	21.70	18.60	15.60	12.60	9.70	7.10	4.50
190	200	35.90	32.90	29.80	26.80	23.80	20.70	17.70	14.70	11.70	8.90	6.30
200	210	38.10	35.00	31.90	28.90	25.90	22.80	19.80	16.80	13.80	10.70	8.10
210	220	40.40	37.10	34.00	31.00	28.00	24.90	21.90	18.90	15.90	12.80	9.90
220	230	42.70	39.30	36.10	33.10	30.10	27.00	24.00	21.00	18.00	14.90	11.90
230	240	45.10	41.60	38.30	35.20	32.20	29.10	26.10	23.10	20.10	17.00	14.00
240	250	47.80	43.90	40.60	37.30	34.30	31.20	28.20	25.20	22.20	19.10	16.10
250	260	50.50	46.60	42.90	39.60	36.40	33.30	30.30	27.30	24.30	21.20	18.20
260	270	53.20	49.30	45.40	41.90	38.60	35.40	32.40	29.40	26.40	23.30	20.30
270	280	56.20	52.00	48.10	44.20	40.90	37.60	34.50	31.50	28.50	25.40	22.40
280	290	59.30	54.80	50.80	46.90	43.20	39.90	36.60	33.60	30.60	27.50	24.50
290	300	62.40	57.90	53.50	49.60	45.70	42.20	38.90	35.70	32.70	29.60	26.60
300	310	65.50	61.00	56.50	52.30	48.40	44.60	41.20	37.80	34.80	31.70	28.70
310	320	68.60	64.10	59.60	55.10	51.10	47.30	43.50	40.10	36.90	33.80	30.80
320	330	71.70	67.20	62.70	58.20	53.80	50.00	46.10	42.40	39.10	35.90	32.90
330	340	74.80	70.30	65.80	61.30	56.90	52.70	48.80	44.90	41.40	38.10	35.00
340	350	78.30	73.40	68.90	64.40	60.00	55.50	51.50	47.60	43.70	40.40	37.10
350	360	81.80	76.80	72.00	67.50	63.10	58.60	54.20	50.30	46.40	42.70	39.40
360	370	85.30	80.30	75.30	70.60	66.20	61.70	57.20	53.00	49.10	45.20	41.70
370	380	88.80	83.80	78.80	73.70	69.30	64.80	60.30	55.90	51.80	47.90	44.00
380	390	92.30	87.30	82.30	77.20	72.40	67.90	63.40	59.00	54.50	50.60	46.70
390	400	95.80	90.80	85.80	80.70	75.70	71.00	66.50	62.10	57.60	53.30	49.40

MARRIED Persons—WEEKLY Payroll Period

And the wages are—		And the number of withholding allowances claimed is—										
At least	But less than	0	1	2	3	4	5	6	7	8	9	10 or more
		The amount of income tax to be withheld shall be—										
$100	$105	$14.10	$11.80	$9.50	$7.20	$4.90	$2.80	$.80	$0	$0	$0	$0
105	110	14.90	12.60	10.30	8.00	5.70	3.50	1.50	0	0	0	0
110	115	15.70	13.40	11.10	8.80	6.50	4.20	2.20	.10	0	0	0
115	120	16.50	14.20	11.90	9.60	7.30	5.00	2.90	.80	0	0	0
120	125	17.30	15.00	12.70	10.40	8.10	5.80	3.60	1.50	0	0	0
125	130	18.10	15.80	13.50	11.20	8.90	6.60	4.30	2.20	.20	0	0
130	135	18.90	16.60	14.30	12.00	9.70	7.40	5.10	2.90	.90	0	0
135	140	19.70	17.40	15.10	12.80	10.50	8.20	5.90	3.60	1.60	0	0
140	145	20.50	18.20	15.90	13.60	11.30	9.00	6.70	4.40	2.30	.30	0
145	150	21.30	19.00	16.70	14.40	12.10	9.80	7.50	5.20	3.00	1.00	0
150	160	22.50	20.20	17.90	15.60	13.30	11.00	8.70	6.40	4.10	2.00	0
160	170	24.10	21.80	19.50	17.20	14.90	12.60	10.30	8.00	5.70	3.40	1.40
170	180	26.00	23.40	21.10	18.80	16.50	14.20	11.90	9.60	7.30	5.00	2.80
180	190	28.00	25.20	22.70	20.40	18.10	15.80	13.50	11.20	8.90	6.60	4.30
190	200	30.00	27.20	24.30	22.00	19.70	17.40	15.10	12.80	10.50	8.20	5.90
200	210	32.00	29.20	26.30	23.60	21.30	19.00	16.70	14.40	12.10	9.80	7.50
210	220	34.40	31.20	28.30	25.40	22.90	20.60	18.30	16.00	13.70	11.40	9.10
220	230	36.80	33.30	30.30	27.40	24.50	22.20	19.90	17.60	15.30	13.00	10.70
230	240	39.20	35.70	32.30	29.40	26.50	23.80	21.50	19.20	16.90	14.60	12.30
240	250	41.60	38.10	34.60	31.40	28.50	25.60	23.10	20.80	18.50	16.20	13.90
250	260	44.00	40.50	37.00	33.60	30.50	27.60	24.70	22.40	20.10	17.80	15.50
260	270	46.40	42.90	39.40	36.00	32.50	29.60	26.70	24.00	21.70	19.40	17.10
270	280	48.80	45.30	41.80	38.40	34.90	31.60	28.70	25.80	23.30	21.00	18.70
280	290	51.20	47.70	44.20	40.80	37.30	33.90	30.70	27.80	25.00	22.60	20.30
290	300	53.60	50.10	46.60	43.20	39.70	36.30	32.80	29.80	27.00	24.20	21.90
300	310	56.00	52.50	49.00	45.60	42.10	38.70	35.20	31.80	29.00	26.10	23.50
310	320	58.40	54.90	51.40	48.00	44.50	41.10	37.60	34.10	31.00	28.10	25.20
320	330	60.80	57.30	53.80	50.40	46.90	43.50	40.00	36.50	33.10	30.10	27.20
330	340	63.60	59.70	56.20	52.80	49.30	45.90	42.40	38.90	35.50	32.10	29.20
340	350	66.40	62.40	58.60	55.20	51.70	48.30	44.80	41.30	37.90	34.40	31.20
350	360	69.20	65.20	61.10	57.60	54.10	50.70	47.20	43.70	40.30	36.80	33.40
360	370	72.00	68.00	63.90	60.00	56.50	53.10	49.60	46.10	42.70	39.20	35.80
370	380	74.80	70.80	66.70	62.70	58.90	55.50	52.00	48.50	45.10	41.60	38.20
380	390	77.60	73.60	69.50	65.50	61.50	57.90	54.40	50.90	47.50	44.00	40.60
390	400	80.40	76.40	72.30	68.30	64.30	60.30	56.80	53.30	49.90	46.40	43.00
400	410	83.20	79.20	75.10	71.10	67.10	63.00	59.20	55.70	52.30	48.80	45.40
410	420	86.30	82.00	77.90	73.90	69.90	65.80	61.80	58.10	54.70	51.20	47.80
420	430	89.50	84.80	80.70	76.70	72.70	68.60	64.60	60.50	57.10	53.60	50.20
430	440	92.70	88.00	83.50	79.50	75.50	71.40	67.40	63.30	59.50	56.00	52.60
440	450	95.90	91.20	86.60	82.30	78.30	74.20	70.20	66.10	62.10	58.40	55.00
450	460	99.10	94.40	89.80	85.20	81.10	77.00	73.00	68.90	64.90	60.90	57.40
460	470	102.30	97.60	93.00	88.40	83.90	79.80	75.80	71.70	67.70	63.70	59.80
470	480	105.50	100.80	96.20	91.60	87.00	82.60	78.60	74.50	70.50	66.50	62.40
480	490	108.70	104.00	99.40	94.80	90.20	85.60	81.40	77.30	73.30	69.30	65.20
490	500	112.20	107.20	102.60	98.00	93.40	88.80	84.20	80.10	76.10	72.10	68.00
500	510	115.80	110.60	105.80	101.20	96.60	92.00	87.40	82.90	78.90	74.90	70.80
510	520	119.40	114.20	109.10	104.40	99.80	95.20	90.60	86.00	81.70	77.70	73.60
520	530	123.00	117.80	112.70	107.60	103.00	98.40	93.80	89.20	84.50	80.50	76.40
530	540	126.60	121.40	116.30	111.10	106.20	101.60	97.00	92.40	87.70	83.30	79.20
540	550	130.20	125.00	119.90	114.70	109.50	104.80	100.20	95.60	90.90	86.30	82.00
550	560	133.80	128.60	123.50	118.30	113.10	108.00	103.40	98.80	94.10	89.50	84.90
560	570	137.40	132.20	127.10	121.90	116.70	111.50	106.60	102.00	97.30	92.70	88.10
570	580	141.00	135.80	130.70	125.50	120.30	115.10	109.90	105.20	100.50	95.90	91.30

Social Security Employee Tax Table

5.85 percent employee tax deductions

| Wages | | Tax to be withheld | Wages | | Tax to be withheld | Wages | | Tax to be withheld | Wages | | Tax to be withheld |
At least	But less than		At least	But less than		At least	But less than		At least	But less than	
93.94	94.11	5.50	105.05	105.22	6.15	116.16	116.33	6.80	127.27	127.44	7.45
94.11	94.28	5.51	105.22	105.39	6.16	116.33	116.50	6.81	127.44	127.61	7.46
94.28	94.45	5.52	105.39	105.56	6.17	116.50	116.67	6.82	127.61	127.78	7.47
94.45	94.62	5.53	105.56	105.73	6.18	116.67	116.84	6.83	127.78	127.95	7.48
94.62	94.79	5.54	105.73	105.90	6.19	116.84	117.01	6.84	127.95	128.12	7.49
137.53	137.70	8.05	148.64	148.81	8.70	159.75	159.92	9.35	170.86	171.03	10.00
137.70	137.87	8.06	148.81	148.98	8.71	159.92	160.09	9.36	171.03	171.20	10.01
137.87	138.04	8.07	148.98	149.15	8.72	160.09	160.26	9.37	171.20	171.37	10.02
138.04	138.21	8.08	149.15	149.32	8.73	160.26	160.43	9.38	171.37	171.54	10.03
138.21	138.38	8.09	149.32	149.49	8.74	160.43	160.60	9.39	171.54	171.71	10.04
138.38	138.55	8.10	149.49	149.66	8.75	160.60	160.77	9.40	171.71	171.89	10.05
138.55	138.72	8.11	149.66	149.83	8.76	160.77	160.95	9.41	171.89	172.06	10.06
138.72	138.89	8.12	149.83	150.00	8.77	160.95	161.12	9.42	172.06	172.23	10.07
138.89	139.06	8.13	150.00	150.18	8.78	161.12	161.29	9.43	172.23	172.40	10.08
139.06	139.24	8.14	150.18	150.35	8.79	161.29	161.46	9.44	172.40	172.57	10.09
181.12	181.29	10.60	192.23	192.40	11.25	203.34	203.51	11.90	214.45	214.62	12.55
181.29	181.46	10.61	192.40	192.57	11.26	203.51	203.68	11.91	214.62	214.79	12.56
181.46	181.63	10.62	192.57	192.74	11.27	203.68	203.85	11.92	214.79	214.96	12.57
181.63	181.80	10.63	192.74	192.91	11.28	203.85	204.02	11.93	214.96	215.13	12.58
181.80	181.97	10.64	192.91	193.08	11.29	204.02	204.19	11.94	215.13	215.30	12.59
181.97	182.14	10.65	193.08	193.25	11.30	204.19	204.36	11.95	215.30	215.48	12.60
182.14	182.31	10.66	193.25	193.42	11.31	204.36	204.53	11.96	215.48	215.65	12.61
182.31	182.48	10.67	193.42	193.59	11.32	204.53	204.71	11.97	215.65	215.82	12.62
182.48	182.65	10.68	193.59	193.77	11.33	204.71	204.88	11.98	215.82	215.99	12.63
182.65	182.83	10.69	193.77	193.94	11.34	204.88	205.05	11.99	215.99	216.16	12.64
226.42	226.59	13.25	237.53	237.70	13.90	248.64	248.81	14.55	259.75	259.92	15.20
226.59	226.76	13.26	237.70	237.87	13.91	248.81	248.98	14.56	259.92	260.09	15.21
226.76	226.93	13.27	237.87	238.04	13.92	248.98	249.15	14.57	260.09	260.26	15.22
226.93	227.10	13.28	238.04	238.21	13.93	249.15	249.32	14.58	260.26	260.43	15.23
227.10	227.27	13.29	238.21	238.38	13.94	249.32	249.49	14.59	260.43	260.60	15.24
227.27	227.44	13.30	238.38	238.55	13.95	249.49	249.66	14.60	260.60	260.77	15.25
227.44	227.61	13.31	238.55	238.72	13.96	249.66	249.83	14.61	260.77	260.95	15.26
227.61	227.78	13.32	238.72	238.89	13.97	249.83	250.00	14.62	260.95	261.12	15.27
227.78	227.95	13.33	238.89	239.06	13.98	250.00	250.18	14.63	261.12	261.29	15.28
227.95	228.12	13.34	239.06	239.24	13.99	250.18	250.35	14.64	261.29	261.46	15.29
270.86	271.03	15.85	261.97	282.14	16.50	293.08	293.25	17.15	304.19	304.36	17.80
271.03	271.20	15.86	282.14	282.31	16.51	293.25	293.42	17.16	304.36	304.53	17.81
271.20	271.37	15.87	282.31	282.48	16.52	293.42	293.59	17.17	304.53	304.71	17.82
271.37	271.54	15.88	282.48	282.65	16.53	293.59	293.77	17.18	304.71	304.88	17.83
271.54	271.71	15.89	282.65	282.83	16.54	293.77	293.94	17.19	304.88	305.05	17.84
271.71	271.89	15.90	282.83	283.00	16.55	293.94	294.11	17.20	305.05	305.22	17.85
271.89	272.06	15.91	283.00	283.17	16.56	294.11	294.28	17.21	305.22	305.39	17.86
272.06	272.23	15.92	283.17	283.34	16.57	294.28	294.45	17.22	305.39	305.56	17.87
272.23	272.40	15.93	283.34	283.51	16.58	294.45	294.62	17.23	305.56	305.73	17.88
272.40	272.57	15.94	283.51	283.68	16.59	294.62	294.79	17.24	305.73	305.90	17.89

Cash Benefit Payments

Examples of monthly cash benefit payments (effective June 1974)

Average yearly earnings after 1950*	$923 or less	$3,000	$4,000	$5,000	$6,000	$7,000	$8,000	$9,000	$10,000
Disabled worker	$ 93.80	$194.10	$228.50	$264.90	$299.40	$335.50	$372.20	$393.50	$412.40
Wife under 65 and one child	47.00	102.70	162.00	224.00	249.90	262.40	279.20	295.20	309.40
Widowed mother and one child	140.80	291.20	342.80	397.40	449.20	503.40	558.40	590.40	618.60
Widowed mother and two children	140.80	296.80	390.50	488.90	549.30	597.90	651.40	688.70	721.80
One child of retired or disabled worker	46.90	97.10	114.30	132.50	149.70	167.80	186.10	196.80	206.20
One surviving child	93.80	145.60	171.40	198.70	224.60	251.70	279.20	295.20	309.30
Maximum family payment	140.80	296.80	390.50	488.90	549.30	597.90	651.40	688.70	721.80

MODEL

Jerome Hector, age 54, is disabled. His wife is 53 and they have one child, age 13. Hector's average yearly earnings were $8,700. What is their total monthly benefit payment?

$8,700 is between $8,000 and $9,000.

For $8,000

$372.20 ⟵ Disabled worker ⟶ $393.50

+ 279.20 ⟵ Wife under 65 and 1 child ⟶ + 295.20

$651.40 ⟵ Total cash benefit ⟶ $688.70

For $9,000

$688.70 ⟵ Cash benefit for $9,000

− 651.40 ⟵ Cash benefit for $8,000

$ 37.30

× .7 ⟵ $\frac{\$700}{\$1,000}$

$26.110

+ 651.40

$677.51 ⟵ Cash benefit for $8,700

Table 1 —Returns claiming ONE exemption (and not itemizing deductions)

| If the amount on Form 1040A, line 12, is— | | And you are— | | Married filing separate return claiming— | |
At least	But less than	Single, not head of house-hold	Head of house-hold	Low income allow-ance	%Stand-ard deduc-tion
			Your tax is—		
4,950	5,000	486	467	609	591
5,000	5,050	495	476	619	599
5,050	5,100	505	485	628	607
5,100	5,150	514	494	638	615
5,150	5,200	524	503	647	623
5,200	5,250	533	512	657	631
5,250	5,300	543	521	666	639
5,300	5,350	552	530	676	647
6,900	6,950	874	826	1,026	949
6,950	7,000	884	836	1,037	960
7,000	7,050	895	845	1,048	971
7,050	7,100	905	855	1,059	982
7,100	7,150	916	864	1,070	993
7,150	7,200	926	874	1,081	1,004
7,200	7,250	937	883	1,092	1,015
7,250	7,300	947	893	1,103	1,026
9,100	9,150	1,352	1,261	1,561	1,474
9,150	9,200	1,362	1,271	1,574	1,486
9,200	9,250	1,372	1,280	1,586	1,499
9,250	9,300	1,382	1,289	1,599	1,511
9,300	9,350	1,392	1,299	1,611	1,524
9,350	9,400	1,403	1,308	1,624	1,536
9,400	9,450	1,413	1,317	1,637	1,549
9,450	9,500	1,423	1,327	1,651	1,561

Table 2 —Returns claiming TWO exemptions (and not itemizing deductions)

| If the amount on Form 1040A, line 12, is— | | And you are— | | ✱ | Married filing separate return claiming— | |
At least	But less than	Single, not head of house-hold	Head of house-hold	Married filing joint return	Low income allow-ance	%Stand-ard deduc-tion
				Your tax is—		
4,950	5,000	343	332	318	467	448
5,000	5,050	353	341	326	476	457
5,050	5,100	362	350	334	486	465
5,100	5,150	372	359	342	495	473
5,150	5,200	381	368	350	505	481
5,200	5,250	391	377	358	514	489
5,250	5,300	400	386	366	524	497
5,300	5,350	410	395	374	533	505
6,900	6,950	716	684	644	861	784
6,950	7,000	727	693	653	872	795
7,000	7,050	737	703	663	883	806
7,050	7,100	748	712	672	894	817
7,100	7,150	758	722	682	905	828
7,150	7,200	769	731	691	916	839
7,200	7,250	779	741	701	927	850
7,250	7,300	790	750	710	938	861
9,100	9,150	1,172	1,096	1,049	1,374	1,286
9,150	9,200	1,182	1,106	1,057	1,386	1,299
9,200	9,250	1,192	1,115	1,065	1,399	1,311
9,250	9,300	1,202	1,124	1,073	1,411	1,324
9,300	9,350	1,212	1,134	1,081	1,424	1,336
9,350	9,400	1,223	1,143	1,089	1,436	1,349
9,400	9,450	1,233	1,152	1,097	1,449	1,361
9,450	9,500	1,243	1,162	1,105	1,461	1,374

Table 3 —Returns claiming THREE exemptions (and not itemizing deductions)

| If the amount on Form 1040A, line 12, is— | | And you are— | | ✱ | Married filing separate return claiming— | |
At least	But less than	Single, not head of house-hold	Head of house-hold	Married filing joint return	Low income allow-ance	%Stand-ard deduc-tion
				Your tax is—		
4,900	4,950	205	200	196	315	299
4,950	5,000	213	208	204	324	306
5,000	5,050	221	216	211	334	314
5,050	5,100	229	224	219	343	322
5,100	5,150	238	232	226	353	330
5,150	5,200	246	240	234	362	338
5,200	5,250	255	248	241	372	346
5,250	5,300	263	256	249	381	354
6,900	6,950	571	548	514	696	628
6,950	7,000	581	557	522	707	638
7,000	7,050	590	566	531	718	647
7,050	7,100	600	575	539	729	657
7,100	7,150	609	584	548	740	666
7,150	7,200	619	593	556	751	676
7,200	7,250	628	602	565	762	685
7,250	7,300	638	611	573	773	696
9,100	9,150	1,006	946	906	1,186	1,103
9,150	9,200	1,015	954	914	1,199	1,114
9,200	9,250	1,024	962	922	1,211	1,125
9,250	9,300	1,033	970	930	1,224	1,136
9,300	9,350	1,042	978	938	1,236	1,149
9,350	9,400	1,051	987	947	1,249	1,161
9,400	9,450	1,060	995	955	1,261	1,174
9,450	9,500	1,069	1,003	963	1,274	1,186

Table 4 —Returns claiming FOUR exemptions (and not itemizing deductions)

At least	But less than	Single, not head of house-hold	Head of house-hold	Married filing joint return	Low income allow-ance	%Standard deduc-tion	At least	But less than	Single, not head of house-hold	Head of house-hold	Married filing joint return	Low income allow-ance	%Standard deduc-tion	At least	But less than	Single, not head of house-hold	Head of house-hold	Married filing joint return	Low income allow-ance	%Standard deduc-tion
4,800	4,850	74	74	74	173	161	6,950	7,000	438	422	398	562	495	9,100	9,150	849	804	764	1,015	938
4,850	4,900	81	81	81	181	168	7,000	7,050	448	431	406	571	505	9,150	9,200	858	812	772	1,026	949
4,900	4,950	89	88	88	189	175	7,050	7,100	457	440	414	581	514	9,200	9,250	867	820	780	1,037	960
4,950	5,000	96	95	95	197	182	7,100	7,150	467	449	422	590	524	9,250	9,300	876	828	788	1,048	971
5,000	5,050	104	102	102	205	188	7,150	7,200	476	458	430	600	533	9,300	9,350	885	836	796	1,059	982
5,050	5,100	111	109	109	213	195	7,200	7,250	486	467	438	609	543	9,350	9,400	893	844	804	1,070	993
5,100	5,150	119	116	116	221	202	7,250	7,300	495	476	446	619	552	9,400	9,450	902	852	812	1,081	1,004
5,150	5,200	126	123	123	229	209	7,300	7,350	505	485	454	628	562	9,450	9,500	911	860	820	1,092	1,015

Table 5 —Returns claiming FIVE exemptions (and not itemizing deductions)

At least	But less than	Single, not head of house-hold	Head of house-hold	Married filing joint return	Low income allow-ance	%Standard deduc-tion	At least	But less than	Single, not head of house-hold	Head of house-hold	Married filing joint return	Low income allow-ance	%Standard deduc-tion	At least	But less than	Single, not head of house-hold	Head of house-hold	Married filing joint return	Low income allow-ance	%Standard deduc-tion
4,800	4,850	0	0	0	60	49	6,900	6,950	289	280	271	410	343	9,200	9,250	709	677	637	872	795
4,850	4,900	0	0	0	67	55	6,950	7,000	297	288	279	419	353	9,250	9,300	718	685	645	883	806
4,900	4,950	0	0	0	74	61	7,000	7,050	306	296	286	429	362	9,300	9,350	727	693	653	894	817
4,950	5,000	0	0	0	81	67	7,050	7,100	315	305	294	438	372	9,350	9,400	736	702	662	905	828
5,000	5,050	0	0	0	89	73	7,100	7,150	324	314	302	448	381	9,400	9,450	745	710	670	916	839
5,050	5,100	4	4	4	96	80	7,150	7,200	334	323	310	457	391	9,450	9,500	754	718	678	927	850
5,100	5,150	11	11	11	104	86	7,200	7,250	343	332	318	467	400	9,500	9,550	763	726	686	938	861
5,150	5,200	18	18	18	111	92	7,250	7,300	353	341	326	476	410	9,550	9,600	772	734	694	949	872

Table 6 —Returns claiming SIX exemptions (and not itemizing deductions)

At least	But less than	Single, not head of house-hold	Head of house-hold	Married filing joint return	Low income allow-ance	%Standard deduc-tion	At least	But less than	Single, not head of house-hold	Head of house-hold	Married filing joint return	Low income allow-ance	%Standard deduc-tion	At least	But less than	Single, not head of house-hold	Head of house-hold	Married filing joint return	Low income allow-ance	%Standard deduc-tion
5,600	5,650	0	0	0	67	39	6,800	6,850	149	144	144	255	197	9,200	9,250	709	677	637	872	795
5,650	5,700	0	0	0	74	45	6,850	6,900	157	152	151	263	205	9,250	9,300	718	685	645	883	806
5,700	5,750	0	0	0	81	51	6,900	6,950	165	160	159	272	213	9,300	9,350	727	693	653	894	817
5,750	5,800	0	0	0	89	57	6,950	7,000	173	168	166	280	221	9,350	9,400	736	702	662	905	828
5,800	5,850	4	4	4	96	63	7,000	7,050	181	176	174	289	229	9,400	9,450	597	572	537	751	676
5,850	5,900	11	11	11	104	69	7,050	7,100	189	184	181	297	238	9,450	9,500	605	580	544	762	685
5,900	5,950	18	18	18	111	75	7,100	7,150	197	192	189	306	246	9,500	9,550	613	587	551	773	696
5,950	6,000	25	25	25	119	82	7,150	7,200	205	200	196	315	255	9,550	9,600	621	595	559	784	707

Tax Rate Schedules

SCHEDULE X—Single Taxpayers Not Qualifying for Rates in Schedule Y or Z

If the amount on Form 1040A, line 16, is:

Enter on Form 1040A, line 17.

Not over $500.... 14% of the amount on line 16.

Over—	But not over—		of excess over—
$500	$1,000	$70+15%	$500
$1,000	$1,500	$145+16%	$1,000
$1,500	$2,000	$225+17%	$1,500
$2,000	$4,000	$310+19%	$2,000
$4,000	$6,000	$690+21%	$4,000
$6,000	$8,000	$1,110+24%	$6,000
$8,000	$10,000	$1,590+25%	$8,000
$10,000	$12,000	$2,090+27%	$10,000
$12,000	$14,000	$2,630+29%	$12,000
$14,000	$16,000	$3,210+31%	$14,000
$16,000	$18,000	$3,830+34%	$16,000
$18,000	$20,000	$4,510+36%	$18,000
$20,000	$22,000	$5,230+38%	$20,000
$22,000	$26,000	$5,990+40%	$22,000
$26,000	$32,000	$7,590+45%	$26,000
$32,000	$38,000	$10,290+50%	$32,000
$38,000	$44,000	$13,290+55%	$38,000
$44,000	$50,000	$16,590+60%	$44,000
$50,000	$60,000	$20,190+62%	$50,000
$60,000	$70,000	$26,390+64%	$60,000
$70,000	$80,000	$32,790+66%	$70,000
$80,000	$90,000	$39,390+68%	$80,000
$90,000	$100,000	$46,190+69%	$90,000
$100,000	....	$53,090+70%	$100,000

SCHEDULE Y—Married Taxpayers and Certain Widows and Widowers

If you are a married person living apart from your spouse, see page 5, paragraph 1(d), of the instructions to see if you can be considered to be "unmarried" for purposes of using Schedule X or Z. If you can, your tax may be lower.

Married Taxpayers Filing Joint Returns and Certain Widows and Widowers (See page 5)

If the amount on Form 1040A, line 16, is:

Enter on Form 1040A, line 17.

Not over $1,000.... 14% of the amount on line 16.

Over—	But not over—		of excess over—
$1,000	$2,000	$140+15%	$1,000
$2,000	$3,000	$290+16%	$2,000
$3,000	$4,000	$450+17%	$3,000
$4,000	$8,000	$620+19%	$4,000
$8,000	$12,000	$1,380+22%	$8,000
$12,000	$16,000	$2,260+25%	$12,000
$16,000	$20,000	$3,260+28%	$16,000
$20,000	$24,000	$4,380+32%	$20,000
$24,000	$28,000	$5,660+36%	$24,000
$28,000	$32,000	$7,100+39%	$28,000
$32,000	$36,000	$8,660+42%	$32,000
$36,000	$40,000	$10,340+45%	$36,000
$40,000	$44,000	$12,140+48%	$40,000
$44,000	$52,000	$14,060+50%	$44,000
$52,000	$64,000	$18,060+53%	$52,000
$64,000	$76,000	$24,420+55%	$64,000
$76,000	$88,000	$31,020+58%	$76,000
$88,000	$100,000	$37,980+60%	$88,000
$100,000	$120,000	$45,180+62%	$100,000
$120,000	$140,000	$57,580+64%	$120,000
$140,000	$160,000	$70,380+66%	$140,000
$160,000	$180,000	$83,580+68%	$160,000
$180,000	$200,000	$97,180+69%	$180,000
$200,000	....	$110,980+70%	$200,000

Married Taxpayers Filing Separate Returns

If the amount on Form 1040A, line 16, is:

Enter on Form 1040A, line 17.

Not over $500.... 14% of the amount on line 16.

Over—	But not over—		of excess over—
$500	$1,000	$70+15%	$500
$1,000	$1,500	$145+16%	$1,000
$1,500	$2,000	$225+17%	$1,500
$2,000	$4,000	$310+19%	$2,000
$4,000	$6,000	$690+22%	$4,000
$6,000	$8,000	$1,130+25%	$6,000
$8,000	$10,000	$1,630+28%	$8,000
$10,000	$12,000	$2,190+32%	$10,000
$12,000	$14,000	$2,830+36%	$12,000
$14,000	$16,000	$3,550+39%	$14,000
$16,000	$18,000	$4,330+42%	$16,000
$18,000	$20,000	$5,170+45%	$18,000
$20,000	$22,000	$6,070+48%	$20,000
$22,000	$26,000	$7,030+50%	$22,000
$26,000	$32,000	$9,030+53%	$26,000
$32,000	$38,000	$12,210+55%	$32,000
$38,000	$44,000	$15,510+58%	$38,000
$44,000	$50,000	$18,990+60%	$44,000
$50,000	$60,000	$22,590+62%	$50,000
$60,000	$70,000	$28,790+64%	$60,000
$70,000	$80,000	$35,190+66%	$70,000
$80,000	$90,000	$41,790+68%	$80,000
$90,000	$100,000	$48,590+69%	$90,000
$100,000	....	$55,490+70%	$100,000

SCHEDULE Z—Unmarried (or legally separated) Taxpayers Who Qualify as Heads of Household (See page 5)

If the amount on Form 1040A, line 16, is:

Enter on Form 1040A, line 17.

Not over $1,000.... 14% of the amount on line 16.

Over—	But not over—		of excess over—
$1,000	$2,000	$140+16%	$1,000
$2,000	$4,000	$300+18%	$2,000
$4,000	$6,000	$660+19%	$4,000
$6,000	$8,000	$1,040+22%	$6,000
$8,000	$10,000	$1,480+23%	$8,000
$10,000	$12,000	$1,940+25%	$10,000
$12,000	$14,000	$2,440+27%	$12,000
$14,000	$16,000	$2,980+28%	$14,000
$16,000	$18,000	$3,540+31%	$16,000
$18,000	$20,000	$4,160+32%	$18,000
$20,000	$22,000	$4,800+35%	$20,000
$22,000	$24,000	$5,500+36%	$22,000
$24,000	$26,000	$6,220+38%	$24,000
$26,000	$28,000	$6,980+41%	$26,000
$28,000	$32,000	$7,800+42%	$28,000
$32,000	$36,000	$9,480+45%	$32,000
$36,000	$38,000	$11,280+48%	$36,000
$38,000	$40,000	$12,240+51%	$38,000
$40,000	$44,000	$13,260+52%	$40,000
$44,000	$50,000	$15,340+55%	$44,000
$50,000	$52,000	$18,640+56%	$50,000
$52,000	$64,000	$19,760+58%	$52,000
$64,000	$70,000	$26,720+59%	$64,000
$70,000	$76,000	$30,260+61%	$70,000
$76,000	$80,000	$33,920+62%	$76,000
$80,000	$88,000	$36,400+63%	$80,000
$88,000	$100,000	$41,440+64%	$88,000
$100,000	$120,000	$49,120+66%	$100,000
$120,000	$140,000	$62,320+67%	$120,000
$140,000	$160,000	$75,720+68%	$140,000
$160,000	$180,000	$89,320+69%	$160,000
$180,000	....	$103,120+70%	$180,000

Metric Tables

LENGTH

1 kilometer (km) = 1,000 meters (m)
1 hectometer (hm) = 100 meters
1 dekameter (dam) = 10 meters
1 decimeter (dm) = .1 meter
1 centimeter (cm) = .01 meter
1 millimeter (mm) = .001 meter

CAPACITY

1 kiloliter (kl) = 1,000 liters (ℓ)
1 hectoliter (hl) = 100 liters
1 dekaliter (dal) = 10 liters
1 deciliter (dl) = .1 liter
1 centiliter (cl) = .01 liter
1 milliliter (ml) = .001 liter

WEIGHT AND MASS

1 kilogram (kg) = 1,000 grams (g)
1 hectogram (hg) = 100 grams
1 dekagram (dag) = 10 grams
1 decigram (dg) = .1 gram
1 centigram (cg) = .01 gram
1 milligram (mg) = .001 gram

APPROXIMATIONS

1 centimeter $\doteq$ .4 inch (in.)
1 meter $\doteq$ 1 yard (yd)
1 kilometer $\doteq$ .6 mile (mi)
1 liter $\doteq$ 1 quart (qt)
1 kilogram $\doteq$ 2 pounds (lb)
1 inch $\doteq$ 2.5 centimeters
1 mile $\doteq$ 1.6 kilometers
1 gallon (gal) $\doteq$ 4 liters
1 pound $\doteq$ .5 kilogram
1 ounce (oz) $\doteq$ 30 grams

GLOSSARY

The explanations given in this glossary are intended to be brief descriptions of the terms listed. They are not necessarily definitions.

Accessory   An accessory is extra equipment that is not really needed. An accessory usually adds to the convenience, comfort, safety, appearance, etc. An air conditioner is an accessory in cars.

Accountant   An accountant is a professionally trained person who keeps business records. He or she advises clients on their financial management.

Addends   Addends are numbers to be added.

MODEL   In $5 + 3 = 8$, 5 and 3 are addends.

Amortization schedule   An amortization schedule shows the repayment of a loan with a series of equal payments. It also shows the breakdown for interest and principal for each payment.

Annual   Annual refers to a period of 12 months or one year.

Annually   Annually means yearly or every year.

Appliance   An appliance is a machine or device, usually using electrical power. A washing machine is a large appliance; a toaster, a small appliance.

Area   Area is the number of square units needed to cover a region on a surface. The area of a rectangle 2 feet by 3 feet is 6 square feet.

Assessed value   The assessed value is the value at which a property is taxed. The assessed value is usually given as a percent of the original or market value.

Associative property of addition   When adding any three numbers, you may group them in any way.

MODEL $8 + 6 + 5$

$$\begin{array}{c|c} (8 + 6) + 5 & 8 + (6 + 5) \\ \hline 14 + 5 & 8 + 11 \\ 19 & 19 \end{array}$$

Associative property of multiplication   When multiplying any three numbers, you may group them in any way.

MODEL $3 \times 4 \times 2$

$$\begin{array}{c|c} (3 \times 4) \times 2 & 3 \times (4 \times 2) \\ \hline 12 \times 2 & 3 \times 8 \\ 24 & 24 \end{array}$$

Average   The average of two or more numbers is the sum of the numbers divided by the number of addends.

MODEL   The average of 5, 10, and 9 is $\frac{5 + 10 + 9}{3}$, or 8.

Balance   A balance is a weighing device using two pans. The pans are at opposite ends of a horizontal beam.

Banker's interest   In banker's interest, it is assumed that there are 12 months of 30 days each, or 360 days in each year.

Bank statement   A bank statement is a form prepared by the depositor's bank. The form lists all checks cashed and deposits made for a particular period of time (usually one month).

Beneficiary   A beneficiary is a person named to receive the benefits or income from an insurance policy, a will, etc.

Board of directors   A board of directors is a group of persons who are responsible for managing the business of a corporation, organization, or agency.

Bodily injury insurance   Bodily injury insurance provides financial protection for a car owner. Payments are made if the car causes injury or death to other people.

Bond   A bond is a certificate, issued by a government or company. It promises to pay the holder a specified sum at a certain date. A bondholder receives interest in this period.

Boutique   A boutique is a specialty shop dealing in fashionable ready-to-wear clothes and accessories.

Broker   A broker is an agent who buys and sells stocks and bonds for others.

Brokerage fee   A brokerage fee is the amount charged by a broker for buying and selling stocks and bonds.

Budget   A budget is a financial plan for future spending of one's income.

Business administration   Business administration is a course of study which prepares one for a career in managing and operating a business.

Buyer   A buyer for a business is a person who determines which items should be purchased for sale to customers.

Canceled checks   Canceled checks are the checks drawn by a depositor and cashed by his or her bank. The checks are marked ''paid'' and returned to the depositor with the bank statement.

Capacity   Capacity is the amount of liquid that a container will hold.

Career   A career is an occupation, lifework, or vocation.

Carrying charge   A carrying charge is the interest that the dealer adds to the balance due. The charge is made on the amount due after the down payment.

Cash advance   A cash advance is an amount of money given in advance to an employee by a company to pay for expenses.

Cash discount   A cash discount is the deduction that is allowed on an invoice price. Payment must be made within a specific period of time to get the discount.

Cash sale   A cash sale is a business transaction in which the buyer pays by cash or by check at the time of purchase.

Cash surrender value   The cash surrender value of an insurance policy is the amount of money which can be collected by the insured if the policy is canceled.

Catalog   A catalog is a book which describes goods for sale. It suggests prices to be charged the consumer and offers the middleman a trade discount.

Catalog price   The catalog price is the price which the manufacturer recommends that the consumer be charged. It is sometimes called the *list* or *retail price*.

Charge account   A charge account customer uses a credit card to purchase goods or services. It allows the customer to take possession of the goods and to pay at some future date.

Charge sale   A charge sale is a business transaction in which the buyer charges the cost to his or her account.

Check   A check is a written order in which a bank is directed to pay out money from the depositor's account.

Checkbook   A checkbook contains blank checks for payment orders and stubs on which the depositor keeps a record of his or her checking account.

Checking account   A checking account is an arrangement made by a depositor and a commercial bank, whereby written payment orders will be made to third parties from the depositor's account.

Checking division   Checking division uses the following rule:

Divisor × quotient + remainder = dividend.

Closing costs   Closing costs refer to the legal costs needed to complete the purchase of real estate. They include attorney's fees, title search, federal stamps, insurance, and part of the year's taxes.

Coinsurance clause   A coinsurance clause in a fire insurance policy requires that the property owner share some of the loss with the insurance company. This is the case if the amount of insurance carried is less than the required percent, usually 80% of property value.

Collision insurance   Collision insurance covers damages to the driver's automobile in case of an accident.

Commercial bank   A commercial bank specializes in loans to business people. It is often called *a full service bank*. It provides most banking services such as savings and checking accounts, auto loans, long and short term loans, trusts, payment of taxes and utility bills, safe deposit boxes.

Commission   Salespeople may be paid a commission based on the amount of their sales. It acts as an incentive to increase sales. It may be a percent of the sales or an amount per item sold.

Common factor   A common factor is a number that is divisible into each of 2 or more numbers.

MODELS   3 is the common factor of 12 and 15   because $12 \div 3 = 4$ and $15 \div 3 = 5$.

4 is the common factor of the numerator and the denominator of $\frac{12}{16}$ because $\frac{12 \div 4}{16 \div 4} = \frac{3}{4}$.

Commutative property of addition   When adding any two numbers, you may add them in either order.

MODEL $5 + 3 = 3 + 5$

Commutative property of multiplication When multiplying any two numbers, you may multiply them in either order.

MODEL $5 \times 3 = 3 \times 5$

Comparison shopping In comparison shopping a buyer of goods or services attempts to determine which is the best buy among several similar offers.

Competitive To be competitive, the seller of goods or services must offer them at a price which will attract possible buyers.

Compound interest Compound interest is interest paid on both the principal and previous interest remaining on deposit.

Comprehensive insurance Comprehensive insurance provides financial protection to the car owner. It pays for damages resulting from causes such as fire, theft, and vandalism.

Congruent Congruent figures are exact copies of each other in shape and size.

Consumer A consumer is a person who uses goods and services.

Conventional loan Conventional loans are loans which are made by banks. They carry a higher rate of interest than government backed loans.

Cost of goods sold The cost of goods sold is the estimated or actual cost value of goods which have been sold.

Cost of living The cost of living increases or decreases as the amount of money needed to buy goods and services changes.

Credit card A credit card is issued by certain companies and banks for the convenience of their customers. It enables the holder to make purchases and to postpone payment for approximately 30 days. After that time a carrying charge is added to the balance due.

Credit risk A person with a reputation for paying debts promptly is considered a good credit risk.

Credit union A credit union is a savings and loan organization formed by a group of employees with a common interest or employer.

Dealership A dealership is a business which has the exclusive right to sell a particular product or service in a given area. For example, an appliance or automobile dealership.

Decimal Decimal means based on ten.

Deductible clause A $50 or $100 deductible clause in an insurance policy means that the insured pays the first $50 or $100 of damages.

Deductions Deductions refers to money that is withheld from a person's pay. Deductions also refers to the various amounts a person may subtract from the gross income when computing his or her income tax.

Degree Celsius Degree Celsius (°C) is the metric unit used to measure temperature.

Denominator The denominator of a fraction is the number written below the horizontal bar. The denominator of a fraction cannot be 0.

MODEL In the fraction $\frac{7}{8}$, 8 is the denominator.

Depreciation Depreciation is a decrease in the value of an article or property due to wear and age.

Disability Disability benefits may be paid to an employee who is unable to work due to a physical or mental condition. This condition is expected to last at least 12 months, or possibly result in death.

Discount A discount is a deduction from the original price of an article which is usually offered for early or cash payment.

Distributive property of multiplication over addition The distributive property links the operations of multiplication and addition.

MODEL $3 \times (5 + 2) = (3 \times 5) + (3 \times 2)$

Dividend (in division) The dividend is the number to be divided.

MODEL In $6\overline{)18}$, 18 is the dividend.

Dividend (stock) A dividend is the earnings on shares of stock. The dividend may be paid to stockholders in cash or in stock.

Divisor The divisor is the number that is used to divide a number.

MODEL In $6\overline{)18}$, 6 is the divisor.

Down payment A down payment is the amount of money that must be paid at the time of an installment purchase. It is applied toward the total price.

Endowment policy An endowment insurance policy provides protection for a specified period of time. Benefits are paid to the insured if he or she is still living after this period of time.

Equivalent fractions Equivalent fractions are 2 or more fractions that have the same value.

MODEL $\frac{1}{2}, \frac{2}{4}, \frac{3}{6}, \frac{4}{8}$, and $\frac{5}{10}$ are equivalent fractions.

Estimate To estimate means to determine roughly or approximately.

Estimated life The estimated life of an object or machine is the time that the object is expected to last with average use and care.

Extended coverage Extended coverage is insurance which protects the homeowner against losses due to lightning, windstorms, hail, rain, water, riot, explosions, etc.

Extremes The extremes are the first and fourth terms in a proportion.

MODEL In the proportion $\frac{5}{8} = \frac{10}{16}$, 5 and 16 are the extremes.

Face value The face value is the amount written or stamped on a note, bond, or insurance policy.

Factors Factors are numbers to be multiplied.

MODEL In $5 \times 7 = 35$, 5 and 7 are factors.

F.I.C.A.   The initials F.I.C.A. stand for *Federal Insurance Contributions Act*. This plan commonly known as *Social Security*. It is a federal law which provides retirement income, disability insurance, medical care, and survivors' benefits for those who qualify.

Finance contract   A finance contract is a legal, written agreement. In this agreement a buyer promises to make payments as specified.

Financing   Financing is a method by which a consumer obtains money or credit to buy articles. The purchases are usually on an installment plan.

Fire insurance   Fire insurance provides financial protection against loss of property due to fire.

Fixed expenses   Fixed expenses are necessary living costs that occur regularly. For example, one's monthly rent or mortgage payment.

Form 1040   Federal income tax Form 1040 is for those taxpayers who have earned more than $10,000 and who wish to itemize deductions. Usually in these cases the deductions will amount to more than 15% of the taxpayer's adjusted gross income.

Form 1040A   Federal income tax Form 1040A is primarily for those taxpayers who have earned less than $10,000 or who do not have deductions which amount to more than $2,000.

Frequency of repair   Frequency of repair tells how often an object, car, appliance, etc., has to be repaired.

Fully covered   Fully covered means that a homeowner has taken out enough fire insurance to be completely insured for losses due to fire.

Greater than   The symbol for greater than is $>$.

MODEL $10 > 6$ is read ''10 is greater than 6.''

Gross profit   Gross profit is the difference between net sales and the cost of goods sold. It is sometimes called the *margin* or *markup*.

Guarantor   A guarantor for a loan is a person who agrees to assume any financial liability for someone else.

Health insurance   Health insurance provides financial protection against hospital and surgical expenses. It also provides protection against loss of income if a person becomes disabled and cannot work.

Homeowner's insurance policy   A homeowner's insurance policy provides financial protection against property damage and personal liability.

Incentive plan   An incentive plan encourages employees to increase their productivity in order to earn more money.

In-hospital expenses   In-hospital expenses include costs for the use of the operating room, drugs, X-rays, in-hospital laboratory tests, blood, and so on.

Installment   An installment is a part of a debt to be paid at regular times for a specified period of time.

Installment plan   An installment plan is an arrangement for credit to buy goods. The buyer agrees to make regular payments for a specified period of time until the debt is paid.

Installment purchase   In an installment purchase, a consumer agrees to pay the purchase price of goods or services over an extended period of time.

Insurance policies   Insurance policies provide protection against financial loss due to accident, illness, fire, property damage, personal liability, and so on.

Interest   Interest is the amount of money that the lender of money, goods, or service charges the borrower. It is also the amount of money earned through investing in savings accounts and bonds.

Interest bearing note   An interest bearing note is one to be paid on its due date with interest. Interest is calculated for the term of the note.

Interest formula   The interest formula is: Interest equals principal times rate times time.

$$I = p \times r \times t, \text{ or } I = prt$$

Inventory   An inventory is a listing of items on hand at a particular time. It indicates quantities and their actual or estimated value.

Investing   Investing means putting money into banks, stocks, bonds, property, and so on, to obtain income or profit.

Invoice price   The invoice price is the difference between the catalog, or list price, and the trade discount.

Invoice terms   The invoice terms give the percent of cash discount allowed, the number of days in the discount period, and the number of days in the credit period.

MODELS   2/10, n/30 allows a 2% cash discount if paid in 10 days; otherwise the amount of the invoice is due in 30 days.

3/10, 1/20, n/30 allows a 3% cash discount if paid in 10 days, a 1% cash discount if paid from the 11th to 20th day; otherwise the amount of the invoice is due within 30 days.

Itemize   To itemize means to list in a certain order.

Itemized deductions   Taxpayers who use the 1040 tax form may list all allowable deductions. These include medical expenses, other taxes paid, interest payments, contributions, etc.

Joint account   A joint account is a single checking or savings account which is shared by 2 or more people.

Joint tax return   A joint tax return is one prepared by a husband and wife whether one or both have earned taxable income. It will usually result in a smaller tax liability than if each prepared a separate tax return.

Kilowatt hour   A kilowatt hour (kwh) is a unit for measuring the amount of electricity used. 1 kilowatt hour = 1,000 watts. If a 100-watt bulb is left burning for 10 hours, 1 kwh of electricity will have been used.

Lending agency   A lending agency is any business that loans money.

Less than   The symbol for less than is <.

MODEL   5 < 8 is read, "5 is less than 8."

Levy   A government or organization may levy (impose) certain charges to raise funds.

Life insurance   Life insurance provides protection for the insured's entire life. Money is paid to the beneficiary upon the death of the insured. In some cases money may be paid to the insured when he or she reaches a specified age.

Limited payment life policy   A limited payment life insurance policy is paid for in a limited period of time such as 20 or 30 years. It provides protection for the insured's entire life. It is sometimes called *whole life insurance*.

List price   The list price is the price which the manufacturer advises that the retailer charge. It is sometimes called the *catalog* or *retail price*.

Major medical insurance   Major medical insurance is a type of health insurance. It protects the insured against large medical expenses of a serious injury or a long illness.

Maker   The maker of a promissory note is the borrower who signs the note. The maker's signature usually appears in the lower right-hand corner.

Manager   A manager is a person who is placed in charge of a particular area of operations.

Market price   The market price of a stock or a bond is the current price on the stock exchange. It is sometimes called the *market value*.

Markdown   A markdown is the amount by which the price of goods has been reduced, usually at a sale.

Markup   The markup is the amount by which the selling price is greater than the cost. It is sometimes called the *gross profit* or *margin*.

Maturity value   The maturity value of a note is the total amount due on the date of payment.

Means   The means are the second and third terms in a proportion.

MODEL   In the proportion $\frac{5}{8} = \frac{10}{16}$, 8 and 10 are the means.

Metric system   The metric system is a system of measurement based on the decimal system. Commonly used units for length, capacity, weight, and temperature are the meter, liter, kilogram, and degree Celsius respectively.

Middleman   A middleman is one who has a service to perform between the manufacturer and the final consumer.

Mileage   Mileage means the total number of miles traveled. Gasoline mileage refers to the number of miles traveled per gallon of gas.

Minimum wage   A minimum wage, set by the federal and state governments, is the lowest legal rate of hourly pay allowed in most types of work.

Monthly   Monthly means each month or per month.

Mortgage   A mortgage is a legal claim to certain property of the borrower. It gives the lender the right to ownership if payments are not made according to the agreement.

Multiple   A multiple of a number is the product of that number and another number.

MODEL   15 is a multiple of 5 because $5 \times 3 = 15$.

Necessity   A necessity is an item without which a person could not live, such as food.

Net loss   A net loss results when the cost of goods sold and the operating expenses are greater than the gross profit.

Net profit (net income)   The net profit (net income) is found by subtracting the operating expenses from the margin, or gross profit. If these expenses are greater than the gross profit, a net loss results.

Numerator   The numerator is the number written above the horizontal bar in a fraction.

MODEL   In the fraction $\frac{3}{5}$, 3 is the numerator.

Octane rating   An octane rating of gasoline is a number used to show the anti-knock quality of the gasoline.

Odometer   An odometer is an instrument used to measure the distance traveled by a car.

Option   An option is a choice or alternate method.

Overdrawn   An account is overdrawn when a depositor has written checks for more money than is available in his or her checking account.

Overstocked   To be overstocked means to have more than enough goods on hand than are needed for sale.

Overtime   Overtime is time worked beyond the regular hours per day or per week for employees on a hourly pay basis. A higher rate is usually paid for overtime.

Partnership   A partnership is a business organization owned and operated by 2 or more people.

Par value   Par value is the value which is printed, written, or stamped on the face of a stock or bond certificate. It is sometimes called the *face value*.

Payee (of a note)   The payee of a promissory note is the lender to whom payment will be made.

Payee (of a check) The payee of a check is the person to whom the check is made payable.

Percent Percent, meaning hundredths, represents a fraction with a denominator of 100. The symbol for percent is %.

MODEL $45\% = .45 = \frac{45}{100}$

Perimeter The perimeter of a polygon is the total distance around the polygon. It is found by adding the lengths of the sides.

Periodic Periodic means occurring or appearing at regular times. Periodic premium insurance payments may be made monthly, quarterly, semi-annually, or annually.

Personal liability insurance Personal liability insurance protects homeowners. It pays for legal defense and bodily injuries of others. It also pays for damage, caused by the homeowner, to other property.

Piece-rate wages Piece-rate wages are wages based on the number of units of work completed.

Place value Place value refers to the position or placement of number symbols which are used to name a number.

MODEL In 512.6, 5 is in the hundreds place, 1 is in the tens place, 2 is in the units place and 6 is in the tenths place.

Principal The principal is the amount of money borrowed. It sometimes refers to the value of goods and services loaned.

Promissory note A promissory note is written evidence of a debt. It is signed by the borrower and shows to whom, how much, and when payments will be made.

Property damage insurance Property damage insurance is a form of liability insurance. It provides financial protection and legal defense when your car damages the property of others.

Proportion A proportion is a statement of equality of 2 ratios.

MODELS $\frac{1}{2} = \frac{2}{4}, \frac{2}{3} = \frac{8}{12}, \frac{4}{5} = \frac{12}{15}$

Public liability insurance Public liability insurance is a combination of two types of automobile liability insurance: bodily injury and property damage.

Public utilities Public utilities are essential services such as electricity, gas, water, and telephone. Companies that provide these services are often called *public utilities*.

Quarterly Quarterly means one-fourth of a year, or once every 3 months.

Quotient Quotient is the number obtained when a number is divided by another number.

MODEL In $3\overline{)6}^{2}$, 2 is the quotient.

"Ragged" decimals   "Ragged" decimals refer to numbers whose decimal place values are different. To add "ragged" decimals, line up the decimal points.

MODEL   65.7834, 752.1, 2.17

$$
\begin{array}{r}
65.7834 \\
752.1 \\
+\ \ \ 2.17 \\
\hline
\end{array}
$$

Rate   Rate is a relative amount, usually expressed as a ratio or percent.

Rate of return   The rate of return on an investment shows how profitable it is.

Ratio   A ratio is a comparison of 2 numbers by division. A ratio is usually stated as a fraction, a decimal, or a percent.

MODEL   The ratio 4 to 5 may be expressed as $\frac{4}{5}$, .8, or 80%.

Real estate   Real estate refers to permanent and immovable things such as land and buildings. It is often called real property.

Reciprocal   The product of any number and its reciprocal is 1.

MODEL $\frac{2}{5} \times \frac{5}{2} = 1$, so $\frac{5}{2}$ and $\frac{2}{5}$ are reciprocals of each other.

Reconciliation statement   A reconciliation statement is prepared by a depositor to determine the correct balance. This balance is the amount which is available in the bank and against which future checks may be drawn.

Regular time   Regular time provides for a specific number of working hours in a work week or day.

Related rate   A related rate is the percent equivalent of a given ratio.

MODEL $\frac{1}{4} = 25\%$

Retailer   A retailer is a person who sells goods in small quantities directly to the consumer.

Retail price   The retail price is the price at which goods are sold to consumers. It is sometimes called the *catalog* or *list price*.

Return   The return on an investment is the profit, or loss, that is made on the investment.

Round to   Round to means to give an approximate answer.

MODELS   541.784 rounded to the nearest tenth is 541.8.

15.3 cm rounded to the nearest cm is 15 cm.

Sale   A sale is a business transaction in which property or services is exchanged for an agreed amount of money or other considerations.

Sales slip   A sales slip is a form prepared by the seller. It shows the customer's name and address, the items sold and their selling prices, the sales tax, and the total amount due.

Sales tax   A sales tax is a charge made on the retail price of certain goods and services. It may be imposed by certain state and local governmental units.

Savings bank   A savings bank is a financial institution that specializes in savings accounts. It also specializes in loans for personal reasons or for mortgages.

Savings and loan associations   Savings and loan associations are organized under special government charters. They may offer savings accounts, mortgage loans, and improvement and construction loans. They are not allowed to offer checking accounts, short-term loans, and trusts. They usually pay higher interest rates on savings accounts than commercial or savings banks.

Scale   A scale is a ratio between a dimension on a drawing and the same dimension of the object it represents.

Scale drawing   A scale drawing is a drawing with the same shape as the object it represents. It may be smaller or larger in size.

Second-hand   A second-hand item is one which has been owned by more than one person when it is offered for sale to another customer.

Securities   Securities are written documents of ownership such as stock and bond certificates.

Semiannual   Semiannual means once every 6 months or twice a year.

Service charges   Service charges are fees charged by a bank for handling a depositor's checking account and preparing a bank statement.

Share (of stock)   A share of stock is a legal document showing part ownership in a corporation. The document is sometimes called a *stock certificate*.

Shareholder   A shareholder (or stockholder) is a person who owns shares of the capital stock of a corporation.

Statement   A statement, or bill, is a form sent once a month to a charge customer. It indicates any balances owed to the company from whom the goods or services were purchased.

Stock exchange   A stock exchange is a place where the actual buying and selling of stocks and bonds occurs.

Stockroom   A stockroom is a place where large quantities of goods are stored prior to being sold to customers.

Straight-life insurance   Straight-life insurance provides protection for life. It requires that the insured pay premiums for life. It has a cash surrender value.

Straight-line depreciation   The straight-line method of depreciation of an object is based on an average annual depreciation.

$$\text{Average annual depreciation} = \frac{\text{total depreciation}}{\text{estimated life}}$$

Surgical expense insurance Surgical expense insurance pays for all or part of the surgeon's fees for an operation.

Tax refund A tax refund is the amount of income tax overpayment to which the taxpayer is entitled. The refund will be returned to the taxpayer or applied to the next year's tax liability, as indicated by the taxpayer.

Template A template is a pattern or mold that is used as a guide in a design.

Term insurance Term insurance offers financial protection for a specified period of time, usually 5 or 10 years. It can be renewed at higher rates without a medical examination. It has no cash surrender value.

Term of a note The term of a note is the time between the date of a note and the date on which it must be paid.

Theft insurance Theft insurance provides financial protection against losses of personal property due to theft. The theft might occur at home or away from home. This insurance is part of a homeowner's policy.

Time-and-a-half Time-and-a-half is a rate of pay for overtime which is $1\frac{1}{2}$ times the regular hourly rate.

MODELS Hourly rate: $2.90 Overtime rate $1\frac{1}{2} \times$ $2.90, or $4.35 per hr

Hourly rate: $2.75 Overtime rate: $1\frac{1}{2} \times$ $2.75, or 4.12\frac{1}{2}$ per hr

Trade discount A trade discount is the reduction in the list price. A trade discount is given by a manufacturer to retailers.

Trade-in value The trade-in value is the amount allowed on a used article as part of the purchase price of a new one.

Trade securities To trade securities means to buy and sell stocks, bonds, notes, and certificates.

Unit price The unit price of an item is a way of restating the selling price in terms of a single unit. For example, 2.3¢ per gram.

Variable expenses Variable expenses are flexible items which change from time to time. For example, medical expenses.

Vocation A vocation is a career chosen by a person as a way of earning a living.

W-2 form A W-2 form is the tax withholding statement that an employer issues to each employee. The form indicates the total wages earned and all amounts withheld during the previous tax year.

Wholesaler A wholesaler is one who buys in large quantities from the manufacturer or producer. A wholesaler then sells in smaller quantities to retailers or other dealers.

Workmen's compensation Workmen's compensation provides for insurance benefits. These are payable to employees in case of accident or death as a result of their employment.

ANSWERS

Page 2

16	2	9	7
3	13	6	12
5	11	4	14
10	8	15	1

Page 4　**1.** 6　**3.** 15

5.

$8 + (4 + 6)$	$(8 + 4) + 6$
$8 + 10$	$12 + 6$
18	18

7. $(38 + 62) + 91$　**9.** 366　**11.** 3,514 doz
13. $1,860; $698

Page 5　**1.** 137　**3.** 332　**5.** 962　**7.** $1,452
9. $7,674; $4,283; $9,279; $8,448; $15,428;
$14,256

Page 6　**1.** Three thousand, four hundred
seventy-five　**3.** Six hundred forty-seven
million, eight hundred two thousand, one
hundred eleven　**5.** 65,875
7. 24,000,024,024　**9.** $38,665; $36,704;
$42,833; $51,496; $37,335; $75,127;
$139,160; $143,000　**11.** 1,171 lb

Page 9　**1.** 15　**3.** 18　**5.** 229　**7.** 114
9. 3,363　**11.** 1,100　**13.** 6,964　**15.** 1,124
17. 1,152 mi　**19.** 2,107 gal　**21.** $486
23. $138　**25.** $2,888; $1,897; $766; $7,723;
$2,172　**27.** $1,705; $2,509; $1,000; $6,503;
$1,289

Page 10　**1.** $9　**3.** 7,005 lb　**5.** $152
7. lose; 1,689　**9.** $13　**11.** $156; $123;
$250; $596; $67　**13.** $148; $136; $168;
$565; $113

Page 11　**1.** $26,376; $1,220; $26,000; $400;
$1,260; $39,673; $15,583　**3.** $2,147; $1,708;
$3,785; $1,150; $5,545; $3,245　**5.** 27
7. $22; $336

Page 15　**1.** 7　**3.** 17

5.

$8 \times (4 \times 6)$	$(8 \times 4) \times 6$
8×24	32×6
192	192

7.

$8 \times (10 - 6)$	$(8 \times 10) - (8 \times 6)$
8×4	$80 - 48$
32	32

9. 360,696　**11.** 448,400　**13.** 1,140
15. 85

Page 16　**1.** 40 in.　**3.** 104 meters
5. 476 sq ft　**7.** 1,615　**9.** 8,100
11. $390,525　**13.** 324 sq ft

Page 17　**1.** $260; $160; $172; $240; $200;
$1,290; $258　**3.** $220; $168; $220; $172;
$975; $195　**5.** $893　**7.** $2,775
9. 7,128 mi

Page 19　**1.** 427　**3.** 987　**5.** 975　**7.** 85
9. 640 r17　**11.** 440 r 85　**13.** 183

Page 20　**1.** 14　**3.** 18 hr　**5.** 75 gal　**7.** 90
9. 33　**11.** $2,742　**13.** 169

Page 21　**1.** 12 meters　**3.** 118 meters
5. 48 sq meters　**7.** 2,464 sq meters
9. $160; $114; $175　**11.** 20 meters
13. 16　**15.** $143　**17.** 21

Page 22　**1.** $10,498　**2.** 20,498　**3.** $3,683
4. 7,674　**5.** 377,254　**6.** 290,016　**7.** 975
8. 57 r 48　**9.** 79　**10.** $230　**11.** $3,956;
$5,075; $1,302; $5,907; $4,426; $10,333
12. $116; $261; $315; $872; $180; $692
13. $176　**14.** $114

Page 24　**1.** 40　**3.** 50　**5.** 90　**7.** 100
9. 800　**11.** 1,000　**13.** 1,010　**15.** 1,700

Page 26

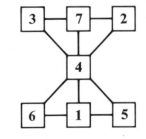

Page 28   **1.** Eight tenths   **3.** Seventy-one and six tenths   **5.** Eight and three hundred seventy-six thousandths   **7.** .04   **9.** 3.0207   **11.** .35 = .350   **13.** .308 < .380   **15.** .06 < .60   **17.** .8 = .80

Page 29   **1.** Ten and five hundredths   **3.** Five and five hundred fifty-five thousandths   **5.** Five hundred fifty-five and five tenths   **7.** .005   **9.** .106   **11.** 49.149   **13.** $107.03   **15.** 27.5 inches   **17.** 4.6 lb   **19.** 8.9 inches   **21.** 4.5 miles   **23.** <   **25.** >   **27.** .095, .015, .001   **29.** .49, .151, .08   **31.** 15.5, 15.425, 15.05

Page 30 $475; $675; $700; $670; $710; $730; $790; $980; $730   **1.** $146   **3.** $177.50   **5.** <   **7.** <   **9.** <   **11.** <   **13.** >   **15.** >   **17.** 35   **19.** 167   **21.** 1,961

Page 33   **1.** 13.487   **3.** 15.133   **5.** 89.67   **7.** 586.17   **9.** 54.45   **11.** 207.272   **13.** 25.62   **15.** 4.737

Page 34   **1.** $2,975.70   **3.** $726.83; $785.30; $548.32; $848.36   **5.** $279.36   **7.** .255 in.   **9.** 15.75

Page 35   **1.** $104.76; $45.24   **3.** $65.00; $35.00   **5.** $283.30; $33.30   **7.** $189.00; $86.00   **9.** $27   **11.** $700   **13.** $2,333

Page 39   **1.** 3,453.373   **3.** 2,044.4326   **5.** $3,049.20   **7.** $19,534.90   **9.** 32,900   **11.** 59.585   **13.** 9.625 sq ft   **15.** 9.7375 sq mi

Page 40   **1.** $105.88; $140; $116.25; $121.10; $483.23   **3.** 26.25   **5.** $26.25   **7.** $118.50   **9.** $106.56   **11.** 651.375 sq ft; 85 sq in.; 26.875 sq yd; 7.5 sq ft

Page 41   **1.** 13.26   **3.** .004   **5.** 306.192   **7.** 3 lb   **9.** 36.2 kilometers   **11.** .06 centimeters   **13.** 231   **15.** 1,258   **17.** 333.938   **19.** $703.13   **21.** $2,566.81   **23.** .13721   **25.** 125 sq ft   **27.** $5,310   **29.** $2,700

Page 43   **1.** 7.572   **3.** 3   **5.** .34   **7.** .15   **9.** 63.64   **11.** .173   **13.** .069   **15.** 14.6   **17.** .03   **19.** 5.39

Page 44   **1.** 73   **3.** 27,410   **5.** 1.46   **7.** 740   **9.** $5.36   **11.** $.49   **13.** 125   **15.** .00015   **17.** .6500   **19.** 6.200   **21.** 270.0   **23.** 84.53 mph   **25.** $2.08   **27.** 4.215 in.   **29.** $.73

Page 45   **1.** 32   **3.** 114.875   **5.** 3,017.56   **7.** .129668   **9.** 858   **11.** 1,348   **13.** 3.05   **15.** $1,149.94   **17.** $201.24   **19.** 200; 600   **21.** 45,635   **23.** $163.63; $180; $264.65

Page 46   **1.** One hundred five ten thousandths   **2.** One and forty-six hundredths   **3.** 2.05   **4.** .407   **5.** >   **6.** <   **7.** 1.421   **8.** 47.956   **9.** 3.111   **10.** 23.68   **11.** 5.076   **12.** .090034   **13.** 9,200   **14.** 18.4   **15.** 45 sq ft; 1.04 sq yd; 127.5 sq yd   **16.** $520.63; $601.99   **17.** $6.05   **18.** $5.48   **19.** $.23   **20.** 192

Page 48   **1.** 3,450   **3.** 3,160   **5.** 7,200   **7.** 14,900   **9.** 87,000   **11.** 100,000   **13.** 470,000   **15.** 3,020,000   **17.** 15   **19.** 234   **21.** 4,260   **23.** 867.3   **25.** 628   **27.** 67.9   **29.** $3.90   **31.** $22.50   **33.** $65   **35.** $603   **37.** 5,760; 57,600; 576,000   **39.** .06; .6; 6   **41.** $93.60; $936; $9,360

Page 50

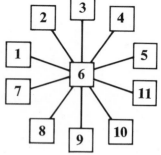

Page 52   **1.** 7 cm; 68 mm   **3.** 4 cm; 42 mm   **5.** 5,600   **7.** 3,000   **9.** 152,000   **11.** 350   **13.** .26   **15.** 25 cm   **17.** 60 cm   **19.** 750 cm   **21.** 6 in.   **23.** 40 in.   **25.** 400 in.

Page 53   **1.–3.** Answer may vary.
5. 8,582.7 km; 8,582,700 m   **7.** $14.76
9. 10   **11.** 12   **13.** Jack; 1.2 mi   **15.** 24
17. 80

Page 54   **1.** 658.392   **3.** 97.414
5. 45,706.508   **7.** 19,446   **9.** 61,172
11. $40.36   **13.** $330.43   **15.** $1,105,020
17. $3,212; $770; $832; $1,350

Page 57   **1.** 1,000   **3.** .001   **5.** .1
7. 3,600   **9.** 8.956   **11.** 3,850   **13.** 3,000
15. 2,000   **17.** 42.8ℓ; 42,800 mℓ
19. .075ℓ; 75 mℓ **21.** 30ℓ **23.** 200ℓ
25. 4 qt; 1 gal   **27.** 20 qt; 5 gal   **29.** 50 qt;
$12\frac{1}{2}$ gal

Page 58   **1.** 1,000 cc; 1 ℓ 1,000 mℓ
3. 376.3 cc; .3763 ℓ 376.3 mℓ **5.** .946 ℓ
7. 215 mℓ **9.** 21,960 mℓ; 21.96 kℓ
11. 60,000 ℓ; 60 kℓ **13.** $.80   **15.** Lula
17. 60 qt   **19.** 7 gal

Page 59   **1.** $172.40; $209.27; $515.69;
$48.33   **3.** net pay $125.79; $137.52; $94.11;
$161.10; $112.77; $761.64; $130.35
5. .89 m   **7.** 8   **9.** 234 lb   **11.** 60

Page 63   **1.** 1,000   **3.** .001   **5.** .326
7. 4.265   **9.** .09   **11.** 50 kg   **13.** 15 kg
15. 1,080 g   **17.** 2.5 kg   **19.** 110 kg
21. 400 lb

Page 64   **1.** 850 g; .85 kg   **3.** 1,763 g;
1.763 kg   **5.** 8.6 kg; 8,600,000 mg   **7.** 840
g; .84 kg   **9.** 3,600 lb   **11.** $9.00
13. $1.89   **15.** kilogram

Page 65   **1.** 2.13   **3.** 95,450   **5.** 14.5
7. 710.52   **9.** 80.8665   **11.** 85.4   **13.** .7392
15. 432   **17.** $9   **19.** $95   **21.** $33.90
23. $24.20   **25.** 58   **27.** $.96   **29.** 22.9
31. 36.72 cm

Page 67   **1.** 22°C   **3.** 15°C   **5.** 38°C
7. warm   **9.** cool   **11.** very hot
13. dropped 15°   **15.** rose 10°

Page 68   **1.** 17°   **3.** 28°   **5.** 46°   **7.** 80°
9. 12°   **11.** −10°C   **13.** 25°C

Page 69   **1.** 83.75   **3.** 84   **5.** .46   **7.** 6.014
9. 103.8   **11.** >   **13.** <   **15.** <
19. $36.82; $3.18   **21.** $316.75; $33.25
23. $73.70; $23.70   **25.** $198.95; $38.95
27. $128.65; $21.35

Page 70   **1.** 6 cm   **2.** 22 mm   **3.** .042
4. 4   **5.** 362   **6.** .042   **7.** .06   **8.** 22,000
9. .143   **10.** 1,400   **11.** .043   **12.** 10 cm
13. 29   **14.** 14   **15.** 10   **16.** 8   **17.** 900
18. very cold   **19.** hot   **20.** drop of 15°C
21. 30 mi   **22.** Anna, 124 miles or 186 km
23. $21.93   **24.** 1.462 kg   **25.** $2.50
26. $.02 per gal or $.005 per liter   **27.** 2,460
28. 9°C

Page 72   **1.** .25   **3.** .006   **5.** 6.2   **7.** .48
9. .0062   **11.** .0004   **13.** 2.562   **15.** .00246
17. .0009   **19.** 2.5; .25; .025   **21.** 2.85;
.285; .0285   **23.** .0015; .00015; .000015
25. $2.40; $.24; $.024   **27.** $.349; $.0349;
$.00349   **29.** $.004; $.0004; $.00004

Page 73   **1.** 9,335   **2.** 88.7   **3.** 3,611
4. 2,129   **5.** 5,232   **6.** .08072   **7.** 13
8. 2.24   **9.** .05   **10.** 18   **11.** 360
12. 45,000   **13.** .045   **14.** 4,830   **15.** 20
16. 8   **17.** 4   **18.** 30°C   **19.** Marita
20. $7.85   **21.** 182 miles   **22.** $157.85;
$132; $96; $385.85   **23.** $2,314; $618; $1,425;
$2,797; $1,560

Page 74   **1.** October 7–11 Sales   **3.** Sales in
thousands   **5.** Abni; Tony   **7.** $53,000
9. Ben's   **11.** $167,000   **13.** $28,000

Page 76   RATIO; DIVIDE; FRACTION;
SUBTRACT; NUMERATOR; CONSUMER

Page 78   **1.** B: $\frac{12}{16}$, $\frac{6}{8}$, $\frac{3}{4}$; C: $\frac{16}{16}$, $\frac{8}{8}$, $\frac{4}{4}$, $\frac{2}{2}$; D: $\frac{24}{16}$,
$\frac{12}{8}$, $\frac{6}{4}$, $\frac{3}{2}$; F: $\frac{56}{16}$, $\frac{28}{8}$, $\frac{14}{4}$, $\frac{7}{2}$ **3.** $\frac{2}{3}$ **5.** $\frac{3}{8}$ **7.** $\frac{1}{3}$
9. $\frac{7}{11}$ **11.** $\frac{1}{2}$ **13.** $\frac{4}{7}$ **15.** 1   **17.** $\frac{7}{8}$ **19.** 15
21. 27

Page 79   **1.** $\frac{1}{3}$ **3.** A, $\frac{5}{8}$; B, $1\frac{3}{8}$; C, $1\frac{7}{8}$
5. A, $\frac{9}{16}$; B, $1\frac{9}{16}$; C, $2\frac{7}{16}$ **7.** $\frac{2}{3}$ **9.** $\frac{13}{20}$ **11.** $\frac{5}{9}$
13. $\frac{2}{4}$, $\frac{3}{6}$, $\frac{4}{8}$ **15.** $\frac{6}{8}$, $\frac{9}{12}$, $\frac{12}{16}$

Page 80   **1.** 2.76 sq m   **3.** 118.44 sq m   **5.** \$163.63; \$180; \$264.65; \$190.55   **7.** 4,000   **9.** .423   **11.** 13.6   **13.** .43   **15.** 870   **17.** \$2.76   **19.** \$27.10   **21.** \$7.77

Page 83   **1.** $\frac{1}{4}$ **3.** $\frac{1}{2}$ **5.** $\frac{3}{5}$ **7.** 3, 12; 8, 5; 36; 40; no   **9.** 45   **11.** 56   **13.** 100   **15.** >   **17.** <

Page 84   **1.** \$45.90   **3.** 144   **5.** 3,040   **7.** 32,400   **9.** 126 m   **11.** 9,000   **13.** 2 out of 25

Page 85   **1.** 5   **3.** 12   **5.** $\frac{1}{2}$ **7.** $\frac{4}{5}$ **9.** $\frac{1}{3}$ **11.** 10   **13.** 100   **15.** 400   **17.** 1,300   **19.** 1.463   **21.** 17.5   **23.** \$2.60   **25.** 288   **27.** 81.45; .08145   **29.** \$.013 per ℓ

Page 87   **1.** 10   **3.** 36   **5.** 40   **7.** $\frac{7}{8}$ **9.** $\frac{9}{10}$ **11.** $1\frac{1}{4}$ **13.** $3\frac{2}{3}$ **15.** $3\frac{1}{2}$ **17.** $2\frac{1}{8}$ **19.** $1\frac{13}{30}$ **21.** $26\frac{5}{12}$ **23.** $14\frac{9}{40}$

Page 88   **1.** $15\frac{3}{4}$ gal   **3.** $9\frac{1}{3}$ in.   **5.** $27\frac{1}{4}$ doz; 29 doz   **7.** $4\frac{3}{4}$ **9.** $11\frac{3}{4}$; 15; $11\frac{2}{3}$; $13\frac{3}{4}$; $13\frac{1}{12}$; $21\frac{5}{12}$; $22\frac{7}{12}$; $21\frac{1}{4}$

Page 89   **1.** 20   **3.** 126   **5.** 160   **7.** <   **9.** <   **11.** 2,730   **13.** .3467   **15.** 1.248   **17.** \$7,363; \$5,711; \$8,599; \$10,193; \$17,378; \$24,315; \$19,125; \$34,120; \$20,314   **19.** 836,000   **21.** 5.5   **23.** 755

Page 91   **1.** $\frac{2}{5}$ **3.** $\frac{3}{8}$ **5.** $\frac{1}{6}$ **7.** $\frac{7}{20}$ **9.** $\frac{3}{16}$ **11.** $\frac{1}{4}$ **13.** $2\frac{5}{3}$ **15.** $5\frac{6}{5}$ **17.** $3\frac{11}{9}$ **19.** $11\frac{11}{7}$ **21.** $2\frac{1}{3}$ **23.** $3\frac{3}{8}$ **25.** $4\frac{7}{12}$ **27.** $3\frac{1}{4}$ **29.** $7\frac{3}{8}$ **31.** $2\frac{7}{8}$

Page 92   **1.** $\frac{7}{10}$ m   **3.** $3\frac{53}{100}$ m   **5.** $1\frac{5}{12}$ ft   **7.** $\frac{1}{30}$ **9.** $1\frac{1}{4}$ cups   **11.** $7\frac{2}{3}$ **13.** $9\frac{7}{10}$ **15.** $15\frac{3}{4}$

Page 93   **1.** $1\frac{5}{12}$ **3.** $1\frac{1}{20}$ **5.** \$13,999; \$14,136; \$17,538; \$15,839; \$64,044; \$2,532   **7.** 16; 16; $16\frac{1}{4}$; 16; $15\frac{3}{4}$; 16; 32; 32; 32   **9.** 4,522   **11.** cold   **13.** warm   **15.** very, very hot

Page 97   **1.** $1\frac{1}{3}$ **3.** $\frac{21}{40}$ **5.** $\frac{2}{3}$ **7.** $\frac{17}{12}$ **9.** $\frac{19}{8}$ **11.** $\frac{65}{4}$ **13.** $19\frac{1}{4}$ **15.** $13\frac{1}{8}$ **17.** $\frac{1}{4}$ **19.** $\frac{5}{18}$ **21.** $16\frac{5}{8}$ **23.** $1\frac{3}{4}$ **25.** $1\frac{5}{16}$

Page 98   **1.** \$20.63   **3.** $40\frac{1}{2}$ **5.** \$4.00   **7.** 459   **9.** \$97.50; \$103.06; \$177.23; \$169.50; \$153.00; \$145.69; \$127.50; \$180.00; \$1,153.48   **11.** $15\frac{5}{6}$ sq ft   **13.** $46\frac{7}{8}$ sq yd

Page 99   **1.** 4.678   **3.** 36,420   **5.** 8.7   **7.** 1,063,936   **9.** 2,089,356   **11.** $\frac{3}{5}$ **13.** $\frac{5}{8}$ **15.** \$588; \$2,628; \$1,512   **17.** $6\frac{11}{24}$ **19.** $14\frac{1}{6}$ **21.** \$10,186   **23.** 40.2

Page 101   **1.** $\frac{2}{1}$ **3.** $\frac{4}{3}$ **5.** $\frac{72}{50}$ **7.** $\frac{6}{18}$ **9.** 96   **11.** $\frac{1}{18}$ **13.** $\frac{2}{3}$ **15.** $\frac{5}{6}$ **17.** 2   **19.** $1\frac{1}{2}$ **21.** $\frac{9}{10}$

Page 102   **1.** 24   **3.** 32   **5.** 640   **7.** 21   **9.** 60 kmph   **11.** $14\frac{6}{11}$ **13.** \$.50   **15.** 111   **17.** $5\frac{7}{9}$

Page 103   **1.** .036   **3.** 42,000   **5.** 780   **7.** 201   **9.** 3,708   **11.** $\frac{1}{6}$ **13.** $\frac{1}{5}$ **15.** 48   **17.** 28   **19.** 80   **21.** $20\frac{1}{4}$; \$81; 20; \$60; $20\frac{3}{4}$; \$83; $9\frac{3}{4}$; $9\frac{3}{4}$; $10\frac{1}{2}$; $9\frac{1}{4}$; $8\frac{1}{4}$; $13\frac{1}{2}$

Page 105   **1.** $\frac{1}{48}$ **3.** $\frac{1}{10,000}$ **5.** 1″   **7.** $2\frac{2}{5}$″   **9.** $2\frac{1}{2}$″   **11.** 72   **13.** 126   **15.** 432   **17.** $\frac{1}{500}$

Page 106   **1.** 2″ × $1\frac{1}{2}$″   **3.** about 12 ft   **5.** $25\frac{1}{2}$ in.   **7.** $\frac{1}{36}$; 8″ × 6″   **9.** $\frac{1}{24}$; 9″ × 6″   **11.** 36′; 60′; 24′; 42′; 12′; 18′

Page 107   **1.** 42,000   **3.** 1.467   **5.** .033
7. $\frac{2}{3}$ **9.** $2\frac{7}{16}$ **11.** 31   **13.** $334   **15.** $3\frac{3}{7}$ hr
17. 15   **19.** 3,000

Page 108   **1.** $\frac{2}{3}$ **2.** $\frac{3}{4}$ **3.** $\frac{2}{6}, \frac{3}{9}, \frac{4}{12}$ **4.** $\frac{4}{10}$,
$\frac{6}{15}, \frac{8}{20}$ **5.** 24   **6.** 40   **7.** >   **8.** =   **9.** $\frac{3}{4}$
10. $3\frac{7}{10}$ **11.** $\frac{3}{8}$ **12.** $\frac{3}{4}$ **13.** $\frac{3}{10}$ **14.** $3\frac{1}{8}$
15. $\frac{3}{4}$ **16.** $3\frac{1}{3}$ **17.** 12 cm   **18.** 15 cm
19. 12 ft   **20.** 7 ft   **21.** $10\frac{2}{5}$ gal   **22.** $1\frac{1}{5}$ gal
23. $22\frac{1}{2}$ hr   **24.** $1\frac{5}{13}$ mph   **25.** $6'' \times 5\frac{1}{4}''$
26. 15 in.

Page 112   UNITS; SOLVE; METRIC;
FACTOR; PERCENT; PROFESSION

Page 114   **1.** 25%   **3.** 63%   **5.** 300%
7. 50%   **9.** $16\frac{2}{3}$%   **11.** 37.5%   **13.** .28
15. .001   **17.** 1.40   **19.** $\frac{1}{20}$ **21.** $\frac{1}{100}$
23. $1\frac{2}{5}$

Page 115   **1.** .25; 25%   **3.** $\frac{3}{4}$; 75%
5. $\frac{123}{1,000}$; .123   **7.** 1.45; 145%
9. $.33\frac{1}{3}$; $33\frac{1}{3}$%   **11.** $\frac{22}{25}$; 88%   **13.** $\frac{8}{125}$; .064
15. .72; 72%   **17.** $\frac{7}{25}$ **19.** .50   **21.** 50%
23. 42.5%   **25.** $\frac{3}{20}$

Page 116   **1.** 2.8 cm   **3.** 20 cm   **5.** 16.8 cm
7. 60'   **9.** 35'   **11.** 400'   **13.** 19   **15.** 1.1
17. $\frac{13}{25}$ **19.** $\frac{1}{4}$ **21.** $\frac{2}{5}$ **23.** $2.44   **25.** 10.9
27. a 9.2 cm × 6.2 cm drawing   **29.** about
5 ft tall   **31.** a bit over 6 ft tall

Page 119   **1.** 30   **3.** 19   **5.** 8.45   **7.** 80%
9. 200%   **11.** 160   **13.** 560

Page 120   **1.** 60 or more   **3.** $64   **5.** 30%
7. $1,200   **9.** 30%   **11.** $3,750
13. $97.13   **15.** 20%   **17.** $250
19. $45.05

Page 121   **1.** 26%   **3.** 30%   **5.** .8%
7. 80%   **9.** $37\frac{1}{2}$% or 37.5%   **11.** $33\frac{1}{3}$%

13. $\frac{1}{10}$ **15.** $\frac{3}{25}$ **17.** $1\frac{1}{2}$ **19.** .67   **21.** 1.6
23. .005   **25.** $\frac{17}{20}$ **27.** $5\frac{1}{4}$ **29.** $\frac{3}{8}$ **31.** 4
33. 70%   **35.** $\frac{47}{100}$ **37.** 18 mi   **39.** $10\frac{1}{2}$ sq ft
41. $4,648\frac{1}{8}$ m²

Page 125   **1.** 25%   **3.** 25%   **5.** 50%
7. 20%   **9.** $33\frac{1}{3}$%   **11.** 50%   **13.** 25%
15. $16\frac{2}{3}$%

Page 126   **1.** 4,000; 24,000; $16\frac{2}{3}$%   **3.** 10%
5. 12%   **7.** 10% decrease   **9.** 11% increase
11. 5% increase   **13.** +100; 25%; −.8;
80%; +300; 12.5%; −125; 50%

Page 127   **1.** 150   **3.** 1,776.599   **5.** 42%
7. 400   **9.** $\frac{1}{6}$ **11.** $1\frac{7}{12}$ **13.** $2\frac{1}{2}$ **15.** $5\frac{1}{4}$
17. $\frac{3}{5}$ sec   **19.** $9,373.20   **21.** $830
23. $264.50   **25.** 20%

Page 129   **1.** $2,025; $2,025; $675;
$337.50; $675; $472.50; $540; total $6,750
3. 25%; $33\frac{1}{3}$%; $12\frac{1}{2}$%; $12\frac{1}{2}$%; 10%; $6\frac{2}{3}$%

Page 130   **1.** 126; 90; 36; 54; 36; 18
3. 2,750; 1,815; 550; 165; 220   **5.** 30%;
20%; 10%; 10%; 30%   **7.** 25%; 15%; 30%;
10%; 8%; 7%; 5%   **9.** 2,790; 1,860; 3,720;
2,232; 2,790; 2,418; 2,790

Page 131   **1.** 120   **3.** 150   **5.** >   **7.** >
9. $33\frac{1}{3}$%   **11.** 12.5%   **13.** 20%   **15.** 10%
17. 5%   **19.** 5%   **21.** 240   **23.** 11,750
25. 25%   **27.** 15%

Page 132   **1.** 7%   **2.** .9%   **3.** 400%
4. 75%   **5.** $66\frac{2}{3}$%   **6.** 350%   **7.** .426
8. .057   **9.** .007   **10.** $\frac{7}{100}$ **11.** $\frac{29}{100}$ **12.** $1\frac{4}{5}$
13. 86.4   **14.** 460   **15.** 25%   **16.** 6.25%
17. 288   **18.** 64   **19.** 10%   **20.** 2%
21. $2,912; $2,496; $1,664; $1,560; $1,768;
100%; $10,400   **22.** $62.68   **23.** 87%

Page 134   1. $\frac{1}{10}$ 3. $\frac{3}{4}$ 5. $\frac{1}{6}$ 7. $\frac{1}{8}$ 9. $\frac{5}{8}$
11. $7   13. $42   15. $12   17. $9
19. $48   21. $210   23. $140   25. $240
27. $6,500

Page 136   Answers may vary.

Page 138   1. $315; $1,815   3. $120; $2,120
5. $63; $288   7. $70.50; $540.50   9. $134;
$804   11. $106.25; $4,356.25   13. $16.64;
$640.64   15. $.75; $150.75   17. $27; $927

Page 139   1. $90   3. $52.50   5. $5,152
7. $3,540   9. $57.20; $497.20
11. $1,522.50   13. $613.50   15. $305

Page 140   1. 25%   3. 60%   5. $58\frac{1}{3}$%
7. 43%   9. 140%   11. 48.5%   13. $\frac{7}{50}$
15. $\frac{1}{10}$ 17. $\frac{1}{200}$ 19. .87   21. .0003   23. 2
25. .046   27. 1.64   29. 4.2   31. 14
33. 6.4   35. $8,000; 25%; 24%; 9%; 5%;
6%; 9%; 12%; 1%; 3%; 2%; 4%

Page 143   1. Evelyn Roedema   3. 7%
5. 30 days   7. 86 days   9. June 17
11. Feb. 28

Page 144   1. May 1; $604   3. $1,005.56
5. $911.25   7. Mar. 4; $364.20   9. May 7
of the following year; $1,854   11. $380

Page 145   1. 14,000   3. 36,000   5. .036
7. 2.88   9. 20%   11. 400   13. $8,280;
$54,280   15. $337.50; $4,837.50   17. $9;
$309   19. $8; $608   21. $37.50; $1,537.50
23. $1,541.48   25. $6,240   27. $437.50
29. 15%

Page 149   1. $1,120.61   3. $186.76
5. $450.60; $382.83; $382.83; $397.83;
$381.14

Page 150   1. $691.76   3. $202.30; $187.98;
$187.98; $187.98; $162.90; $162.90; $162.90;
$138.88; $138.88; $138.88; $38.78

Page 151   1. 460   3. .048   5. 1,360
7. 18%   9. $16\frac{2}{3}$%   11. 4.6 kg   13. 510
15. Aug. 7   17. May 4 of the following year;
$1,860

Page 153   1. correct available balance,
$170.62   3. correct available balance,
$123.33

Page 154   1. correct available balance,
$1,649.25   3. correct available balance,
$438.70   5. $262   7. $1,038.92

Page 155   ·1. cool   3. very hot   5. $2,125;
$2,550; $1,700; $1,020; $680; $340; $85
7. $415.06; $399.96; $399.96; $702.11;
$622.51   9. $636.53

Page 156   1. $663; $2,223   2. $3.50;
$283.50   3. 60 days   4. Feb. 6
5. $344.02; $333.92; $333.92; $333.92;
$312.40   6. $356.43; $341.33; $341.33;
$341.33; $321.73   7. $377.51
8. $250.62   9. $757.50   10. Aug. 6,
$914.63   11. $456   12. $361.08

Page 158   1. $1   3. $17.65   5. $78.09
7. $25.50   9. $2.50   11. $5   13. $32.80
15. $9

Page 159   1. 233.25   2. $6\frac{1}{4}$ 3. 3,184
4. $2\frac{3}{8}$ 5. 8,512   6. $28\frac{1}{6}$ 7. 3.04   8. 2
9. <   10. <   11. 16   12. 12   13. $225;
$1,725   14. Jan. 31   15. 1,105   16. 48
17. 20%   18. 10%   19. .04   20. 360
21. .118   22. 9 m   23. 14 m   24. 25%;
30%; 15%; 20%; 10%   25. correct available
balance, $377.82

Page 160   1. Closing Price Per Share of Bon
Stock   3. market value   5. Some values
between 0 and $25 are not shown.   7. $25\frac{3}{4}$,
or $25.75   9. 10th and 13th   11. $\frac{1}{2}$, or
$.50   13. $260   15. $25

Page 162   Arrange dots in shape of a triangle.

Page 164   1. $14.38   3. $15.60   5. $56.25
7. $10.84   9. $562.75   11. $828.38
13. $1,343.90

Page 165   1. $107.69   3. $210.18
5. $535.95   7. $634.10   9. $1,813.32
11. $1,481.25   13. compounded quarterly

Page 166   **1.** 50% **3.** $33\frac{1}{3}$% **5.** $116\frac{2}{3}$%
7. 50% **9.** 130% **11.** .1% **13.** 5,040.29
15. 90.1742 **17.** $1\frac{1}{12}$ **19.** $33\frac{3}{8}$ **21.** $27\frac{5}{24}$
23. $430.92; $465.89; $547.02; $561.83
25. $53.57
Page 169   **1.** $725 **3.** $922.50 **5.** $322.50
7. $745 **9.** $992.50 **11.** $780 **13.** $110
15. $100 **17.** $82.50 **19.** $55 **21.** $73.75
23. $470; $20 **25.** $170; $27.50
27. $288.75; $22.50 **29.** $185; $21.88
Page 170   **1.** $5,840; $600 **3.** $4,275;
$481.25 **5.** $2,730; $232.50 **7.** $1,575
9. $900 **11.** $3,455 **13.** $1,242.50
Page 171   **1.** $\frac{1}{20}$ **3.** $\frac{1}{40}$ **5.** $\frac{1}{3}$ **7.** .04
9. .0525 **11.** .003 **13.** 413.61
15. 31.2001 **17.** $\frac{5}{8}$ **19.** $1\frac{11}{12}$ **21.** $25\frac{3}{4}$
23. $956.48 **25.** $1,101.34 **27.** $1,793.40
29. 6% compounded quarterly
31. $8.01
Page 173   **1.** $1.82 **3.** 4 **5.** $412.40
7. $150
Page 174   **1.** $360 **3.** $1,101.86 **5.** 30
7. 200; $400 **9.** $605
Page 175   **1.** $\frac{1}{20}$ **3.** $\frac{1}{6}$ **5.** $\frac{1}{14}$ **7.** 25
9. .5 **11.** $60 **13.** $72.50 **15.** $65
17. $495; $50 **19.** $470; $27.50 **21.** $425;
$37.50 **23.** $3,900 **25.** $1,987.50
27. $532.50 **29.** $75.60
Page 179   **1.** 5% **3.** 8.3% **5.** 8.2%
7. 8% **9.** 10.3% **11.** 6.7% **13.** 15%
Page 180   **1.** 5.6% **3.** 8.2% **5.** $125
7. 4% bond at 110 **9.** $5 at 37
11. $150,000
Page 181   **1.** 188.3529 **3.** 58.475
5. .029442 **7.** $\frac{1}{20}$ **9.** $4\frac{3}{8}$ **11.** $\frac{3}{40}$
13. $17\frac{1}{10}$ **15.** $1,383.75 **17.** $11,866
19. $118.63; $110; $115.50; $111.36; $455.49
21. 71 shares **23.** $160
Page 183   **1.** $15.50 **3.** $332 **5.** $80.60

Page 184   **1.** $1,825 **3.** $4,743
5. $309.40 **7.** $1,680 **9.** $25,212
Page 185   **1.** 3 **3.** 2 **5.** 15 **7.** $82\frac{2}{27}$
9. 73.6 **11.** 60% **13.** 28 **15.** 4.4%
17. 6.7% **19.** 9% **21.** 8.3% **23.** 40%
25. $200,000
Page 187

		Company	You
1.	Room	$1,200	$150
	In-Hospital	490	0
	Surgical	200	50
3.	Room	$1,800	0
	In-Hospital	245	0
	Surgical	200	0
	TV and Tel.	0	$35

Page 188   **1.** $1,250; $375 **3.** $190
5. $4,000 **7.** $2,100 **9.** $7,400; $1,500
Page 189   **1.** 356.3 **3.** 365 **5.** 12.5%
7. 10% **9.** 10% **11.** 15% **13.** $199.80
15. $316.80 **17.** 10% **19.** $6\frac{2}{3}$%
21. $19,500
Page 190   **1.** $784.19 **2.** $580.40
3. $850; $42.67 **4.** $970; $65 **5.** $976.55
6. $2,296.63 **7.** $540 **8.** $82.50 **9.** 15%
10. 8.3% **11.** $393.75 **12.** $150
13. $18.37 **14.** $277
Page 192   **1.** $600 **3.** 30° **5.** 75° **7.** 84°
9. 171° **11.** 100% **13.** 360°
Page 194   11, 25, 4; 14, 17, 9
Page 196   **1.** $73.99 **3.** $144 **5.** $75.50
7. $200 **9.** $7.50 **11.** $1,500 **13.** $1.95
Page 197   **1.** $.60; $.25 **3.** $5.50; $2.50
5. $5.00; $2.50 **7.** $2.50; $.55 **9.** $7.95;
$1.00 **11.** $17.40 **13.** $47.60 **15.** $6; $2
17. $5,300; $1,900 **19.** $4 **21.** $4
Page 198   **1.** 1,794 **3.** 1,153 **5.** 938
7. 8,200 **9.** .082 **11.** 823 **13.** .146
15. $1,200; $200 **17.** $240 **19.** $9.24
21. $3,525
Page 201   **1.** 1.2¢ **3.** 83.3¢ **5.** $1.385
7. 65-g box for $.75 **9.** 10-oz can for $.65
11. 1.5-kg can for $2.79

Page 202   **1.** 45.6¢ **3.** 15.4¢ **5.** 42.0¢
7. $1 **9.** 30.9¢ **11.** 42.5¢ **13.** 7-oz for
$.89 **15.** 3.5-box at $5.95 **17.** 5 for $1.99
19. 3 cans for $.89 **21.** 10-oz for $1.43
23. 7.3 ℓ for $4.15
Page 203   **1.** $32.90 **3.** $10 **5.** $1
7. 47,253 **9.** 85,785 **11.** .042 **13.** .036
15. 48,000 **17.** $14.70 **19.** .078 ℓ
21. $3,985; $5,452; $4,217; $16,033; $2,379
Page 205   **1.** $45 **3.** $90; $4.10 **5.** $139;
$13.60
Page 206   **1.** $210; $11.75 **3.** $675;
$708.75; $39.38 **5.** $60; $1,260; $1,410
7. $499.88; $524.87; $34.99; $624.87
9. $5.63; $78.83 **11.** $5.94; $165
13. $19.60 **15.** 1st offer; $16
Page 207   **1.** 15,296 **3.** 50,901 **5.** 46,000
7. 87,000 **9.** 4.467 **11.** 1.4¢ **13.** $1.23
15. half-gallon for $.79 **17.** 8-pack for $1.35
19. 789 g **21.** 1,554 sq m **23.** 8,976 sq cm
Page 211   **1.** $1.04 **3.** $.29 **5.** $.07
7. $16.61 **9.** $42.29 **11.** $95.40
13. $27.22 **15.** $4.39
Page 212   **1.** $59.43 **3.** $45.68 **5.** $12.48
7. $16.64 **9.** $183.71
Page 213   **1.** 387 **3.** 415 **5.** $160; $1,160
7. $253.50; $1,553.50 **9.** $8; $408
11. $3.96; $503.96 **13.** $900; $1,050;
$43.75; $1,150 **15.** $1,020; $231; $1,251;
$1,431 **17.** $40 **19.** $547.20 **21.** $32.50
Page 215   **1.** $58.62 **3.** $90.40 **5.** $78.44
Page 216   **1.** $30.60 **3.** $78.10 **5.** $17
7. $41.60
Page 217   **1.** Jean Rising Sun **3.** 8%
5. 30 days **7.** 60 days **9.** July 20
11. $2.10 **13.** $196.20 **15.** 85
Page 218   **1.** $3.50 **2.** $52.20 **3.** $4,000;
$1,600 **4.** $1.48; $.43 **5.** 7.9¢ **6.** 0.3¢
7. $41.50 **8.** $60.50 **9.** $400; $50
10. $255; $30 **11.** $.20 **12.** $.26
13. $2,625 **14.** $18.85 **15.** 42 oz for $2.09
16. 2 lb 10 oz for $1.19 **17.** $130.63
18. $147.25

Page 220   All answers are approximate.
1. −40° F **3.** 32° F **5.** 88° F **7.** 140° F
9. 195° F **11.** −40° C **13.** −20° C
15. 32° C **17.** 60° C **19.** 88° C
Page 222   GRAPH; ORDER; CHART;
RECORD; CHEAT
Page 224   **1.** $300 **3.** $1,047.67 **5.** $720
7. 28% **9.** 40%
Page 225   **1.** $15.60 **3.** $5,755.20 **5.** 24%
7. 31.6% **9.** $5,280; $6,720 **11.** $80,000
13. $6,783 **15.** $113.05
Page 226   **1.** 10 **3.** 75 **5.** $126.24
7. $697.16 **9.** $306.21; $286.11; $286.11;
$286.11; $270.06
Page 229   **1.** $202.02; $477.99; $798.49;
$1,478.50 **3.** $17,300 **5.** $25,600
7. $1,711
Page 230   **1.** $2.70; $5.64; $8.97; $30.80;
$4.34; $2.86; $55.31; $219.69; $165.91
3. $53,000; $22,000 **5.** 50%; $16\frac{2}{3}$%
Page 231   **1.** 6 m; 4 m; 7 m **3.** $3\frac{3}{4}$ in.
5. $2\frac{1}{2}$ in. **7.** 48% **9.** $207.90
11. $115.79
Page 235   **1.** 3% discount within 10 days;
full amount within 30 days **3.** 3% discount
within 10 days; 2% discount 11–20 days; full
payment within 30 days **5.** March 31
7. Oct. 6 **9.** May 14; May 19 **11.** 5; $3;
$147 **13.** 21; none; $300
Page 236   **1.** Nov. 9; Nov. 29 **3.** June 4;
June 14; June 24 **5.** $245; $247.50; $250
7. $171.24 **9.** $126.44 **11.** $688.05
Page 237   **1.** 32 **3.** 75% **5.** 280
7. $15,000; $9,000 **9.** $695.82
11. $1,612.68 **13.** 5% compounded annually
15. $47,310; $21,118
Page 238   **1.** 41.5% **2.** 40.5% **3.** $36,300
4. $29,350 **5.** March 20 **6.** Aug. 9
7. $85.50 **8.** $288; $312 **9.** $22,000
10. $7,500 **11.** 12; none; $400 **12.** 10;
$22; $528

Page 241   **1.** $855.48   **2.** $890; $55
3. $57.12   **4.** 5.4¢   **5.** $385; $35
6. $4,500; $2,000   **7.** 3,600,000   **8.** 64,000
9. .0046   **10.** May 4   **11.** $331.20
12. $608.95   **13.** $136.07   **14.** 9.5%
15. $900   **16.** 20%   **17.** Nov. 3; $555.50
Page 244   You would earn $1.50 more than
your friend.
Page 246   **1.** $3.30   **3.** $3.60   **5.** 3.82\frac{1}{2}$
7. 2.62\frac{1}{2}$ **9.** $105.80   **11.** $124.70
13. $97.28; $11.52; $108.80   **15.** $118.80;
$19.80; $138.60
Page 247   **1.** $129.05   **3.** Simpson: $159.10;
Case: $161.50   **5.** $123.53   **7.** $126.83
9. $215.80
Page 248   **1.** Feb. 23   **3.** May 5   **5.** $1,150;
$70   **7.** $870; $80   **9.** 10%   **11.** 10%
13. $250   **15.** $291; $294; $300
17. $1,417.50
Page 251   **1.** $66   **3.** $94.50   **5.** 38; $57
7. 46; $73.60   **9.** $124   **11.** $370
Page 252   **1.** $130   **3.** $118.47   **5.** $101.25
7. $635   **9.** $192   **11.** $104
Page 253   **1.** $108; $8.10; $116.10
3. $118.50; $11.25; $129.75   **5.** $1,900;
$2,375; $1,710; $1,140; $1,425; $950
7. $122.96   **9.** $2,153.83   **11.** $144
13. $255
Page 255   **1.** $821.93   **3.** $646.43
5. $824.85   **7.** $807.30   **9.** $500.18
11. $5.54   **13.** $8.13   **15.** $14.59
17. $289.05
Page 256   **1.** $1,497.60   **3.** $2,421.90
5. $1.38   **7.** $630
Page 257   **1.** 119.530   **3.** 203.560   **5.** 6.8%
7. 8.2%   **9.** $200   **11.** $153   **13.** $164.80
15. 16$\frac{2}{3}$%
Page 261   **1.** $31.90   **3.** $52.50   **5.** $49.60
7. $20.80; $8.05; $1.38; $1.75; $105.71
9. $10.50; $6.81; $1.16; $1.75; $96.18
Page 262   **1.** $187.90   **3.** $191.17
5. $142.53   **7.** $126.11   **9.** $113.84;
$116.84

Page 263   **1.** 4.0647   **3.** 12.77   **5.** $45.50
7. $306.00   **9.** $591.44   **11.** $671.58
13. $593.22   **15.** $153.00   **17.** $.59
Page 265   **1.** $844   **3.** $1,049
5. $1,862.89
Page 266   **1.** $3.60 due   **3.** $16.20 refund
5. $140.09 refund
Page 267   **1.** .17468   **3.** 47.5551   **5.** $49
7. $38.30   **9.** $1,800; $300   **11.** $7,150;
$1,750   **13.** $27.20; $11.32; $1.93; $150.22
15. $34; $12.63; $2.16; $165.37
Page 269   **1.** yes   **3.** $8,795
Page 270   **1.** yes   **3.** no   **5.** $10,722
7. $4,545
Page 271   **1.** 1.04   **3.** 3.14   **5.** $66.70
7. $1,350   **9.** $2   **11.** $1,057   **13.** $30.99
due   **15.** $4; $1.90
Page 272   **1.** $117.76   **2.** $672.75
3. $587.10   **4.** $56.50   **5.** $178.85
6. $147.00   **7.** $271.60   **8.** $287.50   **9.** no
10. $8,424   **11.** $947   **12.** $1,448.54
Page 274   **1.** $1,800   **3.** $25   **5.** $7,900
7. 72$\frac{1}{2}$¢   **9.** $350
Page 276   0 red sides: 1, 1 red side: 6, 2 red
sides: 12, 3 red sides: 8, 4, 5, or 6 red sides:
none
Page 278   **1.** $3,960.08; $660.08
3. $3,101.44; $501.44   **5.** $57.78
7. $110.63
Page 279   **1.** $3,036   **3.** $676
5. $4,320.12   **7.** $65.47   **9.** $288; $75.52
11. no; Bank A interest = $552; Bank B
interest = $441.60
Page 280   **1.** 500-g box for 99¢   **3.** 10 for
$1.79   **5.** yes   **7.** $11,315   **9.** 8-pack for
$1.49   **11.** 3 for 25¢
Page 283   **1.** $1,550; 14.6¢ per mi
3. $1,690; 14.7¢ per mi   **5.** 8.9 $\frac{\text{km}}{\ell}$; 1.7¢
per km   **7.** 24 $\frac{\text{mi}}{\text{gal}}$; 1.9¢ per mi
Page 284   **1.** 297.6 mi   **3.** $349.44
5. $169.30   **7.** $1,558.62; 10.3¢ per mi
9. $126.72   **11.** 17.2 $\frac{\text{mi}}{\text{gal}}$

Page 285   **1.** $37   **3.** $94; $8   **5.** $3,129.88; $629.88   **7.** $100   **9.** $128.78   **11.** $124; $18.60; $142.60   **13.** $110; $24.75; $134.75

Page 289   **1.** $825   **3.** $272.22   **5.** $37.67   **7.** $600   **9.** $492.86   **11.** $2,215.13   **13.** $4,239.71   **15.** $250.09   **17.** $41.68

Page 290   **1.** $509.62   **3.** $929   **5.** $11.11   **7.** $2,400   **9.** $2,100   **11.** $1,668.75   **13.** $1,238.57

Page 291   **1.** $64.84   **3.** $642.66   **5.** $234.28   **7.** $112.25   **9.** $157   **11.** $1,586.97; about 11¢ per mi   **13.** about 7.8 km per liter

Page 293   **1.** $38.27   **3.** $65.28   **5.** $57.80   **7.** $25.90   **9.** $19.28   **11.** $39.50

Page 294   **1.** $90.41   **3.** $109.94   **5.** $268.39   **7.** $262.71   **9.** He pays $50; Insurance Co. pays $550   **11.** $5,000; $3,500

Page 295   **1.** $149.71   **3.** $2,087.98   **5.** $708.56   **7.** $850   **9.** $3,700

Page 296   **1.** $4,760; $1,000   **2.** $4,640; $640   **3.** $1,400   **4.** $750   **5.** $1,620; 9¢ per km   **6.** $1,500; $12\frac{1}{2}$¢ per mi   **7.** $12.5 \frac{km}{\ell}$; about 1.3¢ per km   **8.** $88.50   **9.** $69.98   **10.** $257.48

Page 298   **1.** $850   **3.** 169 cm   **5.** $5\frac{2}{3}$ yd   **7.** 13.6 ℓ **9.** $204.86   **11.** $11,625

Page 300   8; 13

Page 302   **1.** $23,188   **3.** $45,528   **5.** $37,934.80   **7.** $251.76, $225, $26.76, $29,973.24; $251.76, $224.80, $26.96, $29,946.28

Page 303   **1.** $179.95   **3.** $261.45   **5.** $335.92   **7.** $144.76, $125, $19.76, $14,980.24; $144.76, $124.84, $19.92, $14,960.32; $144.76, $124.67, $20.09, $14,940.23; $144.76, $124.50, $20.26, $14,919.97

Page 304   **1.** $65.47   **3.** $52.66   **5.** $40.60   **7.** 37%   **9.** 46.8%   **11.** $2,880; $3,120   **13.** $3,400   **15.** $43.90; $14.59; $3.74; $187.13

Page 307   **1.** $.03125, or 3.125%   **3.** $2.14285   **5.** $285.71   **7.** $236.25

Page 308   **1.** $.006, or .6%   **3.** $5.10   **5.** $33.50   **7.** $368,000   **9.** $286.88   **11.** $107.10   **13.** $867.20   **15.** $2,215.20

Page 309   **1.** $17,500; $7,500   **3.** $4,554.60; $454.60   **5.** $45,528   **7.** $302.48   **9.** no; Bank A, $462; Bank B, $369.60   **11.** $11,400

Page 311   **1.** 28¢   **3.** 30¢   **5.** $4.04   **7.** $17.01   **9.** $5.68   **11.** $53.37

Page 312   **1.** $3.02   **3.** 16¢   **5.** 424 kwh   **7.** $46.57   **9.** $24.41

Page 313   **1.** March 18   **3.** $237.60   **5.** 6.25; $.024   **7.** $2,065; $.1475   **9.** $.064   **11.** 12; none; $480   **13.** 7; $16.38; $529.62

Page 317   **1.** $28.80   **3.** $160.16   **5.** $56,250

Page 318   **1.** $36.40   **3.** $324   **5.** $1,672   **7.** $35,000   **9.** $25,000   **11.** $9,375

Page 319   **1.** $23.65   **3.** $54.97   **5.** 41¢   **7.** $1,300   **9.** $1,479.41   **11.** $75 due

Page 321   **1.** $62.40; $158.50   **3.** $48; $130.20   **5.** $66.56; $161.26   **7.** 40%; 60%

Page 322   **1.** $647.15   **3.** $505.50   **5.** Newton, $33\frac{1}{3}$%; Mutual, 20%; National, $46\frac{2}{3}$%;   **7.** Hersey, $12,000; Sanford, $20,000

Page 323   **1.** $132.62   **3.** $208.28   **5.** $36.30   **7.** $13,500   **9.** $8,469   **11.** no

Page 324   **1.** $45,528   **2.** $23,188   **3.** 6%, or $.06   **4.** 2.5%, or $.025   **5.** 44¢   **6.** 14¢   **7.** $35   **8.** $44   **9.** 40%; 60%   **10.** $33\frac{1}{3}$%; $66\frac{2}{3}$%   **11.** $1,912.50   **12.** $37,500   **13.** $25.03   **14.** $449.45

Page 326   **1.** 16   **3.** 24

Page 327   **1.** $4,160; $660   **2.** $1,040   **3.** $30,352   **4.** $5, or 5%   **5.** $35   **6.** 80%; 20%   **7.** .1¢   **8.** $252; $1,452   **9.** $640.70   **10.** $235   **11.** $161.20   **12.** $602.55   **13.** $135.75   **14.** $400

Page 328   **1.** $\frac{1}{6}$; $\frac{1}{6}$ **3.** $\frac{4}{7}$; $\frac{3}{7}$ **5.** $\frac{2}{6}$, or $\frac{1}{3}$ **7.** 0   **9.** $\frac{3}{6}$, or $\frac{1}{2}$ **11.** $\frac{3}{8}$ **13.** $\frac{7}{8}$